Evaluation and Management of Infants and Young Children with Developmental Disabilities

Evaluation and Management of Infants and Young Children with Developmental Disabilities

by

Mildred E. Copeland, M.S., O.T.R.
Kansas University Affiliated Facility at
    Lawrence
Bureau of Child Research
The University of Kansas
Lawrence

and

Judy R. Kimmel, M.A., O.T.R.
Stormont Vail Regional Medical Center
Topeka

·P·A·U·L·H·
BROOKES
PUBLISHING CO

Baltimore • London • Toronto • Sydney

Paul H. Brookes Publishing Co.
Post Office Box 10624
Baltimore, Maryland 21285-0624

Typeset by Brushwood Graphics, Inc., Baltimore, Maryland.
Manufactured in the United States of America by
The Maple Press Company, York, Pennsylvania.

Photography Credits:

Dave Lutz: Figures 3.4, 3.6, 3.10, 3.14, 3.30, 4.2, 4.3, 4.4, 8.1, 8.3, and 10.3.

Nancy Peterson: Figure 8.2.

Mildred E. Copeland: 3.1, 3.2, 3.5, 3.7, 3.8, 3.12, 3.19, 3.23, 3.25, 4.1, 6.1, 8.4, 9.5, 10.1, 11.4, 11.5, and 11.6.

All drawings were done by Judy R. Kimmel, with the exception of Figure 10.2, which was drawn by M. G. Hermetet.

Library of Congress Cataloging-in-Publication Data
Copeland, Mildred E.
 Evaluation and management of infants and young children with
developmental disabilities / by Mildred E. Copeland and Judy R.
Kimmel.
   p.   cm.
 Bibliography: p.
 Includes index.
 ISBN 0-933716-82-6
 1. Developmental disabilities. I. Kimmel, Judy R. II. Title.
RJ135.C66 1989
618.92′8—dc 19   88-8141
                                                             CIP

Contents

Preface

Teaching another person a new skill is an exciting, joyful, and rewarding experience. The authors have experienced that reward when teaching occupational therapy students, teachers, teacher aides, and the parents of infants and young children with developmental disabilities. This book was written to expand upon and to enhance those individuals' present knowledge about the abnormal motor development and the subsequent motor training methods designed for infants and young children with developmental disabilities. The professional staff and parents should view the information about the assessment procedures and management techniques as guidelines and suggestions, keeping in mind that they may need to be adapted to fit each child's specific needs.

Many infants and children with developmental disabilities have more than one significant problem that requires special management techniques. The reader may need to integrate information from several different chapters when planning management strategies and developing either individual or family goals and objectives.

Since the enactment of Public Law 94-142, professionals no longer work in segregated environments. Instead, the Individualized Education Program (IEP) process for developing educational goals and objectives for children is a shared responsibility among teachers, therapists, and parents. A child, for example, does not develop communication and language skills apart from the development of motor or cognitive skills. Therefore, the speech therapist, when working either with an infant or a child, needs to be taught by the physical or occupational therapist what sitting or lying position(s) may promote better lung expansion that in turn may aid in more speech productions. The speech clinician must also learn from the teacher what materials to use and how best to present them in a way that will stimulate the child's interest to want to communicate and thus increase his or her present level of communication or language skills. The parents in turn provide valuable suggestions and information about how the infant or child communicates at home. They may know how their child responds to certain events or materials but need the training from the professionals as to how to get their child to appropriately and effectively respond. Information that is shared among parents and staff members will help ensure continuity and consistent training across various domains (language, motor, cognitive, self-help, and social).

With the signing of Public Law 99-457 in 1986, it is now paramount that the professionals not only continue to be knowledgeable about normal and abnormal development, evaluative techniques, and functional activities designed for infants and young children, but also to recognize and understand the needs of the family both as an entity (looking at each family member's needs) and as a group of individuals working together. It is hoped that the information contained in this book that reflects some of the new changes brought on by recent legislation and research will be shared with parents and other colleagues so that techniques will be adapted and/or incorporated into the infant's or child's total daily schedule. The handling techniques selected for this book could also be used by all individuals who have a part in developing the child's potential independent skills.

The authors have attempted to present clear and concise descriptions of selected developmental disabilities and the assessment and management of those conditions for those students, teachers, and parents who have accepted the challenge of teaching and managing children with special needs.

The book is divided into three parts. Part I describes general assessment and management techniques for the areas of movement, feeding, dressing, toileting, health and safety concerns, physical transfers, and ways to enhance new behaviors or skills. These are techniques that can be applied to a number of specific conditions and can be used by numerous disciplines. Part II explains the specific conditions of at-risk infants, cerebral palsy, mental retardation, and neural tube defects. In this section, unique characteristics as well as specific assessment and management strategies for each condition are described. Part III, the appendices, includes a partial listing of assessments for at-risk infants and children with mental retardation and cerebral palsy.

Acknowledgments

One does not put together all the information contained in a book such as this without the guidance and assistance of numerous individuals. Encouragement and assistance has come in many forms from typing the manuscript, to developing the numerous table formats, to critiquing the manuscript, and, most importantly, to providing moral support. A special thank you goes to Carol Brown, Dorothy Anne Elsberry, Angela Fosnough, Pat Green, Debbie Greenspan, Dorothy Johanning, Ellen Mellard, Lorraine Mixon-Page, Sarah Potter, Barb Schwering, Alberta Wright, and Joane Wyrick for their most valued assistance and support in this special endeavor of ours. Our gratitude also goes to Dave Lutz and Nancy Peterson for taking time out of their busy schedules to photograph some of our children and parents. Special recognition and the "patience" award is given to Kathryn Keyes for showing the senior author the wonders of a computer over a typewriter.

We are deeply indebted to all the parents who have shared with us the rewarding times as well as those frustrating and depressing moments while striving to work toward a more independent level of functioning for their children and themselves.

Very special appreciation is due Melissa A. Behm and her staff at Paul H. Brookes Publishing Co. for their never-ending patience and skillful professional guidance in seeing this manuscript to its completion.

To the many parents, infants, and young children who have taught us much more than we have taught them.

Evaluation and Management of Infants and Young Children with Developmental Disabilities

INTRODUCTION

CHAPTER 1

Children, Parents, and Professionals

The developmentally disabled child has significant and chronic disabilities that are attributable to mental and/or physical impairment, with the onset of the disability any time between conception and the age of 22 years. Each child may have multiple problems that are related to more than one etiological factor (Wiegerink & Pelosi, 1979). The parents of the developmentally disabled child have the challenging task of providing care for their child as well as helping their child reach the highest level of function possible. The parents need to address the emotional and biophysical needs that all children have as well as those needs directly related to their child's disability. This is a large, long-term task for parents and they should not be expected to undertake it alone. The professionals (i.e., therapists, teachers) have the important tasks of treating and teaching the child and teaching and supporting the parents.

The ultimate goal of the parents and the therapy and education professionals is to help the developmentally disabled child reach his or her maximal level of development. This includes not only physical development but psychosocial development. The successful interaction of parents, professionals, and the child in order to attain this goal depends on certain factors specific to each. This chapter discusses these factors for each member of the triad.

The discussion of the child addresses the development of body image and self-esteem in normal and abnormal children. The developmentally disabled child's self-awareness and how the child feels about that self are important parts of his or her development as a whole person. In order to function at an effective level, humans need to feel good about themselves. Studies have demonstrated that atypical children and adolescents have impaired body image and lower self-esteem than normal peers. Illness, injury, congenital anomalies, and impaired interpersonal relationships do have an effect on the individual's perception of his or her body and self-esteem. The child's perception of illness, hospitalization, and treatment and the effect of the parent-child interactions on the development of body image and self-esteem are also discussed.

3

The discussion of the parents covers factors that influence parental reactions and coping behaviors when a child has a disability as well as parental reactions to the birth of a disabled child. A child's self-concept can be a reflection of the kind of care or lack of care received from the parents or significant caretakers. Parental overprotection is usually the result of good intentions. Overprotected children are often not self-reliant, are poor problem solvers, and are uncomfortable with even healthy risk-taking. Parents who reject their child may be unconsciously rejecting a child who has a short life expectancy. Parental rejection can also stem from denial that the parents have produced a less-than-perfect offspring. Rejected children may also be overprotected by parents who are overcompensating for their negative feelings. Children who are coldly cared for may have the perception that they are bad or unworthy and may have an indecisive idea of how they should behave.

The discussion of professionals includes health and educational personnel as well as those persons in related disciplines who play a role in the life of a developmentally disabled child (e.g., social workers). There must be communication and cooperation among all these persons if a comprehensive and appropriate plan for a given child is to be designed and implemented. A team approach, whether multi-, inter-, or transdisciplinary, is the best means of achieving this. In addition, professionals can have a positive or negative influence on parental cooperation. This is only one reason that parents must be included as part of the child's planning and management team.

THE CHILD

What do you see when you observe a child on the playground, at home, in the grocery store, or in the classroom? Do you see bright, wide-open eyes soaking in all there is to see? Do you see a face that smiles or frowns or communicates in some way with people? Do you see a body that is full of movement, exploring the environment and striving to master itself and all it contacts? Do you see evidence that the child has feelings not only about that physical body and all that is in it and on it, but also thoughts and feelings about being a good child or a bad child? It is hoped that you will see a child who is confidently interacting with people and objects in the environment.

Development of Body Image and Self-Esteem

What do normal children know and think of themselves? What factors affect the development of healthy body image and self-esteem? The study of body image, body concept, body perception, self-concept, and self-esteem is complicated by the use of many different terms and the lack of standard use of these terms and their definitions. For the purpose of this chapter, the following definitions are used.

Body image is a conscious awareness or a mental picture that the individual has of the internal and external body. This awareness is based on the child's experience of the body and the perception of others and of the child's own body. A child's body image develops through the child's visual, tactile, and kinesthetic experiences of his or her body. Body image includes viewing the body as attractive or unattractive. Traditionally, the child's self-drawing has been used to obtain a pictorial representation of the child's body image (Figures 1.1 and 1.2) (Atwater, 1983; A. Henderson & Coryell, 1972; Ottenbacher, 1981).

Body concept is the abstract, intellectual knowledge a child has of his or her own body. This is acquired through conscious learning and includes the ability to locate and label body parts and surfaces. The cognitive awareness of "me" and "not-me" is based upon sensory experience of one's own body in comparison with the same kind of sensory experience with the bodies of other people and objects. Specific sensory experience would include visual and tactile experiences. Body concept can be evaluated by asking the child to point to and name his or her body parts and the body parts on other people. Gilfoyle, Grady, and Moore (1981) refer to this as body sense.

Body perception can be compared to an unconscious map of the body that is based on tactile, proprioceptive, and vestibular information that has been received, interpreted, integrated, and stored in the central nervous system and enables the human to know how the body is positioned and moving without relying on visual cues (Ayres, 1979). Vision also provides important information to the central nervous system and further enhances the human's body perception/schema. Body perception assists the human in maintaining posture, performing automatic movements, and coordinating voluntary movements (A. Henderson & Coryell, 1972; Smythies, 1953). Since body perception is an unconscious mechanism, it can only be assumed that it is properly integrated by observing the individual's appropriate motor response to stimuli (Smythies, 1953).

Body perception and body schema are the same according to Ayres (1979). A. Henderson and Coryell (1972) described body schema as an unconscious mechanism that underlies the spatial motor control, providing the central nervous system with information about the relationship of the body and its parts to environmental space.

Self-perception, self-image, self-concept, self-identification, and *self-esteem* refer generally to the individual's cognitive awareness that he or she is separate and unique from others. Self-esteem encompasses the individual's evaluation of himself or herself and the perception of how others judge the individual.

Self-awareness or self-perception is enhanced when the child engages in purposeful activities that allow him or her to interact with the environment. Playing with toys and other objects in the environment also assists the child in

Figure 1.1. Self-portrait by nondisabled male, age 3 years.

developing a sense of what is "mine" and "not-mine" as the child is developing a sense of pride in the body and the accomplishments of that body. Autonomy or self-mastery is very important to most individuals throughout life. Autonomy is particularly important to the 2-year-old child and the adolescent.

Self-image or self-identity evolves from self-awareness or self-perception (Gilfoyle et al., 1981) and includes the child's view of present accomplishments as well as the child's dreams of what he or she would like to become. Self-identification is the result of the integration of one's past and present with what one wishes to become in the future. Small children pretend to be firemen or teachers, and adolescents begin to try out different roles through employment and new kinds of social interactions.

The individual's self-concept and self-esteem consist of what the individual consciously thinks of himself or herself, including unique characteristics and what he or she is capable of doing. This evolves from past experience, including interactions with parents, siblings, and peers and contact with institutions such as school (Gilfoyle et al., 1981). Self-esteem is the value the individual places on his or her own worth (J. Coopersmith, 1967; S. Coopersmith, 1959; Teplin, Howard, & O'Connor, 1981). Ayres (1979) stated that self-esteem, self-control, and self-confidence come from feeling the body is a competent sensorimotor being and from good neurological integration and the ability to direct oneself.

Self-actualization is a process whereby we become whatever we have the potential to become through our own efforts (Le Francois, 1983).

In summary, body perception is the unconscious sensory construct that allows us to maintain antigravity posture, perform unconscious movement, and plan and execute voluntary movement effectively. Body image and body concept are the conscious, cognitive awareness of the body, its parts and surfaces.

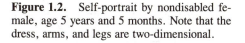

Figure 1.2. Self-portrait by nondisabled female, age 5 years and 5 months. Note that the dress, arms, and legs are two-dimensional.

Self-awareness, -perception, -image, -concept, and -esteem are the individual's assessment of the thinking, feeling part of the person and relate to the individual's evaluation of how well or how poorly he or she measures up to others. Also included in the complete picture the individual has of the self is a projection of the individual into future roles and identities.

Chronological Development of Body Image and Self-Esteem

How does the human evolve from an infant—who is assumed to not have a sense of separate body or a sense of unique personal identity—to the adolescent or young adult who is comfortable with whom he or she is becoming (self-identity and self-esteem) and who is on the way to performing at his or her maximal level of potential (self-actualization)? Two basic components, body perception or schema, which allow us to know where we are in space and allow us to move efficiently, and self-esteem, which is how we feel about our physical and emotional selves, develop over a long period of time. The changes brought about by these components are ongoing throughout our lives, and bring the infant from a state of no personal identity to self-actualized adulthood.

In the early hours and days after birth, the infant receives from the mother or other caring individuals a great deal of visual, auditory, gustatory, tactile, proprioceptive, and vestibular input through such ordinary activities as feeding, bathing, cuddling, and rocking. The reception and organization of stimuli by the baby's central nervous system of what the baby sees, hears, tastes, smells, and feels is the basis for the development of a map of the external and internal body as well as perceptual maps of the environment. The infant begins to learn to distinguish between what is part of the body and what is external and separate from the body through such means as touching his or her own body and that of others, experiencing discomfort, and seeing his or her own reflection and that of others in the mirror. Experiencing voluntary movement is also vital to the development of body concept and perception and a developing sense of personal self-identity (Anthony, 1979).

The human infant is no longer viewed as a passive recipient of stimulation. Brazelton and Als (1979) described the neonate's initial major task as one of achieving homeostasis while receiving great amounts of stimulation from the environment. However, even the neonate shows evidence of affective and cognitive response soon after birth. Self-quieting behaviors such as placing a fist in the mouth and sucking on it have been observed in the neonate.

If the infant is cared for by an adult who is perceptive of the infant's needs to be fed, changed, and talked to, the infant begins to experience the feeling of being able to exert some control over the environment and develop trust in that environment. This is the foundation for a sense of personal identity and self-esteem and is the beginning of viewing oneself as competent and worthwhile.

Body Image and Body Concept

Body image and body concept are the conscious components of body perception. They include the conscious awareness of the individual parts of the body. The child can not only locate or point to specific parts but can name them as well. Body image and concept are based upon body perception.

Mans, Cicchetti, and Sroufe (1978) have studied infants and their ability to recognize themselves in a mirror. This is one part of the process of developing awareness of the self as distinct from others, which is a major developmental task in infancy. Initially, in the first month of life, the infant responds to the mirror image with little affect and little sustained attention. Soon the response changes and becomes more social. The infant smiles, laughs, vocalizes, and touches the reflection of his or her own face in the same way the baby would respond to the faces of other people. By about 6–12 months the infant will also interact with the self-reflection in a more repetitive and deliberate manner. When the baby is 12–15 months old the responses to the mirror self-image become more sober and even avoidant in nature. This response to the mirror images resembles the stranger anxiety responses seen in many children of this age. The infant recognizes that the self-reflection in the mirror is not the face or faces viewed as often as the primary caretaker's face is viewed. Self-recognition of the mirror image begins to emerge in some normal infants between 15 and 18 months and is well established by 22 months of age.

The recognition of one's own mirror image parallels the development of the child's ability to draw his or her own self-portraits. The preschooler's earliest drawings (Figure 1.3) of the human form initially include those parts that were first verbally labeled—head, some facial features, arms, and legs. These earliest drawings include a primitive face with eyes, mouth, and arms and legs

Figure 1.3.   Early self-portrait by nondisabled male, age 3 years.

added directly to the head. Later the facial features are more detailed, with definite eyes, nose, mouth, ears, teeth, and eyebrows, and arms and legs may have hands and feet added. Eventually there will be a torso between the head and the upper and lower extremities (Figure 1.4) and the drawings will be two-dimensional (Figure 1.2).

Body Perception

Body perception is the "unconscious awareness" of where the body begins and ends, the relationship of one part to other body parts, and the relationship of the whole body to the environment, especially the body's relationship to the pull of gravity. This is how our brain knows when the body is right side up or falling.

The acquisition of intentional, independent movement and the attainment of bowel and bladder control contribute to the development of body perception and are major milestones from the child's and the parents' perspectives. Intentional movement is vital to the child's acquiring knowledge of his or her own body, how to control that body, and the body's relationship to space. Intentional movement is an important factor in the development of autonomy (B. J. Lewis, 1978). Behavioral autonomy is the ability to perform age-appropriate tasks in an independent manner, and emotional autonomy involves relying on one's own inner reserves of esteem and confidence when involved in interpersonal relationships (Atwater, 1983).

Self-Image

According to Gardner (1978), the following components contribute to a sense of self: the individual must be aware of his or her own body and its dimensions,

Figure 1.4. Self-portrait, nondisabled female, age 4 years and 3 months.

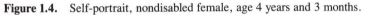

appearance, and condition; the individual must be able to refer to the self using appropriate language such as his or her own name or words of personal reference; and the individual must know his or her own personal history, which includes an awareness of individual needs. Gardner states that a mature sense of self involves being comfortable with what one has done, what one is like now, and what one will become.

The development of the individual's sense of self (self-perception and self-esteem) evolves out of the individual's interactions with the environment, especially interpersonal contacts. Although body sense (body perception) remains a foundation for self-perception/awareness throughout life, it is not enough by itself (Gilfoyle et al., 1981). A major task of the infant and toddler is the development of an awareness that the self is separate from that of others and that the child can cause things to happen, have feelings, and express feelings (Oppenheim, 1984).

Through the experience of hearing his or her own cry, feeling his or her own body with his or her own hands, and seeing his or her own image in a mirror, the infant eventually realizes that his or her body is separate from that of others and can, by itself, cause things to happen. For example, when a mother allows her infant to stop sucking and look around during feeding, the infant is given the opportunity to choose between one activity or the other. This contributes to the development of autonomy and the feeling of competence (Brazelton & Als, 1979). By 10 months, the infant has developed a sense of identity

(Caplan, 1973). The development of autonomy is well under way in the 2-year-old child who has experienced volitional movement and speech (responding to a request with the word "No!") in an environment that has encouraged self-initiated action. The 2-year-old has a sense of "me" and what is "mine" or a sense of ownership of body parts, actions, objects, and significant people. The young child is proud of what he or she can do (Gilfoyle et al., 1981). Object permanence and the cognitive readiness to imitate the actions of others and internalize the behavior of others are also prerequisites to the development of a sense of self (Offer, Ostrow, & Howard, 1981).

Different aspects of autonomy develop over a period of years. The 2-year-old is preoccupied with self-initiated movement, whereas the 4-year-old is acquiring an idea of what is good and bad in the self and others through interactions with others and through role playing (Brazelton & Als, 1979; Garwood, 1983; Kaluger & Kaluger, 1979). The 6-year-old enters school, is exposed to the influence of peers, and acquires an increasing sense of independence from parental influence. The 7–8-year-old demonstrates increasing self-criticism and some insight as to what makes him or her special or unique. The 7–8-year-old child's self-image is related to the physical self, such as attributes of height, weight, and hair style or how he or she is clothed. Children this age frequently compare these same features to those of their peers (Gesell, Ilg, & Ames, 1977). If a friend has a specific kind of sweater or record album then they should have the same if they are to be as good as the friend.

When 9-year-old children answer the question "Who am I?", they will answer by describing concrete physical characteristics such as where they live. The 11-year-old will describe the self in terms of personality traits such as "I am truthful" (S. Coopersmith, 1959; Gesell, Ilg, & Ames, 1956; Le Francois, 1983).

Self-identity is an abstract concept, and we can infer an individual's self-concept/identity only by observing what the individual does or tells us. The young adolescent has an increasing awareness that the self is a part of the total being and the self is the planner and initiator of the individual's thoughts and actions as well as the recipient of feelings, and the sources of personal judgments. Eventually, the individual acquires a sense of honor and self-respect, and takes responsibility for the thoughts and actions of the self. Self-identity also includes impulse control, emotional tone, values, sexual identification, and the individual's identification with a vocation (Offer et al., 1981). There are many factors that affect self-concept. A few are the individual's health, experience of success or failure, parental behaviors toward the child, and interactions with siblings, peers, and teachers.

Body Image and Self-Concept in the Developmentally Disabled Child

The developmentally disabled infant may not be able to receive, process, and integrate the sensory input that is so necessary for development. This child may not be able to experience normal automatic and voluntary movements. The disabled infant is also at risk of being cared for in a less supportive emotional environment, so that his or her development of a healthy body image and good self-esteem is impaired. A sensorimotor deficit can distort what a child learns about the body (Figures 1.5 and 1.6). The deficit and the reactions of significant others such as parents and teachers can affect how the child feels about the body and the worth the child assigns to the self that "lives" in the body.

Studies of children with cerebral dysfunction (cerebral palsy or neurological dysfunction secondary to hydrocephalus), but with normal intelligence, indicate that these children experience increased incidence of emotional and behavioral problems when compared to children without brain damage (Seidel, Chadwick, & Rutter, 1975).

Teplin et al. (1981) found that 4–8-year-old children with cerebral palsy and normal intelligence appeared to maintain positive self-esteem until early elementary school. At that time, students began to compare themselves with their nonhandicapped peers and became upset about the differences in ability.

Early adolescence may also be a time when the disabled individual re-evaluates the effect of the disability on present and future life and may exhibit increased feelings of depression and pessimism (Harper, 1978). Adolescents with myelodysplasia exhibit lower self-esteem than normal peers and regard being different as a negative characteristic (P. W. Hayden, Davenport, & Campbell, 1979; McAndrews, 1979).

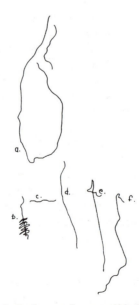

Figure 1.5. Self-portrait by male, age 5 years, with diagnosis of cerebral palsy, mental retardation, and severe bilateral hearing impairment. The child labeled the parts as he drew: *a,* head; *b,* eyes; *c,* nose; *d,* mouth; *e,* arms; and *f,* legs.

Figure 1.6. Self-portrait by male, age 7 years and 7 months, with diagnosis of left spastic hemiparesis and mental retardation. Note that body parts on the left side of the drawing are less complete.

In studies comparing adolescents with cleft lip and palate to adolescents with orthopedic impairments, Harper and Richman (1978) concluded that the type of disability does have some effect on the adolescent's personality characteristics. The individuals with cleft lip and palate demonstrated greater self-concern and self-doubt about interpersonal interactions, whereas orthopedically impaired adolescents demonstrated an isolative and passive orientation to interpersonal interactions.

When Harper (1978) compared adolescents with congenital deficits to age peers with traumatic impairment, data did not support the hypothesis that there are disability-specific personality traits. The fact that physical impairment was present was more significant than the types of disability. Male adolescents in this study tended to reflect a more passive personality style than did females. This was possibly related to a lack of identification with male sexual models and limited social experiences.

In their extensive study of the self-perception of adolescents, Offer et al. (1981) found that physically ill adolescents had lower body image and poorer emotional tone than healthy age mates. These adolescents, with severe acne, marked pubertal delay, hypertension, kidney disease, and cystic fibrosis, felt badly about themselves and viewed their bodies as less attractive than the bodies of normal peers. These young people also stated that they were a burden to their families more often than did healthy adolescents.

The mentally retarded individual demonstrates aberrant body image through self-drawings and also has a poor self-concept (Ottenbacher, 1981).

Moen, Wilcox, and Burns (1977) described 10 8–15-year-old individuals with phenylketonuria (PKU) as having lowered self-esteem when compared with their normal siblings. Lowered self-esteem was present even when the effects of lowered intelligence were removed and may be related to the constant reminder of a special condition and the necessity for a special diet.

The effect of parental attitudes on the self-perception of a handicapped individual cannot be discounted. An individual's self-love will often be a mirror image of the love that person has received from other significant people. Lussier (1980) described an adolescent client born with both arms significantly deformed. In analysis it was determined that the young man's low self-esteem was not related to the presence of deformed arms but to the discouragement and shame his mother had expressed.

The Child's Perception of Illness, Hospitalization, and Treatment

The developmentally disabled child is a child with chronic problems, some of which will necessitate repeated hospitalization and outpatient follow-up. Studies have shown that there is a higher incidence of later behavioral problems among children who have experienced frequent and extended hospitalization. Handicapped children are also the victims of a higher incidence of child abuse.

Rutter (1976, 1979) found that there is not an increased risk for later emotional or behavioral disturbances in children who experience a single hospital admission of 1 week or less in duration. However, repeated hospital admissions are related to a high incidence of emotional disturbance in later childhood, especially if the child came from a disadvantaged environment. Rutter's study supported the earlier findings of Douglas (1975), who reported that hospitalization before age 5 years of more than 1 week's duration was associated with an increased risk for behavioral problems and poor reading in adolescence. This was especially true if, at the time of hospitalization, the child was highly dependent on the mother or under stress.

When a child is admitted to the hospital, whether for a planned, short-term stay or an unplanned, sudden admission, the experience is disruptive. Hospitalization disrupts the familiar routines and relationships of the child and the parents. Hospitalization always produces some stress even if the parents are allowed extensive visiting privileges. Other variables such as the child's age and adequate parental support will have an effect on how the child copes with the stress of being ill and in the hospital. Children between the ages of 6–7 months and 5–6 years are particularly stressed when separated from their parents. Other factors having an effect on how a child copes with illness and hospitalization are the illness, the treatment, and the young child's difficulty in cognitively understanding the purpose of hospitalization and treatment.

Acute distress syndrome has been observed in young children admitted to hospitals or residential nurseries (Rutter, 1979). Acute distress syndrome is characterized by increased anxiety and crying when the child has been left by the parents. Rutter proposed that the distress behaviors are related to an interference in attachment behaviors, possibly because the separation of the child and the mother disrupts an existing bond or the hospitalization does not facilitate the mother-child attachment process.

Petrillo and Sanger (1972) described three phases of reaction to separation from the parents. These three phases of reaction can be observed in children deposited by the parents with a babysitter, a preschool teacher, or a therapist as well as in hospitalized children. During phase one the child is restless, cries a great deal, and may appear to be searching for familiar sights and sounds. This child is protesting being left in a strange place and may reject the attempts of others to offer comfort. In the second phase of reaction to separation, crying will diminish because the child has discovered that protesting is not successful. The child may appear apathetic and disinterested in the surroundings and play. This child may be mourning the loss of the parents, especially if object permanence and trust in the parent is not well established.

The third phase is characterized by interest in the surroundings. The child may begin to play and interact with people. This "settling-in" is a false adjustment because it can be easily reversed by the reappearance of the parents. The reappearance of the parents may serve as a reminder to the child of the previous abandonment. It is not unusual to observe children cry when the parents reappear but not cry when the parents leave again. This may contribute to the development of impaired trust of adults and may be a factor in the behavioral problems in older children who have experienced repeated hospitalizations.

Brewster (1982) determined that children acquire an understanding of information about their illness in a predictable cognitively maturational sequence. Brewster's findings indicate that a child's understanding of an illness is primarily determined by cognitive maturation, not by an extensive educational program. Providing excessive information about the causes of an illness or the purpose of a treatment or the consequences of a potentially harmful action usually will not elicit the desired cooperation from the child.

Children who are 2–6 years old and are functioning at a preoperational cognitive level usually believe that the disease is the result of human actions. A preoperational child might state that, "I got sick because I didn't wear my hat." Typically this child will perceive uncomfortable treatment, immobilization, and isolation as a punishment for a real or an imagined wrongdoing.

Children age 7–10 years no longer attribute all illness to direct human action but rather to other physical causes such as germs. Some children will assume that all illnesses are caused by the same germ. This child knows that treatment is designed to help but is not always able to perceive empathy in the treatment giver. Some children may believe that the only way a therapist will know that the treatment hurts is if the child cries.

Children age 9 years and above can now understand that diseases may have more than one cause or different causes. This child can also infer both intention and empathy in the treatment giver. For example, most 9-year-old children understand that a painful treatment is not being administered as a punishment and will realize that the treatment giver can empathize with the child in his or her discomfort.

It should be noted that if an older child is highly stressed a less mature understanding of the cause of the disease may be retained and expressed. A child who understands that the illness was caused by a germ may still wonder if it was really related to some wrongdoing committed by the child. A child may feel more comfortable with having guilt feelings about causing the illness than with feeling helpless about the situation.

Brewster (1982) concluded that children should not be forced to understand information that is at a higher level than their emotional needs require. The coping style of the child's family appeared to be a more significant predictor of the child's adjustment than repeated explanations about the purpose of hospitalization and treatment.

Some parents are surprised to observe behavioral disturbances when the child returns home from the hospital. Douglas (1975) reported a higher incidence of behavioral deterioration or disturbed behavior, especially in children ages 6 months to 5 years who have been admitted to the hospital three or more times and for more than a month in duration. In those cases where unrestricted parental visits were allowed, there was a lower incidence of behavior deterioration.

In summary, in addition to the illness or injury that precipitated the hospitalization, two major factors appear to have negative effects on the developing child's self-esteem and parent-child relationships: 1) separation from the parents is traumatic and interferes with the attachment process, and 2) young children cognitively cannot understand what has happened and may have unrealistic perceptions of the purpose of treatment.

In order to reduce the trauma of hospitalization, some hospitals allow unlimited parental visitation and assign only a few staff to specific children. While in the hospital and after dismissal the young child will need many opportunities to receive appropriate education about his or her illness and treatment as well as opportunities to express anxieties and fears through play. The hospitalized child will also need continued reassurances that he or she is a valued person.

Parent-Child Interaction and Development of Body Image and Self-Esteem

Since body image and self-esteem are based upon the child's sensory and interpersonal experiences, parental care, including physical and emotional interaction, that expresses respect and love will usually result in a child with a healthy body image and good self-esteem. It is believed that the result of early parent-infant attachment is the emergence in the child of self-reliance, achievement of maturity, and the ability to eventually form similar attachments with others. Failure to form an early attachment may result in a child who lacks a feeling of security in his or her environment, is often anxious, and will have difficulty forming enduring relationships with others (Gardner, 1978). According to Rosen and D'Andrado (1959), parents of high-achieving children set higher standards, encouraged competitiveness, demonstrated concern, encouraged warmly, and displayed great affection. Parents of low-achieving children were likely to be highly directive, made decisions for their children, reacted with annoyance and anger when the children did not immediately behave appropriately and successfully, and were more domineering and authoritative.

THE PARENTS

When a couple has a normal baby they are faced with the necessity of making many changes so that they can meet the needs of their new family member. Some of these changes or adjustments include assuming the new role of parent and reorganizing priorities for time use and financial resources. Parenthood is a role that is not automatically or comfortably assumed by all couples. Establishing a family requires that the husband and wife strive to accomplish many new and overlapping developmental tasks (Tables 1.1 and 1.2).

Developmental tasks are skills that are mastered within a specified time frame according to the expectations of the society in which the individual lives. Developmental tasks are based on the individual's physical maturation and on cultural influences (Duvall, 1971). In the American culture, a young child is expected to walk and achieve bowel and bladder control by a certain age, and young adults are expected to be responsible for their own actions. The developmental task of walking is based primarily on biophysical maturation, whereas those of bowel and bladder continence and self-responsibility are based on biophysical maturation as well as cognitive and cultural expectations.

Table 1.1. Developmental tasks of the new mother

1. Reconcile conflicting conceptions of roles (i.e., wife, mother, employee).
2. Accept and adjust to the stresses and pressures that accompany motherhood and learn how to competently take care of an infant with assurance.
3. Provide appropriate opportunities that will facilitate the development of the infant's motor, cognitive, emotional, and social skills.
4. Share responsibilities of child care with the husband and maintain a satisfying relationship with the husband.
5. Maintain a sense of personal autonomy throughout the parenting period.

Adapted from Duvall (1971) and McBride (1973).

Table 1.2. Developmental tasks of the new father

---
1. Reconcile conflicting conceptions of roles as husband, breadwinner, and father.
2. Learn how to take care of an infant.
3. Encourage the child's full development.
4. Maintain a mutually satisfying relationship with the wife.
5. Maintain a satisfying sense of autonomy and self-concept.

Adapted from Duvall (1971).

Duvall (1971) stated that the successful achievement of developmental tasks leads to happiness and success with later tasks, whereas failure may lead to unhappiness within the individual, disapproval by society, and difficulty with later development tasks. Some of the developmental tasks for the parents and the family unit include physical and emotional maintenance of all the members of the family and socializing the children so that they can eventually be released into society as self-supporting, contributing members of the society (Duvall, 1971).

Brazelton and Als (1979) stated that one developmental task of a new mother is to provide a sensitive environment in which the mother learns to interpret the baby's messages and to meet the baby's needs. Interviews of prospective mothers during their first pregnancy revealed an almost pathological degree of anxiety. After the baby was born, the anxiety appeared to have been an important facilitator in helping the new mother move from a prenatal state of homeostasis into the reorganized state necessary for being able to meet the baby's needs. The prenatal anxiety had been a stimulus for preparing the woman for the new role of mother and for the mother-infant attachment process. The mother-infant attachment or bonding process is believed to be a very important factor in the creation of an appropriately sensitive environment that will meet the infant's physical and emotional needs.

Once the baby is born the new parents must come to terms with the discrepancies that may exist between the child they hoped for and the actual child. Even a normal, healthy baby may not look like or behave like the dreamed-of child (Solnit & Stark, 1961).

The birth of a handicapped child may disrupt and interfere with the achievement of the parental developmental tasks, and occurs at a time when the mother has to cope with a great deal of psychological and physiological change (Sensky, 1982). The parents, in dealing with the disparity between the desired child and the actual child, will be grieving for the lost child while attempting to adjust to the disabled child and his or her unique problems and needs. The parents' adaptive capacities are stressed because they have failed to create a perfect child and may feel they have been damaged by that child. The birth of a handicapped child may stigmatize the parents as also being abnormal (L. G. Miller, 1968; Sensky, 1982).

Parental Reactions to the Birth of a Developmentally Disabled Child

The feelings experienced by the parents who have produced a handicapped child are many and varied. Some of the feelings described in the literature include hopelessness, despair, pessimism, revulsion, inadequacy, fear, anger, guilt, and embarrassment. These feelings are sometimes legitimate reactions to a crisis that may be perceived as a blow to parental self-esteem and a disappointment of parental goals (Kolin, Scherzer, New, & Garfield, 1978; MacKeith, 1973; Taylor, 1982).

There are many reasons why a couple decide to have a child (Taylor, 1982):

1. The child represents the couple's love and the synthesis of man and wife.
2. The child represents a continuation of the family, the family name, and the culture.
3. The child represents success of the parents in fulfilling their adult roles.
4. Society expects this of a married couple.

Regardless of the reasons for having a child, the birth of a handicapped baby disappoints that reason and may be perceived by the parents as failure to meet major life objectives. Under these circumstances, many parents experience several phases or levels of reaction to the crisis.

The first phase may be referred to as a period of *disintegration* and may be characterized by irrational behavior, crying, feelings of helplessness, a desire to escape the situation, and a reluctance to become attached to the child. Some parents also report feelings of shock and denial. These are viewed by some as necessary defense mechanisms that protect the parents during the early hours and days after learning about their child's problem. Acute feelings of sadness and grief over the loss of the desired child sometimes extend into later phases and become a chronic grief. This is especially true when the parents are frequently faced with the evidence of their child's long-term or recurring problems. All of these feelings are disorganizing and exhausting. It is important to remember that during this first phase the parents may have difficulty absorbing or remembering diagnostic information or home program instructions. Forgetting information is a defense against the emotional pain the parents are feeling (McCollum, 1975; L. G. Miller, 1968).

The second phase is one of *adjustment,* during which the parents may express partial acceptance as well as denial. Often the parents will seek for a source of blame or will "shop" for many different diagnostic opinions, particularly if the first diagnosis or prediction of outcome is unacceptable to them. Each new crisis or setback may reactivate previous feelings of anger, sorrow, or depression.

The reintegration phase is characterized by a reorganization of priorities and resources as well as a reorganization of the parental self. It is hoped that the parents can function effectively and realistically when dealing with their child's special needs and future plans. A realistic acknowledgment of the child's and family's situation makes it possible for the parents to assign the child to a place within the family. This takes a great deal of energy and time, and not all parents can achieve this (Drotar, Baskiewicz, Irvin, Kennell, & Klaus, 1975; Herskowitz & Marks, 1977; L. G. Miller, 1968; Taylor, 1982).

The family may be able to give the care of the defective part of the child to professionals and reserve the more normal attributes for themselves and thus provide "normal" loving care for their child. This may help the parents see their child as a person first and a person with a disability second (Herskowitz & Marks, 1977).

Some families cannot progress through the different stages of family development (Table 1.3) and are frozen in an earlier stage, especially if their disabled child remains dependent. Sibling order may be reversed with the disabled child forever being the "youngest" child (L. G. Miller, 1968). Families of premature and sick infants are at increased risk for divorce, child abuse, abandonment, and the infant's failure to thrive (Trause & Kramer, 1983). It has also been demonstrated that the premature child is at risk for later physical and developmental deficits, including behavioral abnormalities (Minde, Whitelaw, Brown, & Fitzhardinge, 1983).

Table 1.3.   Stages of family development

Stages	Family status	Description
1	Married couple without children	The couple will be settling into marital roles (i.e., masculine and feminine roles); adjusting to the kin network; learning how to establish and manage resources such as money.
2	Childbearing family	The couple will be nurturing infants and coping with the needs of both the infants and adults in the family unit economically and socially.
3	Family with preschool and school-age children	The couple will create an atmosphere that facilitates the development of autonomy in their children.
4	Family with teenage and young adult children	The couple will prepare the children for independent living and serve as a launching center for the children; begin to establish postparental interests and roles.
5	Middle-age parents without children at home	The couple will continue to establish postparental roles and reorganize marital relationships and roles.

Adapted from Duvall (1971), L. G. Miller (1968), and Petrillo and Sanger (1972).

When working with developmentally disabled children, the needs of the parents must also be addressed. Helping the parents create an appropriate environment for their disabled child is a legitimate goal. Besides being cognizant of the individual parental development tasks (Tables 1.1 and 1.2), an awareness of the stage of development that the family is currently in and the degree of family integration will help the professional to more effectively assist the family of a disabled child (L. G. Miller, 1968). The stages of family development are listed and described in Table 1.3. The degree of family integration refers to the amount of agreement or conflict that exists between the husband and the wife and other family members pertaining to child management and values.

Factors That Influence Parental Behavior and Adaptation to Having a Disabled Child

Why are developmentally disabled children more likely to be victims of child abuse? What are the factors that influence a parent's ability to cope with the birth of a handicapped child? The severity of the child's physical impairment does not appear to be a significant factor affecting how the parents cope with their child's problem. A significant influence on parental coping abilities appears to be the level of family development (Table 1.3). Kolin et al. (1978) found that only those parents who had had the opportunity to develop a stable relationship over a minimum of 5 years of marriage were able to cope successfully with the crisis of having a handicapped child. Most of the successful parents had had at least one normal child prior to the birth of the handicapped child and the pregnancy had been planned. All of the children in Kolin et al.'s study who were poorly adjusted were the offspring of poorly adapted parents.

Crnic, Friedrich, and Greenberg (1983) found that, although marital disintegration increased with the presence of a severely mentally retarded child, the outcome was more strongly related to the stability of the marriage before the retarded child was born.

Other factors having an effect on parental coping abilities are the parents' own childhoods, events in the immediate postnatal period, characteristics of the child, prior child-rearing experiences, and the social environment (Rutter, 1979).

Parental Childhood

It has been frequently reported that abusing parents were more likely to have been the victims of child abuse. Collingwood and Alberman (1979) reported that the mothers of rejected children tended to have had poor relationships with their own fathers, were unhappy with their present life-styles, and perceived their child as having difficulty or as having an unlikeable personality. The rejected child in this study was more likely to have had poor health or significant behavioral problems such as severe temper tantrums.

Postnatal Events

It is believed that events in the immediate postnatal period may have a significant effect on the development of the parent-child relationship and on subsequent child development (Lamb & Hwang, 1982). Lamb and Hwang proposed that in the human mother there exists a sensitive period occurring in the first minutes and hours after childbirth. During this sensitive period certain experiences such as close physical contact between the mother and newborn infant are more likely to produce affectionate attachment or bonding of the mother and infant than at any other time. (It should be noted that the maternal sensitive period is the optimal time for maternal-infant attachment but is not the only time such attachment can occur.) It is proposed that when the bonding process is disrupted, behavior such as child abuse and neglect will occur.

Lamb and Hwang also stated that there is a belief that the hormonal changes occurring with pregnancy, labor, and delivery biologically "prime" human mothers to behave maternally as soon as the child is born. If the newborn infant is made available to the mother when she is primed, maternal behaviors and thus attachment will be established more easily and the mother will be more responsive and competent. It is hypothesized that the hormones have a facilitating rather than a determining effect on human maternal behavior.

During a predischarge feeding, Leifer, Leiderman, Barnett, and Williams (1972) found that the mothers of full-term infants demonstrated more affectionate touching, held their infants closer, and smiled more than the mothers of separated and nonseparated premature babies. The mothers of premature babies, especially those separated from their infants in the immediate postnatal period, demonstrated less confidence in their own parenting abilities.

K. Grossman, Thane, and Grossman (1981) suggested that early rather than extended mother-infant contact facilitated attachment. However, de Chateau (1979) observed that 1 year after the birth the mothers who were allowed early and extra contact time with their newborn infants were holding their child closer to their body, and fewer had returned to work or initiated toilet training. More of the extra contact children were demonstrating advanced motor, adaptive, language, and social skills than those children who were cared for in a traditional newborn nursery.

Gomes-Pedro, deAlmeida, daCosta, and Barbosa (1984) reported that additional early mother-infant contact had a positive effect on maternal behavior but also significantly increased the interaction behavior of the infant. Several other studies support the hypothesis that early close contact between the mother and her newborn child promotes attachment behavior (Ali & Lowry, 1981; Hales, Lazoff, Sosa, & Kennell, 1977).

An infant's illness may make it impossible or difficult for parents to hold and feed their child. If the baby is perceived as very fragile or vulnerable, the parents may inadvertently begin a lifelong pattern of relating to their child in a way that promotes undesirable results. For example, an overprotected child may not have learned to take responsibility for himself or herself later in life.

Premature and sick infants are less responsive to social stimulation than their healthy, full-term peers. Acutely ill infants show less movement of their body parts and open their eyes less than healthy infants. Mothers of ill infants tend to touch their babies less and have been observed to smile less and do not look directly at their infant's face as often (Minde et al., 1983).

The parents of very ill children may not think of the child as being completely theirs as long as the child is under professional care (M. Green & Solnit, 1964). These parents may also feel sorry for their child as well as extremely apprehensive for their child's welfare even in safe situations. Parents who perceive their child as fragile or vulnerable are often reluctant to leave their child with a babysitter. As a result, the child may experience separation anxiety long after the age when most children are comfortable with reasonable amounts of separation from their parents.

Some parents of handicapped children may infantilize their "fragile" child by not setting limits and by being overindulgent, solicitous, and overprotective. As a result, the child is more likely to be overly dependent, disobedient, and uncooperative. If undue overconcern has been expressed about bodily function or malfunction, the child may become hypochondriacal, with frequent absence from school (M. Green & Solnit, 1964).

Sigal and Gagnon (1975) found that severely ill children exhibited more conduct problems and a tendency toward excessive dependence as compared to moderately ill children. The more intense the parents' preoccupation with the child's survival and health, the less capacity the parents had for setting limits for their child.

Characteristics of the Child

The baby's physical appearance may be viewed as attractive or unattractive by the parents. The baby's level or quality of responsiveness to stimulation will also have an effect on parental behavior toward the child (Solnit & Stark, 1961). An alert baby who cuddles when held will elicit a reciprocal response in the parent. On the other hand, an irritable baby or an unresponsive baby is more likely to solicit a negative response in the parent.

The sex of the child may also be an important factor. Crnic et al. (1983) found that retarded male children had a more significant negative impact on the parent's marriage than retarded female children.

Parents have reported that responsiveness, temperament, repetitive behavior patterns, and the presence of additional or unusual caregiving demands were significantly related to the amount of stress they felt when caring for their handicapped child (Beckman, 1983).

Previous Child-Rearing Experience

Parents who have already produced a normal child are more likely to have a healthy self-concept. These experienced parents are more likely to be comfortable with the responsibilities of parenthood and are better equipped to cope with the needs of a handicapped child. In contrast, parents whose first baby is born with a handicap have not yet demonstrated that they can produce a normal child. The first-time parent must adjust not only to a new child but to the new role of parent. These parents may have less confidence in themselves as capable people and may feel insecure in the role of parenting a normal child let alone a child with special needs.

Social Environment

Social environment includes cultural, religious, and economic influences. Cultural heritage may have an effect on how parents react to the birth of a handicapped child. In a culture that emphasizes the present, past, and future, in that order, the parents may be more concerned with the cause of the handicap than its future implications. In a culture that emphasizes the future and present more than the past, more concern about the prognosis and future expectations may be exhibited than concern for cause or even immediate treatment goals (Petrillo & Sanger, 1972).

Individual religious beliefs can be a source of strength and hope or a stimulus for self-condemnation. A higher incidence of marital discord and maternal depression has been reported in inner-city, working-class groups (Rutter, 1979).

THE PROFESSIONALS

The Team Approach

During the 1950s and 1960s most team approach concepts were nonexistent, and the efforts of a given professional were primarily an isolated or single approach with little knowledge of what other disciplines were providing for the client. Parental involvement in program planning was not encouraged at this time, either. Since the enactment of Public Law (P.L.) 94-142, which mandates a free and appropriate public education for all handicapped children from age 3 to 21, there has been a shift in professional role expectations (L. McCormick & Goldman, 1979). The more the child is physically impaired, the more likely that professionals with specialized training will be involved in the part of P.L. 94-142 called the individualized education program (IEP) process. The number of disciplines involved with any one child can be numerous, and in addition to special education, can include recreational therapy, speech therapy, physical therapy, occupational therapy, parental training, and nutrition and psychological counseling. These and other disciplines (including the family doctor) may have had, to some degree, contact with the handicapped child and the parents.

Basically, three team approaches have been used over the years to develop effective treatment programs for the family and their child, with varying levels of success.

Multidisciplinary Approach

The multidisciplinary approach to the intervention program with orthopedically and mentally impaired children has evolved from the medical model (Hart, 1977; Sirvis, 1978a). Here each member of the team assesses the child's ability as it relates to that team member's particular discipline. Each subsequently written report has been done independently of the other professionals' evaluations. It is common that communication that would allow opportunities for comparison of behavior or results, a concern about possible overlapping of treatment activities, and a discussion of an integrated program plan is nonexistent (Bennett, 1982; L. McCormick & Goldman, 1979). Sparling (1980) suggested that the outcome of this approach results in professional contradictions and client frustrations. Buckley (1983) stated that too often the written evaluation report is sent to one person (psychologist, physician, social worker) who has only a superficial knowledge of all the disciplines, but still is expected to interpret the results even beyond what has been written.

The multidisciplinary team approach does not provide any effective means of prioritizing the needs of the child via a group discussion. Also, since there is no group presentation there is no chance for feedback or revision of the original recommendations based on other findings (L. McCormick & Goldman, 1979). Basically, each discipline works separately for the purpose of assessing the child's ability in a particular area and then forwarding the information to a central figure. Current use of this approach may be in the form of a consultant who is called in to provide additional information not available in the present setting. This information is then filtered to other staff members via the inter- or transdisciplinary process.

Interdisciplinary Approach

In the interdisciplinary approach, the basic format of the multidisciplinary approach is expanded with coordinated team interaction. The expansion of this approach comes from the fact that there are often several informal interactions among the staff members where a pooling of knowledge and ideas results in an integrated program geared for a particular child's individual needs. The final formulation of a program plan is led by a case manager during a formal meeting. It is the case manager who communicates with the parents and is their contact member to funnel questions and answers to and from other staff personnel during the assessment and treatment phases (Fewell, 1983).

It is during the team meetings that the results of all the interviews and evaluations are discussed. Each team member provides input relating to his or her own field of expertise, with a final consensus of who is responsible for each category of the child's training. Levitt (1984) described how dressing may be taught by all staff members but each one is teaching a different aspect of the training program. For example, the occupational therapist may teach arm position or spatial awareness, the speech therapist teaches prepositional concepts such as front/back or top/bottom, and the teacher leads discussions about different types of clothes. The interawareness of what everyone was teaching made possible a smoother independent progress for the child. Sirvis (1978b) advocated that, for every child seen, the interdisciplinary team should make sure four main developmental areas are included in the child's overall goals:

1. Physical independence, including mastery of daily living skills
2. Self-awareness and social maturation
3. Academic growth
4. Career education, including constructive leisure activities (p. 392)

Peterson (1982), a strong advocate of early childhood education for the handicapped (ECEH) program, believes the interdisciplinary team approach is applicable for young handicapped or at-risk children because of several factors. First, the identification of this population requires the skills of every professional discipline. Second, the screening process should consist of all the developmental domains, including information about the medical and family status. Next, an effective treatment program needs the numerous methodologies of the practitioners, who are also working with the parents. Finally, a successful team requires a great deal of cooperative and shared planning time.

The major advantage of this system over a multidisciplinary style is that the child's program is not fragmented nor are there unnecessary overlaps of treatment across domains. A disadvantage to this system stems from the possible development of the "professional turf" syndrome (Heward & Orlansky, 1980). Since this approach stresses that certain areas are to be covered by specific disciplines, any "crossing over" may create professional jealousy. Also, with so many people making a variety of recommendations, the case manager may need to take extra time to understand the reasoning for the decisions so the parents' questions about their child's treatment are answered clearly. Too often feedback to the parents or to other professionals is slow or lacking.

Transdisciplinary Approach

S. R. Harris (1980) has indicated that the transdisciplinary model is but another step toward the ultimate treatment approach by extending the interdisciplinary team idea. W. M. Magrun and Tigges (1982) thought the term stresses both professional role release and role exchange. This concept is difficult for many professionals whose roles have been set in a particular mold for many years. Newly graduated therapists from the allied health field are still learning their "trade" and may be hesitant or may not feel confident enough to take on the responsibility to train others how and when to use specific techniques. At the same time, new graduates or new employees may be more open or willing to change over to different working procedures than the long-time employee.

The transdisciplinary model (also called integrated model or integrated therapy) becomes part of the child's care no matter if that care takes place in the home, around the neighborhood, or at school (L. McCormick & Lee, 1979; Sternat, Messina, Nietupski, Lyon, & Brown, 1977). Therefore, the parents are an important member of that team and give valuable input during the IEP process and treatment development. The actual composition of the group depends upon the needs of the child and support required for the family.

In order to minimize confusion and/or professional conflicts, one individual whose "discipline is most closely aligned with the major needs of the child" is designated (at some centers, several professionals are identified) to implement the child's IEP goals (S. R. Harris, 1980, p. 421). The care of the child and implementation of the program goals are the direct responsibility of one individual, thus reducing the number of staff needing extensive "hands-on" time with the child. This means the person in charge will need in-service sessions with various disciplines learning how to carry, position, feed, communicate with, or teach that child to increase his or her functional skills. Since in some centers this system will require all the staff to be in charge of several children, there will be both general in-service sessions and the individual training time the administration must allow for this approach to be successful. As Hart (1977) stated, each person is held accountable for what he or she teaches, how well the other person has learned the techniques, and the quality and rate of the child's performance.

To attain a successful transdisciplinary approach, Hart (1977) and Sternat et al. (1977) have listed several necessary guidelines:

1. In order to answer questions and make appropriate decisions, each team member must be knowledgeable in their own discipline.
2. There should be a consultative backup system available.
3. Assessment should be done if at all possible in the child's natural environment (home/ward rather than the therapy clinic).
4. Therapeutic techniques should be incorporated into the child's everyday life.
5. Skills should be generalized as much as possible. This means teaching a skill over several materials, persons, and cues.

The continued progress of this type of approach can only be attained by "persuading those professionals used to the traditional role to share their expertise without feeling that their own personal and professional scrutiny are threatened . . . a difficult but challenging task" (L. McCormick & Goldman, 1979, p. 159).

According to Hart (1977), L. McCormick and Goldman (1979), and Sparling (1980), the advantages of the transdisciplinary approach include the development of a staff reinforcement system in which each discipline depends on and supports the efforts of the others, thus building in a framework for continuing education. Because the fragmentation of services is reduced, there is better consistency of therapy throughout the day. Since a lot of the training is done within the classroom environment, there is no time wasted in transporting the children to the "traditional" therapy rooms. This system acknowledges the adult's needs and strengths, which allows for professional growth because of the increased contact time with other disciplines. One of the problems encountered within the other approaches, inconsistent management, is greatly reduced with the transdisciplinary approach. Ottenbacher (1983b) believes there is an appropriate time to develop a positive attitude toward the transdisciplinary idea. College students should be exposed to this system prior to graduation as part of their preclinical training. Without this exposure, Ottenbacher believes the students will develop narrow professional views.

Holm and McCartin (1978) think that a danger of the transdisciplinary idea is that it may be used exclusively by a practitioner who has a smattering of skills from other disciplines but who does not include or consult with other people associated with the child development field. Other disadvantages to this system include: 1) the difficulty of letting go of the traditional therapy/teacher roles; 2) the reluctance of administrators who do not know the advantages of this system to agree to in-service time; 3) the difficulty for some parents to take an active part in being a team member; and 4) professionals who are resistant to change and who impose their own value system on the team (Sparling, 1980).

Problems Relating to the Team Approach

Despite the recognition that closer cooperation and better communication are essential in running an effective team, a number of problems can be expected when first trying to put theory into practice (Levitt, 1984). One of the most frequently encountered issues is professional jealousy or the reluctance to role release certain acknowledged duties. For decades a standard way of describing the differences between physical therapists and occupational therapists was topographical: the occupational therapist works with an individual from the waist up and the physical therapist works from the waist down. Both professions would agree this is not only a poor explanation but an inaccurate definition. Table 1.4, which lists the basic similarities and differences of the complementary skills of occupational and physical therapists, should help to explain the roles of both. When either discipline begins to encroach on or invade the other's "domain," that individual is in violation of the other practitioner's territorial rights and professional jealousy can develop. With the cost of services continuing to rise, parents and/or third-party agencies can no longer afford all the services needed for every child. Many rural communities do not have the composite of disciplines found in the centers within the urban environment.

Table 1.4. Basic differences and similarities between occupational and physical therapists

Occupational therapy	Overlapping areas	Physical therapy
Splinting	Feeding	Ambulation
Psychological and social behavior	Range of motion	Posture—static and dynamic
Eye-hand coordination	Fine motor development	Bracing—trunk, legs
Play	Transfers	Exercise, including strengthening trunk, neck, limbs
Prevocational evaluation/ training	Gross motor development	
Homemaking	Dressing/bathing	
Learning difficulties	Adaptive equipment	
	Strengthening	
	Patient/family education	
	Behavior management	

Reprinted with permission from Prensky, A. L., & Palkes, H. S. (1982). *Care of the neurologically handicapped child* (p. 123). New York: Oxford University Press.

Other agencies have found it more economical in time and expense to have one person cover and train several areas rather than have a number of people all at one time visit parents and their child.

Another problem likely to develop is professional insecurity. Levitt (1984) described this as a person's unwillingness to show that he or she has professional deficits. This person does not want to acknowledge a lack of information about certain techniques or a particular syndrome and will often resist the change to the transdisciplinary approach.

Occasionally fear that someone else can perform a person's job equally well, if not better, creates self-doubt about professional capability and the necessity of one's position. The person feels safe if the team approach remains as is and no changes are instituted, since there would then be no reason to question the person's qualifications.

The ultimate goal of program planning should be directed toward the child and how the handicapping condition affects the family—not the professional's ego. Haring (1975) believes that the therapists (speech, physical, and occupational) should bring their intervention techniques together in the same room (generally the classroom). There each therapist has a chance to share his or her own skills and will often gain valuable techniques in other areas, which only increases and strengthens their own professional worth. No one has all the answers, and by pooling everyone's knowledge and skills, the benefit will be directed where it should be placed, on the child and family. L. McCormick and Lee (1979) advocated that, when everyone on the team works together, the objectives of P.L. 94-142 will become a working reality.

An effective team does not occur spontaneously. It takes time, requires careful planning, and is made possible by maintaining a positive attitude and a desire to seek solutions to problems, be it in one's own area or elsewhere

(Fewell, 1983; Howard, 1982; Levitt, 1984). Howard (1982) believes there are five points each team member must individually and collectively address to assure the development of an effective team:

1. Acceptance of differences in skills.
2. Acceptance of differences in approach.
3. Willingness not to try to know everything.
4. An ability to call on others for assistance.
5. Nonthreatening opportunities for discussion of these areas. (p. 320)

Those involved with the team approach, primarily the transdisciplinary model, in the ensuing years will have to deal with issues of legality. Ottenbacher (1983b) questioned the degree of legal reponsibility of therapists when they are required by their employer to instruct others how to perform technical procedures without the other individuals having the proper credentials or being frequently supervised. This will be an especially sensitive topic in view of different state licensure requirements for various professions. Ottenbacher concluded that there is a fine line between sharing the correct amount of information with others and still being able to maintain control over methods that are exclusive to a particular discipline. On the other side of the fence is the dilemma of knowing when to ask for assistance and when to double-check on technical procedures that are outside one's expertise. This balance of give and take can be achieved if each individual feels secure enough in his or her own field and can comfortably release control of exclusivity to certain skills the child needs help with throughout the day. No one specialty member can be with any one child all day long.

No matter what type of disability an infant or child may have, the team approach will provide the optimal services so long as there is collaboration, cooperation, and a two-way communication channel established between the disciplines and the parents. Holm and McCartin (1978) expressed this appropriately in stating that no specialist is so knowledgeable and so experienced that others cannot improve and broaden his or her skills. Peterson (1982) reminded us that there has to be cooperation not only on the local level but also across agencies (state and federal) that fund programs. There will be mistakes, personal and professional struggles, and sacrifices, but it must be remembered that no matter what type of approach is chosen (inter- or transdisciplinary), the child and the family derive the benefits.

Influence of Professionals on Parental Cooperation

The parents and the professionals share the responsibility for providing opportunities for the disabled child to develop to his or her maximum level of potential in all areas of life. Besides the management of physical needs, the child's needs in the development of body image and self-esteem must also be addressed. The professionals and parents must work together as a team. The following letter to professionals summarizes a parent's needs and suggestions (Salcedo, 1985).

An Open Letter to Professionals

As the parent of a multihandicapped child, I meet with you every day. Without you, my child would never have blossomed as she has; indeed she may not have survived. Nonetheless, at times I leave our sessions feeling angry or defeated. Please take a moment to consider the following "ten commandments" for dealing with parents.

1. Beware of the first positive test result—it sticks. If the first result is positive, I may hesitate to acknowledge when something is wrong. If it is negative, I may hesitate to acknowledge how well things are progressing.
2. Work with me, not against me. I will help give you a complete picture of my child. I probably won't make the first conciliatory move—I've been hurt before by insensitive professionals. I will respond to your kindness.
3. Think carefully about what you put in writing. A professional's record can follow a child forever. Please include something positive about my child— even if it's just a physical characteristic. The forms we use are not sacred so note where my child is near completion of a goal, or where she shows extra effort. This boosts my self-esteem and my child's self-esteem. It also provides those who read your report with a balanced picture of a child with a glaring negative side.
4. Consider how my child's sensory disability interferes with your assessment tools. Such interference is illegal. And unfair—just because my visually impaired child can't read the test question doesn't mean she doesn't know the answer. (Hint: Be creative. We parents need to be inventive continually to adapt everyday living for our children.)
5. Alleviate my fear of labels. Use them carefully and with accompanying personalized descriptions. Labels can be restrictive. They can lead to predictions of the future that are so specific that they are often incorrect.
6. Don't condescend or patronize me. I do not possess expertise in your field but I do know my child better than you do.
7. Don't use jargon. Teach me. Not knowing the language confuses, even degrades me. You are my window to the professional world. By teaching me terms and theories, I can better locate resources and communicate with other professionals and agencies. Share what you learn at conferences and in-services. I have a personal interest.
8. Don't call me Mother. In most cases, this is a physical impossibility. I have a name. Please respect me and address me properly.
9. Don't pity my child. I try daily not to focus on the tragic aspects of my child's disability. Don't force me to do this needlessly.
10. Consider the whole child. She has good days and bad days, strengths and weaknesses, likes and dislikes just like any other person. Respect that and we will all go farther in maximizing her potential. (p. 3)

Involvement of Parents in Planning/Management Team

Arnold (1978) suggested that any successful management program will require the parents' cooperation. For a program to be successful the professional should remember that the parents have been trying to improve their child's condition longer than the professional has. Parents who are involved in the planning for and the management of their child's special needs are usually more knowledgeable about their child's condition and more motivated to do their part in meeting those needs. Parental input helps the professional maintain more practical realism in planning management strategies that can be successfully implemented. Parental involvement helps prevent the professional from planning a program that is overwhelming and impractical.

PART I

Assessment and Management Techniques

CHAPTER 2

Assessment

Although the terms "assessment" and "evaluation" are used interchangeably, several sources (Mulliken & Buckley, 1983; Simeonsson, 1986; H. D. Smith & Tiffany, 1983) describe them as having different but related meanings. Assessment is viewed in a broad sense as the composite of the results of the different evaluation tools or procedures used (i.e., interview, observation, testing). Assessment is the process of collecting, studying, analyzing, and programming specific and relevant information about a child so that a management or treatment plan can be formulated and implemented.

The assessment, in combination with a treatment program and subsequent reassessment, is basically a questioning and problem-solving process that is ongoing throughout the period of time the child is followed by an agency. Accurate assessment and evaluation are important in order to properly identify the child's skills and problems; to ensure that the appropriate treatment program is selected; and to evaluate the effectiveness of the selected intervention approach. In assessing normal children and children with mild handicaps, accuracy has been assured by using standardized tests in which reliability and validity have been verified. However, it has been difficult to use traditional, standardized tests with children with severe and multiple handicaps. In order to assess the skills and the potential for learning in such a child, it has been necessary to be more flexible and creative in adapting the standardized tests or in designing new tests that will evaluate skills in children with sensory and motor handicaps. Simeonsson (1986) stated that although the assessment of special children is fundamentally a clinical rather than a technical activity, it should also have a firm empirical and theoretical basis.

Other criteria for the evaluation process are also mandated by Public Law 94-142 (the Education for All Handicapped Children Act of 1975):

1. Test and other evaluation materials must be provided and administered in the pupil's primary language.
2. Test instruments must be reliable and properly validated for the specific purpose for which the administrator uses them. Although the tests are to be administered in conformance with the test instructions, it is understood

35

that modifications must be made for many children with multiple handicaps. If modifications must be made, the examiner must report and justify them.
3. A battery of tests must be administered so that placement is not made on the basis of a single score or a single test.
4. Tests are to be selected so that the scores or results accurately reflect the pupil's aptitude and achievements and not the extent of their impairment, unless it is the dysfunction that is being measured (Mulliken & Buckley, 1983).

THE ASSESSMENT PROCESS

Purposes of Assessment

The specific purposes of the assessment process include the following (Banus, Kent, Norton, Sukiennicki, & Becker, 1979; P. N. Clark & Allen, 1985; Illingworth, 1975; Knoblock & Pasamanick, 1974; Simeonsson, 1986; H. D. Smith & Tiffany, 1983):

1. Diagnosis and establishment of a baseline or identification of the child's present level of performance, including skills and deficits, for the purpose of providing a foundation for a management program.
2. Identification of those problems that can or cannot be remedied by a therapy or educational program or parent training so that a referral to an appropriate resource can be made.
3. Demonstration of potential for change in order to justify the placement of the child in a certain kind of program.
4. Enlisting the cooperation of the child and parents by establishing rapport and helping the clients begin the process of mastering the presenting problems.

Depending on the presenting problems of the child, the purpose of the evaluation may require the use of one or more of the following methods: screening, testing, diagnosis, treatment planning, and evaluation of the child's existing treatment or educational program.

Phases of the Assessment Process

Pre-Evaluation Data Collection

A study of the child's developmental and medical history may provide important clues pertaining to the presenting problem as well as precautions that need to be noted. Information about a history of seizures, anesthetic areas of the skin, allergies, or side effects of medication is necessary for anyone who is evaluating a child. A study of the existing records may provide clues as to what type of assessment will best meet the needs of the child and the parents. The examiner must be professional enough not to theorize on the basis of only pre-evaluation data and thus come to inaccurate or inappropriate conclusions.

Selection of Assessment Method and Tools and Preparation of Testing Environment

As stated before, assessment methods can include observation, interview, and test administration. There are thousands of different assessments, each designed for a specific population or designed to assess certain behaviors. Selection of the most appropriate assessment method and tool is based on the child's chronological age, and apparent functional level, the nature of the disability, and the purpose of the assessment. Those evaluations designed for specific ages are not appropriate for older or younger children. The functional level of a child's motor and cognitive skills will also determine the kinds of tasks to which he or she can successfully respond. The nature of the disability will mandate the administration of certain kinds of tests and will require certain adaptations. Muscle tone and the effect of involuntary, primitive movement patterns should always be examined when evaluating children with cerebral palsy. Tactile awareness and discrimination should always be examined in children with spina bifida. Visually disabled children may have certain lighting requirements. Physically disabled children will have positioning needs that must be provided for if the children are to perform at their optimal level. If the purpose of the evaluation is to aid in the diagnostic process, certain kinds of assessment may be necessary. If the purpose of the evaluation is educational placement the assessment may need to focus on education-related domains of function.

The testing environment, including lighting, temperature, size of tables and chairs, and test equipment, must be adjusted so that the child will be able to perform at his or her optimal level. The room and test equipment should be stimulating enough to elicit an appropriate response but not over- or under-stimulating. Furniture should be appropriate for the child's size and disability. Proper preparation of the test environment will also allow the examiner to function at his or her optimal level and focus more attention on the child.

Orientation of Child and Parents to Testing Environment

It is important for the examiner to take time to introduce himself or herself and the environment to the client if rapport is to be established and maximal cooperation from the client is to be elicited. Gessell (quoted in Knobloch & Pasamanick, 1974) stated that when a child truly accepts a toy from your hands, the child has accepted you. It may take time to establish rapport with a child; however, it is time well spent.

Interaction with the parents will provide clues as to what their priorities are for their child. Parents are very often uneasy when their child is evaluated by a professional because they may view the process as an evaluation of parental effectiveness. One way of easing parental anxiety is to explain the purpose of the evaluation and explain that the child may not be expected to pass all of the items on the test.

Administration of Selected Tests

If the examiner has not already done so, observation of the child's spontaneous behavior just prior to initiating a standardized test will be helpful for two reasons. Spontaneous play may allow the child a chance to become familiar and comfortable with the testing room and allow the examiner to confirm that appropriate assessment tools have been selected. If the child's spontaneous play is at a higher or lower level than the examiner anticipated, the examiner can then select more appropriate assessment tools.

If a standardized test is being used the examiner should use the standard instructions and standard manner for presenting items to the child. Many standardized tests are designed to be presented to a specific population, in a specific manner, and in a set sequence if valid results are to be obtained. If unstandardized but formal tests are used, the examiner will usually be able to find administration suggestions in the administration manuals.

Regardless of the type of test used, if the test or the method of administration has been adapted in any way, the examiner should carefully document and justify the changes. Careful, accurate recording of the child's responses is essential during the assessment process. Do not wait until the assessment is completed before attempting to write down observation of spontaneous behavior or behavior elicited during a test.

Most assessment administration manuals will instruct the examiner as to at what level or with what test item the assessment should begin or end. Many assessments are designed to begin at a level where the child will experience success.

The examiner must be familiar enough with the administration procedures, including the sequence of test item presentation, that items can be quickly presented and the child's attention and motivation maintained. A helpful rule to follow is "Hurry yourself, but not the child." In other words, the examiner must be prepared to present the next test item as soon as the child finishes the previous item but, at the same time, must allow the child an appropriate amount of time to respond.

An appropriate examiner role should be maintained during the assessment. Although one does not want to intimidate or frighten the child, the examiner is not the child's buddy or playmate. The examiner should speak honestly, using good manners toward the child, and should set and maintain limits for behavior or time allowed for a certain kind of activity. The examiner will need to be able to distinguish between real and pretend fatigue or illness. Some children who fear failure will feign fatigue or illness in order to avoid certain kinds of activities. If the child is really ill or very tired, the evaluation should be discontinued for the time being. If the child is pretending illness, the examiner can move on to other items on the test. Although a child's inappropriate behavior should not be allowed to control the situation, the examiner does need to respect the child's legitimate reasons for refusal to perform a task. Legitimate reasons are fear, real fatigue, and real illness (Banus et al., 1979).

In order to effectively assess children, the examiner needs the following skills and characteristics:

Thorough knowledge of normal development, the variations in normal development, and deviations from normal development so that abnormalities can be recognized

Thorough knowledge of a sufficient number of evaluation tools and methods used with a broad range of ages and covering a broad range of tasks and skill components

A questioning mind that will constantly seek answers to problems

Good observation skills and the ability to actively listen

Flexibility, spontaneity, and creativity in using media and activities appropriate for children at different ages

Ability to analyze the developmental tasks so that the appropriate performance components or prerequisite skills can be thoroughly evaluated

Ability to organize time, space, activity, and collected data; prioritize client problems; and problem solve

Scoring, Interpreting, and Organizing Assessment Data

As the examiner integrates the data from the different tests into a written report, it must be remembered that this report becomes a legal document and therefore must be written in precise and appropriate language. Written evaluation reports usually include recommendations for remediation and follow-up.

Sharing Evaluation Results with Other Disciplines and Parents at Staff and Interpretation Meetings

It is during the discussions with professionals from other disciplines, the parents, and, when appropriate, the child, that the child's strengths are recognized and his or her problems are prioritized. Ideally, the end result of these sharing and planning meetings is a holistic plan that meets all of the child's needs in a timely manner.

Effects of Development Process and Environment

Evaluation is an information-gathering, problem analysis process that must be based on a thorough knowledge of child development and pathological processes, including the effects of environmental experiences (P. N. Clark & Allen, 1985). The information gathered during the evaluation process must be relevant to the child's chronological age and relevant to the expectations of the child's social environment (i.e., it must be referenced to the developmental tasks established as appropriate for a normal child at a given age). The child's mental age, functional level, diagnosis, and home and school environment must also be considered when selecting evaluation tools and tasks as well as in the analysis of the collected data. The specific tasks or items that have been selected for a screening or comprehensive assessment are based on normal sequences of development, established developmental tasks, and the necessary performance components or prerequisites for completing tasks.

Developmental Sequences

Some of the widely applied normal developmental sequences include the cephalocaudal sequence, the proximal-to-distal or medial-to-lateral sequence, the gross motor–to–fine motor sequence, and the simple-to-complex sequence. These normal developmental sequences can also be applied to the assessment of atypical children because, although the atypical child's development has been disrupted or arrested, development does continue to occur and often follows normal sequences.

Prenatal as well as postnatal development occurs in a *cephalocaudal,* or head to foot, sequence. Babies develop head control before trunk control. If it is observed during an assessment that a child has poor head control, poor trunk control will usually also be observed. Development of selective finger movement prior to development of the ability to wiggle the toes is also an example of the cephalocaudal sequence of development.

Proximal-to-distal or *medial-to-lateral* development can be illustrated by observing that a child develops control of the body at the midline (medial) in static standing before being able to shift weight to the side (lateral) and walk sideways along a table. Another example is that trunk and shoulder stability (proximal) develop before fine hand and finger use (distal) develops.

Development of gross motor or large muscle control and movement precedes the development of fine motor or small muscle control and movement. Also, children understand simple, concrete concepts (e.g., prepositional concepts) before they can understand complex and abstract concepts (e.g., time). These principles of development are the frame of reference for many assessment tools, especially criterion-referenced tests, as well as for most remedial programs.

Developmental Tasks

Developmental tasks are those tasks or behaviors that are expected of an individual by a certain age according to the criteria established by the individual's social environment.

Havighurst (1972) suggested the developmental tasks listed in Table 2.1 as appropriate for the indicated age levels. Many criterion-referenced and some norm-referenced tests will include similar tasks (see "Types of Assessment," below).

For the developmentally disabled child the achievement of all of the age-

Table 2.1. Developmental tasks of life phases

Age level	Developmental tasks
Infancy and early childhood (0–6 years)	Learn to walk
	Learn to take solid food
	Learn to talk
	Control eliminating of body wastes
	Learn sex differences and sexual modesty
	Form concepts of form, space, and time and learn language to describe social and physical reality
	Get ready to read (shape and symbol recognition)
	Learn to distinguish right and wrong and begin to develop a conscience
Middle childhood (7–12 years)	Learn physical skills necessary for ordinary games (running, skipping, jumping)
	Build wholesome attitudes toward oneself as a growing organism
	Learn to get along with age-mates
	Learn an appropriate masculine or feminine social role
	Develop fundamental skills in reading, writing, and calculating
	Develop concepts necessary for everyday living (time, memory, problem solving)
	Develop conscience, morality, and a scale of values
	Achieve personal independence (dressing, toileting)
	Develop attitudes toward social groups and institutions (conformance vs. nonconformance)
Adolescence (13–19 years)	Achieve new and more mature relations with age-mates of both sexes
	Achieve a masculine or feminine social role
	Accept one's physique and use body effectively
	Achieve emotional independence from parents and other adults
	Prepare for marriage and family life
	Prepare for economic career
	Develop ideology—a set of values and an ethical system as a guide to behavior
	Achieve socially responsible behavior

Adapted from Havighurst (1972).

appropriate developmental tasks listed in Table 2.1 may be difficult or impossible. During the assessment and program planning processes, therapists, educators, parents, and, when appropriate, the child may have to decide which tasks are important and must and can be mastered, which tasks can be mastered in an adapted form, and which tasks are unnecessary or unrealistic for the child.

Most developmental tasks are mastered in an established sequence over a period of months and years. For example, to achieve personal independence in dressing, toileting, and bathing takes a minimum of 6 years in a normal child. The mastery of the developmental tasks also requires the integration of many performance or skill components.

Performance Components

Performance components are the prerequisite skills or components necessary for the achievement of developmental tasks. Most tasks, such as self-feeding, dressing, or playing on playground equipment, require the development and integration of motor, sensory, sensory-integrative, cognitive, psychological, and social performance components.

In order to show the complexity of the hierarchy of skills involved, let us take as an example the area of personal independence. One task that is part of developing personal independence is undressing. Removing a pair of socks is just one small part of undressing. Table 2.2 presents a brief list of the steps necessary for eventually mastering the task of removing a pair of socks. (These steps are listed so that the child masters the last step of sock removal first [backward chaining].) Listed in Table 2.3 are some of the performance components necessary for the accomplishment of only step 1 in Table 2.2.

A comprehensive assessment will not only examine a child's ability or inability to perform a developmental task such as pulling a sock off or copying a circle with a pencil, but will also examine the performance components necessary for successful completion of the task. An examination of the performance components often provides clues as to why the child has been unsuccessful with a complex task such as undressing or writing.

TYPES OF ASSESSMENT

There are many different types of assessments, each designed to test a specific population (i.e., specific age or disability group) or specific kinds of skills or tasks (i.e., motor, sensory, self-care). Some assessments are designed to identify those children who are most likely to be at risk for certain kinds of problems, such as learning problems. For example, a developmental assessment is designed to appraise the maturity and integrity of the child's nervous system in combination with the behavioral domain and within the context of the child's past and present history (Knoblock & Pasamanick, 1974).

Table 2.2. Sock removal using the backward chaining teaching technique

1. Child removes sock from toes. Thumbs grasp each side of sock.
2. Child removes sock when just below heel. Thumbs grasp each side of sock.
3. Child removes sock when just above heel. Thumbs grasp each side of sock.
4. Child removes sock. Thumbs grasp each side of sock.

Adapted from Fredericks, Riggs, Furey, Grove, Moore, McDonnell, Jordan, Hanson, Baldwin, and Wadlow (1976).

Observation, administration of tests (which might include presenting specific tasks to the child), and interviewing are some of the methods used for assessment. Screening tests are designed to sample the child's behavior in order to determine if a problem exists, to determine if further assessment is necessary, and to aid in the selection of appropriate tests. Comprehensive assessments are designed to thoroughly examine a specific domain of behavior, such as visual-perceptual skills or feeding, or to examine a large sample of behaviors across all domains (motor, cognitive, communication, etc.).

Screening and comprehensive assessment tools can be in the form of criterion-referenced tests or norm-referenced tests. *Criterion-referenced tests* (also called content-, domain-, or objective-referenced tests) are designed so that the individual child's scores are evaluated in terms of specific objectives or tasks that have been accomplished or failed. The child's future performance is compared against his or her own past performance, not the performance of a standardized population. Criterion-referenced test items are usually listed in developmental sequence with the average age of accomplishment provided for each task. This type of test is more adaptable to the needs of the developmentally disabled child and the data gathered are often more easily translated into a management program than are the data from norm-referenced tests. Some criterion-referenced assessments are accompanied by a curriculum plan that provides suggestions on how to help each child master the tasks on the assessment.

Table 2.3. Performance components necessary for removing a sock from the toes of the foot

Motor	Head control, trunk control/sitting balance
	Ability to reach toes with hands
	Adequate muscle strength to maintain grasp on sock while pulling it off
	Motor coordination
Sensory	Visual acuity
	Visual-perception skills
Sensory integration	Eye-hand coordination
Cognitive	Body concept
	Concept of off versus on
	Sequential concepts (shoes must come off before socks)
	Attention span

The Hawaii Early Learning Profile (HELP) and the Learning Accomplishment Profile (LAP) are examples of criterion-referenced assessment tools (Garwood, 1983).

Norm-referenced tests evaluate a child's performance by comparing it to the performance of a larger population of children who have characteristics similar to the child being tested (e.g., age). Most norm-referenced tests are based on the performance of normal children and the data do not always accurately serve the needs of the child with developmental disability (Mulliken & Buckley, 1983). Also, many norm-referenced tests were not designed for use with a severely physically impaired population. The Denver Developmental Screening Test, the Bayley Scales of Infant Development, and the Miller Assessment for Preschoolers are examples of norm-referenced assessments.

Many developmental assessments do not assess specific neuromotor prerequisites such as the status of muscle tone or reflex integration. Instead these assessments focus on what could be called "end products" of neuromotor development (e.g., head control, sitting balance, ability to stack blocks, and ability to dress oneself) (see Table 2.4). For the child with significant motor impairment the therapist will need to take into account the effects of abnormal muscle tone and other problems on the child's overall developmental level.

The following sections discuss various aspects of the assessment process in critical areas of development, including coordination and movement, feeding, and dressing and personal hygiene. Assessment in *specific* developmental disabilities is then subsequently discussed.

ASSESSMENT OF GENERAL SKILL AREAS

Gross and Fine Motor Control and Movement

The development of control and movement occurs in cephalocaudal, medial to lateral, and proximal to distal sequences. In the human infant control and movement begins in the form of reflexes and other automatic reactions in response to specific stimuli. Eventually reflexes evolve into finely tuned automatic reactions and coordinated voluntary movement. A prerequisite to the development of control and movement away from the pull of gravity is the development of head control at the body's midline. Assessment of infants and young children usually begins with observation and testing of head control in different body positions (supine, prone, and sitting), as well as noting the effects of body position on functional motor control. Next, the status of the primitive reflexes and the higher level automatic reactions are tested, followed by the status of specific skills such as rolling, sitting, standing, walking, and food use (Table 2.5). The Milani-Comparetti Motor Development Screening Test and the Bayley Scales of Infant Development, Motor Scale are just two of many screen-

Table 2.4. Examples of items on two developmental assessment tools[a]

Gross motor skills	Neck-righting reaction is present (H)
	Lifts head while lying on stomach (D)
	Rolls prone to supine (H)
	Gets into sitting (D)
	Walks well (D)
Fine motor skills	Visually regards colorful object (H)
	Visually follows object to midline (D)
	Transfers object from one hand to the other (H)
	Stacks tower of two cubes (D)
	Points with index finger (H)
Cognitive/visual-perceptual skills	Finds hidden object (H)
	Dumps raisin from bottle spontaneously (D)
	Initiates several gestures (H)
	Imitates vertical line with pencil (D)
	Copies circle with pencil (D)
Speech and language skills	Laughs (H)
	Imitates speech sounds (D)
	Uses two-word sentences (H)
	Names pictures (H, D)
	Answers questions (H, D)
Self-care skills	Opens and closes mouth in response to food stimulus (H)
	Brings hand to mouth (H)
	Drinks from cup (D)
	Dresses without supervision (D)
	Takes responsibility for toileting (H)

[a]D = Denver Developmental Screening Test; H = Hawaii Early Learning Profile.

ing or evaluation tools designed to assess motor skills. Specific gross and fine motor skills are also evaluated within the context of functional skills such as walking up and down stairs, eating, dressing, and the execution of play and school tasks.

Positioning and Functional Motor Control

In *Positioning the Handicapped Child for Function,* Ward (1984) provided several examples of assessments used when evaluating a child's positional needs for motor function. Assessment of positional needs should include observation of the child in horizontal and antigravity positions. Horizontal positions include prone, supine, and side-lying. Antigravity positions include long-sitting, side-sitting, chair sitting, kneeling, and standing. The effect of each position on muscle tone and functional control of all body parts should be assessed. Some questions to ask when assessing functional control in each position might include the following:

Table 2.5. Assessment of developmental motor sequences

Positions	Normal movement	Abnormal movement
Rolling	Uses body righting, which allows a smooth segmental roll where the child begins to turn toward the left or right, initiating the movement with the opposite shoulder or hip.	1. The child's body will be stiff when rolling (called log rolling). 2. The arm on the face side extends when the head turns sideways, thus preventing rolling movement (ATNR influence). 3. With the tonic labyrinthine prone reflex dominating, flexor tone will be prominent in hips and knees. This will draw the body up so only the buttocks are touching the floor, making rolling very difficult. 4. Under tonic labyrinthine reflex influence in supine, hyperextension dominates (neck, back, legs) making the whole body arch backward and making rolling impossible.
Crawling	Normal crawling is done in a reciprocal pattern. The right leg and left arm move together and the opposite limbs follow.	1. *Homolateral*—Arm and leg of the same side of body move followed by opposite side. An indication of poorly integrated ATNR. 2. *Homologous*—Both arms moving together followed by simultaneous movement of the legs. Movement such as this means poor integration of the STNR. 3. Legs remain straight and only arms are used to pull child. The Landau reflex is dominant in this pattern of movement.
Creeping	Child is up on hands and knees. Movement is reciprocal, similar to the crawling pattern described above.	1. *Bunny hop* (homologous)—Same-arm-together movement as in crawling. The legs work together, which makes the child look like a bunny hopping. If head moves up and down, it may be because of the STNR influence. 2. Homolateral—Arm and leg of same side move as a unit followed with some movement on other side. The ATNR influence will be noted when head turns: the arm on the face side will extend for support and the other arm (skull side) will bend.

46

Sitting	1. Child sits on tiltable surface such as a tiltboard or inflatable pillow. Even a small chair will suffice. Quickly tilt the surface upward at an angle and repeat action to other side. The child will lean with trunk and head toward the high side and the limbs on the opposite side will extend for support.	1. Abnormal reaction is the inability to stay on the surface; child may fall off.
	2. Good sitting balance is the result of normal equilibrium reactions and should be achieved by 18 months of age.	2. Flexing or turning (rotating) the head while doing a fine motor task may mean a strong ATNR, STNR, or tonic labyrinthine influence.
	3. Observe sitting balance on floor to see if there is good head and trunk control.	3. One hand may mirror or do the same thing as the other hand (associated reactions)
	4. Watch arm movements that are not noted in other positions.	4. May have difficulty doing bilateral fine motor tasks (e.g., cutting).
Kneeling	Have child maintain upright kneeling position to count of 10. Normal ability means good hip stability, equilibrium reaction, and protective extension.	Poor integration results in child unable to protect himself or herself when falling or to use kneeling position as a step toward standing.
Standing	1. Evaluate static and dynamic posture while child maintains balance.	1. Children who walk with arms bent up and high (high guard) are beginning to walk.
	2. Check position of head and spine when standing and walking.	2. Three types of abnormal curvatures of the spine: swayback (lordosis) humpback (kyphosis) lateral curvature (scoliosis)
	3. While walking, there should be a heel-toe foot pattern and reciprocal arm movement.	3. Child who toewalks may be tactually defensive.
	4. Movement of head should be free and independent from rest of body and extremities while maintaining an upright position.	4. When head and eyes are directed toward the floor, it may be because of poor equilibrium.

Adapted from Montgomery and Richter (1978b).

1. Is the head at midline and can the child visually focus on the desired target?
2. Is the trunk symmetrical and well aligned with the rest of the body?
3. Are the lower extremities properly aligned? If seated, kneeling, or standing, are the lower extremities bearing weight equally?
4. Are the upper extremities properly aligned and in functional positions for weight bearing or manipulation of objects?
5. Does this position promote the development of tightness, contractures, deformity, or pressure sores?

Some preliminary experimentation may be necessary in order to determine which positions will allow the child to perform at the highest functional level possible in different tasks. For example, sitting may be the best position for being fed, and side-lying may be the best position for play and other eye-hand coordination tasks.

Status of the Reflexes and Reactions

The purpose of this part of the assessment is to determine the child's level of motor development as it relates to the maturation of the reflex mechanisms. Most primitive reflexes should be integrated by the age of 4–6 months, and the higher level reactions such as head righting and equilibrium begin to emerge soon after birth and persist throughout life. The specific reflexes and reactions to be tested depend on the child's chronological age and the severity of the disability. Figures 2.1 and 2.2 are examples of the two most commonly used reflex evaluation forms: the Milani-Comparetti Motor Development Screening Test (Barnes, Crutchfield, & Heriza, 1977) and the Reflex Evaluation (Kliewer, Bruce, & Trembath, 1977). There are many excellent resources for detailed information on assessing reflexes and reactions in children (Barnes et al., 1977; Fiorentino, 1973; Kliewer et al., 1977; Prechtl & Bientima, 1984).

The procedure for assessing the status of the reflexes and reactions usually consists of first placing the child's body or a body part into a specific position (stimulus). The examiner then observes for involuntary changes in specific body parts (response). The following is a list of some reflexes and reactions with their specific stimuli and expected responses described. Refer to figures 2.1 and 2.2 for the ages at which these reflexes and reactions are elicited in normal children.

Reflexes

1. Palmar hand grasp (Figure 2.3)
    Stimulus—Without touching the back of the child's hand, the examiner will apply pressure to the palm of the child's hand.
    Response—The child's fingers will automatically flex around the examiner's finger.
2. Tonic labyrinthine reflex (Figure 2.4)

Stimulus—The prone or supine position.

Response—Prone: increased flexor muscle tone; supine: increased extensor muscle tone.

3. Asymmetric tonic neck reflex (Figure 2.5)

Stimulus—The infant is supine, although older children can be tested in all-fours position or standing. The examiner turns the child's head to the right or left.

Response—If the child's head is turned to the right there will be increased extensor muscle tone in the right arm and leg and increased flexor tone in the left arm and leg. When the child's head is turned to the left, the opposite response may occur in the extremities. Responses are usually stronger in the arms than in the legs.

4. Symmetric tonic neck reflex (Figure 2.6)

Stimulus—The prone position or all-fours position for older children. The child's head is extended or flexed.

Response—When the head is extended, extensor tone will predominate in the arms, and flexor tone will predominate in the legs. When the head is flexed, flexor tone will predominate in the arms, and extensor tone will predominate in the legs.

5. Moro reflex (Figure 2.7)

Stimulus—With the child usually placed or held in the supine position, this reflex is elicited by a sudden change in the position of the head in relationship to the trunk, and is accomplished by dropping the child's head backward from the trunk about 30 degrees.

Response—Phase one: extension and abduction of the arms with opening of the hands (sometimes associated with crying); phase two: flexion and adduction of the arms across the chest.

6. Landau reflex (Figure 2.8)

Stimulus—The prone position while the child is suspended horizontally.

Response—The child's head, trunk, and extremities will move away from the pull of gravity into extension.

Reactions

1. Head-righting reactions (labyrinthine, optical) (Figure 2.9)

Stimulus—Hold the child in the vertical position (to test for labyrinthine head righting the child should be blindfolded) and slowly tilt the child's body to one side.

Response—The child's head will "right" itself in the direction opposite from the direction of the tilt, or the head will move away from the pull of gravity.

2. Parachute or protective extension reaction (sideways) (Figure 2.10)

Stimulus—With the child seated, the examiner will tilt the child rapidly to one side.

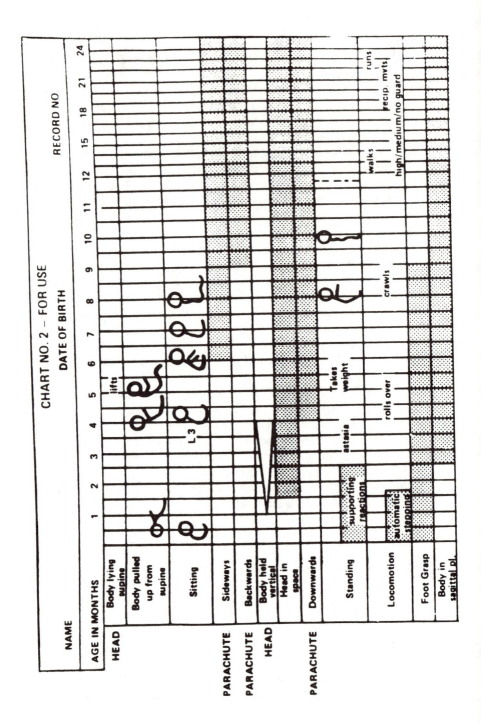

CHART NO. 2 – FOR USE

NAME

DATE OF BIRTH

RECORD NO.

50

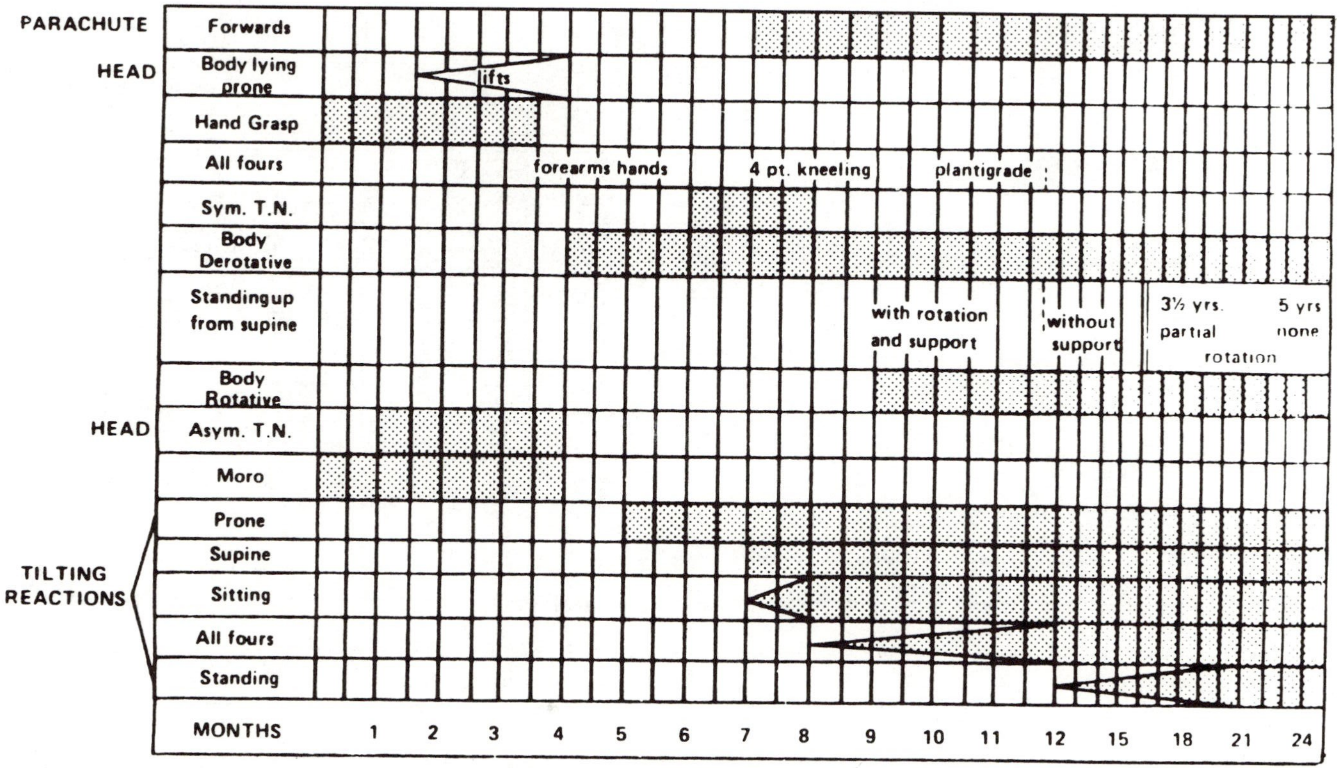

Figure 2.1. Milani-Comparetti Motor Development Screening Test. (From Kliewer, D., Bruce, W., & Trembath, J. [1977]. *The Milani-Comparetti motor development screening test.* Omaha, NE: Meyer Children's Rehabilitation Institute; reprinted by permission of Meyer Children's Rehabilitation Institute, University of Nebraska Medical Center.)

51

Reflex Evaluation

Name: _____

Birth Date: _____ **Age** _____ **Sex** _____ **Physician:** _____

Diagnosis: _____

Examiner: _____ **Date of Testing:** _____

Scoring: + presence of a response or finding
− absence of a response or finding
A asymmetry
+ + obligatory or dominant response or finding

Reflex/Reaction	Age Span Onset	Integration	Score + +, + −, A	Comments
Primitive Reflexes				
Rooting	*28 weeks	3 months		
Sucking - Swallowing	*28 weeks	2-5 months		
Moro	*28 weeks	5-6 months		
Traction	*28 weeks	2-5 months		
Crossed extension	*28 weeks	1-2 months		
Flexor withdrawal	*28 weeks	1-2 months		
Plantar grasp	*28 weeks	9 months		
Galant	*32 weeks	2 months		
Neonatal neck righting (NOB)	*34 weeks	4-5 months		
Neonatal body righting (BOB)	*34 weeks	4-5 months		
Neonatal positive supporting (LE)	*35 weeks	1-2 months		
Proprioceptive placing (LE)	*35 weeks	2 months		
Spontaneous stepping	*37 weeks	2 months		
Proprioceptive placing (UE)	Birth	2 months		
Asymmetric tonic neck	Birth	4-6 months		
Palmar grasp	Birth	4-6 months		
Tonic labyrinthine	Birth	6 months		
Symmetric tonic neck	4-6 months	8-12 months		
Associated movements	Birth-3 months	8-9 years		
Prehensile Reactions				
Avoidance	Birth	6-7 years		
Instinctive grasp	4-11 months	Persists		

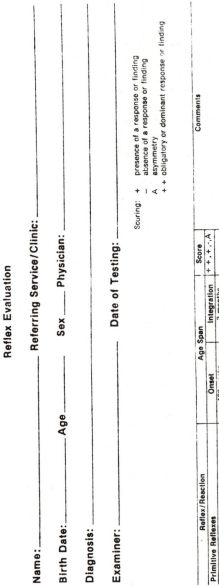

52

53

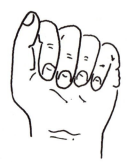

Figure 2.3. Palmar hand grasp. This grasp becomes suppressed by 2–3 months; it can also be elicited by the beginning of the sucking movement.

Response—The child's arm on the side toward which the child was tilted will extend toward the surface to "break" the fall.

3. Equilibrium or tilting reactions in sitting (Figure 2.11)

    Stimulus—With the child seated on an unstable surface (i.e., tilt board), the examiner will slowly tilt the surface to either side, backward, or forward.

    Response—The child's head, trunk, and extremities will move away from the direction of the tilt in order to maintain the original position on the unstable surface.

Sensory Abilities

Assessment of sensory status is important since dysfunction in visual, tactile, kinesthetic, and proprioceptive awareness can have a profound effect upon motor control. If the child is unresponsive to visual stimuli, the therapist and teacher will need to use auditory, tactile, and other kinds of stimuli to elicit movement and interaction with the environment. The child's ability to perceive

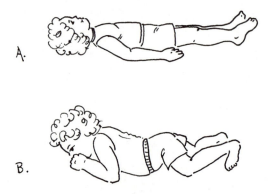

Figure 2.4. Tonic labyrinthine reflex. A, supine; B, prone. If this reflex persists beyond 6 months, the child will have difficulty obtaining the hands/knees (quadraped) position.

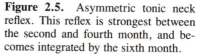

Figure 2.5. Asymmetric tonic neck reflex. This reflex is strongest between the second and fourth month, and becomes integrated by the sixth month.

light touch, deep pressure, pain, and temperature are important for safety reasons as well as for the development of body perception and body concept. Kinesthesia and proprioception are important for the perception of movement and awareness of one's posture or position in space. Vestibular input is necessary for maintaining balance.

Accurate sensory testing requires a cooperative child. With very young or severely involved children only gross sensory testing may be possible. One reason accurate sensory testing is difficult is because vision must be occluded by using a blindfold or some kind of shield so that the child cannot see the body part being tested. Most young children do not tolerate a blindfold or shield well. Severely disabled children may not be able to consistently let the examiner know what sensory information they are receiving. The following are brief descriptions of two sensory tests. For more complete descriptions of sensory testing procedures, the reader is referred to the following sources: Ayres (1980), L. J. Miller (1982), and Scott (1983).

Light Touch

With vision occluded or when the child is not looking, lightly touch a spot on the back of the child's hand with the examiner's fingertip or a cotton swab. After removing the shield, ask the child to point to the spot that was touched. Repeat the procedure by touching different parts of the body. If the child does

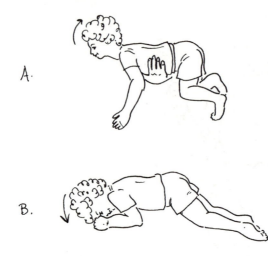

Figure 2.6. Symmetric tonic neck reflex. A, head extended; B, head flexed. This reflex can be facilitated as early as 4 months, and is suppressed by 6–7 months.

not respond, this may indicate that light touch is impaired. The examiner can then apply a stronger stimulus. However, the record should show that light touch is impaired. With severely physically disabled children who cannot point, the examiner will need to observe for other signs that the child felt the stimulus. Behavior that might indicate the child could feel the stimulus would include looking at the part touched, moving the part touched, or a change in facial expression.

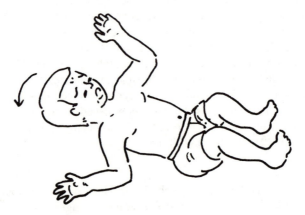

Figure 2.7. Moro reflex. This reflex becomes integrated by 4 months and is considered to be a vestibular reflex.

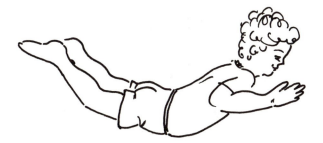

Figure 2.8. Landau reflex. This reflex is normally elicited after 6 months, and becomes suppressed between 12 and 24 months.

Kinesthesia

With vision occluded, the examiner moves the child's arm or another body part into a specific position and then returns the arm to the original position. Next the child is asked to repeat the movement without looking. If the child can repeat the movement accurately without looking, kinesthesia is assumed to be intact in that body part. Children with abnormal muscle tone will have difficulty performing this kind of task, which requires controlled and accurate movement. If a child has abnormal muscle tone and uses predominately abnormal or poorly planned movement patterns, it can be assumed that sensation is probably impaired.

Self-Care Skills

A comprehensive assessment will include the assessment of feeding, dressing, and other self-care tasks. The effect of abnormal muscle tone, predominance of

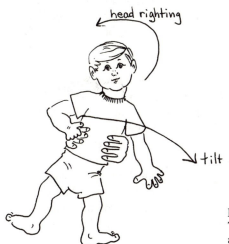

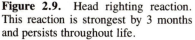

Figure 2.9. Head righting reaction. This reaction is strongest by 3 months and persists throughout life.

Figure 2.10. Parachute or protective extension reaction. This reaction appears between 4 and 9 months and remains throughout life. It is required for a safe sitting posture.

primitive reflexes, and delayed motor development along with any sensory impairment and cognitive/visual-perceptual impairment must be considered when assessing the complex self-care tasks.

Feeding Skills

Many children with neurological impairments present a mixture of abnormal and normal motor patterns, which, according to P. H. Campbell (1979), explains why documenting specific feeding problems can be so difficult. This is especially true for the beginning therapist or teacher. A lot more is involved than observing whether a child, for example, is able to maintain his or her balance, independently manage utensils, or verbally indicate favorite foods. Both handicapped and nonhandicapped children may be able on their own to come to the table, select cinnamon bread in preference to white bread, and spread butter on the bread. The difference may be in the rate, quality, and quantity of the two children's performances. The child with physical limitations may require a longer time to ambulate with crutches to the table, may have difficulty enunciating his or her bread preference, and may manage to get the butter not only on the bread but also over a wide area of the tablecloth and himself or herself. This focus on rate, quality, and quantity of performance does not imply that a beginning staff member cannot identify and prescribe accurate programs while gaining valuable insight in assessing a wide variety of feeding problems.

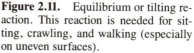

Figure 2.11. Equilibrium or tilting reaction. This reaction is needed for sitting, crawling, and walking (especially on uneven surfaces).

Prior to administering any type of evaluation, the therapist or parent may need to recognize that a problem really does exist. Schmidt (1976) described several observational guidelines that may help the therapist determine if further testing is necessary:

1. Choking and coughing more than once or twice during each meal.
2. Inability to keep most food and liquid inside the mouth and swallow it.
3. Tendency to bite down on the spoon.
4. Intolerence of solid foods beyond the developmental age of six to nine months (inability to chew, tactile sensitivity).
5. Abnormal sitting posture (i.e., head tilted back or to the side, body tilted laterally)
6. High muscle tone.
7. Great effort expended by parent or child resulting in unpleasant mealtimes.
8. Persistent tongue thrust beyond the age of six months (in and out movement of the tongue); usually goes along with inability to chew, choking, and other findings.

Duration of Assessment

Braun, Palmer, and Salek (1983) stated that in order to obtain a successful treatment program one must have used good observation techniques. In assessing feeding skills good observational technique involves a commitment from the examiner to spend numerous sessions assessing both child and feeder. Although there is no documentation in the literature as to how long one must assess oral feeding skills, it is suggested that a 2-week period should provide adequate information. This would involve taking data once a day during a 5-day period for 2 weeks. The author has spent up to 4 months determining the oral-muscular ability for a 4-year-old girl with profound retardation. Although not recommended, this exaggerated length of time was necessary in part because of the frequent illnesses and extreme total body hypersensitivity displayed by this girl. This type of assessment became an ongoing evaluation/treatment until a stable attendance was established.

Content of Evaluation Form

The type of clinical observation form currently being used to assess feeding varies but generally fits into one of two different styles: a descriptive format or a checklist. According to P. H. Campbell (1979), both have advantages and disadvantages that must be recognized by the evaluator. Although a descriptive documentation (Morris, 1977) is very specific and explicit in identifying the feeding problems, it may be too time consuming or too difficult to determine the priority needs. The checklist, although the easiest to administer, provides the least amount of information in relationship to rate, quantity, and quality of performance. The answer to how a child performs a task is not derived from most checklists.

What is needed is a feeding assessment tool that combines both a shortened version of a descriptive form and an expanded checklist with a criterion component added. A first step toward filling that need is an evaluation developed by Stratton (1981). Her evaluation covers areas of oral-muscular strengths and assesses how food and liquid affect the child's chewing, biting, and swallowing ability. Stratton's evaluation is easy, quick, informative, and objective. Table 2.6 shows how each area is graded from a dependent or passive level to a self-sufficient or normal level. This type of criterion-based assessment quickly identifies strengths and weaknesses to a greater degree than does a pass-or-fail checklist. It also helps the inexperienced staff member set treatment plan objectives. Guesswork as to the next level of training is minimized using this type of form. Adaptations or extensions such as those noted in Table 2.7 (Kansas Neurological Institute, 1985) facilitate developing treatment techniques for positioning and textures of food.

Direct Child Contact

Through assessment with direct child contact, the evaluator learns about motor development, gross reflexive movement, eye-hand coordination, general muscular tone, sensory stimulation, oral-pharyngeal reflexes, oral hygiene, and feeding behaviors.

Table 2.6. Feeding evaluation of oral function

J. N. ADAM DEVELOPMENT CENTER
OCCUPATIONAL THERAPY
Evaluation of Oral Function in Feeding

Name _____

Consecutive Number _____

Living Unit _____

Diagnosis: MR _____ Evaluation Data

Physical _____ Reflex Patterns

Positioning Device _____ Oral Structures/Reflexes

Head _____ Lips _____ Teeth _____ Bite _____

Trunk _____ Gums _____ Gag Reflex _____ Reflex _____

Upper Extremities _____ Palate _____ Sucking Reflex _____

Lower Extremities _____ Tongue _____ Rooting Reflex _____

Diet _____

Utensils _____

Average Feeding Time _____

Function	0 "Passive"	1	2	3	4 "Functional"	5 "Normal"
Jaw Closure — extension	Jaw remains open; no noticeable movement in response to utensil.	Jaw thrust: jaw opens as far as possible; difficult to close.	Jaw thrust: jaw opens less than 2"; difficult to close.	Jaw thrust; jaw opens less than 2"; closes easily with manual assistance.	Jaw thrust: corrects itself within few seconds.	Able to open and close jaws smoothly over utensil.
flexion	Jaw remains closed; no noticeable movement in response to utensil.	Bite reflex: holds spoon tightly; cannot voluntarily release.	Bite reflex: easily corrected by jaw control.	Bite reflex: immediate active release without use of jaw control.	Bite reflex: not strong enough to retain utensil in mouth.	Able to open and close jaws smoothly over utensil.
freq.	Response occurs every time.	7 out of 10 times per meal.	5 out of 10 times per meal.	3 out of 10 times per meal.	1 out of 10 times per meal.	No abnormal response.

continued

61

Table 2.6. *continued*

Function	0 "Passive"	1	2	3	4 "Functional"	5 "Normal"
Lip Closure Over Spoon	Mouth remains open; no noticeable movement in response to utensil.	Initial jaw thrust or bite reflex on contact with utensil.	Slight active movement of lower jaw toward spoon.	Jaws close over spoon but not lips.	Lips approximate spoon with no attempt to remove food.	Lips purse together to actively remove food from bowl of spoon.
Tongue Control	Tongue remains at bottom of mouth; no noticeable response to food.	Tongue rolls to side or retracts back; not functional for swallow.	Tongue protrudes horizontally forward & out between lips in swallowing.	Tongue protrudes horizontally forward (but remains in mouth) when swallowing.	Tongue moves forward & upward in attempt to swallow.	Tongue elevates to the roof of the mouth (behind front teeth) and moves food back to swallow.
Lip Closure While Swallowing	Mouth remains open; no noticeable movement during swallow.	Slight active movement of lower jaw/lip during swallow.	Lips partially close during swallow; tongue may occlude opening.	Lips open & close repeatedly during swallow.	Lips approximate during swallow—not tight seal.	Lips close tightly to prevent food loss during swallow.
Swallows Food Without Excess Loss — amt.	100% food loss	70% loss	50% loss	30% loss	10% loss	No excess food loss with average-sized spoon
freq.	Excess loss with every swallow	Excess loss 7 out of 10 times	Excess loss 5 out of 10 times	Excess loss 3 out of 10 times	Excess loss 1 out of 10 times	

62

Chews Food (Tongue/Jaw Control)	Able to bite off solid piece of food and chew functionally. Tongue able to control position of bolus.	Vertical movement with minimal rotary movement.	Vertical jaw movement. Some lateral tongue control.	Minimal jaw movement; not functional for chewing.	No jaw movement.	No noticeable movement of jaws or tongue in response to food.
Sips Liquids	Lips over rim of glass and sips liquid and swallows repeatedly.	Lips over rim of glass; sips liquids but cannot swallow repeatedly.	Lips approximate rim of glass; does not initiate intake.	Slight active movement of lower jaw toward rim of glass.	Initial jaw thrust or bite reflex on contact with glass.	No active movement of jaws, lips & tongue in response to liquid.
Swallows Liquids Without Excess Loss (amt.)	No excess liquid loss.	10% loss	30% loss	50% loss	70% loss	100% liquid loss
(freq.)	No excess loss.	Excess loss 1 out of 10 times.	Excess loss 3 out of 10 times.	Excess loss 5 out of 10 times.	Excess loss 7 out of 10 times.	Excess loss with every swallow.
Swallows Food Without Coughing (sensitiv.)	No coughing or hypersensitivity noted.	Coughing or hypersensitivity only with textures.	Coughing or hypersensitivity noted with textures.	Coughing or hypersensitivity noted with textures, temperature changes.	Coughing or hypersensitivity noted regardless of food consistency.	
Coughing (freq.)	No coughing or gagging noted.	Coughs 10% of the time.	Coughs 30% of the time.	Coughs 50% of the time.	Coughs 70% of the time.	Coughs every mouthful.

From Stratton, M. (1981). Behavioral assessment scale of oral functions in feeding. *The American Journal of Occupational Therapy, 35*(11), 719–721. Copyright 1981 by the American Occupational Therapy Association, Inc. Reprinted by permission.

Table 2.7. Feeding evaluation of oral function—adapted form[a]

Function		0 "Passive"	1	2	3
Jaw Closure	extension	Jaw remains open; no noticeable movement in response to utensil.	Jaw thrust: jaw opens as far as possible; difficult to close.	Jaw thrust: jaw opens less than 2″; difficult to close.	Jaw thrust: jaw opens less than 2″; closes easily with manual assistance.
	flexion	Jaw remains closed; no noticeable movement in response to utensil.	Bite reflex: holds spoon tightly; cannot voluntarily release.	Bite reflex: easily corrected by jaw control.	Bite reflex: immediate active release without use of jaw control.
	freq.	Response occurs every time.	7 out of 10 times per meal.	5 out of 10 times per meal.	3 out of 10 times per meal.
Lip Closure Over Spoon		Mouth remains open; no noticeable movement in response to utensil.	Initial jaw thrust or bite reflex on contact with utensil.	Slight active movement of lower jaw toward spoon.	Jaws close over spoon but not lips.
Tongue Control		Tongue remains at bottom of mouth; no noticeable response to food.	Tongue rolls to side or retracts back; not functional for swallow.	Tongue protrudes horizontally forward & out between lips in swallowing.	Tongue protudes horizontally forward (but remains in mouth) when swallowing.
Lip Closure While Swallowing		Mouth remains open; no noticeable movement during swallow.	Slight active movement of lower jaw/lip during swallow.	Lips partially close during swallow; tongue may occlude opening.	Lips open & close repeatedly during swallow.
Swallows Food Without Excess Loss	amt.	100% food loss	70% loss	50% loss	30% loss
	freq.	Excess loss with every swallow	Excess loss 7 out of 10 times	Excess loss 5 out of 10 times	Excess loss 3 out of 10 times

4 "Functional"	5 "Normal"	*	Additional Feeding Evaluation Information		
			A. Physical Assist	B. Position Change	C. Food Change
Jaw thrust: corrects itself within few seconds	Able to open and close jaws smoothly over utensil.				
Bite reflex: not strong enough to re- tain utensil in mouth.	Able to open and close jaws smoothly over utensil.				
1 out of 10 times per meal.	No abnormal response.				
Lips approx- imate spoon with no at- tempt to remove food.	Lips purse together to actively re- move food from bowl of spoon.				
Tongue moves for- ward & upward in at- tempt to swallow.	Tongue ele- vates to the roof of the mouth (be- hind front teeth) and moves food back to swallow.				
Lips approx- imate during swallow— not tight seal.	Lips close tightly to pre- vent food loss during swallow.				
10% loss _____ Excess loss 1 out of 10 times	No excess food loss with average-sized spoon				

continued

Table 2.7. *continued*

Function	0 "Passive"	1	2	3
Chews Food (Tongue/ Jaw Control)	No noticeable movement of jaws or tongue in response to food.	No jaw movement.	Minimal jaw movement; not functional for chewing.	Vertical jaw movement. Some lateral tongue control.
Sips Liquids	No active movement of jaws, lips & tongue in response to liquid.	Initial jaw thrust or bite reflex on contact with glass.	Slight active movement of lower jaw toward rim of glass.	Lips approx-imate rim of glass; does not initiate intake.
Swallows Liquids Without Excess Loss — amt.	100% liquid loss	70% loss	50% loss	30% loss
— freq.	Excess loss with every swallow.	Excess loss 7 out of 10 times.	Excess loss 5 out of 10 times.	Excess loss 3 out of 10 times.
Swallows Food Without Coughing — sensitiv.	Coughing or hypersensitivity noted regardless of food consistency.		Coughing or hypersensitivity noted with textures, tem-perature changes.	
— freq.	Coughs every mouthful.	Coughs 70% of the time.	Coughs 50% of the time.	Coughs 30% of the time.

From Kansas Neurological Institute. (1985). *Feeding evaluation of oral function—adapted form.* Topeka: Author; adapted from Stratton (1981). Reprinted by permission.

*Indicate if performance was without assist or any adaptations by entering a checkmark.

ªKey to Additional Feeding Evaluation Information:
Indicate by letter the appropriate additional information in each category.

A.   Physical Assist
A.   Manual open/close
B.   Quick stretch—upper lip
C.   Quick stretch—lower lip
D.   Quick stretch—both lips
E.   Quick stretch—corners of mouth
F.   Massage–orbicularis oris muscle
G.   Ice to orbicularis oris muscle
H.   "Desensitization"—tongue blade
I.   "Desensitization"—child's fingers
J.   "Desensitization"—trainer
K.   Disc against lips
L.   Massage to temporalis muscle
M.   Quick stretch to temporalis muscle

N.   Massage to masseter muscle
O.   Quick stretch to masseter muscle
P.   Massage to medial pterygoid muscle
Q.   Massage to medial pterygoid muscle
R.   Food to anterior tongue + pressure
S.   Food to middle tongue + pressure
T.   Food to lateral tongue + pressure
U.   Food between molars
V.   Head forward _____ degrees
W.   Head extended _____ degrees
X.   Push in on chin
Y.   _____ open/close
Z.   Other _____

			Additional Feeding Evaluation Information		
4 Functional"	5 "Normal"	*	A. Physical Assist	B. Position Change	C. Food Change
Vertical movement with minimal rotary movement.	Able to bite off solid piece of food and chew functionally. Tongue able to control position of bolus.				
Lips over rim of glass; sips liquids but cannot swallow repeatedly.	Lips over rim of glass and sips liquid and swallows repeatedly.				
10%loss	No excess liquid loss.				
Excess loss 1 out of 10 times.	No excess loss.				
Coughing or hypersensitivity only with textures.	No coughing or hypersensitivity noted.				
Coughs 10% of the time.	No coughing or gagging noted.				

B. Position Change

A. + Hip/knee flexion (feet positioned)
B. + Hip extension rotation/abduction (feet positioned)
C. + Hip/knee flexion (feet free)
D. + Hip extension rotation/abduction (feet free)
E. + Thumb extension
F. + Hand extension/finger abduction
G. + Supination
H. All items listed in E–G
I. Supination/opposite shoulder
J. Lateral support _____
K. Capitol extension‡
L. No input to back of head

C. Food Change

A. To pureed
B. Pureed + 2 tsp. of mashed potatoes
C. Pureed + 4 tsp. of mashed potatoes
D. To mechanical
E. To mechanical + 2 tsp. of mashed potatoes
F. To regular
G. Other _____

‡Refers to the position of the cervical spine that is neutral (measured as 0°) with respect to flexion and extension.

67

As part of the motor development section of the feeding assessment, Morris (1977) suggested looking at the degree of overall postural control as well as head, trunk, and arm control. Do not observe the child just during mealtimes or in just one position. What happens to the postural tone at rest or when the child is moved? Does the total tone improve in any particular position? Be sure to check the degree of head control with and without physical and verbal cues.

How much trunk control does the child have when he or she is sitting unsupported? Is there lateral protective reaction in the sitting position? Check to see what amount of arm/hand control the child is using during meals. Is there a difference from his or her other daily activities? Can the child handle bilateral as well as unilateral tasks? Are there overflow movements noted in other parts of the body as the child is picking up or using a cup/spoon? Does the presence of certain reflexes interfere with the total body symmetry during feeding?

The persistence of several of the primitive reflexes seriously impedes the continuing advancement of development of feeding skills, and assessment of these reactions must be done. The Moro reflex interferes with trunk balance, arm symmetry, and isolated arm control. In checking the normal reaction to the asymmetric tonic neck reflex (ATNR), one must also observe whether it is creating a lateral jaw shift. This can add to swallowing, sucking, and chewing difficulty. The ATNR certainly interferes with maintaining the head in midline as well as controlling the movement of taking the spoon, scooping the food, and bringing the spoon to the mouth. The tonic labyrinthine reflex forces the child into an extensor pattern, making swallowing difficult.

The maturity level of eye-hand coordination must be evaluated as the child handles food and utensils. Each general stage in the development of hand/finger control (prehension)—regard, approach, grasp, manipulation, and release—also has various levels of maturity, as noted in Table 2.8. Cliff (1979) noted several identifying components that should assist therapists/teachers in determining whether a child has a mature or an immature level of prehension. By observing the position of the thumb in relation to the fingers, the type of grasp, the manner in which an object is manipulated, and the control used to release a toy, one can assess the level of development in regard to independent feeding skills.

The effect sensory input has on the child's eating ability can be determined by observing the child's reaction to sounds, images, tastes, temperatures, smells, and touches. Can the child tolerate loud sounds? One of our client's problems centered around his reaction to certain sounds. Every time an adult coughed, it would trigger a brief seizure-like episode in the child. There would be a sudden body stiffening, internal rotation of the extremities, slight body extension, and an upward roll of the eyes. During lunch, this would interrupt the feeding training. If the child has visual problems, how much does it limit his or her independent eating ability? What happens when a spoon approaches

Table 2.8. Development of prehension during the first year

Age	Regard	Approach	Grasp	Manipulation	Release
0–16 weeks	Can fixate on objects. ATNR directs gaze toward extended hand.		*Reflexive grasp*— After stimulus is made, fingers quickly close around object with a tightening response that follows. *Ulnar grasp*— Little finger next to surface; it is a clumsy grasp and does not maintain grip.		Unable to release toy voluntarily.
16 weeks	Looks at objects and hand.	Head held in midline and hand comes to center of body.	*Hand grasp*—In pronate position grasps in paw-like fashion. Thumb remains next to index finger while fingers curl down.	Mouths toy placed in mouth.	
28 weeks	Takes time to visually inspect toys.	Uses one hand to approach toy. Aims directly over toy.	*Palmar grasp*—Thumb points down. First time for thumb opposition but little control over position or movement. *Superior palmar grasp*—First two fingers have more active part in picking up cube with thumb in opposition with two fingers. Cube rests on radial portion of palm.	Holds, looks at, and brings toy to mouth. Sometimes shakes, bangs, or transfers toy.	One hand pulls toy from other hand.
32–40 weeks		One-hand approach becomes more frequent. Has good directional control.	*Inferior forefinger grasp*— Cross between superior palmar grasp and superior forefinger grasp. Cube still rests near palm. Does not have to rest any part of arm on surface.	Spends more time inspecting, poking, transferring, dropping and regaining.	36 weeks—resists release. 46 weeks— cannot yet release hand on cube.
52 weeks	Vision is used to locate toy but does not direct the hand to the toy.	Movement is now a single fluent action.	*Forefinger grasp and superior grasp*—Two types of adult grasps using distal portion of fingers and thumb.	Can work small item (e.g., pellet). Enjoys playing with toys and will spend lots of time exploring.	Can release cube in cup. Has trouble with two-block tower.

Adapted from Cliff (1979).

69

the child's mouth? Will the mouth open, will the body become tense, or will there be no reaction at all? How does the introduction to a variety of tastes, smells, or temperatures affect biting, tongue thrust, or swallowing? When the child is touched, what kind of response does it set off? Is there a difference between being touched on the outside or inside of the mouth? Does the placement of a spoon on the tongue cause a gag reflex? The response to touch is one of the most important of all senses because of the wide range of responses possible.

Information relating to the child's oral hygiene is also necessary in designing an effective treatment program. Knowledge of medications the child is taking is important because their side effects may interfere with feeding skills. Dilantin, for example, when taken over a long period of time, can produce swelling of the gums, which interferes with chewing and general oral health. Is bruxism (teeth grinding) a problem, and can a cause be identified? Does the child drool? How often and in what position? The child's ability to bite down assumes a normal dental occlusion. If the child has difficulty biting, it may be because of an over- or underbite. A number of children have delayed dental eruption, which will affect the choice and type of food that can be managed. Children with Down syndrome commonly have teeth that are slow to come in as well as irregularly shaped teeth.

Additional bits of information about the child's eating behavior will help in developing a thorough feeding program. How long does it take to complete a meal? Are certain meals easier for the child to handle? Morris (1982) thinks it is important to know the parents' expectations about the quantity of food the child should consume. What is their reaction when the child cannot consume that amount? Are their goals realistic? What type of food is given to the child? If pureed foods are given instead of table foods, what is the reason? Will the child only eat certain foods? In what position is the child usually fed? Many times just correcting the positioning corrects the feeding problems of swallowing, chewing, and jaw and tongue control. (Descriptions of effective feeding positions are given in Chapter 3.)

How the food is handled once it is near or inside the mouth is of prime importance to assess. Does the child bite the food and, if so, how? Is there active jaw and tongue movement? If so, are the patterns normal or abnormal? Farber and Huss (1974) suggested that evaluators should watch for the child who may have a hollowed temple area. The cause may be a poorly developed temporalis muscle that is also creating jaw instability and poor chewing patterns. Specific tongue movements to watch for are the amount of active tongue thrusting observed throughout the entire day versus just at mealtimes. This action plays an important part in the quality of chewing. The type of lip movement a child exhibits is another important clue in the amount of normal control found when the child bites, sucks, chews, swallows, and tongue thrusts. Utley

(1982) indicated that training independent lip closure will result in increased nasal breathing, tongue retraction instead of tongue protraction (tongue thrusting), and less food spillage on the child's face and clothing. The overall effect is a clean, pleasant-smelling child who is more independent in eating skills and a joy with whom to socialize.

Indirect Child Contact

An indirect child contact assessment basically looks at the effect the environment has on the functional eating skills and the rapport between the feeder and the child.

Just as important as the position used to feed the child is the time and place a child is fed. Does the child join the rest of the family at the table? Is the feeding time prior to the regular time and away from the dining room? What are the reasons given for either time and placement? Every family has their own procedures and temperament in getting everyone fed. The evaluator may be able to suggest shortcuts or guidelines to follow or replan the time and place to include the child's participation at meals and still provide a positive social atmosphere.

What do the parents think is their child's feeding problem? The assessment may uncover situations where there is disagreement between the professional staff and the immediate family members. A home visit during mealtime should answer the question of what has been done to alleviate the problem. This is also a good time to observe the verbal and nonverbal interaction between parent and child. Does the parent make the child feel comfortable, or does his or her body and verbal language reflect onto the child an added tension and increased tone?

It may be equally important when working with an older child to find out what bothers the child. What are the child's concerns about the people who do the feeding? Individuals doing the feeding who are not part of the immediate family must be aware of the child's personal territorial boundaries (personal space). How does the child use this space when interacting with new professional staff, strangers, family members, or other children? What happens when an adult invades this territory when the child is unprepared or will not accept that individual so close to his or her face?

It is not uncommon for a child with mild or moderate feeding difficulties to learn (consciously or unconsciously) to change the way a task is performed. Too often this compensation only increases the abnormality. The athetoid child who has poor sitting balance typically learns to sit with hips bent, legs straight, and head and back hyperextended (Finnie, 1975). This posture pulls the shoulders back (retracted) and flexes and externally rotates the arms. As Finnie stated, this makes it impossible for the child to be an active participant in the feeding process. If forward movement is attempted, the compensated balance posture is lost. Corrected positioning with legs flexed and shoulders brought forward will allow the child to direct movement and attention toward the midline for feeding or academic tasks. The child no longer has to exert excess energy just to maintain balance, however atypical it may be.

Dressing and Personal Hygiene Skills

Evaluating the functional dressing ability of a child is best done during appropriate times, such as in the morning while dressing, during the day when the child needs to go to the bathroom, when going outdoors wearing a sweater/coat, and upon going to bed at night. If the assistance of the parents within the home environment is not possible, it is best to select a room or an area in the classroom or clinic with privacy and a minimum of distractions to allow the child to practice self-dressing.

A number of commercial criterion-referenced and norm-referenced assessments as well as informal checklists are available in varying degrees of detail from simple observation (Johnson-Martin, Jens, & Attermeier, 1986; Rogers, D'Eugenio, Brown, Donovan, & Lynch, 1977) to more extensive evaluations of the child's dressing ability (Balthazar, 1971; Coley, 1978; Furuno et al., 1985; Vulpe, 1977). For the older child, further assessment of perceptual discrimination ability, which is needed for independent dressing, is helpful. Is the child aware of the difference between the front/back, inside/outside, and top/bottom of a garment? Must the child be given added visual and tactile support, such as colored corduroy tabs sewn onto a shirt's bottom edge, in order to complete independent dressing and/or undressing?

Associated skills necessary for self-dressing that need to be evaluated include the degree (or qualifying amount) of arm movement, eye-hand coordination, sitting and standing balance (this refers to the status of reflex integration), and social skills (Bailey & Wolery, 1984). This additional information will help establish priorities for the training of more complex dressing skills (primarily closures such as snaps, buttons, belts, and shoelaces). S. Henderson and McDonald (1973) stated that in addition to setting priorities with parents, evaluating or recording any special problems that may require specific adaptation or training methods should be included in the assessment report. Personal hygiene skills to be assessed include bathing, oral hygiene, hair and nail care, management of toileting, and, for females, the management of menstruation. Children with tactile impairment and children who are immobile (spina bifida, spastic cerebral palsy) will also need to include special skin care if skin breakdown (decubiti) due to impaired circulation is to be avoided. For example, children with spina bifida will need to check the skin over weight-bearing parts (buttocks) and skin over bony parts (heels, ankles, hips) for signs of impaired circulation and signs of developing decubiti. Associated skills for independence in this area include an awareness of body parts, color discrimination in order to rate red skin, and an ability to change position.

Cognitive and Visual-Perceptual Skills

Basic cognitive processes and prerequisites for understanding the environment include selective visual and auditory attention; perception, or the ability to assign meaning to sensory stimuli; memory of objects and events; understanding basic concepts such as shape, color, size, prepositions, sequencing, and time; and problem solving. Higher level cognitive functions include abstract thought and reasoning. In assessment, cognitive abilities are observed in verbal and nonverbal (motor) problem-solving tasks, expressive and receptive language tasks, and tasks requiring perceptual and informational processing (P. N. Clark & Allen, 1985; Molnar, 1985; Scherzer & Tscharnuter, 1982).

The psychologist will be the primary evaluator of cognitive functions in many settings. However, parents, teachers, and therapists also need to understand how the individual child perceives the environment and events within the environment. An understanding of the child's level of perception and cognition is essential if the adults caring for the child are going to communicate effectively with that child.

Standardized tests of cognition provide information about how the individual child is functioning in comparison to age peers. However, the physically disabled child may not be able to respond verbally or with the required motor skills to the standardized assessment tasks. This means that what the child perceives and comprehends about the evaluation task or environment is trapped inside that child. It may be appropriate to supplement the data obtained on a standardized test with data obtained through observation of the child in less structured situations and through adapted assessments designed to compensate for the child's physical dysfunction (Lyons, 1984).

The *Psychoeducational Evaluation of the Preschool Child: A Manual Utilizing the Haeussermann Approach,* by Jedrysek, Klapper, Pope, and Wortis (1972), has been designed for the child who is nonverbal or has significant motor impairment. According to Langley (1983) this test, which is based on the work of Else Haeussermann as described in *Developmental Potential for Preschool Children* (1958), is one of the most relevant and practical assessment tools for educational screening of the child with physical disabilities. This assessment is designed to assess the educational potential of preschool children or individuals who appear to be cognitively functioning at the preschool level. The following areas are addressed in this assessment: 1) physical functioning and sensory status, 2) perceptual functioning, 3) competence in learning for short-term retention, 4) language competence, and 5) cognitive functioning. The main items in each section are arranged in ascending order of difficulty with the last item at a level appropriate for entry into the first grade. If the child is unable to respond successfully to a main item, there are probes, which are tasks requiring less abstract cognitive processing and less complex motor responses. The test is begun only after the child is positioned so that maximal functional abilities are possible and the child's method of communication (e.g., verbalizations, pointing, smiling) has been established.

The following is one main test item from the section assessing perceptual functioning. Here the reader can see the concept of downward modification of a test item through the use of the probe items.

> *Main Item #7: Color Matching*
> Materials: Six pairs of colored squares
> Procedure: Display all six colored squares randomly. Ask the child to pick out the square that matches the one the examiner is holding.
> *Probes:* (used if child fails main item)
> 1. Reduce number of colored squares the child must choose from.
> 2. Should the child fail the probe item the examiner can make the task more concrete. For example, a doll with colored socks can be used. The examiner can put one of the pair of socks on the doll and ask the child to point to or look at the sock that should go on the doll's other foot. (Jedrysek et al., 1972, p. 18)

This type of assessment can provide information about the child's level of cognitive and perceptual functioning and information about what type of stimuli or teaching materials are meaningful to the child.

ASSESSMENT IN SPECIFIC DEVELOPMENTAL DISABILITIES

The At-Risk Infant

The process of administering assessment tests and interpreting their results in infants below 1 year of age is a difficult task. It requires knowledge beyond just memorizing what verbal instructions are required. Too many variables, not under the infant's or examiner's control, have an effect on each infant's behavior in an unpredictable manner (Fewell, 1983) (Table 2.9). In fact, the completion of any type of assessment may take several days for a number of reasons. It may also require that procedures or certain items be modified, especially for medical problems. Interpretations must reflect these changes. The examiner must be cognizant of the way the infant reacts just before feeding time, or to strangers when tired or fatigued, and when the infant is overstimulated (Erickson, 1976; Farber & Williams, 1982). Depending on the examiner's expertise, the session can either be therapeutic or stressful for the infant and adult alike.

Although any assessment tool will not totally forecast specific future problems, there is some consensus regarding the usefulness of early testing. First, it identifies where the infant is within the developmental process. Next, it provides an easy way of screening those infants who require additional in-depth testing. Third, the testing results yield strengths and weaknesses that can be used as a basis for developing an intervention program. Finally, the effective-

Table 2.9. Important variables influencing test results in at-risk infants

Variable	Reason
Position	1. The infant's position will determine whether the task is difficult or easy to perform. 2. Position of material will indicate if the infant can adequately select the correct response.
Size	The dimensions of the materials or toys will have an effect on the results if the infant cannot hold or see the materials.
Color	Too many colors in close approximation of each other or too bright colors will be distracting to the infant.
Duration	Length of time of the test may be more than the infant can handle and poor performance may result toward the end of the session.
Attention span	Ability of infant to attend and perform a task will be determined by the attention span.
Physical environment	The amount of furniture, clutter, noise, and movement within the immediate surroundings will determine the amount of concentration in the infant.
Rapport	1. Informing or telling the infant/toddler what is to be done will result in a positive response as opposed to asking if the infant would like to do the task. 2. Allow the infant to accumulate to the surroundings and to the examiner. A relaxed atmosphere will aid in relaxing the infant.
Order of assessment	1. First administering a few items that will produce success (such as items below infant's age) will set a positive atmosphere and result in higher performance. 2. Present activities that lower the activity level (cognitive or fine motor). Initiating gross motor activities first will lessen attention span during the latter part of the testing period.

Adapted from Harbin (1977).

ness of the program can be determined from prepost testing (Horowitz, 1982; Sheehan & Gallagher, 1984). Since different assessments have been developed to effectively evaluate the above goals, the selection of a test must be done after reviewing the parameters of the purpose and the age range of the test.

Gentry and Adams (1978) indicated that the accuracy of a determination of the extent of a problem improves with age of the infant. However, the longer intervention is delayed, the more difficult it may be to ameliorate the handicapping condition. The reader also must keep in mind that an early assessment will not predict future problems. Reasons for this, according to Horowitz and Dunn (1978), are as follows:

1. The inherent instability of the infant.
2. The changing nature of the test items in IQ tests across different ages.
3. Insufficiency of testing techniques. (p. 23)

According to Bailey and Wolery (1984), a comprehensive evaluation will result when, in addition to following the assessment protocol, several considerations are remembered. First, in order to elicit the infant's best performance, the assessment process should be nonthreatening. Second, assessments should be conducted during the infant's alert arousal state, which may mean the test will be conducted over several sessions. When scheduling the initial evaluation, therapists would be wise to ask the mother what time during the day is the best responsive time for the infant. Bailey and Wolery believe that, although multiple-session assessment can be time consuming, the end results can be both optimal performance and effective program planning. In order for this to happen, a third consideration is to limit the time period for each assessment session to no more than 30–45 minutes. A fourth useful consideration that helps achieve optimal ability is to modify the test items. Simplifying the instructions, adapting the materials, or reinforcing correct responses may give the needed cues necessary for optimal performance. Examiners should be warned that tampering with a standardized test will make the final score invalid and should be done only when the score itself is unimportant and the emphasis of the test is on possible instructional methods. Whenever possible a fifth consideration should be made: Implementing an interdisciplinary process will lessen the stress of having one person responsible for making decisions outside his or her professional expertise. As has been mentioned, parental involvement should be a prime consideration in assessing the infant's strengths and weaknesses. Unless proven otherwise, the information parents provide should be regarded as accurate and reliable.

Issues of Interpretation

Difficulties with test interpretations will inevitably develop when examiners stretch the parameters of a test. The appropriate selection of a test for an infant will result in valid interpretations, thus avoiding false assumptions (see below). Every test on the market has certain limited capabilities and was designed for a specific reason. Too frequently, screening instruments are given to infants who do not fall within the instrument's age bracket or cannot verbally or physically compete the test (Lewko, 1976).

Examiners must keep in mind that many tests can only indicate what the infant is doing at the time of testing with a particular person at a specific time of day. Certain factors such as hunger or illness will help determine the attention span of an infant. In the presence of such factors it would be better to formally assess an infant on another day when the health of the infant would produce a higher social level.

To predict an infant's progress only on the basis of test results is to overlook the effect that early intervention training has on independent motor ability. Fewell and Sandall (1983) have questioned any test's predictive validity on the basis of many of the topics discussed above. A more relevant predictor of future developmental delays of an at-risk infant is the home environment, which includes the parents' attitude toward the child, the parents' education, the stability of the home, the socioeconomic level of the family, and the infant's temperament (Fewell & Sandall, 1983; Ramey & Brownlee, 1981).

Other problems commonly confronted by therapists and teachers are the relative objectivity of behavioral-type checklists and the tendency to teach just to the test items in many developmental checklists (Fewell & Sandall, 1983). Too often this leads to or develops splinter skills. Knowing how each skill fits into or develops from a broader focus area enables the therapist or teacher to train or emphasize a developmental process.

Selection of Assessments

The selection of assessments is determined by several factors. Based on the referral concerns or current difficulties, the examiner has dozens of infant tests among which to select. A sampling of infant assessments are described in Appendix A; a smaller portion of those listed are described here in more detail.

Apgar Scoring System

The Apgar test, designed by Dr. Virginia Apgar (1960), is probably the first assessment every newborn encounters. It is administered by the medical staff in the delivery room at 1 minute after birth. Follow-up exams are usually done at 5 and/or 15 minutes; not all hospitals check the infant at all three times (Jennett, Warford, Kreinick, & Waterkotte, 1981).

The five components of the test measure neonatal physical responsiveness, development, and overall state of health (Fewell & Sandall, 1983). As noted in Table 2.10, the test assesses the infant's muscle tone, heart rate, reflex irritability, skin color, and respiration. A maximum score for each category is 2 points, for a total score of 10; the normal range is between 7 and 10. A neonate

Table 2.10. Apgar scoring system

	2	1	0
Appearance (color)	completely pink	body pink, extremities bluish	blue body
Pulse (heart rate)	higher than 100	less than 100	absent
Grimace (reflex irritability)	reflex responsiveness	grimace or slight cry	no response
Activity (muscle tone)	active motions	some movement of arms and legs	limp, motionless
Respiration (respiratory effort)	strong efforts	slow, irregular breathing	no respiration

Adapted from Apgar and Beck (1974).

who scores between 4 and 6 is considered moderately depressed, and a neonate who scores less than 4 is considered severely depressed.

Although the Apgar is completed quickly, it does have a few drawbacks. Sheehan and Gallagher (1984) indicated that at the 1-minute scoring period, the skin color is difficult to correctly assess because very few infants are entirely pink. Also, studies have indicated that low scores in themselves are not strong predictors of future development (Fewell & Sandall, 1983).

There have been attempts to use the results from the Apgar to predict future handicaps. Nelson and Ellenberg (1981) followed 49,000 children to the age of 7 years, checked their physical status, and compared that status to their Apgar scores. Fifty-five percent of the children with high Apgar scores (7–10) at 1 minute and 73% of those with high scores at 5 minutes later developed cerebral palsy. Of those children who scored 0–3 at 10 minutes and survived, 80% had no major handicap.

Several studies have attempted to show a correlation between the Apgar score and intelligence scores (Broman, Nichols, & Kennedy, 1975; Edwards, 1968; Servnian & Broman, 1975; Shipe, Vandenberg, & Williams, 1968). The conclusion is that the relationship of the Apgar score to intelligence scores, or any similar predictive comparison, is still inconclusive and that the Apgar is best at assessing fetal and perinatal factors only (Fewell & Sandall, 1983; Horowitz, 1982).

Denver Developmental Screening Test

The Denver Developmental Screening Test (DDST) was developed by Frankenburg and Dodds (1969) to screen for developmental delays from birth to 6 years. The four areas of developmental skills measured are personal-social, fine motor–adaptive, language, and gross motor. Each of the 105 items is depicted as a horizontal bar broken into four parts (25%, 50%, 75%, and 90%) whose sizes depend upon the age at which each of the sample groups accomplished the task (Figure 2.12). The infant's performance is scored as a pass or fail through observation, direct testing, and parent response. Developmental delays are identified if the item was failed and the infant's score was entirely to the left of the age line on the horizontal bar (Figure 2.12). This test, which is relatively easy to learn, can be administered by both professionals and nonprofessionals. A thorough description of and guidelines about the DDST have been written by Erickson (1976).

Since the introduction of the DDST, people have questioned whether the test could be used as a predictor of developmental problems. The results from S. K. Campbell and Wilhelm's (1985) study revealed that the DDST is much less sensitive in correctly identifying children with deviant neurological potential than is the Bayley Scales of Infant Development.

The question of whether the DDST could be a predictor of kindergarten difficulties was looked at by Cadman et al. (1984). The test was administered by

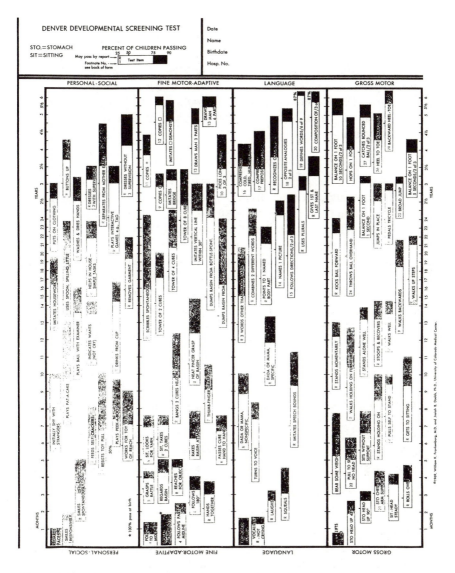

Figure 2.12. Denver Developmental Screening Test. (From Frankenburg, W. K., & Dodds, J. B. [1969]. *Denver developmental screening test.* Denver: LADOCA Project and Publishing Foundation; reprinted by permission.)

public health nurses to 2,569 children served by four school districts in Southern Ontario. The children, who were within 5–7 months from entering kindergarten when given the DDST, also received a teacher rating report at the end of that school year. The teachers rated learning abilities, classroom behavior, amount of special attention required, and special education referrals. The DDST was able to correctly rank only 5%–10% of the problems in those four areas.

The Denver Developmental Screening Test should not be used as a predictor of later intelligence or behavior, nor should it be used as a foundation for programming. The users of this assessment tool would be better off to stick to the original intent, that of being a valuable screening for developmental delays across four domains.

Neonatal Behavioral Assessment Scale

Birth to 1 month is the age range of the Neonatal Behavioral Assessment Scale (NBAS), commonly called the Brazelton Scale after the principal developer, T. Berry Brazelton (1984). This neonatal tool assesses a normal full-term infant's neurological (reflex) and behavioral reaction with 46 items. It tests the infant during several arousal states, including sleep, drowsiness, crying, and active alertness. During these times, the examiner evaluates the infant's best reaction to visual, auditory, and tactile stimuli on graded 4- and 9-point scales. Some of the specific reflexes assessed include the plantar grasp, automatic walking, Moro, rooting, and sucking. The infant's behavioral responses cover the degree of alertness, irritability, and cuddliness. A supplemental (NBAS-Kansas) version makes it possible to obtain a score that reflects the difference between the modal (the quality of performance) and the best behavior (Horowitz, 1982).

Gorski (1984) described a study of 53 infants and the follow-up assessment 7 years later. Although the Brazelton correctly identified 87% of the neurological and 80% of the behavioral problems, there was an equally high percentage (80) of infants diagnosed as normal who 7 years later had neurological problems; only 24% of those diagnosed as normal later had a behavioral deficit. Continued research is needed to ascertain the Brazelton's predictability.

Bayley Scales of Infant Development

As Horowitz (1982) stated, the Bayley is "currently the best and most widely used general instrument to evaluate infant developmental status" (p. 109). There are three parts to the Bayley: the mental and motor indices plus the infant behavior record (IBR) (Bayley, 1969). The IBR is completed after administering the mental and motor sections. It describes how the infant responded to objects and adults as well as giving an impression of the infant's emotional and developmental status. The results are derived from a pass-fail scoring system that gives a basal and a ceiling subscore and a final mean developmental index score of 100 at any given age. The test provides a developmental quotient, not an intelligence score (Horowitz, 1982; Murphy, Nichter, & Liden, 1982).

The Bayley is frequently used to compare the effectiveness of another assessment tool or used to evaluate a program's progress. Eipper and Azen (1978) found the Bayley to have significantly larger developmental lags than the Gesell Developmental Schedules when administered to 21 boys and girls with Down syndrome with an age range of 8 to 33 months. The differences between the two tests stem from the manner in which the tests are presented to the infants. In the Gesell there is more latitude given in the verbal instructions, many items are passed on the basis of a parent's comments, the refused items do not count against the child, and the scoring procedure is more lenient than that found in the Bayley. Eipper and Azen's conclusion is that, for research purposes, the test of choice is the Bayley. They also felt that the Gesell test tends to overestimate the developmental level in a child with existing delays.

It is not uncommon for only the mental and motor portions of the Bayley to be used and not the IBR. In the study done by Lasky and his coworkers (1983) only the IBR was used to compare three experimental infant groups with varying weights and ventilatory therapy requirements and a normal infant control group. All three experimental groups received lower ratings than the control group. Within the high-risk groups there were interesting differences. Regardless of the weight, the ventilated infants obtained the lowest overall performance; the very low birth weight and ventilated infants were described as being overly active with a short attention span; and those newborns who were never ventilated and had a very low birth weight were characterized as being happy, passive, and delayed.

Additional Assessments

In addition to the assessment tools just discussed and the other tests listed in Appendix A, there are a number of motor actions that need to be evaluated with regard to their functional level.

Muscle Tone

In order to explore and expand one's environment, one must have movement and postural control. Even communication during infancy is done primarily through movement, such as pointing or raising an arm (Fetters, 1981). In order for the infant to control movement, there must be adequate muscle tone.

Bailey and Wolery (1984) described Swanson's four methods for assessing the quality of muscle tone and noted that the most effective way is to feel the consistency of the muscle. A soft feel (hypotonic) or a hard/stiff (hypertonic) feel indicates abnormal tone. Observing the degree of movement within an arc or range of motion (ROM) will indicate the type of tone. Limited ROM indicates hypertonicity and exaggerated and hyperextended ROM should be rated as hypotonicity. Shaking an extremity at a joint (knee or elbow) will also assess muscle tone. When the extremity appears to resist shaking or is difficult to shake, hypertonicity is indicated. Hypotonicity is indicated when the extremity has no control and is so loose that the hands or feet are floppy. A final way to evaluate muscle tone is to observe the infant's posture. If the infant is unable to lift and maintain control of the head and trunk while in prone, sitting, or standing, that is evidence of floppy, hypotonic tone. The infant who feels more comfortable in the "W" or reserved sitting position (see Figure 3.7) has hypotonicity. Hypertonic muscles are noted when the posture is very rigid or flexed. Crawling may be very difficult because the legs cannot flex voluntarily. Balance, as indicated by Morrison, Pothier, and Horr (1978), is closely related to muscle tone and the ability to cross the midline.

Sensorimotor Ability

Various sensorimotor inputs give valuable information for future programming. Hypersensitivity is noted in direct and nondirect contact with the infant. An infant who does not like to crawl on carpet or who, when attempting to stand, curls the toes or raises up on the toes is exhibiting sensitivity to tactile stimuli. Of equal concern is the infant who does not respond to any type of tactile input. Auditory assessment can be accomplished by ringing a bell, speaking in a loud voice, or making an unexpected loud noise. These are preferably done outside of the infant's visual field so the infant's response would be to turn his or her head because of the noise rather than the visual stimuli. Morrison and her colleagues (1978) believe a general visual examination can be made by observing "how an infant pursues an object with his eyes or how well he coordinates his visual-motor systems" (p. 119).

Reflexes

To help the therapist in determining and interpreting the effects of reflex testing, Molnar (1974, 1978) has described reflex differences between infants with mental retardation and those with cerebral palsy. When primitive reflexes such as the ATNR or the Moro maintain their effect on the infant's response to external stimuli, there is a cascading effect on the rate of development and quality of higher level reflexes. As Molnar (1978) noted in children with cerebral palsy, more often than not the postural adjustment reactions fail to emerge. These automatic reactions allow the individual to develop and maintain throughout life a relationship of proper body alignment no matter what position the body is in and despite the effect of gravity. The reflexes at this level include the positive supporting, protective extension, and tilting reactions. Refer to Chapter 3 for a description of reflexes and the implications when primitive reflexes persist.

What has been noted in infants with mental retardation is not a persistence of the primitive reflexes but a delay in development of the postural reflexes. In contrast to the normal age at which the postural reflexes are attained (6–18 months of age), the infant with retardation attains these responses between 11 and 45 months. The motor milestones of the infant and toddler with Down syndrome (crawling, getting in and out of sitting position, pulling to stand, and walking) are greatly delayed. This is due in part to the low muscle tone level and the effect that gravity has on the movements (Lydic, Windsor, Short, &

Ellis, 1985). Molnar (1974) has noted that the above motor skills were mastered within 1–4 weeks once the postural reflexes emerged.

In addition to the published reflex assessment forms of Capute et al. (1978), Fiorentino (1973), and Pearson (1973), a new approach to reflex testing has been developed by DeGangi, Berk, and Valvano (1983). The content of this assessment tool, the Test of Motor and Neurological Functions (TMNF), is reported to "validly and reliably measure muscle tone, primitive reflexes, automatic and equilibrium reactions and qualitative movement findings" (p. 183). The authors stress to therapists that, although the conclusions should be viewed as tentative, the results can provide valuable information for screening and diagnostic purposes. It is further suggested that the TMNF has the potential for objectively identifying infants with suspected motor and neurological deficits. There is a need for further comparison of the TMNF with other reflex assessments before any final conclusions can be made as to the effectiveness of this test.

Hoskins and Squires (1973) saw a need to develop a form that would assess and compare both voluntary gross motor skills and reflex development. Since there is such a close relationship between the two responses to external stimuli, a deficit in one or both areas could provide valuable treatment clues. Having both sets of information on one sheet makes for easier comparison.

The Child with Cerebral Palsy

Some of the major problems characteristic of cerebral palsy are abnormal muscle tone, persistance of primitive reflexes, and delayed development of higher level motor reactions and skills. These problems will probably interfere significantly with the child's ability to sit, walk, eat, and play. The assessment of muscle tone, status of reflexes, cognitive/visual-perceptual status, and so forth are discussed separately. However, in reality these components are often evaluated simultaneously during the same test situations or tasks. Table 2.11 presents an outline of the components of a comprehensive assessment of the child with cerebral palsy. Some of these components are discussed further below. A listing of various assessments useful for children with cerebral palsy can be found in Appendix B.

Muscle Tone

Muscle tone can be assessed using several methods (P. N. Clark & Allen, 1985). While the child is lying or sitting (position would depend upon child's overall level of development) in a comfortable position, a passive range of motion (P/ROM) can be conducted by moving each joint in the extremities through its full range of movement. For example, the elbow can be flexed or extended and the wrist can be flexed, extended, and moved from side to side (radial and ulnar deviation). The therapist should note any *involuntary* resistance to pas-

Table 2.11. Sample assessment outline for children with cerebral palsy

I. Overall developmental level
    A. Gross motor skills in prone, supine, sitting, and standing (e.g., head control, rolling, sitting balance, walking, running, stair climbing)
    B. Fine motor skills in prone, supine, sitting, and standing, e.g.:
        1. Eye-hand coordination skills, including visual attention, reach, grasp, manipulation, and release (accuracy, speed)
        2. Oculomotor skills
        3. Oral-motor skills
    C. Cognitive/visual-perceptive skills
        1. Memory, attention span
        2. Basic concepts of shape, color, size; prepositional concepts
        3. Visual perception of figure-ground, position in space, and spatial relationships
        4. Problem-solving skills
    D. Speech and language skills
        1. Receptive language
        2. Expressive skills—communication
    E. Self-care skills
        1. Feeding
        2. Dressing
        3. Toileting and hygiene
    F. Play skills (e.g., selection of toy, appropriate use of toys)
    G. Social skills (i.e., awareness of and interaction with others)
    H. Emotional status (i.e., self-esteem, expression of feelings)
II. Pathology
    A. Muscle tone and status of primitive reflexes in prone, supine, sitting, and standing; effect of muscle tone and primitive reflexes on stability and mobility in all items listed in I
    B. Sensory status
        1. Taste and smell
        2. Vision
        3. Hearing
        4. Tactile discrimination
        5. Kinesthesia and proprioception
        6. Vestibular system function
    C. Range of motion, passive and active

Adapted from Cliff (1979), Garwood (1983), and Levitt (1984).

sive movement, which is an indication of hypertonicity. A very floppy extremity of excessively mobile joint would be an indication of hypotonicity. This method (P/ROM) of assessing muscle tone does not take into account any changes in muscle tone that might be related to body position (i.e., supine versus prone) or the effect of exertion or voluntary movement.

    Muscle tone can also be assessed by conducting a P/ROM after placing the child in *each* of the following positions: supine, prone, side-lying, sitting, and standing. While assessing muscle tone in each of these positions, the therapist should also note the presence of tonic (primitive) reflex patterns. For example, in the supine position, the therapist would typically feel increased extensor muscle tone since the supine position is a stimulus for the tonic labyrinthine reflex. The prone position is also a stimulus for the tonic labyrinthine reflex and the result in prone is increased flexor muscle tone. Increased flexor muscle tone would cause a severely involved child's head to pull down and in toward the body, the elbows and hands to flex, and the hips and knees to flex. Side-lying is a neutral position, and the muscle tone of a child with cerebral palsy may be more relaxed and more normal in this position. If the child is more relaxed in side-lying, more voluntary movement of the hands and arms may be possible. When the P/ROM is conducted while the child is sitting or standing, the therapist may feel more hypertonicity than when the child was lying down. This is because the child must exert more effort to maintain sitting or standing, and such exertion of effort will increase muscle tone.

It is also important to assess the effect of voluntary movement on muscle tone. If voluntary movement is possible, the child should be instructed to roll over, move from supine to hands and knees and crawl, move into sitting, and stand up and walk, run, or climb stairs. During movement the therapist should note evidence of changes in muscle tone. For example, a child with right spastic hemiplegia may appear relaxed when sitting on a chair and both arms may be symmetrically positioned. However, as the child starts to walk or run, the right arm will involuntarily flex at the elbow and the hand will close as a result of hypertonicity.

Reflexes and Reactions

The persistence of a primitive reflex such as the grasp reflex beyond the age of 3 months may be a sign of spasticity in the upper extremities. The delayed appearance of a higher level reaction such as protective extension in the arms may also be a sign of abnormal muscle tone. The assessment of the reflexes and reactions may provide information about the type of cerebral palsy and how severely involved the child is (Keele, 1983). Other authorities, such as Bobath (1985), no longer rely on testing individual reflexes because this encourages a tendency to treat the reflexes rather than the whole child. Instead, it is recommended that patterns of reactions and how they interfere with normal activity be assessed.

An example of such an assessment is the Cerebral Palsy Assessment/Basic Motor Control by Semans, Phillips, Romanoli, Miller, and Skillea (1965), which can also be found in Trombly (1983). The selected test postures demonstrate the nature and extent of interference by abnormal muscle tone and abnormal movement patterns. Only two postures are described here. For each posture the examiner first places the child in the designated position and observes whether the child can maintain the position. The examiner also asks the child to get into and out of the position independently. It is important to note whether the child uses normal or stereotyped patterns of movement.

Prone on hands with extended elbows and hips. The examiner will observe the amount of freedom from flexor hypertonus in prone and test the child's ability to support weight on extended arms. When the child moves out of this position, does he do so naturally or does he flex his head thus causing automatic flexion of the elbows? Can the child shift weight from one arm to the other in this position?

Seated with knees extended and hips abducted. The examiner will observe the child's ability to sit erect with flexion at the hips and extension at the knees. Both arms should be relaxed. Other questions to ask include: Does the child need to use the arms for support or can the arms be moved freely and used for object manipulation? Can the child move his head freely without disrupting sitting balance? (Trombly, 1983, p. 84)

Not only should the child's ability to maintain a posture or to get into and out of a posture be tested, but the child's ability to perform activities in a given position should also be assessed. For example, in the all-fours position, can the child crawl? In the sitting or standing position, can the child use both hands freely and easily to pick up and manipulate objects?

Motor Function

The assessment of the motor function of a child with cerebral palsy not only includes the effect of a position on function, but also the effect of handling techniques on function. Handling techniques refer to the examiner manipulating, moving, or stabilizing the child in specific ways in order to attempt to change (normalize) muscle tone and elicit higher level motor reactions. An example of a handling technique that can be used to normalize muscle tone is gently shaking a spastic arm in order to reduce the hypertonicity. A handling technique designed to elicit higher motor reactions is holding the seated child by both shoulders and slowly tilting the child to one side in order to elicit head righting. An excellent resource on the procedure for a neurodevelopmental assessment of the child with cerebral palsy is *Early Diagnosis and Therapy in Cerebral Palsy: A Primer on Infant Developmental Problems* by Alfred L. Scherzer and Ingrid Tscharnuter (1982).

The Child with Mental Retardation

When assessing a child with mental retardation, valuable information can be obtained from a developmental checklist as to the age level at which the child can function. Appendix C lists numerous assessments that have general usage and some that are specific for a certain subgroup of mental retardation (e.g., severely retarded or Down syndrome). The limitations noted on any one of the tests listed in Appendix C, with the exception of the Gross Motor and Reflex Development by Hoskins and Squires (1973), will generally provide a summary of skills that can or cannot be performed at various age levels. Very few of these developmental tests give any clue as to why the child cannot perform a task or even explain why the child does the task in such an unusual manner. The Vulpe Assessment Battery (Vulpe, 1977) does provide information as to what level of assistance (verbal or physical) the child requires in order to complete the task. The disadvantage of the Vulpe is its volume. Many therapists and teachers do not have the time to administer the entire Vulpe test, but even portions of the test would provide valuable bits of information in an area that may be extremely difficult to master.

Many therapists or teachers do not attend in their evaluation of a child to how the child performs a task—specifically, what type of sensory process assists or hinders the child from performing a task. Montgomery (1981) has described and outlined the reasons for attending to the various sensory inputs that are found deficient in the child with mental retardation without physical impairments. Assessments/observations and treatment implications are listed in Table 2.12. Like the child who is physically impaired, the ambulatory child with mental retardation has had limited exposure to and experience with many of the sensory inputs. Without adequate information from the visual, auditory, tactile, gustatory, olfactory, vestibular, and proprioceptive/kinesthetic senses, reflexes will remain at the primitive stage or even fail to emerge. The final outcome is a child with limited or atypical types of reactions to balance and locomotion.

Most developmental assessments provide information on the child's ability to perform tasks compared to other children of the same age and are based on end product tasks. Since the majority of children referred to therapists already have been diagnosed as having a motor problem, it is more helpful to identify the neuromotor and sensory integrative processes that have caused the problem (Richter, 1986). In order for the evaluator to obtain some of this information, the child must be able to comprehend instructions on the more well-known sensory integrative tests such as the Southern California Sensory Integration Tests and the Miller Assessment for Preschoolers. These tests, as noted by Richter, also require a thorough knowledge of the sensory integration process on the part of the therapist when interpreting the results and have questionable reliability scores when used with children with mental retardation who have low IQ scores.

Since therapists need to evaluate and document a child's sensory responses, postural reactions, stability/mobility performance, coordination of motor control, and oral motor development, they need to look for a test covering these areas that does not require a high cognitive level. A new test developed by Richter (1986) called the Sensorimotor Performance Analysis (SPA) is being designed with many of these requirements included for mentally retarded children between the ages of 5 and 18 years with no physical limitations. The advantage of the SPA over other sensory assessments is that it provides information on postural responses, muscle tone, gross and fine motor coordina-

Table 2.12. Sensory input deficiencies in children with mental retardation

Sensory input	Assessment/observation	Therapeutic implications and/or suggestions
Visual	Start with horizontal eye movement, then vertical, and then diagonal. Note if there is jerky movement, or head turning across midline.	1. Use flashlight on wall, or dark paper; can pretend it's a bug or car you're trying to find. 2. Vestibular activities may improve eye movements; have child look at target while swinging or slowly spinning.
Auditory	1. Observe reaction to noise with child who cannot see; eye-blink may be only indication child can hear. 2. Oversensitive reaction— puts hands over ears or talks to self, talks continuously, cries or screams.	1. Include vestibular activities such as rolling, swinging, or spinning and have child sing, talk, or answer questions of adult. 2. Child who is auditorily hypersensitive may be calmed with tactile input because such children are also tactile defensive.
Tactile	1. Responds in negative manner by physically withdrawing or verbally indicating the uncomfortable reactions. 2. May be seen to have a weak hand grip. 3. May reject textured food or flavored food for pureed or bland food.	1. Firm pressure versus light touch is recommended. 2. Relay games on hands and knees or crab walk. 3. Rubbing gums may help to desensitize tactile defensiveness. 4. Have child rub arms/ legs/face with terrycloth.
Olfactory/ gustatory	1. Administer odors cautiously, remove immediately if extreme reactions are observed. 2. Children who constantly mouth hands and toys may do so because of decreased oral sensitivity. 3. Oral hypersensitivity may be observed in children who avoid flavored or textured foods.	1. To avoid overloading system, vary stimulants and limit amount of time spent on this sensory input activity. 2. Perioral stimulation (outside and inside rubbing and/or massage) can help decrease sensitivity. 3. Gradually increasing texture to current food consistency tends to lessen the usual dramatic transition period.

continued

Table 2.12. *continued*

Sensory input	Assessment/observation	Therapeutic implications and/or suggestions
Proprioceptive (info. from muscles, joints, and ligaments) and kinesthetic (info. from joints)	Observe head movement in various positions and check the following actions: a. Turning of head without movement of upper extremities and trunk. b. Maintain balance with vision occluded.	1. Kneeling position—bounce on trampoline or swing on platform swing. 2. Prone position—push self on scooterboard on floor and down ramp.
Vestibular (awareness of where one is in space with or without vision)	1. Should only be done by therapist who has had proper training. 2. Spin child around in one direction, abruptly stop and observe the eye movement (nystagmus). Normal duration is 20 seconds for 10 rotations. Child's normal eye movement will continue after spinning is stopped for 10 seconds (Ayres, 1975).	1. Rolling down incline (large wedge, a hill outdoors) 2. Rolling up in a blanket and then reversing the direction. 3. Rolling in a barrel. 4. Spinning in a platform swing or swing outdoors. Supervision is required for safety precautions and to observe for any dizziness or nausea. 5. Riding on scooterboard on stomach or sitting can be incorporated into relay games.

Adapted from Montgomery (1981).

tion, motor planning, motor development, bilateral integration symmetry, and sensory and neurological processing using verbal instructions, physical assistance, demonstrations, or any combination of the above. Although the SPA is not yet on the market, preliminary information indicates that it has good test-retest reliability as well as a high interrater reliability. This test may prove a valuable tool because of the in-depth information it provides on why a child moves in a certain way, and it also can be used as a guide in developing a more functional treatment program.

Finkle, Hostetler, and Hanson (1983) suggested that, when evaluating the profoundly retarded child, one also observe such things as what attracts the child's attention, by what process the child moves around, what seems to motivate the child (food, physical contact, verbal praise, combination of factors), if the child is absent frequently and why, and how long the child can stay on a task before fatigue sets in. Copeland (1982) has listed questions (see Table 2.13) that are pertinent to the developmental motor sequence (prone, supine, rolling, etc.;

Table 2.13. General questions about motor ability

Questions	Yes	No	Sometimes

Prone
1. Can child raise head 45 degrees?
2. Can child raise head 90 degrees?
3. Is weight supported by forearms?
4. Is weight supported by hands?
5. Can child obtain an all-four position?
6. Can child open hands in all-four position?
7. Can child reach with one hand while shifting weight to other side of body?
8. Can child actively obtain an all-four position?

Supine
1. Are arm movements observable?
2. Are arm movements equal?
3. Is one arm and hand moving more than the other?
4. Are arms bent most of the time?
5. Are leg movements equal?
6. Is one leg moving more than the other?
7. Are leg movements observable?

Head
1. Is head always turned to one side?
2. When head turns sideways, do arms assume the "fencing position"?

Rolling
1. Can child roll from back to side?
2. Can child roll from back to front?
3. Can child roll from front to back?
4. Does child roll as a "log"?
5. Can child roll segmentally?

Sitting
1. Can child attain sitting position from horizontal position?
2. Can child maintain sitting? How long _____?
3. Does child "W" sit?
4. Does child side-sit?
5. Does child "tailor" sit?
6. Does child long-leg sit?
7. Can child maintain posture in a regular chair?

All-Four Position
1. Can child assume this position?
2. Can child maintain this position?
3. Can child crawl once this position is achieved?
4. Can child crawl reciprocally?

Kneeling
1. Can child assume this position?
2. Can child maintain this position?
3. Can child move while kneeling?

(continued)

Table 2.13. *continued*

Questions	Yes	No	Sometimes

Standing
1. Can child actively get to standing?
2. Is weight equally distributed?
3. Can child walk without assistance?
4. Can child balance on one foot? (left _____ or right _____)
5. Can child balance on either foot?
6. Can child stand on uneven surface without losing balance?
7. Can child stand on tiptoes?
8. Can child stand on one foot for five seconds?
9. Can child stand on one foot for ten seconds?
10. Can child walk length of balance board ($2'' \times 4'' \times 6''$)?

Walking
1. Can child walk unassisted?
2. Does child need equipment (walker, crutches, and so on) to walk?
3. Can child walk with a normal gait?
4. Does child lean when walking? If so, how?

Running
1. Does child run stiffly?
2. Can child run on tiptoes?
3. Can child run well with few falls?

Climbing
1. Can child climb into adult chair?
2. Can child climb ladders and/or other types of vertical equipment?

Jumping
1. Can child jump in place with step-tap pattern?
2. Can child jump with two feet together?
3. Can child jump over objects? How high? _____
4. Can child broad jump? How far?

Hopping
1. Can child hop on one foot?
2. Can child hop on either foot? How far?

Skipping
1. Can child skip on one foot?
2. Can child skip on either foot?
3. Are skipping movements smooth and coordinated?

Kicking
1. Does child walk into ball to kick?
2. Can child swing leg to kick stationary ball?
3. Can child kick moving ball?

(continued)

Table 2.13. *continued*

Questions	Yes	No	Sometimes

Throwing
1. Can child hurl ball?
2. Can child throw ball overhand?
3. Can child throw ball at large target?
4. When throwing, does child step forward with leg opposite hand throwing ball?

Catching
1. Does child trap ball with body and arms?
2. Does child catch ball with hands?
3. Can child catch small ball with one hand?

Rolling
1. Does child roll ball using forward motion of arms and hands?
2. Can child roll ball toward adult?

Fine Motor

General hand and arm movements
1. Does child open hands only when body is tilted backwards?
2. Can child open hands voluntarily?
3. Can child touch thumb to each finger?
4. Can child rotate forearm?

Grasping
1. Is child able to maintain grasp?
2. Does child grasp crayon with fist?
3. Does child grasp crayon in adult fashion?
4. Does child grasp small objects using whole hand?
5. Does child grasp objects with neat pincer grasp?
6. Does child grasp with one hand only?

Releasing
1. Does child drop object immediately?
2. Can child voluntarily release object?

Manipulation
1. Is child able to stack blocks? How many? _____
2. Is child able to transfer objects from hand to hand?
3. Is child able to bang objects together?
4. Is child able to complete simple puzzle?
5. Is child able to complete complex puzzle? How many pieces?

From Copeland, M. E. (1982). Development of motor skills and the management of common problems. In K. E. Allen & E. M. Goetz (Eds.), *Early childhood education—special problems, special solutions* (pp. 129–171). Rockville, MD: Aspen Publishers, Inc. Copyright 1982. Reprinted with permission of Aspen Publishers, Inc.

see Table 2.5). These questions can be answered through observing the child as well as from a parent report. In any of these positions, one would like to know the endurance ability of the child: How long can the head remain at a 45-degree angle while in the prone position or while sitting? What is the latency period from stimuli to motor response? These types of questions are more helpful the more severe is the physcial and mental handicap.

A number of mentally retarded children have difficulty coordinating gross and fine motor movements. This can be observed when the infant attempts to roll over and pull to stand, or in the toddler trying to control extensor and rotatory movements while walking, or the older child who is trying to maintain a hand grip while climbing a ladder. The underlying cause for these problems may be poor or weak muscle tone and muscle strength. This is a necessary assessment that is the responsibility of the therapist.

Anyone who communicates with children with mental retardation using signing as the primary means of communication is aware of the frustration both child and adult encounter when the sign is not understood. The problems encountered often result in gross approximations that create a lot of guess work and a loss of interest on the part of the adult because the signing is done so slowly. This is because of the limited fine motor manipulative ability as well as limited cognitive understanding of children with mental retardation (Dennis, Reichle, Williams, & Vogelsberg, 1982). Dennis and her colleagues have paved the way for better training by functionally assessing the motoric hand positions and the movements necessary in forming the letters, words, and numbers. For example, to form the letter "C" the hand and fingers must be in the midposition, with fingers and thumb apart from each other and in an opposed pregrasp that forms the shape of the letter "C." If a child cannot physically get the thumb apart and opposite the fingers or has difficulty in getting the arm and hand in a neutral position (between full pronation and full supination), the poor quality of the sign may cause it to be hard to read. Of equal importance in signing is the ability to move the arms toward and away from the midline, or center point of the body, and to be able to move one arm across that imaginary center line.

The article written by Dennis and her colleagues (1982) also lists commercial assessments that evaluate the unilateral/bilateral motor patterns, prehension, and motor planning. A few of the tests listed that may be familiar to teachers and therapists are the Purdue Perceptual-Motor Survey (Roach & Kephart, 1966), Sensorimotor Integration Program Checklists (Montgomery & Richter, 1978b), and the Southern California Sensory Integration Tests (Ayres, 1980). These authors would also recommend the Erhardt Developmental Prehension Assessment (Erhardt, 1982) as an excellent evaluation of the child's reflex reaction, fine motor manipulation, and related fine motor problem-solving ability. Erhardt's approach to the total child is to assess the developmental level of the fine motor components and how they affect the child's overall level of functioning across general domains.

The Child with Neural Tube Defects

Assessment of the child's neuromotor, cognitive, and social-emotional states should be repeated frequently throughout the developmental period. Repeated assessment will help prevent soft tissue contractures, help monitor the state of a shunt, and assist the child's caretakers in planning a management program that best meets the child's needs (Badell-Ribera, 1985). Assessment of the child's neuromotor states may include the following: sensory testing, especially responses to light touch, deep pressure, and sharp/dull stimuli; reflex testing; passive and active ROM; muscle testing if the child is old enough to cooperate; and observation of spontaneous movements. According to Badell-Ribera (1985), observation of postural attitude and spontaneous movement, along with testing muscle strength and sensory testing, will help determine which muscle groups are intact and which are impaired as well as determine the areas of skin anesthesia. If the child has hydrocephalus, the state of shunt function, sensorimotor function in both upper extremities, and cognitive/visual-perceptual skills should also be assessed. Periodic assessments of bowel and bladder function, of the integrity of the skeletal system, and of the skin over weight-bearing surfaces are all necessary for the child's overall health management.

CHAPTER 3

Coordination and Movement

All of the complex motor tasks that the human executes take place against a background of basic postures and patterns of movement. This includes stability in different positions, head righting, equilibrium, protective reaction, and reach, grasp, manipulation, and release. Prerequisites to the complex patterns of movements are dependent upon the uninterrupted maturation of the central nervous system, which allows the integration of the primitive reflex patterns and the balance between flexor and extensor muscle tone.

Brain damage can cause the release of primitive postures or reflexes from the control of higher centers in the brain. Abnormal movement develops, in part, because the sensation of movement is distorted and shunted or diverted into abnormal patterns (Marks, 1974; Trombly, 1983).

In treatment the abnormal patterns of movement, which are often associated with abnormal muscle tone, are inhibited by helping the child regain or develop control over posture and movement. This is accomplished through careful positioning and handling. Positioning and handling techniques normalize muscle tone, providing the child with more normal sensory experiences of position and movement. Stability in a position is usually emphasized before movement within the position, and movement into and out of the position.

The sensory components of movement—tactile, kinesthetic, proprioceptive, vestibular, and visual input—are essential for controlled voluntary movement.

Tactile input, or the sense of touch, provides the individual with information about where external stimuli are contacting the skin. The sense of touch provides the information that a bug has landed on one's arm or that one's shirt collar is standing up.

Kinesthesia, or the sensation of movement, tells the brain the extent and the direction of movement, especially of body parts such as the extremities.

Proprioception tells the brain about the body's posture, movements, and changes in equilibrium. Proprioception also provides information about the position, weight, and resistance of objects (e.g., a tray full of food) in relation to the body. Also included is the correlation of the unconscious sensations from the skin and joints (Thomas, 1985).

The *vestibular* mechanism, with its receptor located in the semicircular canals in the inner ear, provides information to the brain about the position of the head in space and the head's relationship to gravity. The vestibular mechanism helps maintain equilibrium or balance.

Visual input is also an important stimulus in the early development of normal muscle tone, and the later execution of accurate movement. Children born with severe visual impairment but who are otherwise normal will demonstrate low muscle tone, a delay in the development of head control, and a delay in the development of other forms of antigravity movement such as walking unassisted across an open space.

All of this sensory information is integrated so that the individual is aware of the position of the body and the body parts in relation to each other and in relation to the environment. The sensation of movement and body position in space is perceived by the brain and allows the brain to then program muscles to respond appropriately in order to maintain the desired posture or adjust the posture.

REFLEXES AND MOTOR SKILLS

Early movement in infants is dominated by reflexes or automatic movement patterns in response to specific stimuli such as movement of the head. In association with these primitive reflexes are involuntary alterations in muscle tone. In young infants there is a predominance of flexor muscle tone over extensor muscle tone. Subsequent alterations in muscle tone and modification of the reflexes is the result of central nervous system maturation. Eventually the primitive reflexes become integrated into more refined voluntary movements and a balance between flexor and extensor muscle tone evolves. In children with an immature central nervous system or a developmental disability such as cerebral palsy, the predominance of a primitive reflex can interfere with the development of more advanced motor skills (Table 3.1). For example, if the asymmetric tonic neck reflex and extensor or flexor muscle tone are not modified the child can become stuck in an exaggerated form of this reflex. Predominance of this extreme position would consequently interfere with the development of head control in midline, bilateral hand skills, eye contact with both hands at midline, and other bilateral skills such as walking.

To modify excessive or insufficient muscle tone and the predominance of primitive reflexes, certain positions and specific handling techniques can be used. *Positioning* is the placement of the child in carefully selected positions (e.g., side-lying, sitting, standing) in order to accomplish the following goals: normalization of muscle tone, prevention of deformity, and stabilization of the body. Positioning also includes the careful placement of all body parts. Some

Table 3.1. Effect of persistent primitive reflexes on development

Reflex	Normal infant	Child with cerebral palsy
Sucking	Onset: 28 weeks' gestation Integrated: 2–5 months Allows infant to obtain nourishment when mouth is stimulated	Child cannot stop sucking when he or she wishes to Child sucks food off of spoon instead of using more mature lip patterns to clean spoon
Rooting	Onset: 28 weeks' gestation Integrated: 3 months Allows infant to turn head toward food source when cheek is stroked on one side	Child has difficulty maintaining a midline head position when one cheek is stroked or touched
Grasp	Onset: birth Integrated: 4–6 months Allows hand to automatically close and momentarily hold onto object when pressure is applied to palm	Child cannot voluntarily open hand or let go of an object
Positive supporting reaction	Onset: 35 weeks' gestation Integration: 1–2 months Allows infant to momentarily bear weight on extended legs when soles of feet touch surface	Extensor tone in legs will be excessive and ball of foot will touch ground first (instead of heel). Child will "toe-walk" or will not be able to walk safely because of reduced joint mobility and insufficient balance
Asymmetric tonic neck	Onset: birth Integration: 4–6 months When infant's head is turned to right, the right arm and leg exhibit increased extensor muscle tone and the left arm and leg more flexor tone Allows infant to focus eyes briefly on the hand of the extended arm	Child cannot maintain symmetrical position and cannot bring both hands together at midline Child cannot look at both hands at the same time Interferes with self-feeding, walking
Tonic labyrinthine	Onset: birth Integration: 6 months In the supine position extensor tone predominates, whereas in prone flexor tone predominates	In supine the severely involved child is in stiff extension and cannot lift head, bring hands to midline, or roll over In prone, the child is in excessive flexion and may not be able to lift or turn the head to clear the air passage May not be able to roll over or get into the all-fours position

Adapted from Barnes, Crutchfield, and Heriza (1978), Bobath (1985), and Molnar (1979).

positions can be utilized to increase or decrease muscle tone. Some positions have an inhibitory effect upon undesirable postures and movement patterns, stabilize proximal body parts, and allow better function in distal body parts. For example, the child can be stabilized in a symmetrical sitting position on a chair (with the hips flexed and adducted, knees flexed, and feet well supported to reduce extensor hypertonus) so that he or she is better able to control lips, tongue, and jaw for eating, and control the hands for eating and playing.

Handling is a dynamic process with the goals of normalizing muscle tone, preparing the child for movement, and facilitating movement. The therapist's hands are placed on carefully selected parts of the child's body referred to as key points of control. Key points of control are usually proximal body parts and may include the base of the child's skull or back of the neck, shoulders, trunk, and hips. Use of the hands on an appropriate key point of control can control or inhibit undesirable postures and movements and then promote or facilitate more normal posture and movement (Scherzer & Tscharnuter, 1982).

Handling techniques in combination with certain body positions can be used to normalize muscle tone. Handling can be effective in stabilizing the child in a certain position and then preparing the child to shift body weight in order to reach for an object or to move into another position. Handling techniques are used to facilitate righting and equilibrium reactions and to promote the functional, voluntary movement necessary for play and self-care. Instruction to the child during handling is presented so the child can respond to commands at a subconscious level. For example, if the objective is for the child to shift body weight to one side while seated, the therapist will hold a toy out to that side and say "Get the toy." The child will automatically (subconsciously) shift weight to one side as he or she reaches for the toy. Expecting the child to follow the command "Lean to the side" would require the child to respond at a conscious level and may increase muscle tone excessively and decrease functional ability.

Positioning and handling will be described separately; however, in reality these two techniques are often applied simultaneously.

MUSCLE TONE

Abnormal muscle tone and developmental motor deficits are common in all adaptive behavior levels of mental retardation as well as other developmental disabilities such as cerebral palsy. The type of muscle tone a child exhibits may reflect the reflex stage of the child and the quality of motor skills that the child is able to complete. A child who demonstrates a persistent Moro reflex (causing him or her to fall backward) will have difficulty maintaining a sitting position when his or her center of gravity is shifted. Likewise, when there is evidence of a hyperactive gag reflex, the child will easily choke, gag, refuse textured foods, seriously alter his or her nutritional intake, and be presented with life-threatening health problems. Table 3.2 describes some of the effects of excessive or insufficient muscle tone on motor development.

In order for a child to make volitional movements, there must be balance and coordination between muscle strength and tonus (Sternat, 1987). Factors that Sternat (1987) has found to either hinder or assist in the development of postural tone are internal emotional status, external stimulations, physical environmental changes, and the effect of the tonus state to other muscles. A child who smiles in response to someone talking to him or her and whose muscle tone immediately increases may have no other way of reacting to both internal and external stimuli. The child is happy with the social contact but the adult may have begun talking before visual contact was established. Both factors contributed to the increased muscle tone. Unhappy or angy feelings about having to do an unwanted activity or being massaged or listening to soothing music can also change the quality and quantity of voluntary movement because of the increase or decrease of muscle tone. Utley (1982) defined tone as the "degree of tension of a muscle" (p. 164). Table 3.3 lists similarities and differences in the two abnormal types of muscle tone: hypotonicity and hypertonicity.

Hypertonicity

Increased tension or tone has been termed "hypertonicity" or "spasticity." Montgomery (1981) saw these two terms as different conditions, and it is difficult to determine in the literature if other authors are talking about spasticity or hypertonicity. Unless specified, most people are using the two terms interchangeably. With hypertonia, there is increased muscle tone with a loss of active movement, an increase in abnormal movement, or even involuntary movement (Sukiennicki, 1979). Spasticity refers to "an exaggerated response to muscle stretch, exaggerated deep tendon reflexes or the presence of clonus" (Montgomery, 1981, p. 1270).

Hanson and Harris (1986) indicated that children with hypertonia are at risk for contractures, dislocation, and curvatures of the spine. Hypertonicity and spasticity affect voluntary movement because they restrict flexion, extension, and rotation of the trunk, neck, and upper and lower extremities. Force is exerted downward from the pull of gravity, with the arms and shoulders retracted and the head in protraction or retraction as the child tries to sit up. Connor, Williamson, and Siepp (1978) have noticed a lack of movement in the hands, fingers, feet, and toes, with movement adduction and crossed extension of the legs, in the child with hypertonic muscle tone. While the child, who has been placed over a bolster, is playing with a toy, the therapist or teacher can shift the child's weight by slowly rotating the hips, thereby reducing tone. This is done by placing the adult's hands on the child's back and on either the hips or stomach, then rolling the lower extremity from side to side (Jaeger, 1987).

Table 3.2. Movement and postural problems related to abnormal muscle tone

Abnormal muscle tone	Related problems
Excessive tone (hypertonic, spastic cerebral palsy)	Abnormal amount of involuntary resistance to movement is present and child is trapped in a position or is unable to move easily. This frequently leads to muscle imbalance and subsequent soft tissue contractures. The child: 1. In supine, is prevented from lifting the head up, rolling over, and bringing both arms/hands to midline by excessive extensor tone. 2. In sitting, has difficulty lifting head and looking around, reaching out with one or both hands, and opening hands to pick up a toy because of excessive flexor tone. 3. Has difficulty with respiration, eating, and talking. 4. May have permanent loss of range of motion due to contractures.
Insufficient tone (hypotonic, atonic, floppy child)	Abnormal lack of resistance to movement, with resulting hypermobility of joints, instability, and even subluxation of joints. The child: 1. Is insecure in most antigravity positions such as sitting and standing. 2. Is unable to maintain a position such as holding head up or holding arm out for very long. 3. Is insecure in position for feeding and may not be able to suck or chew adequately for long periods. 4. Has asynchronous, shallow breathing, making sustained vocal production difficult.
Fluctuating tone (dystonic, athetoid cerebral palsy)	Intermittent abnormal resistance alternating with a complete lack of resistance to movement. The range of muscle tone may be from normal to hypotonic, normal to hypertonic, or hypotonic to hypertonic. The child is unable to maintain a stable, still posture and unable to move the body parts smoothly and efficiently. The child: 1. Has poor ability to hold trunk, shoulders, and upper arms still while manipulating object with the hand because of inability to co-contract shoulder girdle muscle and stabilize in midranges of movement. 2. May overshoot when reaching for an object. 3. Has difficulty in maintaining steady, sustained lip closure while sucking or chewing. 4. May grimace when attempting to smile, laugh, or speak.

Adapted from P.N. Clark and Allen (1985), Haynes (1983), Scherzer and Tscharnuter (1982), and Ward (1984).

Table 3.3. Similarities and differences in muscle tone

	Hypotonicity	Hypertonicity
1. Characteristics	Low tone, floppy, "rag doll"	High tone, spastic or rigid
2. Distribution	Generalized, symmetrical	Generalized; often asymmetrical
3. Range of motion	Excessive; joint hyperextensibility	Limited to midranges
4. Risk for contractures	Risk for dislocation (jaw, hip, atlantoaxial joint)	Risks for contractures (flexor), dislocations (hip), and deformities (scoliosis, kyphosis)
5. Deep tendon reflexes	Hypoactive	Hyperactive
6. Integration of primitive reflexes	Hyporeflexive; sometimes delayed integration	Often delayed
7. Achievement of motor milestones	Delayed (amount of delay correlates with severity of tone abnormality)	Delayed (amount of delay correlates with severity of tone abnormality)
8. Influence of body position	Tone remains same	Tone fluctuates with changes in body position
9. Consistency of muscles	Soft, doughy	Hard, rocklike
10. Passivity	Wide-ranging, continuous excursions	Stiff, limited range of excursions
11. Respiratory problems	Shallow breathing; choking secondary to decreased pharyngeal tone	Decreased thoracic mobility; limited inspiration and expiration
12. Speech problems	Secondary to respiratory problems—little sustained phonation	Dysarthria secondary to hypertonicity in oral muscles
13. Feeding problems	Hypoactive gag reflex, open mouth and protruding tongue, incoordination in swallowing	Hyperactive gag reflex, tongue thrust, bite reflex, rooting reflex
14. Change with increasing age	Tone improves; become more normal	Hypertonicity often increases because of use of abnormal reflexes and abnormal movement patterns
15. Therapy techniques (to normalize tone)	Joint compression through spine and extremities Bouncing and tapping	Relaxation in prone position over therapy ball or lap Use of reflex-inhibiting postures and positions
16. Neuropathology	Disturbance in cerebellar function	Release of reflex activity from cortical control

From Harris, S. R., & Tada, W. L. (1985). Genetic disorders in children. In D. A. Umphred (Ed.), *Neurological rehabilitation* (Vol. III, p. 198). St. Louis: C. V. Mosby; reprinted by permission.

When transferring a hypertonic child, three simple carrying techniques used to break up extensor patterns will aid both the infant and the adult. All three carrying positions have the child facing away from the adult for a better view of the environment plus help in developing midline opportunities of the arms and hands. The first position allows for trunk rotation and hip flexion (Figure 3.1); the second holds the child in a side-lying position, which allows the adult to elongate the child's trunk as well as flexing the legs and arms (Figure 3.2); and the third position has the child's back next to the adult's side, which makes it easy to control flexion of the legs and brings the shoulders forward.

Intervention techniques to minimize the degree of hypertonia range from therapeutic handling and positioning (Connor et al., 1978) to relaxation tech-

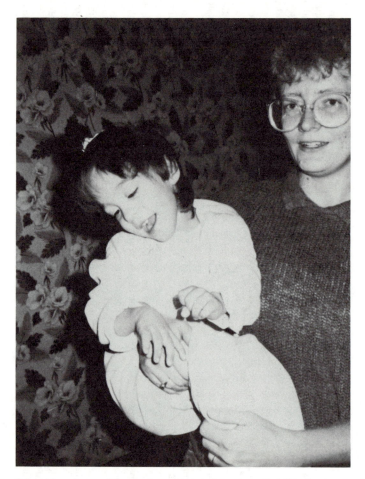

Figure 3.1.   Carrying position for hypertonic infant or small child allowing trunk rotation and hip flexion.

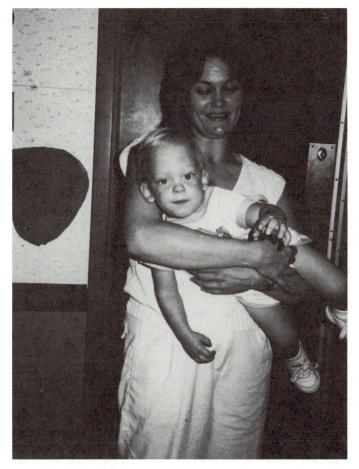

Figure 3.2. Side-lying carrying position for hypertonic infant or small child.

niques (Farber, 1982; Farber & Huss, 1974) and inhibitive casting (S. R. Harris & Tada, 1985). Ice used as an inhibitory technique with hypertonicity should be used by knowledgeable therapists. Following the application of ice on any body part, the therapist must move that extremity in the normal range to avoid a painful return to hypertonicity (Farber, 1982). Also, Farber cautions readers that if the child is scared or fearful about the treatment, muscle tension will only increase. It would be wiser to try other methods with this child.

Hypotonicity

Children who are under the influence of too little or very little muscle tone are unable to move independently, especially against gravity. Such children are slow in developing control in creeping, sitting, pulling to stand, and walking skills. These children are labeled as "floppy" because they have the feel and look of a rag doll. There is no clear definition of the muscles themselves when the arms and legs are felt. When pulled to a sitting position, the child cannot maintain a hand grasp and offers little resistance to being moved, and there may be an extreme head lag (Blackman, 1984c). Once in the sitting position, the child is able to sit only with a slumped or rounded trunk. The head may rest on the shoulders because of a lack of neck control. Other characteristics of hypotonicity include "hypermobile joints and diminished proprioceptive sensation" (Connor et al., 1978, p. 176). The hypermobility of the joints is caused by lax ligaments (ligaments support the joint across bones) that create excessive movement. Because of this excessive movement, there is a tendency for hip, jaw, and neck dislocation to occur (Hanson & Harris, 1986). Poor head control and poor oral sensations are two common feeding problems. The low muscle tone will result in weak sucking and lip closure during mealtimes (Lederman, 1984). When a child is always bathed and dressed in a horizontal position, the visual, kinesthetic, and proprioceptive sensorimotor clues are never developed and the child remains passive and becomes even more babyish as time goes by.

Another posture typical of the hypotonic child in the supine position is called the "frog posture" (Figure 3.3). The legs are slightly flexed, abducted, and externally rotated; similarly, the arms are flexed and externally rotated with the fingers loosely flexed. In order to move around, the young infant in the supine position pushes backward using an extensor thrust (Connor et al., 1978). This mode of ambulation should be discouraged because it only reinforces the persistence of the tonic labyrinthine reflex in supine. While standing, the hypotonic child shows the characteristic pot belly, shoulders that slope downward, arms that are hyperextended at the elbows, and legs that are abducted and hyperextended (Lederman, 1984). A posture that is generally in extension will cause the child to throw the entire body into extensor thrust. This abnormal posture will create difficulty both in a static position and during dynamic move-

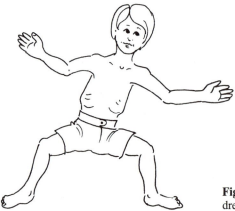

Figure 3.3. Frog posture seen in children with insufficent muscle tone.

ment whether the child is in a supine, sitting, or standing position (Fraser & Hensinger, 1983). A side effect of this increased tone that is noticed in these various positions is that the expanded and rigid rib cage results in shallow and labored breathing (Hanson & Harris, 1986).

Because of the hypotonic level of the muscles, there are delays in the postural and equilibrium reactions (S. R. Harris & Tada, 1985). Since these higher level reflexes are dependent upon the body automatically reacting in the opposite direction to the pull of gravity either in a protective response or to maintain or regain balance, facilitative intervention methods should be employed. Neurodevelopmental facilitative methods of joint compression, tapping, and resistance (S. R. Harris, 1981a, 1981b; S. R. Harris & Tada, 1985) along with sensorimotor stimulation (Connor et al., 1978; Farber, 1982) will help increase muscle tone, which in turn develops head and trunk control.

MOTOR SKILLS

Developmental Motor Activities

Independent motor control can be trained by incorporating sensory integration techniques (emphasizing how sensory input affects motor output) and neurodevelopmental techniques (stressing normal positioning and handling through key points of control). Combining these two essential methods with the child who has either hypotonic or hypertonic muscles is best achieved using a developmental sequential approach. Hanson and Harris (1986) have described several activities parents and professionals can try with children who have various motor delays. Depending on the child's delay, activities can center on the following developmental gross motor skills: head control, trunk control, protective extension reactions, sitting, mobility on the floor, rising to stand with support, standing, walking, running, jumping, and climbing/descending stairs (Hanson & Harris, 1986). Fine motor skills also described by these authors can be developed by incorporating within a home- or center-based program the developmental goals of visual tracking, reaching, grasping, releasing, midline ability, and manipulating objects. This program is strong in the application of behavior management techniques, especially chaining, shaping, and physical and verbal prompts as well as positive reinforcements. The following activities are examples the authors have found successful in achieving the motor milestones. Readers are reminded that several chaining steps must be used before the final skill can be mastered.

Gross Motor Skills

Head Control

Initially, have the child (while in the prone position) turn his or her head from the side to the midline position and back to the side position. For children with excessive tone or limited movement this task may be eased by elevating the head with a firm pillow or wedge. In the prone position, the child can be placed on a blanket or over a rolled towel, with the arms placed forward in a slightly flexed position. The child is then encouraged to look at a toy or an adult who is making noise. The main objectives would be to increase the amount of time the head remains off the blanket and to increase the angle of the head (from 45° to 90°). Head control can also be worked on when the child is in the sitting position by encouraging the child to look at an adult or toy.

Trunk Control

The child needs to control and strengthen his or her trunk muscles not only in a sitting position but also while turning over or when tipping forward or sideways. Good trunk control is derived from the integration of primary reflexes, normal equilibrium reactions, and functioning extensor muscles. Children with developmental disabilities such as mental retardation, cerebral palsy, or spina bifida may display poor integration of equilibrium responses, abnormal muscle tone, inadequate head and trunk extension that results in a loss of balance, poor sitting posture, or spinal deformities (kyphosis, lordosis, or scoliosis).

Montgomery and Richter (1978b) have developed activities that provide sensory stimulation, facilitate equilibrium and protective reactions, strengthen postural muscles, improve flexibility, and improve body image while the child is in the sitting position. Balancing and bouncing on a Hoppity-Hop ball will facilitate extensor tone of the neck and trunk area, provide vestibular stimulation, and develop general motor planning. Sitting on a scooter board will provide good vestibular stimulation as well as proprioceptive stimulation to the buttocks and facilitation of equilibrium reactions. Plumber's plungers can assist the child to pull a scooter board forward and at the same time increase muscular strength and flexibility of both arms. Active exercises (stretching, reaching, rotating, rocking, etc.) in tailor-sitting, long-sitting, and side-sitting all provide a means to stimulate the vestibular system and facilitate motor planning.

Protective Extension Reactions

Once a child can stabilize himself or herself while sitting, the child must then learn to control his or her movements if, for example, while reaching for a toy the child topples over. In whatever direction the child loses control he or she must learn to unconsciously react with extended arms and rotation, flexion, or extension of the trunk area (Figure 3.4). This can be trained by supporting the child at the hips and tipping the child swiftly in one direction. If a child is slow in responding, as happens with children with abnormal muscle tone, physically prompt the child by moving the arm in the correct direction and help stabilize and maintain arm extension by holding around the child's elbow.

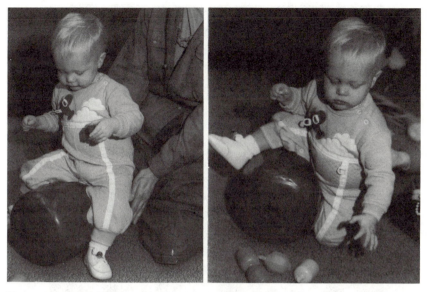

Figure 3.4. Straddling a cylinder develops equilibrium reactions *(left)* and helps teach a child to respond to unexpected movements *(right)*.

Sitting

Normal independent sitting begins with a rounded back and arms resting on the lower legs or on the knees (Figure 3.5). Short periods of this posture are acceptable but for extended amounts of time this will not strengthen the back extensor muscles. The primary concern of the therapist or teacher is to get the infant to depend less (within normal expectations) on arm propping and more on trunk control. This will happen when the child has established good head control and has developed a comfortable and secure feeling while in the prone position.

Mobility on the Floor

The child's ability to creep (stomach off the floor) across the floor as well as going up and down stairs begins by maintaining upper body weight on extended arms for at least 20 seconds (Hanson & Harris, 1986) (Figure 3.6). Next, the child becomes able to pivot on his or her stomach to reach toys. As muscles strengthen, the child learns to be more flexible in his or her motions and begins to venture forward (crawling on stomach). Children with handicaps can be encouraged to alternate leg movements if the adult pushes forward on the bottom of each foot in a reciprocal pattern. Once the normal child is able to get to and maintain a hand/knees (four-point) position with rocking motion, the creeping pattern is not far behind. The child with severe muscle involvement may not be

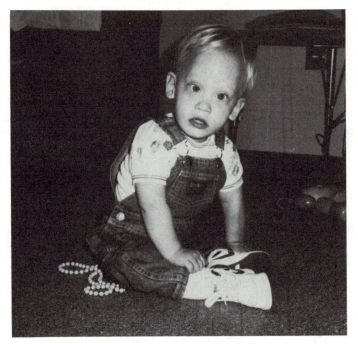

Figure 3.5. Initially, the child can support himself in a sitting position when the arms, extended on the legs, act as a stabilizer for the upper trunk area.

so fortunate in achieving the creeping movement because of the persistence of primitive reflexes. Prior to working on four-point rocking, therapists should stress the inhibition of any abnormal primitive reflexes.

Rising to Stand with Support

Once the child becomes vertical, a vastly different world becomes available to him or her, and most children develop on to the independent standing stage with little fuss. At this stage, one of the most difficult tasks a child has to learn is getting into a half-kneeling position. They tend to pull into standing using toes on extended legs. This places the child standing on the toes with his or her body leaning almost at a 45° angle. A child with abnormal muscle tone cannot move out of this stance without falling down. For this reason, therapists and teachers must stress teaching the half-kneel–to-stand technique because it puts the child a normal distance away from furniture without increasing his or her muscle tone.

Standing

Once the child with handicaps learns the normal technique for getting to a standing position, the next step is to maintain and control equilibrium and bal-

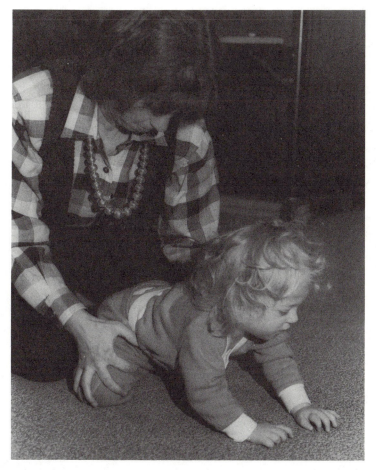

Figure 3.6. Pulling the legs in (adduction) and maintaining the legs parallel to the trunk will facilitate weight bearing on hands and knees.

ance in a static (stationary) and dynamic (moving) posture. Johnson and Werner (1975) suggested therapists begin by supporting most of the child's weight under the armpits or around the chest. Allow the child to support as much weight as possible without the knees bending. The adult's feet can provide support if they are positioned on the outside and next to the child's feet. This will prevent any lateral foot sliding. Next, encourage the child to stand independently next to a couch, coffee table, or chair. This will provide an opportunity for the child to lean forward for additional support when it is needed and it will give the adult time to decrease the amount of physical support, in an inconspicuous manner. When full weight is maintained, stand the child in an open space away from any furniture. Begin by holding one hand and releasing this support slowly, and finally encouraging the child to stand by himself or herself for up to 20 seconds (Hanson & Harris, 1986; Johnson & Werner, 1975). Other variations include rising from a squat position with or without adult assistance. Having the child sit on a small stool and then rise to a stand can be done while singing nursery or finger action songs. Therapists have discouraged parents from using walkers or jumper seats with children displaying excessive muscle tone. These types of equipment tend to reinforce and strengthen toe standing.

Walking

One of the primary motor deficits of concern to parents and therapists is the lack of or delay in achieving independent walking. Several studies have attempted to compare intellectual level and age of walking (Hreidarsson, Shapiro, & Capute, 1983; Shapiro, Accardo, & Capute, 1979; Silva, McGee, & Williams, 1982). It was agreed from these studies that, as a general statement, the age at which a child achieves independent walking is not a good predictor of the level of the child's intelligence, nor can it be said that low intelligence will predict delays in motor milestones. In one study (Hreidarsson et al., 1983) 137 children with severe retardation walked at a mean age of 4.2 years; 127 profoundly retarded individuals in another study (Shapiro et al., 1979) achieved independent walking skill at 2.5 years. In a study conducted by Kaminer and Jedrysek (1983) with 200 children with mild to severe retardation, the age of walking was mastered by 17 months. As can be noted in the above cases, the contributing factors are too variable to be able to definitely predict the age of walking.

When children do begin to walk, practice and neurological maturation generally alleviate the awkward, clumsy, wide gait and high arm guard pattern. For some children the normal gait pattern does not totally develop; instead these children show signs of toewalking without evidence of generalized hypertonicity. A few of the retarded clients of this author and those described in the literature display extreme plantar flexion and internal rotation of the leg (Blockey, 1975). This causes the child to walk up on the toes, creating a very unsteady gait and poor equilibrium reactions. In the static position the children can maintain heel/toe contact with the surface, and under physical control and verbal instruction they can walk a heel/toe pattern if done slowly. The causes of habitual toe walking found in the annotated bibliography of Sweeney and Lydic (1985) included the use of a babywalker during the "imprint" ages of 6–15 months (Blockey, 1975); vestibular dysfunction (Colber & Koegler, 1958; Montgomery & Gauger, 1978); familial conditions (Furrer & Deonna, 1982; J. E. Hall, Salter, & Bhallask, 1967); and a habitual behavioral problem (Griffin, Wheelhouse, Shiavi, & Bass, 1977). Treatment is as varied as the possible causes, including sensory integration, active and passive range of motion exercises, surgery, various kinds of casts, and use of overcorrection behavioral techniques. Not enough research has been written about the success rates of each of these different treatment procedures. Therefore the selection of a treatment modality may very well depend on discovering the cause of the motor deficit, which then will determine the most effective treatment avenue.

The teaching strategies for walking are varied and depend on the physical condition of the child. The child with Down syndrome or cerebral palsy with low tone may need support at the hips. Shifting the child's weight forward can easily be done with the adult's hands over the pelvis (Figure 3.7). Children with spastic muscles often have limited walking ability and may need the additional support of braces or control at the arms. Instead of the legs scissoring (crossing

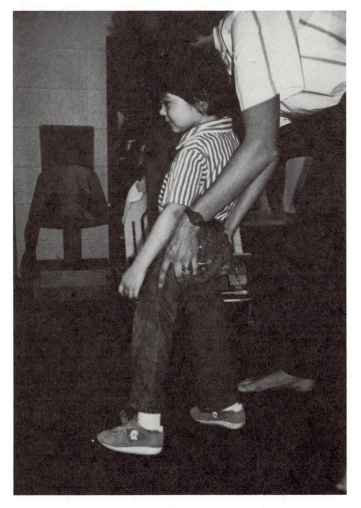

Figure 3.7. Providing support at the child's hips while teaching walking.

over each other) normal alignment can be obtained if the arms are held extended and hands rotated with the thumbs up. This also allows for normal trunk and neck extension, which gives the child a good view of the immediate environment. Parents and staff should provide sufficient practice time for cruising around furniture, pushing a doll buggy or walker, walking with two or one hands held, walking between two adults, and various types of independent walking (sideways as well as backwards).

Running, Jumping, and Other Complex Motor Skills

To develop muscular strength, endurance, flexibility, and coordination, children with retardation must be given an opportunity to develop independent use of their legs and arms in movements that are parallel and opposite each other. This can be done with a trampoline, jungle gym, seesaw, tricycle, slide, tunnels (boxes provide good crawling equipment), and other outdoor equipment. Children with mental retardation also lack the sensory awareness that gives them a sense of where they are in space, and the exposure to activities that require them to make decisions about themselves and the space around them. Activities that will help them include rolling in a blanket, planning how to get through an indoor maze (crawling through, under, and over furniture), placing a ladder on the floor for the child to step into each space, or walking across a balance beam.

General Fine Motor Skills

The components of fine motor development of reaching, grasping, manipulating, and releasing begin with the control of visual fixation and tracking. Final achievement will be reached with the development and control of the shoulder girdle and the upper arms and trunk area. Hanson and Harris (1986) suggested the following goals for the fine motor development: visual tracking and fixation, reaching and hands-to-midline, grasping, releasing, midline activities, and manipulating objects.

Visual Tracking and Fixation

The major emphasis in this area centers on developing smooth eye movements in several directions (up, down, sideways, and circularly). Present brightly colored or black-and-white patterned toys that have an auditory component and move the toy slowly across and within the infant's or child's visual field. Begin this activity with the infant or child's head in midline and move the toy slowly in alternating directions (for example, back and forth and then up and down). Visual fixation is enhanced by attaching objects from the crib or near the bed. The toy's color, pattern, and/or noise will generally attract the infant's or child's attention.

Reaching and Hands-to-Midline

Initially, infants make random lateral arm movements. As control in the shoulders and upper arms develops, the child's ability to bring both arms toward the midline of the body becomes better. Praising the infant's attempts at "swiping" at objects or physically assisting the infant's hands in reaching toward the center of the body will reinforce independent movement. Those infants and children who have limited physical movement may develop independent movements and establish proper positioning if relaxation techniques are administered. First attempts will result in random involuntary reaching out to the side. Advanced movements are direct and under the child's control.

Grasping

An infant's first attempt at maintaining a firm grasp on toys is weak and nonfunctional. Gradually this lack of control is replaced with increased strength and dexterity. Begin by placing small objects in the infant's palm and closing the fingers around the toy, if this does not happen automatically. As independent control develops other variations can be added. Both hands can be used to maintain a grip on larger toys. This can be a fun game if a balloon or large bean bags are passed or tossed between two children with assistance from their mothers. To encourage the pincer grasp, present items with a rough surface and gradually work toward small items that have a smooth surface, thus making them more difficult to pick up.

Releasing

Releasing skills can be trained intially in a supported sitting position while playing with small cubes or rattles. If a child with abnormal muscle tone does not feel secure or comfortable while sitting, increased tension in the arms, hands, and trunk may occur. The practice of having the child place a small toy on a flat surface or giving the item to someone else will provide good opportunities for independent release. The child can place an object in a box, pot, can, or cup. Stacking all kinds of items can become a fun game between adult and child (Figure 3.8).

Midline Activities

The child with physical limitations may have difficulty performing the simplest of tasks. Buttoning a shirt, scooping with a spoon, playing pat-a-cake–type games, or stacking blocks can turn into a futile and frustrating event. The reason for this problem may stem from a persistent asymmetric tonic neck reflex (ATNR), spastic muscle tone, or very weak (hypotonic) muscles that make bringing the arms to the midline difficult or impossible. To provide midline experiences, lay the child on his or her side with a firm pillow behind to minimize the tendency of rolling onto the back. Commercial side-lyers are avail-

Figure 3.8. Copying the therapist's block design can help the child release fingers from around the cube.

able, but a pillow, a rolled towel, a couch, or an adult are less expensive and provide just as adequate support to facilitate bringing the hands together. Start by bringing the shoulders forward and, if necessary, helping the child to touch and hold a toy. Encourage the exploration of the child's own hands. Mittens with interesting attached textured designs may encourage further midline exploration. As control toward the midline increases, place the child in front of a mirror in a supported sitting position such as an adult's lap. Other variations can have the child lying on his or her stomach over the top of a rolled towel or blanket or on his or her back.

Manipulating Objects

Manipulation is the ability to use the hands in a skillful manner. The task of achieving this ability takes on many forms, particularly in quality and quantity, during the first several years of life. Cratty (1979) has found that the emergence of manipulative abilities is closely associated with the exposure and experience of hand-to-mouth exploration. An infant will use the lips and tongue as well as the eyes to make judgments about the various properties of a toy and eventually will be able to identify the specific characteristics of that toy by just looking at it. The child with mental retardation or cerebral palsy who is unable to independently move the upper extremity, to bring the hands to the midline, or to put objects in the mouth may also have difficulty in visually tracking the movements of the hands. This limited ability in manipulating objects will also affect the development of grasp; independent play; social skills; conceptualization of size, form, and color; and problem solving (Bailey & Wolery, 1984). It is essential that the retarded child be exposed to and assisted in manipulating as many different types of toys and materials as possible. Being able to bang, push, pull, pat, lift, squeeze, spin, turn, and slide toys will give valuable information about an object as well as developing muscular strength, endurance, flexibility, and dexterity. The ability to manipulate toys is the prerequisite to the functional skills of dressing, writing, and eating and can pave the way for vocational work and independent living (Johnson & Werner, 1975).

MANAGEMENT TECHNIQUES
USED TO NORMALIZE MUSCLE TONE

Positioning

Positioning is often one of the earliest techniques utilized in therapy and should be an ongoing part of all of the activities in which the child engages—sleeping, feeding, toileting, bathing, play, school, and transportation (Prensky & Palkes, 1982).

The amount of head and trunk control the child has and the nature of the predominating postures and movement patterns will determine the child's positioning needs. Head and body position have a great deal of influence on muscle tone, and a change in the child's position (e.g., change from supine to side-lying) often has an immediate effect on muscle tone.

The child with cerebral palsy often cannot easily get into or maintain an appropriate, stable position and simultaneously participate in an activity such as eating or schoolwork. Instead, the child will use a position that is easier but potentially deformity producing because the position "gives in" to the hypertonus or primitive posturing. A frequently observed example is W-sitting (Figure 3.9), which is used by many children who already have flexor hypertonicity. Although the W-sitting position provides the child with a wide base of support in sitting, it leads to tightness and increases the possibility of contractures in the hip flexors, abductors, and internal rotators, the knee flexors, and the ankle dorsiflexors. The child who tends to sit in the W position can be encouraged to use other methods such as sitting on a low stool (Figure 3.10).

The presence of an obligate ATNR is an example of a primitive posture. The child will not be able to maintain symmetry in most positions. The head will be turned to one side, resulting in an increase of extensor muscle tone in the arm and leg on the face side and in increased flexor tone on the opposite side.

Figure 3.9. The W-sitting position should be avoided or changed whenever possible.

This asymmetrical position makes if difficult for the child to sit up straight with body weight distributed equally on both buttocks and both feet. This position also interferes with the child's ability to maintain eye contact with both hands simultaneously and interferes with attempts to bring both hands together at the midline for bilateral activities. Asymmetrical sitting may result in spinal deformities such as scoliosis. Spinal deformities and poor positioning interfere with the functioning of the internal organs of the chest and abdominal areas.

Careful positioning can be used to alleviate the problems just described. According to Ward (1984), positioning can be used as a treatment modality

Figure 3.10. The typical "W" posture *(left)* and one alternative treatment technique *(right)*.

with the following goals: 1) promote normal development, 2) compensate for lack of functional ability, and 3) prevent, minimize, or delay physical deformity. Careful positioning will allow the child to function optimally during feeding, play, toileting, and other activities (Scherzer & Tscharnuter, 1982).

There is no one ideal position for all children since the human engages in many different kinds of activities requiring many different body positions. Even within the same position, some activities require a stable postural background whereas other activities require weight shift within the position. A variety of positions are necessary for each child in order to provide relief of the skin areas over bony prominences so that pressure sores can be prevented and to allow for changes in muscle and tendon length to prevent contractures.

Each position should provide good body alignment and symmetry, avoid encouraging the development of tightness and deformities, break up mass patterns of flexion or extension, and maximize the child's ability to perform a given task (P. N. Clark & Allen, 1985). If a nontraditional position is used for an activity (i.e., side-lying for reading or looking at a picture book), the position of the activity or the materials must also be adjusted in order to foster maximal performance and reduce frustration.

Several methods for positioning children were suggested by Ward (1984) and include the caregiver using his or her body to support the child, using standard furniture, and using special positioning equipment designed for physically impaired persons. During some play activities and dressing, in which frequent position changes and weight shift are required, it may be more practical for the caregiver to use his or her hands, chest, and legs to support the child. Standard furniture such as a child-size chair or the corner of an adult-size upholstered chair can be used for some activities. Children with severe multiple handicaps may need positioning equipment designed specifically for their use. Positioning equipment is more stable and frees the caregiver's hands for other functions such as presenting food or toys to the child.

It should be noted that prior to positioning the child it may be necessary to normalize muscle tone using various handling techniques designed to reduce hypertonicity or increase insufficient muscle tone. These handling techniques will be described later.

Horizontal Positions

The normal infant begins to develop stability and the ability to move in horizontal positions first. Therefore, for many severely involved children, treatment will begin in the supine, prone, or side-lying positions. In supine, the normal 4- to 6-month-old infant can lie with the head at midline, shoulders forward with both hands engaged at midline, and a balance between flexor and extensor muscle tone throughout the body. In prone the infant can soon lift the head up and bear weight on the upper extremities. Eventually, the child can shift weight from one arm to the other while reaching for a toy. In prone there is an appropriate balance between flexor and extensor muscle tone. Side-lying is often used by the normal child as a transitional position between prone and supine or as a position of rest. For the child who has abnormal muscle tone in prone or supine, the side-lying position often becomes one of the first positions used for normalizing muscle tone, for play, and for rest.

Side-Lying

Equipment Foam wedges, pillows.

Positioning In the side-lying position (Figure 3.11), the head must be supported so it is maintained in alignment with the body's midline and so the bottom shoulder will not bear excessive weight and be pushed into excessive forward or backward positions. If the child cannot maintain side-lying, the back and possibly the front of the trunk will need to be supported with pillows. A pillow between the legs will also help maintain the side-lying position, prevent excessive hip adduction, and protect the bony prominence of the knees and ankles. If extensor tone is excessive it will be best to have the head ⁚ .ed slightly forward with hips and knees flexed. The top hip and knee may be flexed more than the lower hip and knee. If the top shoulder falls too far forward or backward, it will be necessary to support the top arm with a pillow. Supporting the top arm will help maintain the integrity of that shoulder joint, including tendon and muscle tissue, especially if muscle tone is abnormal.

Use of the Position Side-lying is a "neutral" position for those individuals who exhibit excessive flexor muscle tone in prone and excessive extensor muscle tone in supine. In side-lying the severely involved child can be in a

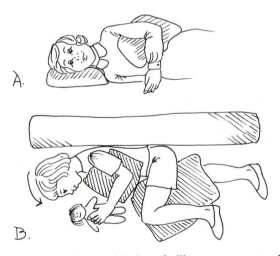

Figure 3.11. Side-lying position: positioning of pillows to support and align body parts. *A*, Front view. *B*, Top-down view.

position that promotes a stabilized midline head position in which the child does not have to work against the pull of gravity, the child is more relaxed, and the upper extremities are more free to manipulate objects (Figure 3.12). With the head stabilized and the hands at midline, good eye contact with the hands and toys is possible. This promotes eye-hand coordination. When seated, the severely involved child is often too tense to use the hands and simultaneously maintain head and trunk control. Poor head control also interferes with eye-hand coordination. Also, in sitting, the arms and hands are frequently used for support rather than for object manipulation. Side-lying can be used as a position for play and sleep.

Precautions Prolonged use of this or any position is contraindicated if pressure sores, contractures, and boredom from the same visual orientation to the environment are to be prevented. The child must be frequently monitored in order to make sure good alignment and circulation are maintained. In side-lying particular care should be used to appropriately position and protect both shoulders.

Supine

Equipment Foam wedges and rolls, pillows.

Positioning In supine (Figure 3.13), with the head at midline and flexed slightly forward, the child can lie on a flat surface or an inclined surface. Pil-

Figure 3.12. The use of a commercial side-lyer is an excellent way of bringing the arms into the midline position.

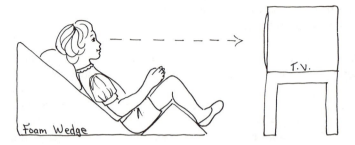

Figure 3.13. Supine position: semi-reclined.

lows or sandbags may be necessary to maintain the head and trunk in midline and the extremities in proper alignment. The maintenance of body symmetry is important if the child tends to have a strong ATNR. If excessive extensor muscle tone is present in supine it will be necessary to flex the head slightly forward and flex the hips and knees. Figure 3.14 shows how the teacher can control the child's tight posture by positioning the child between her legs. Close contact as well as controlled tactile stimulation can be easily provided in this position. These positions are never forced against the involuntary resistance of excessive

Figure 3.14. Teacher using her legs to support child and at same time providing visual and tactile input.

Figure 3.15. Supine position: semireclined with pillows supporting shoulders and upper arms and flexed knees.

extensor muscle tone. Handling techniques or the side-lying position may be necessary for relaxing the child prior to flexing the hips and knees. After the hips and knees are flexed the child is placed in supine. In the child with insufficient muscle tone that allows the shoulders to droop backward onto the surface on which he or she is supine, the shoulders may need to be supported forward (Figure 3.15).

Use of the Position   Supine can be used as a position for sleep, passive activities such as watching television, or some play activities. The semireclined position is sometimes used, with great care, for feeding. If the child is watching television or engaged in other activities while supine, the activity or equipment should be positioned at or below eye level in order to prevent excessive extension of the head. If symmetry is to be maintained, the activity must be placed at midline.

Precautions   Discontinue this position if it triggers excessive extensor muscle tone.

Prone

Equipment   Foam wedges, pillows, prone stander.

Positioning   In prone (Figure 3.16), after carefully selecting the angle and height of the foam wedge, the child's body should be positioned symmetrically with all body parts properly aligned. The incline of the foam wedge is determined by the use of the prone position (rest or activity) and the amount of head righting ability the child possesses. The height of the top of the foam wedge from the floor is determined by whether the child will support himself or herself on the forearms or hands. Pillows or sandbags may be useful in stabilizing the child. The head should be slightly extended, in line with the spine, or slightly flexed. The head should not be extended beyond 45°. Hyperextension of the head may trigger excessive extensor muscle tone in the rest of the body. Too much head flexion in prone may increase flexor muscle tone, which tends to be stronger in prone in some children.

If the child has hip flexor contractures, pillows may have to be used to

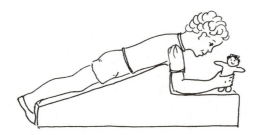

Figure 3.16. Prone position on foam wedges that support the child in the prone-on-forearms position.

accommodate some hip flexion (Figure 3.17). Always allow the ankles to be dorsiflexed to the neutral anatomical position.

If an incline of more than 45° is used, then a prone stander (Figure 3.18), which supports the lower extremities in weight bearing, is more appropriate than lying prone on a foam wedge.

Use of the Position   As noted in Figure 3.19, the prone position can be used to facilitate extensor muscle tone and head control in children who already have some head-righting ability; to reduce flexor muscle tone if the upper extremities are positioned with the shoulders in some forward flexion and the child can utilize some head righting; and to allow practice of weight bearing on both upper extremities and eventually some weight shift (Ward, 1984). The prone position can be used for rest, play, and in some cases eating. The prone stander can be used to promote head righting, extensor muscle tone, and weight bearing on the lower extremities, and frees the hands for manipulations of objects (Figure 3.18).

Precautions   Toys should always be placed carefully so that excessive head flexion or extension does not occur. Monitor the child frequently to make sure proper body alignment is maintained. Reevaluate the use of this position and possibly discontinue if excessive flexor or extensor tone is triggered. Discontinue the position if the child cannot breathe freely and easily.

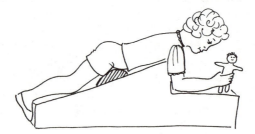

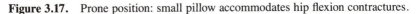

Figure 3.17.   Prone position: small pillow accommodates hip flexion contractures.

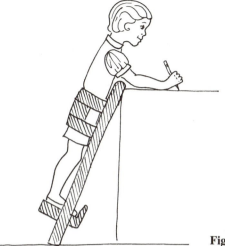

Figure 3.18. Prone stander.

Antigravity Positions

By the age of 8–9 months many normal children are voluntarily assuming the all-fours position and the sitting position. In assuming these positions the child must move his or her head and trunk, as well as other body parts, away from the pull of gravity. Once the position is assumed, the child is eventually able to maintain a stable posture and then shift weight within the position. An impor-

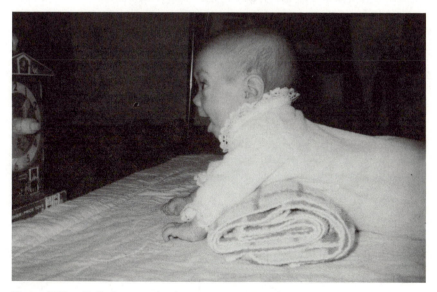

Figure 3.19. Rolled-up towel enhances extensor tone in arms, neck, and back.

tant milestone for the sitting or standing child occurs when the role of the upper extremities shifts from one of support to one of object manipulation. In order to assume, maintain, and shift weight in all-fours, sitting, and standing there must be an appropriate balance of flexor and extensor muscle tone, adequate muscle strength, and adequately developed righting and equilibrium reactions.

For those children who have abnormal muscle tone, these antigravity positions are achieved only with great effort or only with assistance from a caregiver using special handling techniques or positioning devices.

Floor Sitting/Long-Sitting

Equipment   Floor sitter, corner seat, adaptation of the standard environment.

Positioning   In long-sitting (Figure 3.20), the hips are flexed to 90° and the body's weight evenly distributed on both buttocks, and the legs are extended at the knees or straight out in front of the child. Ideally the legs are abducted at the hips with a slight amount of hip external rotation. The child can be stabilized manually or in a floor sitter, corner seat, or the corners of a large stuffed chair. Once stabilized in long-sitting the hands are free to manipulate objects. In order to sit in the long-sitting position the child will need good head control and trunk control. If good righting and equilibrium responses are not present, additional supports need to be considered (Figure 3.21).

Use of the Position   Long-sitting can be used to discourage children from using too much W-sitting or side-sitting. W-sitting promotes the development of tightness in hip flexors, adductors, and internal rotators as well as knee flexors. Side-sitting is an asymmetrical position that also promotes too much flexion in the lower extremities. Long-sitting may also be useful in reducing hamstring or knee flexion contractures. Knee flexion contractures may initially have to be accommodated by putting a small pillow under the knees or raising the long-sitter several inches off the floor (Figure 3.22).

Figure 3.20.   Long-sitting position.

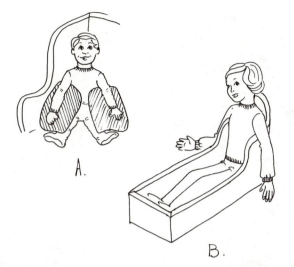

Figure 3.21. Long-sitting: supported. *A*, Small child seated in corner of large chair or couch is supported by pillows under both arms. *B*, Larger child supported in long-sitting in a floor seat.

If the child's shoulders tend to retract or pull back too much, a corner seat or additional adaptations to other types of chairs may be necessary (Figure 3.23). It is important for the shoulders to be forward enough to allow the arms and hands to reach the table surface in front of them. The reader is again referred to Ward (1984) for adapting seating to many different and unique situations.

Long-sitting may be a good position for passive activities such as listening to music or stories or watching television. With an appropriate table surface long-sitting may also be a good position for play or school work.

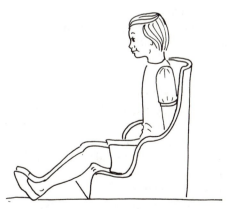

Figure 3.22. Long-sitting: raised floor seat accommodates knee flexion contractures.

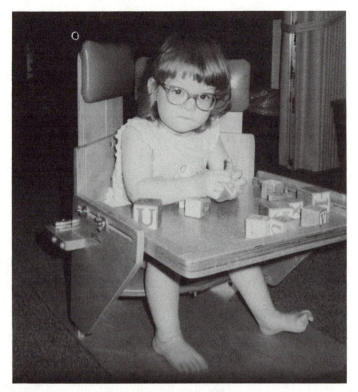

Figure 3.23. Commercial corner chair inhibits shoulder retraction.

Precautions Avoid sitting for prolonged periods of time. Normal children are able to voluntarily shift their weight every few minutes so that circulation to the weight-bearing body parts (buttocks, heels) is sufficient. The severely involved or immobile child should be in any one position no longer than 20–30 minutes without either a change of position or assistance in relieving pressure on weight-bearing body parts.

Floor Sitting/Ring Sitting

Equipment Floor sitter, corner seat.

Positioning The child is seated with the hips flexed at 90° but with more hip external rotation and abduction than seen in long-sitting (Figure 3.24).

Use of the Position This position may be better suited for the child who already has knee flexion contracture but needs to be seated for some activities. Ring sitting provides the child with a wide base of support and symmetry and is a good alternative to W-sitting. Figure 3.25 shows examples of long-sitting and ring sitting. Abduction and external rotation of the hips may break up excessive extensor muscle tone in some children.

Figure 3.24. Ring sitting.

Ring sitting is a good position for passive activities as well as play and school work. Some dressing could be accomplished in ring sitting since the feet are closer to the body and within reach.

Precautions   Same as for long-sitting.

Floor Sitting/Side-Sitting

Equipment   None.

Positioning   The child is seated asymmetrically with both hips and knees flexed and swept to the same side. Often one arm is used for support (Figure 3.26).

Figure 3.25. Examples of long-sitting and ring sitting.

Figure 3.26. Side-sitting.

Precautions   Prolonged use of this position should be discouraged because it promotes asymmetrical and excessive flexion of the lower extremities. In spastic children there is a potential for dislocation of the top hip, which is usually in internal rotation and adduction. Maintaining balance in this asymmetrical position may require excessive expenditure of energy and increase muscle tone to an undesirable level.

Chair Sitting

Equipment   There are numerous types of commercially available chairs for children with special needs. Straight chairs with adjustable foot supports, barrel seats that abduct the hips, and chairs that provide maximal head, trunk, and lower extremities support are just a few examples. Seating devices should be carefully selected so that they meet the individual child's seating needs and do not contribute to further deformity.

Positioning   The ideal position in a chair includes the following components: body symmetry; head at midline and flexed slightly forward; trunk well aligned at midline; hips flexed to 90° and abducted; knees flexed to 90°; ankles dorsiflexed to 90°; and weight evenly distributed between both buttocks, thighs, and feet (Figure 3.27A). The table surface should be positioned at elbow height for those children who have good head and trunk control. For children with poor trunk control and excessive flexor muscle tone in the trunk and upper extremities, the table height should be raised to midchest.

Use of the Position   The seated position is used for play, schoolwork, toileting, eating, and transportation. If the child is to be seated for eating, schoolwork, or play, the following suggestions will help to properly align the body parts, normalize muscle tone, and prevent further deformity:

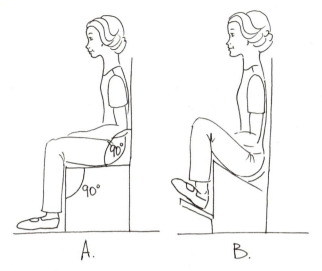

Figure 3.27. Sitting positions. *A*, Standard sitting position with hips, knees, and ankles flexed to 90°. *B*, Jackknife sitting position used to reduce total body extension. The angle of hip, knee, and ankle flexion is less than 90°.

1. Position the child as symmetrically as possible with weight evenly distributed on both buttocks, both thighs, and both feet.
2. The head should be at midline and flexed slightly forward. If the head is flexed too far toward the chest, flexor hypertonicity may result in the rest of the body. If the head extends too far back, extensor hypertonicity in the rest of the body may occur. Improper head position will also interfere with eye-hand coordination, breathing, and swallowing.
3. The hips will need to be flexed if extensor hypertonicity interferes with sitting. This is called the jackknife sitting position, and the hips and knees are flexed to less than 90° (Figure 3.27*B*).
4. Both feet must be well supported, with proper alignment of the lower legs, ankles, and feet.

To achieve the best sitting position, the therapist or caregiver may have to first use handling techniques that reduce muscle tone (see below).

Precautions Same as for long-sitting. For some spastic children, excessive chair sitting is contraindicated because it promotes tightness or contractures in hip and knee flexors.

Positioning Devices

Kneelers

Weight bearing in the kneeling position is used when weight bearing in the hips is desired but total lower extremity extension is not desired (Ward, 1984).

Supine Standers

Supine standers support the child from behind and can be vertical or reclined. Supine standers as well as other standing supports maintain the child in symmetrical, properly aligned weight-bearing positions. Even in children who do not eventually develop the ability to independently stand and walk, weight bearing in standing is important for the maintenance of body integrity. The supported standing position can also be used to decrease flexor muscle tone and increase extensor tone. Precautions include preventing malalignment of joints and ensuring that extensor tone is not excessive.

Handling Techniques

Various handling techniques are designed to reduce excessive muscle tone, increase insufficient muscle tone, stabilize fluctuating muscle tone, reduce or inhibit the effect of undesirable reflex behaviors such as asymmetrical position, and facilitate desirable postures and movements such as head at midline, symmetrical positioning, and good reciprocal movement. Handling techniques may be applied after the child has been positioned (e.g., gentle rocking after the child is placed in the neutral side-lying position) or prior to positioning for activities such as play, eating, or schoolwork.

The descriptions that follow do not provide sufficient information to teach the reader how to treat a child with cerebral palsy. These techniques can be mastered only by observing a therapist and by practicing under the supervision of a therapist. For more detailed step-by-step descriptions of handling techniques used with infants, the reader should refer to *Early Diagnosis and Therapy in Cerebral Palsy* (Scherzer & Tscharnuter, 1982).

To Reduce Excessive Muscle Tone

With the child in a position that is least likely to further increase muscle tone, muscle tone can be reduced by using neutral warmth, slow stroking, gentle shaking, and rocking (P. N. Clark & Allen, 1985; Farber, 1982; Haynes, 1983). If the child has excessive muscle tone in prone and supine, begin with the child in side-lying. Supine is also a good position if extensor muscle tone is not excessive.

If the child is hypersensitive to being touched and does not enjoy contact with various textures, use a firm touch with warm hands. This child's hypersensitive skin may need to be desensitized prior to engaging in play with textured toys or prior to eating. Inhibitory touch can be used to desensitize hypersensitive skin. Examples of inhibiting touch are maintained touch pressure with the palm of the hand on a hypersensitive body part, and stroking (Farber, 1982).

When using any technique to reduce muscle tone, the caregiver must constantly monitor the effect of the technique on the child's muscle tone; state of alertness or wakefulness; rate, quantity, and quality of movement; and emotional well-being. If the child becomes agitated or fearful another technique must be selected. If the child falls asleep or the skin turns blue (cyanotic), inhibition has been excessive—stop using that technique.

The following are examples of specific handling techniques designed to reduce excessive muscle tone.

Neutral Warmth

If the child is extremely hypertonic, wrapping the child's body or body part in a cotton or thermal blanket may have an inhibitory effect on muscle tone. The ultimate goal is to facilitate independent normal movement. The ideal temperature for neutral warmth is $35-37°$ C ($96-98°$ F). It is believed that wrapping the body helps retain body heat, not increase it. Neutral body warmth relaxes the muscles and thus reduces muscle tone. Good positions when the entire body is wrapped are side-lying or supine. Precautions include leaving the face uncovered so the child can breath easily and to reduce the chance of the child being frightened. The caregiver must constantly monitor the effect of the neutral warmth on the child. The goal is to normalize muscle tone, not to put the child to sleep. The length of time required to relax the muscles will vary with individuals and will depend on whether the entire body (except the face) or just one extremity is wrapped. Approximately 15–20 minutes should be sufficient if the entire body is wrapped (Farber, 1982; Farber & Huss, 1974).

Slow Stroking

After positioning the child in the prone position, the therapist uses the pads of the fingertips (fingernails should be short so that the child is not accidentally scratched) to apply a firm but light pressure and stroking motion down the center of the child's back in a cephalocaudal direction. The first and second fingers of each hand stroke on either side of the midline or spine. Stroking is applied in the same direction as the hair grows. Beginning at the base of the child's skull with one hand, the therapist moves that hand to the base of the child's spine. Just before lifting the hand at the base of the spine, the therapist's other hand begins at the base of the child's skull. The continuous, rhythmic stroking is done for not more than 3–5 minutes so that the skin is not irritated and autonomic nervous system rebound is avoided (Farber, 1982).

If the child cannot tolerate the prone position because of excessive flexor muscle tone or inability to turn the head to the side for free breathing, slow stroking can be initiated with the child in the side-lying position.

Gentle Shaking or Rocking

With the child in side-lying, supine, prone, or sitting (whatever position is most relaxing, least deformity producing, or best suited for the activity to follow),

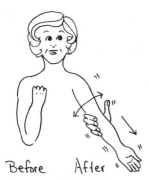

Before   After

Figure 3.28. Gentle shaking of an extremity to reduce flexor hypertonicity. Beginning with the upper arm the extremity is gently shaken. At the same time the therapist will gently externally rotate the shoulder and extend the elbow.

excessive muscle tone can be reduced by gently shaking a body part. For example, to reduce flexor hypertonicity in an arm, the therapist can grasp the top of one or both shoulders. While moving slowly down the arm, the therapist shakes the arms in a rhythmical and rotary movement (Figure 3.28).

Rocking the child's prone body back and forth over a small bolster (Figure 3.29) can be used to reduce hypertonicity in the muscles that pull the arms in toward the body.

Slow Rolling

With the child in the supine position and using the child's pelvis and trunk as key points of control, slowly roll the child from supine to side-lying and back to supine. Repeat the half-roll in the opposite direction. Rolling the child completely over to prone is usually not done when attempting to reduce muscle tone in severely involved children. The slow, rhythmical rolling is repeated until signs of relaxation are observed. Rolling can also be initiated in side-lying instead of supine.

Figure 3.29. Rocking the prone child over a padded bolster to reduce hypertonicity in the muscles of the shoulders that pull the shoulders into the body.

Trunk and Hip Rotation

One of the best handling techniques for the child with hypertonic muscle control is accomplished with trunk and hip rotation (Utley, 1982). Trunk rotation can be incorporated into the movement patterns as the child is being lifted or changed from one position to another (i.e., supine to sitting) as well as in the sitting position. When the child is sitting, the shoulders and upper trunk are turned sideways using one hand of the adult while the other hand is stabilizing the child's waist and hips in a forward direction. Hip rotation is best done while the child is lying on his or her back with a pillow under the head to further break the extensor pattern. With the hips and knees flexed at 90° and 45° angles, respectively, the therapist or teacher slowly moves the legs in as wide a circular motion as the child can tolerate (Figure 3.30). Be sure to stabilize the shoulder on the side opposite to that to which the legs are pointing. Other variations are moving the legs side-to-side and from the chest to the floor. Utley (1982) has provided in detail an excellent description of the adult's hand positions and movements for both rotation techniques.

Positioning

Positioning can also be used to reduce muscle tone. For children who exhibit excessive flexor muscle tone in prone and excessive extensor muscle tone in supine, side-lying is a good neutral position. While the child is in the side-lying position, the caregiver can initiate gentle shaking and rolling to further reduce hypertonicity. If the side-lying position is used for relaxation or eye-hand coordination activities, remember to support the head and neck with a pillow so that the midline of the face is in line with the spine. Having the child resting on a pillow in the side-lying position is an excellent way to restrict the ATNR effect, and allows the child to view his or her environment in a more relaxed manner. Remember to use a pillow whose thickness is the same as the distance from the child's shoulder to the head. Another pillow placed between the flexed legs while in the side-lying position softens the pressure point that tends to occur on the bottom leg and relieves or lessens the stretch of the tight muscles of the top leg. When the child is sitting in a chair, the way to break up the strong extensor pattern is to flex the hips, knees, and ankles (less than 90°) and place an abductor wedge (or firm pillow) between the thighs. An abductor pad can be used also on prone boards and in wheelchairs (S. R. Harris & Tada, 1985).

To Increase Insufficient Muscle Tone

Some of the problems related to abnormally low muscle tone may include hypermobility of the joints, diminished kinesthetic and proprioceptive sensation of movement, and consequent delayed motor development. Hypertonic or floppy infants will often assume unusual postures because they do not have enough muscle tone to maintain good stable joint alignment and body positions

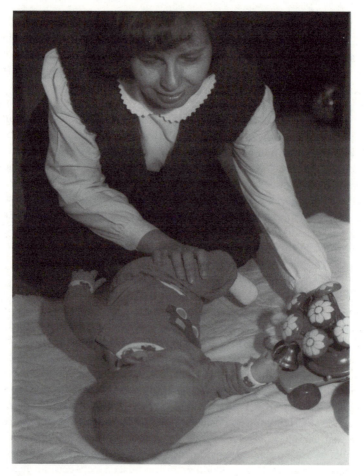

Figure 3.30. Hip rotation.

against the pull of gravity. A posture that is frequently assumed by hypotonic infants is the frog position (Figure 3.3). If the child remains in unusual positions for long periods of time, deformities such as hip dislocation can occur. The hypotonic child tends to prefer the supine position because he or she can see and breathe more easily. However, this position may increase extensor muscle tone abnormally and would delay the development of head control, which occurs in prone (Abell, 1978). Hypotonic children often lack sensory (tactile, proprioceptive, kinesthetic) experiences because of their abnormal muscle tone and reduced opportunity for movement. These children are in danger of experiencing the same level of experiential deprivation as in severely, multiply handicapped children. Impaired sensation will also interfere with the development of body image, body concept, and body perception.

The treatment objective for hypotonic children is to provide appropriate stimulation, usually through specific handling techniques, that will facilitate an appropriate increase in muscle tone and prevent experiential deprivation (Abell, 1978; P. N. Clark & Allen, 1985; Haynes, 1983).

Sensory Integration

Sensory integration, according to Ayres (1979), is defined as the pulling together or organization and interpretation of sensory stimuli into a whole integrated system of sensations for everyday use. We use all of our sensory inputs (sights, sound, taste, touch, smell) as well as the information received from the muscles, joints, gravity, and movement to tell us how to respond motorically, emotionally, and intellectually. Ayres's description of an orange is an excellent example of how the various sensory inputs help stimulate a motor response. Looking at, holding, and smelling the orange triggers the memory of the color, shape, texture, and taste, which in turn starts the individual peeling and eating the orange. Additional information is relayed to let the person know how much muscle strength is needed to peel the orange skin. This process of sharing information is done so quickly on a subcortical level that one is not cognizant of the implications of the sensory stimuli but only aware of when a motor response occurs. If a child must stop, think about, and react to each separate stimulus, the child would not have enough time in an 8-hour day even to do half a day's activities.

For these reasons F. A. Clark and Shuer (1978), Parham (1985), and Richter (1986) have emphasized that children with mental retardation may not have sufficient cognitive ability to respond to standardized sensory assessments, nor do they possess enough inner drive to have a high enough creative level to initiate and choose therapeutic activities. Since the lack of ability to understand instructions given in an assessment procedure may affect the child's score, the type of sensory integration assessment used to diagnose sensory dysfunction should be chosen carefully (Parham, 1985; Richter, 1986). In addition, these authors suggest that the treatment program be altered from the typical sensory integration program to a more structured, therapist-directed activity. Within the last 10 years a number of research studies have investigated the effect of sensory integrative programs on the development of motor and self-stimulatory behavior of mentally retarded children and adults with positive results (Parham, 1985; Urbanik, 1986). According to the literature, the most effective stimulation included vestibular (Bonadonna, 1981; Kuharski, Rues, Cook, & Guess, 1985; MacLean & Baumeister, 1982; W. E. Magrun, Ottenbacher, McCue, & Keefe, 1981), tactile (Kinnealey, 1973; McCracken, 1975), olfactory and gustatory (Storey, Bates, McGhee, & Dycus, 1984), proprioceptive (Montgomery & Richter, 1978a), and kinesthetic (White & Labarda, 1976).

Regardless of the type of sensory input used, the therapist or caregiver must proceed with caution and have proper training. The type and amount of sensory input must be matched to the developmental age of the child and the child's level of physiological stability. For example, a tactually defensive child may respond better to firm touch since light touch may result in avoidance or disorganized behaviors. A child's fear and anxiety may interfere with the central nervous system's ability to properly process stimuli, so time should be taken to establish rapport with the child. Sensation may last longer than the stimuli, and too much stimulation (excessive duration or too strong) may be overcompensated for by the central nervous system in an attempt to regain homeostasis, for example, too much slow stroking to calm or relax a child may be compensated for by the central nervous system's automatically arousing the child and increasing behavior or muscle tone in an attempt to regain neurophysiological balance.

Auditory, visual, tactile, proprioceptive, and vestibular input, if carefully applied, can be used to increase muscle tone. The following suggestions should be carried out only under the supervision of a physical therapist or occupational therapist who understands normal development of the sensory systems and the effects of specific stimulation on the child's central nervous system. If muscle tone tends to fluctuate between insufficient tone and excessive tone, these stimuli should not be administered unless the child is in a position that will inhibit undesirable postural reactions (Trombly, 1983).

Auditory Stimulation   Random, rhythmical sounds such as speech or music, especially if there are changes in pitch and volume, are stimulating. Even continuous auditory input will have a calming or relaxing effect. For example, speaking to a child in an even monotonic voice may calm the child. Speaking with varied inflection may be stimulating enough to increase general alertness and muscle tone. If sound is used to stimulate a child, be sure it is not loud or too sudden. Sudden, loud noises may elicit a startle response, which can have a disorganizing effect on the individual.

Visual Stimulation   Interesting and varied visual stimuli may not only attract the child's attention and motivate the child to attempt movement, but may also result in an increase in muscle tone. Visual stimuli can be in the form of toys and objects of color appropriate for the child's age as well as objects that move and make a noise. Very young infants are more responsive to high-contrast colors and patterns. An infant is more likely to look at black and white concentric circles than at multicolored pastel objects.

Tactile and Proprioceptive Stimuation   The receptors for tactile and proprioceptive stimulation are located in the skin, joints, tendons, and muscles. How a child responds to tactile stimulation may give valuable information toward establishing more appropriate treatment activities. Abnormal reactions can be noticed when the child withdraws from unexpected tactile stimuli, becomes hyperactive after consistent tactile contact, crawls with fisted hands, walks on tiptoes, avoids messy art activities (clay, fingerpaint), gags or chokes on textured food, prefers wearing long-sleeved shirts, or automatically opens his or her mouth when touched anywhere near the mouth area. These signs are evidence of tactile defensiveness or hypersensitivity to light touch.

Examples of desensitization   Activities used to desensitize a child's reaction to tactile input can include:

1. Playing in sand, clay, fingerpaints, shaving cream (pudding had been used with children who tend to put things in their mouths).
2. Rolling inside a blanket or carpeted barrel over a squeaky toy.
3. Placing a hand into a cloth bag and identifying objects of different size, texture, and density.
4. Rubbing parts of the body with different textured materials (terry cloth, sponges, cotton balls, plastic scrubbers) as well as lotions.
5. Playing pillow fight or wrestling games.

Results of tactile preference studies   To determine what type of tactile input was preferred by 12 children (3.7–8.2 years old) who were visually impaired and had multiple handicaps, Danella (1973) presented paired variations of nine different tactile materials, include a vibrator. This was done by placing each child's hand over a different object. The length of time each object was held was recorded. The results indicated a higher preference for vibration, and the lowest preference (shortest contact time) was for fur and yarn. The author acknowledged that the noise and vibratory quality of the vibrator may have been the additional variables (not found with the other objects) that explained why the children were more interested in the vibrator than in any of the other tactile objects.

Selected examples of tactile and proprioceptive stimulation   Brief, moving, light touch with the pads of the fingertips applied to the skin of carefully selected areas of the body may arouse the child and increase muscle tone. This is especially effective when applied to the skin around the lips in order to elicit better lip closure. Beginning at the midline, under the nose, sweep the fingers lightly around the lips to the chin under the lower lip. Precautions include constantly monitoring the effect of light touch on the child by observing the child's facial expressions, skin color, and behavior. If the child attempts to withdraw from the stimulation or his or her facial expression indicates extreme discomfort, it would be better to use a firmer touch pressure instead of light touch.

Proprioceptive stimulation includes quick stretch, traction, tapping, vibration, stretch pressure and resistance of muscle, joint compression, and proprioceptive training (Farber, 1982). Proprioceptive input may increase muscle tone; however, these techniques should be utilized only after obtaining sufficient knowledge of human anatomy and the neurophysiological effect of this type of stimulation. *Quick stretch* applied to an extended muscle after some muscle tone has already been facilitated during vestibular stimulation will further increase muscle tone. Quick stretch is applied to a muscle or muscle group only with great care and only after the body parts are properly positioned. Quick stretch applied to the wrist and finger extensors may facilitate opening of the hand and extension of the wrist. *Traction*, or pulling on a joint, causes separation of the joint's articulating surfaces and is believed to stimulate receptors located in the joints.

Brief, intermittent pressure or *tapping* applied to the belly of a muscle increases muscle tone, whereas pressure applied to the point of muscle insertion on the bone has an inhibitory effect. By tapping quickly, the muscle area in question can be stimulated to achieve the desired action (e.g., tapping around the mouth to achieve mouth closure or puckering). Results are best obtained with isolated problems. According to Lederman (1984), *resistance* facilitates and strengthens muscles. The study by S. R. Harris (1981a) demonstrated the use of neurodevelopmental therapy (NDT) did indeed improve the motor skills of 20 infants with Down syndrome.

Whereas traction on a joint promotes movement, *compression* or approximation of joint surfaces promotes stability of that joint. Compression of joint surfaces can be achieved by manually compressing the joint or by having the child bear weight on that joint. Compression is applied over a joint through the bone's longitudinal axis with the force equal to or less (or sometimes greater) than the body weight (Farber, 1982). Force can be applied with three quick strokes of up to 15 seconds followed by an appropriate activity. This technique builds up co-contraction, which in turn increases muscle tone. Several ways of applying joint compression are the prone-on-elbows, four-point, and sitting positions. In each position, the pressure is applied from the shoulders in a downward direction to the elbow, hand, or hip, respectively. For example, a bolster or small rolled towel can be used under the child's stomach. This places the child's hands and knees on either side of the bolster, which helps increase proprioception through weight bearing and develops stability through joint compression. Farber (1982) gives further details on the techniques and theory of joint compression for the interested reader.

A number of exercises that parents, teachers, and therapists can incorporate into their own settings are easily adapted with several types of instructions and equipment. These exercises include NDT techniques of tapping, resistance, and joint compression as well as developing righting and equilibrium reactions. In one such exercise, with the infant/child on his or her back, the adult should raise and extend one of the child's legs. Place one hand over the knee and hold the foot at the heel with the other hand. With the leg at a 45° angle, apply downward pressure several times, straightening the leg if the child bends it at the knee. Praise is given when resistance is felt. This exercise is repeated several times with both legs to increase muscle tone. A fun game of playing "bicycling" or alternating kicking the legs also develops muscle strength. There are other tactile-proprioceptive techniques that can be utilized to increase muscle tone. The reader is referred to *Neurorehabilitation: A Multi-*

sensory Approach (Farber, 1982) for more information about these and other techniques.

Vestibular Stimulation   The receptors for vestibular input are the semicircular canals located in the inner ear. These receptors are sensitive to movement of the head in linear, circular, and inverted directions as well as to vibration. Appropriate vestibular input is an important factor in the development of muscle tone. Linear movement can be provided through moving forward and backward as in a rocking chair. Circular movement is provided through rolling and spinning activities. Inversion of the head by placing the child prone over an inflated bolster or beach ball has been used to increase extensor muscle tone in order to improve head control, trunk control, and extension, all of which are necessary for standing. Vestibular input is considered to be a strong stimulus and should be provided with caution. Inappropriately applied vestibular input has been known to precipitate vomiting, seizures, and other undesirable reactions in some children. Vestibular input should always be initially applied gently and slowly. The caregiver should always constantly monitor the child's face, skin color, rate of breathing, and verbal comments for signs of adverse reactions to the stimuli. Children with recent head injuries or strokes should not be inverted without prior consultation with the child's physician.

Recent research   A number of studies have dealt with the premise that sensory input via the vestibular system, using a systematic procedure, will enhance postural and equilibrium reactions, muscle tone, and motor performance. In Ottenbacher's (1983a) review of vestibular stimulation, the studies revealed a general consensus regarding the importance and effectiveness of early intervention with at-risk infants, children with Down syndrome, and children with cerebral palsy. Depending on how the therapist administers the stimulation, vestibular input can have either an excitory or a soothing effect on the individual. Combined with other sensory inputs (tactile, visual, auditory) the overall effects have proved to have moderate lasting results. More studies are needed to answer the many questions yet unresolved.

To assist a newcomer to the field of vestibular stimulation in understanding the mechanism of the vestibular system, the writings of Ayres (1972, 1979), de Quiros and Schrager (1978), and Ottenbacher and Short (1985) are highly recommended. The discussion here is centered on a description of several recent studies.

In a study done by Kuharski et al. (1985), vestibular stimulation was administered three times a week to three subjects with chronological ages of 3–5 years with severe handicaps. Two children had fluctuating tone (athetoid) in all extremities as well as neck and trunk area. The third child was described as having increased tone all over (spastic). Each child was supported in a "tumbleform" chair on a square platform and spun in the upright and side-lying positions. Using a large Plexiglas grid in front of the child, measurements of the child's sitting posture after spinning were taken to show the effect of vestibular stimulation. Mean baseline percentage of erect sitting for subjects #1, #2, and #3 were 46, 19, and 10, respectively; following intervention these percentages were 66, 32, and 57. However, 4-month follow-up records indicated a decreased baseline percentage of erect sitting for the spastic child but not for the two athetoid children. The study indicated that the intervention program in future attempts to establish sitting behavior should vary with the existing type of muscle tone.

A study done by Kantner, Kantner, and Clark (1982) investigated what effects vestibular stimulation would have on the language development of children with mental retardation. Different treatment techniques, ranging from vestibular spinning and language training to specific speech therapy or general language stimulation were used with three groups of children. Results failed to support or refute a correlation between vestibular stimulation and language acquisition even though all three groups made some progress in overall communication skills. Further research in this area, with variations, was recommended.

Vestibular stimulation was successfully employed in a study by Bonadonna (1981) that reduced stereotypical rocking behavior in three individuals with severe mental retardation. Each child was placed both prone and supine on a large plastic ball and rocked in three different directions. Similar procedures were applied when the individuals were placed on a platform and hammock swing. Not only was the targeted behavior reduced as early as 6 days into the program, but there was an increase in social behavior and manipulation of objects.

Activities and equipment In order to activate the vestibular system, movement can be initiated sideways, back and forth, and by turning or rotating the head and body on its axis. Equipment that promotes these movements includes a swing, barrel, scooter board and ramp, rocker, large beach ball, waterbed, swinging platform, swinging net, tire or inner tube swing, Kenner Sit-N-Spin, slide, merry-go-round, trampoline, and tiltboard. The scooter board is a popular piece of equipment, especially when the therapy room includes a ramp. Lying prone on the board, the child can push with hands and feet down the ramp and across the floor, which is a good activity to develop extensor pattern in the extremities, neck, and back. The child can also pull himself or herself across the floor using two plumber's plungers. This will strengthen muscle tone and increase the child's endurance level. While prone, the child can also spin the board around using one or two hands.

Rolling down a hill or performing somersaults is popular with older children. All ages enjoy dancing or swaying to music. A common practice with an outdoor swing is to have the child lie on the seat, wind or twist the swing, and then let it unwind. The therapist can control the speed and must observe the child's reaction once the spinning stops. Younger children enjoy being rolled up in a blanket and then unrolling themselves on top of a mat. A squeaky toy can be placed underneath the blanket so that the child can make a noise when on top of the toy. The therapist can also vary the rolled blanket activity by pulling on the blanket quickly or slowly to roll the child out. A three-person game has the child inside a jersey tubing with two adults holding each end of the long tube. Swinging the tube back and forth is enjoyable, and some children like to be swung in a complete circle. These suggested activities are only the beginning of many variations possible.

The amount of spinning, rocking, or rolling, in terms of speed and duration, done with an infant or small child needs to be carefully monitored. Uncomfortable side-effects develop because there is a cumulative effect over time on the whole body. Too much speed or too long a time with any one activity can cause dizziness, loss of motor control, or nausea. Children who have known seizures or who may be prone to a seizure should be introduced to vestibular stimulation slowly and only under close supervision by a therapist who has had experience working with children with seizures or who understands the impact of vestibular stimulation on the entire body and internal organs. Too much stimulation over time (a few seconds up to several minutes) has been known to activate a seizure.

Positioning and Handling

Positioning can also be utilized to increase muscle tone. Supported standing in a prone stander or standing frame may be effective in increasing extensor muscle tone. Care must be taken to ensure proper body alignment in weight-bearing positions.

Although the best position to increase extensor control and to develop muscle tone is when the child is on his or her stomach, there are also other positions that are just as effective. Even in the prone position there is a tendency for the child to go back into the frog-like posture because of fatigue that develops over time. This may be the perfect opportunity to use a variety of positions and activities that reinforce normal alignment of the lower extremity. Connor and her coworkers (1978) suggested using a net hammock (both ends of the hammock are suspended from a single ceiling hook) or semi-inflated air mattress or bean bag. The therapist can align the child's head, trunk, and extremities in flexion. This placement provides adequate midline arm and leg opportunities for sensorimotor stimulation. The primary negative reaction to this position is the fact that the child is limited in overall movement opportunities and sensory development. Also, no child should ever spend extended periods of time (not over 10–15 minutes) in any one of the above activities. Circulation problems are common with many infants and children with mental retardation, cerebral palsy, or spina bifida, so these positions should be used during a transitional phase between activities.

A handling technique that provides proprioceptive and vestibular input and increases muscle tone is carefully bouncing the child while the child is seated on an adult's lap or on an inflated object (pillow, tube, beach ball). The child can also be bounced while prone. Bouncing should be done only if the child has sufficient head control or head support. It is also important that the child's head, trunk, and extremities are all properly aligned (Abell, 1978). The caregiver will have to use appropriate key points of control or hand placement in order to help the child maintain proper body alignment.

To Stabilize Fluctuating Muscle Tone

The predominating problem in children with athetoid cerebral palsy is an involuntary fluctuation between hypertonicity, hypotonicity, and normal muscle tone. The fluctuating muscle tone causes instability in positions such as sitting or standing and results in excessive, extraneous motion when movement is attempted. The goals in management are to improve proximal stability, decrease involuntary movement, and increase controlled movement in the midranges of joint movement (Powell, 1985).

Placing the child in a weight-bearing position is usually used to increase proximal stability and decrease involuntary movements. The child who is prone and bearing weight on both forearms is hoped to be experiencing proximal stability in the upper trunk, shoulders, and head and decreased extraneous movement in the head and arms. The therapist uses key points of control and joint compression to further enhance stability with the child bearing weight on both forearms while in the prone position. In this case the therapist can use both shoulders as key points of control while applying pressure toward the midline of the body. This helps stabilize the head at the midline and helps the child bear weight on stable shoulders and forearms. This also allows the child to experience the sensation of stability. Once the child can maintain the posture, then slow weight shift from one forearm to the other is gradually introduced. This same sequence, using different key points of control, is applied in the all-fours, sitting, and standing positions.

For all types of cerebral palsy initial emphasis is placed on the development of head and trunk control in all positions that are appropriate for the child's chronological and functional age level. Once stability is achieved in each position, then an activity or action can be imposed upon the position. In each position the therapist will continue to use handling techniques to normalize muscle tone, reduce the effect of primitive reflexes, and facilitate the development of more mature motor responses such as head righting, trunk rotation, protective responses, and equilibrium responses.

Once the child is stable in a weight-bearing position such as sitting or standing, the therapist, by using key points of control such as the shoulders, trunk, or hips, can introduce weight shift by gently rocking the child side to side or forward and backward over the weight-bearing joints. Once stability and weight shift (which will include trunk rotation, head righting, and equilibrium responses) are achieved, it is important that the child be encouraged to do something in that position. This could initially be a physically passive cognitive activity such as reaching out to point at a picture. At first the activity should be presented at the child's midline to allow practice of proximal stability before requiring the child to reach out to the side for a toy. Reaching out to the side will require weight shift and possibly some trunk rotation in that direction and head righting in the opposite direction. As the child concentrates on the toy, the therapist, using handling techniques, assists the child in practicing automatic weight shift, head righting, protective responses, and equilibrium reactions.

CHAPTER 4

Feeding

The eating behaviors of normal children follow a certain developmental pattern. Not only does the child grow from a dependency for survival upon an adult to the self-mastery of using utensils, but social communication also develops as a result of the interaction between each member of the family. This is noted by Morris (1977), who indicated that a child with limited motor ability that interferes with independent eating skills also "does not possess the skilled movements of the mouth which will be necessary for producing clear speech" (p. 1). Further evidence of the relationship between the development of feeding skills and language is found in the literature. Farber and Huss (1974) advocated that early intervention treatment programs begin before myelination of the nervous system is complete because it is easier to train "normal speech and feeding patterns" before abnormal patterns are well established and harder to change.

Mealtime is the natural time for teaching and reinforcing independent feeding skills and is said to be a time when prespeech skills can also be facilitated (Mueller, 1972). Generally, all meals except dinner are hurried and/or are spent away from home. Therefore, dinnertime provides an opportunity for the whole family to reinforce the numerous social, language, and motor skills that have been trained earlier in the day. Lunch and snacktime are good times for parent and child to concentrate and work on techniques developed by the therapists and teachers. These techniques are aimed at developing greater independence in feeding, which in turn will increase the child's ability to expand the quantity of his or her expressive language. Disadvantages to feeding the child with the family include the fact that the excessive amount of time and attention to the child required of the parents often results in their not getting to eat or having to wait until the child's dinner is over. Another result of this approach is that other members of the family feel left out or feel that they are being slighted by the parents. One solution would be to begin feeding the child with handicaps before the regular dinnertime. Then, during the meal, the child can be given dessert or a toy, or one parent can complete feeding the child. In this way the child is not as hungry and not as demanding on the parents' time, which allows them to communicate and interact with the rest of the family.

Most children achieve the various developmental feeding skills without too much difficulty or frustration to themselves or their parents. They learn to progress from strained to solid foods; to progress from scooping to cutting with utensils; and to change from a passive to an active participant in mealtime conversations. For some children with handicaps, all aspects of normal eating patterns are difficult if not impossible to achieve from as early as the first day of life (Connor et al., 1978; Mueller, 1975).

Numerous studies reinforce the fact that children with handicaps are extremely slow or, in many cases, never achieve normal feeding patterns. Utley et al. (1977) stated that children with severe multiple handicaps and neurological impairments have "extreme and in some cases life-threatening feeding problems" (p. 290). These include difficulty in swallowing and breathing, choking, vomiting, and the inability to maintain the head in an upright position. Poor neck control interferes with breathing and swallowing, especially if the child's head falls forward or backward.

Parents of normal children take for granted that their children will eventually become independent in their feeding skills. However, parents often find themselves assuming the responsibility for identifying and developing training skills for neurological difficulties without adequate preparation (Matheny & Ruby, 1963). According to Webb (1980), children with a chewing problem become easily tired and bored having to struggle and concentrate continually to control every bite of food. The parents then become frustrated, not knowing how to identify the cause of the problem, let alone how to select the proper treatment technique. It is not surprising that the parents' attitude toward their child and the overwhelming task of finding solutions to these problems greatly affect the child's immediate responses and eventual progress.

The need for early feeding intervention is known by most therapists, nutritionists, and special education teachers, but is not totally known or fully understood by physicians and parents. Since parents first seek help from their pediatrician or family physician, it is crucial that a communication channel be available among all individuals concerned with the child's feeding or eating problems. If done early, this sharing and inclusion of ideas will help minimize any potential habit-forming problems later on. It is therefore the responsibility of the staff member in charge of the feeding program to pass on information about the evaluation, program, and eventual progress of the child not only to the parents but also to the doctor. It must be emphasized that any feeding program should be flexible and open to change as the expertise of the staff develops and the cooperative relationship between the therapist, teacher, physician, parents, and child strengthens.

NORMAL FEEDING DEVELOPMENT

Feeding Patterns

Without a general knowledge of when normal feeding patterns occur, any appraisal of the child's feeding problems will remain primarily subjective (Schwartz, Niman, & Gisel, 1984). Without this basic understanding, it becomes difficult to assess whether a child's feeding ability is age-appropriate or just delayed or actually abnormal (Morris, 1977). Readers wishing a detailed account of the development of feeding skills are directed to the writings of Morris (1977, 1978a, 1978b, 1982) and Parmelee (1963a, 1963b).

As noted in Table 4.1, the ultimate stage of adult eating behavior is dependent upon the development of overlapping areas of function. A normal baby will progress in a predictable pattern in the type of food consumed at various ages, in the preferred position during feeding, in the coordination ability between hand and mouth, and in the various levels of social interaction. The child with a handicap may accomplish these growth patterns at a later age, may perform these skills with great difficulty, or may never master these behaviors at all. It is helpful for the inexperienced evaluator to remember that 11 different normal developmental sequences can be used as guidelines for both assessment and treatment of feeding problems. The following synopsis of normal feeding development is derived from Freeman, Gould, Markley, and Smith (1975) and Morris (1982).

Birth to One Month

Since the normal full-term's baby's overall muscle tone is primarily flexor, it is not surprising to observe this same tone overflowing to other parts of the body. Other behaviors noted at this age are: 1) the lip and suck control are highly efficient and strong; 2) the coordination between sucking, swallowing, and breathing has yet to be developed; and 3) the newborn will exhibit a strong rooting reflex during each feeding, which occurs at 4-hour intervals by the end of the first month. Breast-fed and bottle-fed infants differ with regard to the amount of sucking force required to obtain the milk. Freeman et al. (1975) stated that too often the hole in the commercial nipple is too large or the nipple is too soft, thus allowing the bottle-fed infant to consume large amounts of fluid without becoming tired. This in effect does not allow the infant to force the milk out of the bottle, which means more milk may be consumed than desired in too short an amount of time. The bottle-fed infant, because he or she does not tire, will vomit the excess consumed milk. The breast-fed infant expends more energy in sucking, and will have tired prior to consuming too much milk.

According to Morris (1982), there are several considerations one should keep in mind when evaluating a newborn. She stated that the degree of oral-

Table 4.1. Feeding development in normal children

Age	Skill	Age	Skill
Birth	Sucking and swallowing Incomplete lip closure Unable to release nipple	18 months	Drinks from cup well Hands empty cup or dish to mother—if she doesn't see, child will drop item Chews meat well Better control with spoon
4 weeks	Opens mouth, waiting for food Better lip closure Active lip movement when sucking Takes cereal from spoon	21 months	Handles cup well Very regimented in eating—wants everything on a routine schedule and presented same way each time
6 weeks	Pureed fruit from spoon	2 years	Can handle small glass, partially filled, with one hand Moderate spillage from spoon Refuses previous favorite food Inserts food into mouth without turning over spoon Food preference may stem from taste, form, consistency, or just color
3 months	Anticipates feeding		
4 months	Recognizes bottle, mouth ready for nipple Cup feeding may be introduced—very messy but enjoys process More control and movement of tongue is handled by child —not by reflexes Appetite is more erratic Will not consume three full feedings Tongue thrust seen more with cup feeding than spoon feeding	3 years	Minimum spilling from spoon Dawdles at mealtime Likes to spear food with fork Sets table well
5 months	Mouth opens ready for spoon Uses hands to draw bottle to mouth but releases when nipple is inserted Tongue reversal after spoon removed, ejecting food involuntarily	4 years	Likes to serve self Washes and dries own face and hands
		5 years	Appetite may increase, prefers simple food Beginning to use knife to spread Talkative during meals
5½ months	Good lip closure Overhand grasp with both hands to feed self with cup Good control with lips and tongue	6 years	Doesn't always finish meal by self—may need assistance; often asks for help Very active; cannot sit still Asks for more food than can consume
6 months	Beginning definite chewing motion by gumming food		

Age	Behavior
	Enjoys snacks more than mealtime
	Spills with milk—common at this age
	Breakfast may be most difficult meal
	Not interested in dessert
7 years	May return to finger feeding
	Appetite is less for girls; boys may have tremendous appetite
	May eat formerly disliked dishes
	Interested in desserts
	Use of napkin is spotty
8 years	Girls hold fork in adult fashion; boys hold fork pronated
	Starting to cut with knife
	Shovels food into mouth
9 years	Asks for seconds, even thirds
	Appetite under better control
	Likes to help prepare meals
	Still has difficulty controlling and knowing what to do with napkin
	Difficulty in cutting food to appropriate size, tends to be too big
11 years	Has a satisfied feeling after meals
12 years	Bottomless pit—eating constantly
13 years	Appetite more stable
14 years	More like adult balance

Age	Behavior
7 months	Spoon fed chunky foods
	Feeds self soft foods (banana, vegetables, etc.)
	Drooling noted with mouth activity
	Reaches for food with head
8 months	Uses two hands on cup—messy
	Holds own bottle
	Picks up food with thumb and forefinger
	Finger feeds most of food
	Chokes easily when drinking from cup
9 months	Grows impatient when watching meal preparation
	Enjoys chewing
	Likes to finger feed self—messy
	Appetite finicky
10 months	Lateral movement of jaw
	Grasps and brings bottle to mouth
	Food is to be felt, tasted, smeared, and dropped on floor
	Cup feeding still messy—may want to play with it
11 months	Objects if mother tries to help complete feeding
	Can use cup by self
12 months	More choosy about food
	Independent about finishing meal—may dump remaining food on floor
	Lunch is least motivating meal
15 months	Holds cup with fingers—many spills
	Grasps spoon—poor manipulation
	Spoon inverted before insertion
	Shows definite preference for certain foods

From Copeland, M., Ford, L., & Solon, N. (1976). *Occupational therapy for mentally retarded children* (pp. 146–147). Baltimore: University Park Press; reprinted by permission. Data from Gesell and Amatruda (1947), Gesell and Ilg (1946), Ilg and Ames (1955), Rutherford (1971), Smart and Smart (1967), and Spock (1972).

muscle strength, the ease of initiating a suck, the amount of cupping of the tongue, and the overall efficiency of the suck determine the normal or abnormal feeding condition of the infant.

Two to Three Months

During the second and third month, sucking becomes forceful as the mouth and lips open in a reflexive response due to visual stimuli of the approaching bottle or breast. The rooting reflex is not totally inhibited; that is, the mouth will open whether the infant is hungry or not (Freeman et al., 1975). In addition to the visual recognition, the infant is able to tactually identify the bottle, which often triggers a suckle response. At this age, there is a gap in the corners of the lips but generally very little leakage occurs. Morris (1982) indicates that this is because many infants compensate by increasing the cupping action of the tongue.

The infant uses body language to communicate eating desires. The degree of hunger is exhibited by the child turning toward or away from the food source, opening or closing the mouth, or changing the speed of the suck. This type of behavior is often misinterpreted by adults. Too many times the feeder continues to feed the infant, not realizing the infant's need to pause, aversion to certain foods, or discomforts with a prolonged sitting position. The infant may also be full and wish no more food. Gagging is also a response to too much food. The infant may be saying "I've had enough" or "I don't like the taste" or "I can't handle the added texture of formula." Continued pressure on the infant to stay on the bottle may result in the vomiting of the meal. During this time, it is much easier for the feeder to distinguish between a hunger and a pain cry (Freeman et al., 1975).

Four to Six Months

The infant becomes quite adept at holding the bottle while in a semi-reclined position at the fourth month (displays good head control). By the sixth month, most infants can sit in a high chair without any problems. There is the beginning of a food preference, exhibited by the closing of the mouth to avoid specific foods. The suck remains quite strong by the sixth month. Even though the child is motorically quite active at this age, he or she can coordinate and stabilize jaw movements without slowing down. Since there is greater control of neck muscles against gravity, it is easier to close the mouth and then swallow (Freeman et al., 1975). Morris (1982) further described the tongue action of the 6-month-old infant as being back and forth, preventing a biting action. Therefore, any food presented in the center of the tongue gets caught in a suckling motion and is eventually pushed out of the mouth. A very different response is noted when food is placed on the side of the mouth. The tongue moves sideways with the help of the diagonal movement of the jaw. From the fifth to sixth months, there is greater voluntary movement and control of the tongue and jaw.

Seven to Eleven Months

At 7 months, greater precision of movement of the lips and tongue has developed. These movements of closure and laterality assist in inhibiting the chewing reflex and facilitate food removal using the lips. Independent motor skills allow the child to finger-feed himself or herself and pick up a cup. Further manipulation of the cup usually ends up as a disaster—the contents are spilled all over the child and the high chair. The next 3 months (8th through 10th) show an awareness in tongue movement. It becomes a game to move the food from side to side, up and down, and in and out. The child enjoys making a "raspberry" sound, especially with a mouth full of food.

Physical activity continues at 9 months. Parents may find their children constantly "climbing out of their highchairs, throwing objects on the floor and exploring the food at mealtime" (Morris, 1982, p. 44). This behavior seems to occur when the child is full or just not interested in the meal. Cup drinking is accomplished with the tongue protruding on the lower rim. The cup will be up next to the corners of the mouth, acting as a stabilizer for the jaw and helping to control lip action (Morris, 1982). Although the child is a passive participant in biting the food (actually the parent breaks off the food as the child's jaw holds the food stable), he or she is actively engaged in the beginnings of chewing and finger feeding. The jaw and tongue use an up-and-down motion. This is more of a munching or gumming action than a true chewing pattern.

Twelve to Seventeen Months

By the end of the first year, the chewing ability continues to improve (the child can bite most foods on his or her own) and there is less food spillage from the mouth. Prior to the 18th month, there appears to be a breakdown in motor control (Freeman et al., 1975). Manipulation of any utensil (spoon, cup, dish) creates a gigantic mess. This is the period during which a bowl of cereal may end up on the child's head or on the floor; the wrist action is too quick, thus spilling milk out of the cup; and the spoon is inverted before it approaches the mouth (Freeman et al., 1975). This is the fun time, according to Freeman et al., the time to smear anything and everything all over any surface within close range.

Eighteen to Twenty-Three Months

When the child is 18 months, the previously uncontrollable movements become manageable. The child can remove food with his or her tongue from the corners of his or her mouth. Continuous drinking is done with the rim of the cup between the teeth. The cup is managed without spills and the child will hand the cup and dish to a parent. If the parent does not take the cup or dish, they may get thrown. Although food is scooped up with a spoon, it is still turned over as the spoon approaches the mouth.

Twenty-Four to Thirty-Six Months

Toward the beginning of the second year, spoon feeding is accomplished with moderate spilling. The cup is lifted and returned with one hand. Rotary chewing is much easier to handle. The child is learning to shift food quickly and accurately and feels confident using the circular-rotary jaw pattern (Morris, 1982). This means that by age 3 years, not only does the child have good control of tongue movements, but there is adequate internal jaw stabilization and lip closure to coordinate patterns needed for biting, chewing, and swallowing. It is at this point in feeding development that the child has the adult characteristics needed for basic oral-motor function.

Primitive Oral-Motor Reflexes

The infant's first oral neuromuscular responses are reflexive and therefore involuntary. Table 4.2 lists the various primitive oral reflexes, indicating the importance of each in normal development and the effect they have on feeding behavior if one or all persist beyond the age by which they are normally integrated. For example, problems in controlling jaw, lip, and tongue movements while eating is frequently one of the early signs of cerebral palsy (Tarratt, 1971). Many of these problems are related to the persistence of several primitive reflexes.

Rooting Reflex

The primitive oral reflex that is easiest to elicit in the newborn is the rooting reflex. As the newborn comes in contact with the mother's breast, the infant's head immediately turns toward the source of nutrition. Although this is a survival response, enabling the infant to seek out his or her food source, an examination of the rooting reflex can be elicited simply by touching or stroking the area (sides, top, or bottom) around the mouth. The head will turn in the direction of the stimuli while the mouth opens and energetically moves with one major purpose in mind—to find the food. The onset of the reflex is at 28 weeks gestation, and it becomes integrated by 3 months (later with a breast-fed baby), when the infant is then able to pair his or her responses to his or her own desires.

Because of the persistence of certain other primitive reflexes (asymmetrical tonic neck reflex and tonic labyrinthine reflex) children with cerebral palsy and mental retardation will have a weak or absent rooting reflex. The child will be unable to turn his or her head in response to visual or tactile stimulation. If the rooting reflex remains strong past 5–6 months of age, the child will have little independent control over head movement and the reflex may interfere with a normally strong sucking pattern. The child will keep moving his or her head in search of food even when there is no bottle or breast present and even if the child is not hungry. Mueller (1972) found that inhibiting the tonic labyrinthine reflex brought a normal rooting reflex in line.

Table 4.2. Normal oral reflexes

Reflex	Onset	Integration	Stimulus	Normal response	Implications
Rooting	28 weeks gestation	3 months	Tactile stimulation applied to the oral-facial area in the form of light stroking and/or gentle tapping: 1. From either corner of mouth to cheek area in a lateral direction. 2. From middle of upper lip to the nasolabial area. 3. From middle of lower lip to chin. 4. Around perioral area.	Infant will attempt to find stimulus and suck at it. 1. Head will turn in direction of stimulus. 2. Mouth opens, upper lip and tongue elevate and head extends. 3. Lower lip and tongue depress, mouth opens and head flexes. 4. General head movement follows tactile stimulation around the mouth area and opens mouth.	1. If persists beyond 3 months will interfere with normal feeding development. 2. Reflex persists in children with brain injuries. 3. Response is the strongest when infant is alert and hungry. 4. Weak or absent response in depressed, crying, or satisfied infants—may turn away from stimulus. 5. Assymmetry may indicate neurological damage on one side. 6. Barbiturates may depress response. 7. Response is elicited in sleeping children up to 7 years of age. 8. If absent may interfere with sucking pattern.

continued

153

Table 4.2. *continued*

Reflex	Onset	Integration	Stimulus	Normal response	Implications
Suck/ Swallow	22–28 weeks gestation	2–5 months	Place finger or nipple into infant's mouth. Use a gentle push/pull motion until finger/ nipple makes contact with the tongue.	Lips automatically close around finger/nipple. Rhythmical motion begins alternating with sucking and rest periods. Protrusion and retraction of tongue with tip of tongue elevated. Repeated rhythmical sucking movement followed by swallowing.	1. Pathological after 6 months. 2. Poor or absent suck is found in apathetic babies. 3. Barbiturates may depress response. 4. Failure to obtain response or a persistence after 6 months may indicate general depression of central nervous system or sensorimotor depression. 5. Less intense and irregular during the first few days of life. 6. An increase of palmar grasp is noted during sucking. 7. The rate of sucking increases with age. 8. Response persists beyond the normal 5 months in brain-injured children. 9. A clicking sound on soft palate and/or choking means incoordination. 10. Reflex is replaced by a mature swallowing pattern. 11. May be elicited in sleeping children up to 7 years of age. 12. Easier to elicit if baby is hungry, drowsy, or placed in the feeding position.

continued

Reflex	Onset	Integration	Stimulus	Response	Significance
					13. Difference between nonnutritive and nutritive snacking.
					14. If sucking is absent, parents often enlarge holes in nipple. This should be discouraged—prevents normal oral development of the cheeks, lips, and tongue.
Swallow	10 weeks gestation	Remains throughout life	Intake of liquid or food. Simultaneous pressure to: 1. Soft palate 2. Posterior tongue 3. Pharyngeal walls	Visible elevation of hyoid bone.	1. Poor coordination of breathing and swallowing in brain-injured child. 2. Persistence of infantile suck/swallow pattern occurs in brain-injured children. 3. Drooling is due to poor lip movements and weak swallow.
Biting	Birth	3–5 months	Apply pressure firmly on lateral and anterior part of upper and lower gums.	Immediate jaw closure with vertical biting until stimulus is released.	1. Response not strong in newborn. 2. Even touching teeth of children with cerebral palsy will elicit response. 3. Makes not only feeding but also dental care difficult, unpleasant, and frustrating. 4. Persistence inhibits development of volitional chewing, which includes lateral and rotatory movements of the jaw. 5. Interferes with cup drinking and spoon feeding.

Table 4.2. *continued*

156

Reflex	Onset	Integration	Stimulus	Normal response	Implications
Gag	16.5 weeks gestation	Remains throughout life	Pressure applied along the midline of the tongue to the posterior half of the tongue and soft palate.	Automatic gagging. The floor of the mouth opens, head extends, floor of mouth depresses larynx, diaphragm elevates, and face grimaces.	1. Remains as a safety mechanism throughout life. 2. Considered hyperactive if it occurs within the anterior half of the tongue and hypoactive if elicited as far back as the uvula. A hypoactive response is observed in the floppy tone of children with Down syndrome. 3. In children with cerebral palsy it may be due to inefficient swallowing. 4. Absence or weakness may cause aspiration of food. 5. Normal newborn gags easily. 6. An exaggerated gag response noted in brain-injured children. 7. Becomes weaker after 7 months when chewing begins. 8. A strong gag response is noted when associated with poor suck/swallow response. 9. There appears to be a relationship between the gag reflex and the oral tactile sensitivity. 10. Similar to vomiting response but there is not an increase in pressure during gagging.

Data from Braun et al. (1983), Connor et al. (1978), Ekedahl et al. (1974), Farber & Huss (1974), Morris (1977), Mueller (1972), Ogg (1975), Physical Therapy Department (1976), Tarrat (1971), and Utley et al. (1977).

Suck/Swallow Reflex

The onset of the suck/swallow reflex (sometimes referred to as the suckle/swallow reflex) is between 22 and 28 weeks gestation, and the integration range is from 2 to 5 months. Major problems can occur if the suck/swallow reflex does not develop or if it persists beyond normal expectations. The persistence can interfere with the development of the chewing reflex. Bosley (1965) indicated that before speech sounds can be taught the establishment of the suck/swallow and chewing reflexes must have occurred. The absence of the suck/swallow reflex often creates abnormal eating behaviors such as tongue thrust and jaw retrusion.

It is difficult to think of sucking and swallowing as two separate reflexes. Several references have identified them as one (Braun et al., 1983; Connor et al., 1978; Farber & Huss, 1974; Tarratt, 1971), whereas other authors have singled out each one (Morris, 1977; Utley et al., 1977). Typically, one (sucking) stimulates the other (swallowing). As the stimulus (milk, juice, or water) comes in contact with the mouth, the tongue cups around the nipple and the lips seal in place. The tongue begins an up and backward motion that forces the fluid toward the back of the mouth where swallowing automatically takes place. This action sets up a negative pressure that results in a strong suck. A characteristic of a normal suck pattern is a repeated suck-pause motion. In a normal infant this includes between 10 and 30 repeated sucks followed by a swallow motion (Braun et al., 1983). The amount of pressure and number of sucks varies between a nutritive (breast or bottle) and a nonnutritive (pacifier) suck. Because of the numerous variables found in bottle feeding (type of nipple used, the size of the holes in the nipple, the strength of the formula, etc.), nutritive sucking occurs at half the rate of nonnutritive sucking (Braun et al., 1983).

A weak, slow, arrhythmical or absent suck has been observed in premature infants who have been fed through a nasogastric tube (Lederman, 1984). They have been deprived of normal oral sensory stimulation, which inhibits normal sucking skills. Children with Down syndrome or other hypotonic muscle conditions will have difficulty maintaining a secure lip seal on the nipple, and will have a weak suck and tongue thrusting (J.A. Lewis, 1982). Other variables, such as overall increased tone in children with cerebral palsy, may mask the sucking action. This is done with the protrusion of the tongue over the jaw or, in severe cases, over the lower lip (Mueller, 1972). This will create a clicking sound of the soft palate followed more often than not with choking, which Mueller (1972) believes is due to muscular incoordination. When the suck-swallow reflex remains, this not only prevents development of normal suck-swallow patterns but reinforces a reversed swallow action with an open mouth and thrusting tongue (Lederman, 1984). Associated problems of a persistent suck-swallow reflex relate to a child's later speech patterns and sound productions (Connor et al., 1978).

Swallowing Reflex

A swallowing reaction is elicited when food or liquid (including saliva) is placed toward the back of the tongue and pressure is applied to the soft palate or throat area. Children with abnormal tone find swallowing difficult. Hypertonicity as well as hypotonicity can create choking and gagging because the child cannot adequately control the flow of liquid toward the back of the mouth. Thus these children may bolt down their liquids and eat bird-like portions of their solids in order to avoid swallowing. If the head is thrown backward when given liquids or solids, the child is probably this type of eater (Utley et al., 1977).

Biting Reflex

Applying continuous pressure on the lateral and front part of the gums will produce the biting reflex. The infant will bite down, releasing when the pressure of the stimulus lessens. Ogg (1975) indicated that a normal child does not produce a strong bite reflex but children with cerebral palsy may have a strong and prolonged response. Therapists are cautioned not to place their fingers in such a child's mouth because this may prove to be quite painful and the finger may be difficult to remove. Many times, the harder one attempts to wrest a spoon or finger out of the mouth the stronger the bite becomes. Testing should be done with a plastic-coated metal spoon. The continued presence of this reflex obviously interferes with spoon feeding, cup drinking, food biting, and delays in rotary-type chewing.

Gag Reflex

The gag reflex is a protective or safety mechanism that is present throughout life. Since infants tend to be acutely aware of sensations, it is normal as well as valuable for the infant to engage in oral play (putting objects in the mouth). This not only helps the baby explore his or her surroundings via textures, shapes, size, density, weight, and temperatures but also desensitizes the oral cavity. Thus the region of the tongue in which the gag can be elicited is reduced to that present in an adult (Connor et al., 1978). It can be hypothesized that children who are not allowed nor given the opportunity to mouth toys will lack additional knowledge needed for future development of basic preacademic skills and will maintain the primitive gag reflex. Holding and mouthing objects not only allows for object identification (size, shape, texture, etc.) and desensitization of the perioral area but also the development of midline mobility and stability from the trunk, shoulders, arms, and hands. For a child to be able to perform table activities (putting together puzzles, pointing to and matching colors, feeding himself or herself), these prerequisite skills must be established. If light pressure on the tip of the tongue continues to elicit a gag response, the response should be inhibited. A gag response that is considered weak or absent may allow aspiration of food and must be facilitated. Normally, the gag reflex weakens by 7 months when chewing develops.

Additional Primary Reflexes

A number of primary reflexes, in addition to those preparing the body to maintain an upright position, have an equally important effect on the quality of independent feeding skills.

Babkin and Palmomental Reflexes

Confusion exists in the literature about the similar descriptions between the Babkin and the palmomental reflexes. Basically, a few authors have listed the response of the Babkin and have called it the palmomental reflex. The significance of these reflexes in a child's feeding abilities has yet to be determined, but they are looked at as a sensorimotor learning mechanism.

The *palmomental reflex,* first described by Marinesco and Radovici (1920), is considered to be a primitive reflex. When the thenar or hypothenar eminences of one or both hands are scratched with a rough object or thumbnail, there is a responding contraction of the mentalis muscle, which lifts the chin upward. Reis's (1961) study compares it to an early form of a startle reaction to a nociceptive (painful) stimulus. Reis also notes that the palmomental reflex response could be evoked in other parts of the body but that the strength of the pressure had to be greater than when applied in the infant's hand. Parmelee (1963b) reported that the reflex is found both in adult neurological disorders and in 2%–55% of normal children and adults. Magnusson and Wernstedt (1935) stated that 73% of full-term newborns produced the same movements.

The *Babkin reflex* occurs when both the infant's palms are pressed simultaneously, resulting in flexion of the head forward, rotation of the head toward the midline, closing of the eyes, flexion of the forearms, and opening of the mouth (Parmelee, 1963a, 1963b). Parmelee (1963b) described a study done by Lippman, who encouraged examiners to apply strong, sudden pressure to the infant's palms using the adult's thumb. It was indicated that the response disappears with satiation to repeated elicitations but returns after a short rest period. The onset is at birth and by the fourth month the reflex cannot be elicited. Applying pressure on only one palm will result in a weak response with the head turning toward the side of the stimulus. Wiesser and Domanowsky (1959) mentioned that the Babkin reflex has many of the characteristics of the Moro reflex.

Moro Reflex

The Moro reflex consists of abduction of the arms and extension of the elbows, wrists, and fingers followed by adduction of the arms and flexion of the elbows. Relating these movements to feeding, a prolonged Moro, persisting beyond 2 months of age, will interfere with trunk balance and isolated arm control.

Asymmetrical Tonic Neck Reflex

The *asymmetrical tonic neck reflex* (ATNR; the fencer's position) places the face-side arm in extension and the skull-side arm in flexion when the head is turned to one side. Some children also display a lateral jaw shift that will impede swallowing, sucking, chewing, and holding the head in the midline position. Persistence of the ATNR does not allow the opportunity to learn basic independent feeding skills such as finger feeding and control of utensils.

Tonic Labyrinthine Reflex

Normally, in a semireclined position extensor tone dominates until after 6 months, when the child can use more flexor movement when getting into a sitting position. The prolongation of this *tonic labyrinthine reflex* forces the child into a strong extension pattern, which makes swallowing difficult.

POSITIONING

Schmidt (1976) has identified positioning as "one of the most important parts of the intervention program" (p. 21). Without using proper positioning techniques during feeding, many children with abnormal muscle tone will continue to have problems with gagging, choking, or swallowing. Proper positioning not only helps break up abnormal movement and tone, such as that observed in a child with a prolonged ATNR, but also allows for isolated movements of the upper extremities, head, jaw, tongue, and lips (Connor et al., 1978; Mueller, 1975). The feeding assessment will determine what problems will best be alleviated or minimized with what position.

Freeman and her coworkers (1975) presented a normal developmental guideline as to when and how an infant should be placed for feeding. Between birth and 3 months, the infant is generally placed on the adult's lap or held in the adult's arms. As head control develops at around 3–5 months, an infant seat can be used. By 6 months, trunk control is such that the child can maintain independent sitting in a high chair. The child is able to control his or her movements because of protective and equilibrium reactions. In addition, the well-coordinated movements between hand, trunk, and eye will assist the child in regaining an upright position should balance be interrupted.

In addition to the usual feeding positions (lap, arm, chair), therapists and teachers may need to inform parents of other ways to position their child. Controlling total body tone through adequate positioning is essential in order to establish "normal" feeding habits that inhibit abnormal movements and result in easier control of body symmetry (Connor et al., 1978; Mueller, 1972, 1975; Schmidt, 1976; Tarratt, 1971; Zinkus, no date). The following discussion of positions should assist the staff member in selecting the most appropriate position.

Supine

Many children with handicaps are locked into the supine position because of persistent extensor thrust and ATNR (Tarratt, 1971). Therefore, it may be necessary to begin in this position because the child cannot tolerate the upright position. However, caution must be used in this position to avoid placing the child in a straight horizontal line. The first stage in this process is to make sure that the body (head, hips, and knees) is placed in as much flexion as the child initially is able to tolerate.

Lap Sitting

The lap-sitting position is primarily used for the young infant between birth and 3 months. Face-to-face contact (Figure 4.1) is at its best when the adult makes sure his or her knees are higher than the hips (placing the adult's feet on a small stool or on the rung of another chair can be used). Hyper/hypotonicity of the lower extremity can be corrected by either placing the child's legs on either side of the adult's waist or flexing the child's legs in front of the feeder's stomach

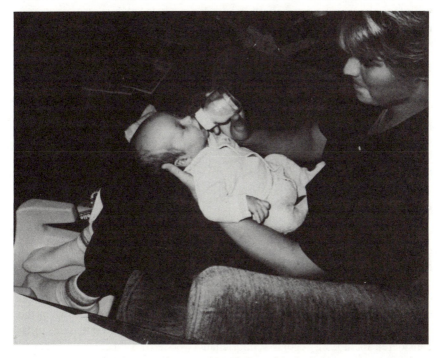

Figure 4.1. Lap feeding can be a great social time for both mother and infant because of the direct face-to-face angle. Any abnormal muscle tone can be controlled by the adult's hands and upper body.

(Connor et al., 1978). Additionally, rolled towels or folded baby blankets can be used to help control abnormal motor problems. Zinkus (no date) discourages this position because it does not give the feeder's hands sufficient control. The present authors contend that it really depends on the extent of the feeding problem(s), the experience of the therapist, and the willingness of the parents to try a new position. By using a wedge the parents can continue to use this direct face-to-face position long beyond the normal suggested age (birth to 3 months).

Side-Lying

The child can be placed sideways on the adult's lap or on a side-lying board, although the former position requires greater independent head, arm, and trunk control from the child. The side-lying board prevents close body contact and makes maintaining mouth control extremely difficult. Remember to provide support to the head and trunk. Requiring the child to maintain this control on his or her own when he or she is not ready will soon produce fatigue and stress, which only increases the already abnormal muscle tone. Side-lying on the adult's lap enables better control of the infant's head and shoulders. Positioning the infant's hips between the adult's legs will prevent leg abduction and external rotation.

Prone

Although not well known or highly recommended, the prone position may be strongly encouraged in order to change sucking, swallowing, or breathing problems (Mueller, 1972; Tarratt, 1971). Placing the child's chest on an incline (wedge, cylinder, or adult's thigh) increases head and trunk extension, thus bringing the lower jaw, lips, and tongue into better alignment for coordinated movements.

Sitting

Sitting is the desired ultimate feeding position. Many children with handicaps could easily tolerate and maintain this position with simple adaptations such as rolled towels tucked next to the child's thighs and/or chest. The apparatus generally used in this position is the high chair. Most high chairs can be changed quickly to correct for the abnormal muscle tone (hyper- or hypotonicity) that creates scissoring of the legs, pulling back of the arms, straightening of the entire body, or complete collapse of the body. Other sitting equipment to be considered includes a regular school chair (wooden), a wheelchair, a barrel chair, and a corner chair (Table 4.3). No matter what type of furniture is used, several general guidelines should be followed to ensure the development of nor-

Table 4.3. Upright sitting equipment[a]

Type	Therapeutic purpose
Corner chair	1. Allows forward positioning of shoulders; hands are brought to midline; eliminates the "high guard" posture with arms. 2. Avoids "rounding" of back; develops "tall" sitting. 3. For floor sitters, encourages leg extension; reduces hamstring contractures. 4. Seat adaptations can correct for hip adductor or abductor tightness.
Barrel seat	1. Reduces hip adductor contractures. 2. Can be designed for either horizontal or vertical positions. 3. Encourages independent sitting.
Straightback classroom chairs (made of wood)	1. Easy to add trunk, head, and leg supports. 2. Inexpensive way to provide needed support without purchasing commercial chair.
Standard wheelchair	If extensive adaptations are needed, best to go to a specialist.

[a]In order to achieve maximum therapeutic value, certain measurements are essential: 1) height of seat from floor, 2) width of seat, 3) height of back, and 4) depth of seat. Referral to a specialist may be warranted if extensive adaptations are required.

mal feeding habits in an upright position (see Table 4.4). Readers wishing a more detailed outline are referred to the work of Ward (1984).

FEEDING PROBLEMS AND SOLUTIONS

Tactile Stimulation

Many children with cerebral palsy have varying degrees of bodily and/or oral sensitivity. This sensitivity tends to compound the problems of sucking/swallowing, lip closure, drooling, tongue thrusting, or chewing. A child with tightness often will increase spasticity, especially while eating. This is the result of a lack of voluntary movement that prevents oral-motor exploration. Mouthing of toys or the child's own fingers is a normal process toward desensitization and helps make the transition from pureed to solid foods.

It is wise to spend several minutes prior to using feeding techniques in order to apply body and oral desensitization techniques. Slow body rolling or firm tactile pressure such as massaging can assist in relaxing the trunk and limbs. For children with hypersensitive oral areas, the safest part of the body to

Table 4.4. Guidelines for development of normal eating skills in a sitting position

Objective	Rationale/method
Develop total body alignment	1. Will provide good head control and proper spinal alignment. 2. Prevents abdominal flexion. 3. Allows isolated movements of head, neck, and arm.
Encourage symmetrical leg posture	Use of abductor pad between legs provides for better base support.
Provide head and shoulder support	1. Eases tension around mouth area. 2. Allows for isolated movement of head, neck, and arm.
Increase hip, knee, and ankle flexion	1. Discourages extensor thrust. 2. To provide stable base of support may need to increase height of knee ($1/2''-2''$) above him.
Provide secure foot support	1. Use of straps across sides of foot and around ankle minimizes plantar flexion. 2. Feet must not be left dangling; increases tendency to hyperextend total body. 3. Simple adaptations: several telephone books or catalogs taped together, small footstool, or wooden platform attached to front chair legs.
Increase independent arm and hand movement	1. Placing "X-" or "H-" shaped straps across shoulders, chest, and waist will allow for increased arm movements. 2. Adapted utensils (built-up handles or straps) decrease feeder assistance.

Adapted from Bergen (1974), Braun et al. (1983), Finnie (1975), Ward (1984) and Zinkus (no date).

massage first may be the feet, legs, or arms. This is borne out in the study by Lemke (1974), in which self-abusive behavior interfered with daily activities, including self-feeding, in a 9-year-old girl who was institutionalized. Treatment sessions included massage applied to the mouth, legs, arms, and soles of both feet. The child was then gradually directed to kinesthetic and vestibular activities. Eighteen months later, the self-abusive behavior occurred only rarely and the child was able to feed herself with only minimal assistance toward the end of the meal.

Oral desensitization, the next step, should always begin on the outside of the mouth with rubbing or patting the cheeks. Gradually work toward the lips. Children with a persistent rooting reflex will automatically open their mouths when touched anywhere near the mouth. Applying firm pressure in downward strokes above the upper lip, upward strokes below the lower lip, and quick stretches at either corner of the mouth using the thumb and index finger are other suggested techniques of desensitization. Once the child accepts this tactile stimulation, proceed to massage the outside surface of the gums. This also should be done gradually, increasing the rate, quantity, and quality of pressure as the child is able to tolerate more stimulation. The amount of time it generally takes for tactile tolerance to develop varies from child to child depending greatly on the level of sensitivity and prior exposure to these techniques. Close observation of subtle changes in the child's behavior will give clues as to when specific techniques may be employed to assist the child toward independent eating skills.

Sucking

Normal Movement

Morris (1982) noted that sucking is the "intake phase of eating and involves ingesting the food/liquid into the mouth" (p. 75). Sucking and swallowing are often regarded as a single reflex (see Table 4.2) that some authors label as the suckle/swallow reflex. Suckling is defined as a primitive form of sucking in which the tongue has a forward-backward movement and brings the jaw forward. The lips are loosely held together, often allowing liquid to escape. Suckling is present up through the fifth to sixth month of life. These actions are gradually replaced by a true sucking pattern where the tongue forms a groove and there is more up-and-down movement and less jaw action (Morris, 1982). Food and liquid are pulled into the mouth because of negative pressure that builds up with the action of the jaw, lips, tongue, and cheek. The neonate shows a strong suck response, loses it for a suckling phase, and regains it between the sixth and ninth month.

Abnormal Movement

When abnormal tone (hypo- or hypertonicity) exists, individual movement is altered. If the suck/swallow pattern is missing the child may compensate, but unfortunately in an atypical fashion with tongue thrusting and/or jaw retrusion (Mueller, 1972). Mueller warned evaluators not to jump to a quick conclusion or to be too general in describing the child's ability. Morris (1982) described children who display both normal and abnormal responses in their oral-motor patterns. A child may have a normal suck but have trouble with all the other phases of eating, or vice versa. What looks normal may be only a coverup for a lack of some important developmental skills.

Assessment

An accurate assessment is crucial in order to prevent the problem from growing and later being impossible to change because of habit, attitude, or increased tone. The child should be checked on sucking using several utensils (bottle, cup, and spoon). Is the movement a reflex response and can it be inhibited? The chewing reflex will not emerge until the child can control the sucking response (Freeman et al., 1975). Check to see in what position the child sucks best. If there is a weak or inefficient suck, check to see if the child's head is in hyperextension or if the tongue is pressed against the hard palate (Morris, 1982). Easy removal of the nipple from the mouth indicates a weak suck. A frequent comment of mothers of these children is that it takes forever for the baby to consume several ounces of formula (e.g., 2–3 ounces in 30–60 minutes). This may be related to too much jaw movement.

Treatment Techniques

Enlarging the holes in the bottle nipple does not increase or develop an independent suck when the problem lies in the fact that the tongue is not forming the necessary groove, is positioned in the wrong place, or is moving too slowly. Larger holes not only increase the quantity of liquid but further decrease the quality of performance. The solution is to find the right nipple for each child to handle best. The shape of the Nuk nipple has numerous advantages for the child with handicaps: 1) the shape helps the lips maintain a good hold on the nipple; 2) the narrow section of the nipple allows for better jaw closure; and 3) the shape provides better tactile input. There are some children who do not have the strength to control even the Nuk nipple, and for them other nipples should be evaluated.

Other types of tactile input may be very effective in improving sucking strength. Very cold objects (popsicles, ice cubes, cold teething toys), sweet-tasting liquids, or strong odors (ammonia, oil of cloves) can initiate the suck reflex (Bosley, 1965; Freeman et al., 1975; Zinkus, no date). Place the child in the prone position over a wedge, a cylinder, or an adult's thigh to lessen the suck/swallow problem. A universal recommendation (especially for older children) for both sucking and swallowing disorders is to teach the child how to drink from a straw. Straw drinking is normally mastered by 4 years. Bosley's (1965) program can be broken down into approximately five steps that, depending on individual needs, can be easily expanded. The type of straw selected will be determined by the amount of involuntary jaw force exerted on the straw (different brands will vary in thickness, so have a variety on hand). If the child clamps down on the plastic straw, it may be better to start with plastic tubing. The walls are thicker and the same procedures can be taught. If there is a strong bite reflex, delay teaching straw drinking until such time as the child can handle multitactile input.

Begin teaching straw drinking by dipping the straw into the liquid. Second, place an index finger over the top of the straw. Third, maintaining the pressure on the top, place the straw bottom between the child's lips. Initially, the straw can be angled upward to about 25°. Fourth, control release of the liquid by manipulating the index finger. Both the speed of flow and quantity of liquid can be manipulated in this manner. The last step is to lower the straw a little below the horizontal line so the child will have an easier time at sucking. We recommend using straw drinking in parallel with other sucking techniques previously mentioned.

Recall that some children have difficulty controlling jaw movement. Any external stimuli near the face will automatically trigger the rooting or bite reflex. In these situations, jaw control procedures applied before any spoon or straw is brought toward the lips will not only minimize the force exerted but also train normal position and movement. Jaw control techniques are described under the swallowing section below.

Swallowing

Normal Movement

Generally, the act of swallowing is accomplished without conscious thought even though the process comprises a complex coordinated movement pattern of the muscles surrounding the mouth, pharynx, larynx, and esophagus (Ekedahl, Mansson, & Sandberg, 1974). The onset or beginning of both the suck and swallow reflex has been identified as early as 5 months gestation. Initially, the two reflexes act as one; the sucking motion immediately sets off a swallow reaction. The infant has no control over when swallowing takes place. As the infant matures, there is a change to more voluntary control as manifested by the observation of more sucking than swallowing. The infant now has the control of how much of the liquid will be swallowed at one time (Bosley, 1965; Farber, 1982).

Basically, swallowing can be separated into three stages: oral, pharyngeal, and esophageal (Ekedahl et al., 1974). The tongue plays an important part in the oral stage by forming a groove or tunnel for the liquid or food bolus to travel toward the pharynx. During the pharyngeal phase, the coordination of muscles around the lips and the tongue helps move the bolus toward the esophagus. In addition to the constriction of the muscles in the oral-pharyngeal area, there is also elevation of the larynx, closure of the nasopharynx, and a momentary stoppage of breathing (Ehrlich, 1970; Farber, 1982; Mueller, 1975). If breathing is continued during this phase, chances are high that food would pass into the lungs, making the child cough and choke. The last phase of swallowing takes the bolus from the esophagus to the stomach.

Abnormal Movement

The cause of poor swallowing can be anything from increased or decreased muscle tone to abnormal facial movements (especially lips and tongue) to delayed reflex action. The overall consensus as to the cause of the gagging, choking, and drooling that occur with poor swallowing appears to be the lack of coordination of the jaw, tongue, lips, and cheeks (Morris, 1982; Mueller, 1972; Wilkie, 1967). Upper lip retraction allows food to spill out of the mouth as well as spreading to all areas of the mouth. If the tongue, instead of forming a groove, remains flat or humps at the wrong time, the bolus remains dispersed and cannot be transferred to the back of the mouth for the second and third phases of swallowing. Swallowing problems appear to center on the oral phase in the majority of cases in which hyper- and hypotonicity are major factors. Sensorimotor difficulties relating to speech and feeding are common with children who have cerebral palsy (Haberfellner & Rossiwall, 1977).

Assessment

Ehrlich (1970) identified three normal swallowing characteristics (see Table 4.5) that should give observers key points to use as a quick screening tool. Mueller (1972) and Morris (1982) have prepared similar lists of observable behaviors that assist the evaluator in identifying not only a swallowing problem but what the cause may be (Table 4.6). The evaluator also must attempt to determine while observing the child swallowing solids whether the problem is due to behavioral or physiological factors.

Treatment Techniques

Because of the lack of lip, tongue, and jaw control (so necessary in carrying out a smooth swallowing pattern), the approach to facilitating a normal swallow needs to incorporate jaw control techniques as the primary method. It may appear to the examiner that the major problem is poor swallowing ability. After using quick checklists of what is normal and the specific reasons for swallow difficulties (Tables 4.5 and 4.6), the majority of cases of difficulty will be related to inability to coordinate, control, or activate one or all of the following: lips, tongue, jaw, and cheeks. Thus improved swallowing skills will be the result of facilitating (or inhibiting as the case warrants) isolated problems or groups of problems. A child who has poor lip action can improve through the application of jaw control techniques. The adult can control lip closure from either the front or side position. Sitting in front of the child requires that the thumb be resting below the lower lip, the index finger on the jaw joint, and the middle finger behind the chin. Jaw control, lip closure, and swallowing can be

Table 4.5. Normal swallowing characteristics

1. The facial muscles are not used (the face is relaxed with lips together).
2. The back teeth (molars) are together.
3. The tongue tip remains behind the upper anterior teeth and the dorsal portion is against the hard palate.

Adapted from Ehrlich (1970).

Table 4.6. Causes of swallowing difficulties

Difficulty	Cause
Coughing or gagging	Food remains in the vallecula or pharyngeal area.
Widening of eyes, followed by coughing and choking	Food is piling up on back of tongue; can cause a gag reflex.
Head extended backward	1. Poor lip control. 2. Prevents liquid/food from falling out of mouth. 3. Occurs when swallowing solids.
Lip retraction	Difficulty swallowing semisolid or solid food.
Tongue thrust	Difficulty swallowing semisolid or solid food.
Loud or labored breathing	1. Difficulty coordinating swallowing and breathing. 2. May gasp for air and start to choke.

Adapted from Braun et al. (1983) and Morris (1982).

regulated by sitting to the right of the child. The left arm goes behind the child's neck, bringing the hand up next to the face. The thumb is on the jaw joint, the index finger is below the lower lip, and the middle finger is behind the chin applying pressure (Mueller, 1975). P. H. Campbell (1979) cautioned not to maintain jaw control (keeping the mouth closed) for prolonged periods because this may cause choking, especially if the child is a mouthbreather,

Additional techniques for the development of swallowing include gentle stroking in an upward and/or downward direction on the throat or rubbing the cheeks. It is important to know in which direction to stroke the child's throat. P. H. Campbell (1976) also cautioned that, with a child whose jaw is already pulled back, pressure may retract the jaw even more. In that case, going upward may help to bring the jaw into better alignment. Teaching the child to take smaller bites or sips followed by an immediate swallow may be all that is required.

Stimulation to the inside of the mouth generally produces an increase of saliva, which then may require jaw control in order for the child to handle the entire swallowing process. Tactile stimulation techniques used inside the mouth will create a normal swallow pattern provided the amount of saliva is sufficient to trigger a swallow (P. H. Campbell, 1976). A controlled tactile program is essential if the child is going to be able to control swallowing and tolerate more textured foods. Campbell finds that increasing a prescribed set of oral stimulations does not increase the effectiveness or develop a tolerance toward food inside the mouth. Instead, the neurophysiological system shuts down and any preceding attempts lose their effectiveness. If this procedure continues, over time no type of stimulation will elicit a response from the child. The following sequence has been recommended by Campbell (1976): 1) using the index finger, rub each side of the upper gums from the center to the back and return to the center point; 2) rub each side of the lower gums, from the center to the back and return to the center point; and 3) using a swivel stick or spoon, apply downward pressure on the tongue to the halfway point (this is called "walking the tongue"). Rub each side of the gums four times and walk the tongue three times (total of 19 stimulations). Initially, going through the full program may be too much stimulation for the child to handle. Therefore, it is best to begin gradually (rubbing just the upper gums or applying pressure only twice on each side instead of four times). Be sure to wait for a response before continuing with the next application.

A long-term goal of independent swallowing will be achieved if the only time the child swallows is when he or she is physically reminded. Swallowing should be done at the unconscious level, and any technique used should assist the child to respond to the stimulation by swallowing automatically (P. H. Campbell, 1976).

Drooling

Etiology

Drooling is normally observed in infants as early as 6 weeks, but is not associated at this time with teething, which generally begins around 4 months (Rutherford, 1971). Drooling increases with the periodic teething process but normally stops by the end of the first year. A normal developmental drooling sequence according to Morris (1982) is depicted in Table 4.7. Excessive saliva spillage at this early age may be the result of "oral exploration and stimulation" or because of increased bodily movement that creates an overflow reaction resulting from the concentration needed when learning new skills (Colangelo, Bergen, & Gottlieb, 1976). Infants do not have the muscle control or coordination established to control drooling. Morris (1978a) indicates that normal infants go through periods of uncontrolled drooling, especially when the stability of the head and trunk area has not been mastered. For example, if an infant has good head control in the prone position but has wobbly trunk stability in sitting, drooling will be seen in the latter position and not in the prone position. Many children with abnormal postural tone are unable to gain control of their head and trunk and therefore maintain this excessive drooling stage after infancy.

Drooling is a common problem associated with abnormal feeding patterns found in children with neurological impairments. The cause of such drooling is as varied as the treatment procedures. Several studies (Ekedahl, 1974; Ekedahl et al., 1974; Rapp, 1980; Wilkie, 1967) alluded to hypersalivation, or the excess production of saliva, as the cause of drooling. Crysdale (1980) and Ekedahl (1974) also made reference to the fact that the hypersalivation factor is contingent on the ingestion of tranquilizers and/or anticonvulsants. During the as-

Table 4.7. Stages of normal development of drooling

Age (months)	Drooling pattern
0–3	Not observed because of the small amount of saliva produced
4–6	Seldom observed in supine position, observed in other positions Decreases with control in sitting position Increases with teething
7–9	Occurs when performing new motor tasks Increases with teething
10–15	Same as 7–9 months
18	Control of lips and tongue greatly improved but may still drool occasionally

Adapted from Morris (1982).

sessment phase of a child's feeding program, information about medications may be a valuable clue to a possible contributor to the drooling problem.

Other contributing factors to the cause of drooling in children with mental retardation and cerebral palsy are poor lip closure (Sittig, 1947), inefficient swallowing movements (Ekedahl et al., 1974), infantile tongue thrusting (McCracken, 1978), uncontrolled jaw stability (Ray, Bundy, & Nelson, 1983), and low tactile sensation and/or mouth breathing (Schmidt, 1976). M. F. Palmer (1947) and Sittig (1947) are not proponents of the hypersalivation theory but rather advocate that drooling is due to a lack of control of lip closure and abnormal swallowing reflexes. Infantile tongue thrusting is observed in children and adults when the tongue is pushed upward and outward, causing a "clean" area as the tongue presses against the incisor teeth (McCracken, 1978). Jaw control assists in normal swallowing movements, helps the tongue move saliva to the back of the mouth or oral-pharyngeal area, and decreases tongue thrusting (Ray et al., 1983). Abnormal muscle tone may interfere with the normal feeding process, thus creating a feeding problem. Hypertonicity interferes with active lip movement (the mouth remains open) and allows saliva to collect and overflow down the chin (Crysdale, 1980; M. M. Harris & Dignam, 1980).

Normal and Abnormal Drooling

The function of saliva is to furnish lubrication of the food, as in preparation for swallowing. When food enters the mouth, or even in anticipation of eating, fluid is secreted into the mouth by three large salivary glands (parotid, submandibular, and sublingual) plus many groups of smaller salivary glands (buccal, palatine, and lingual) (Guerin, 1973). The larger glands respond to the stimulus of food or liquid and the smaller groups secrete continuously, thus providing a normal level of moisture to the internal area of the mouth.

During the normal act of swallowing, the mandible is lifted during the first two stages of swallowing. At the same time, the anterior portion of the tongue forms a "cupped" shape that traps the food and saliva. Next, the tongue tip and sides are pressed forward and upward against the hard palate, pushing the food matter back to the pharyngeal area. At this point, the "tongue-cupping" position is no longer necessary because a combination of convulsive and constrictive motions of the superior and middle pharyngeal muscles continue the transportation of food until the involuntary peristalsis of the esophageal musculature completes the swallowing process (Wilkie, 1967).

A different picture is observed in children with neurological impairments. Instead of the normal tongue-cupping movements, the tongue remains flat and stiff. The back-and-forth movement is replaced with an up-and-down motion. This action disperses the food and saliva in all directions. Drooling occurs as some of the material remains in the oral cavity, eventually spilling out of the mouth. Inability to maintain jaw control, lip closure, and tongue immobility as well as abnormal reflexes and muscle tone tend to facilitate the tongue action described above. Each of these symptoms is described in detail elsewhere in this chapter.

Assessment

The how and why of drooling is multifaceted and it is difficult to isolate and identify just one or two ways drooling can occur. An extensive assessment should not be relegated to just one profession. A team approach must be used, drawing upon the expertise of the medical staff (physician, neurologist, nurse, dietitian, nutritionist), therapists (speech, occupational, and physical), educational staff (special education teachers, paraprofessional aides), and the immediate family. An effective interdisciplinary approach requires each team member to work together, to respect each other's knowledge, and to be flexible and open-minded to change. McCann (no date) aptly stated that "the threatened and defensive staff member will not be able to function in an interdisciplinary team setting" (p. 3).

Because each child's muscle tone is different, each reason for the drooling will vary. Since drooling is a clinical symptom, it is difficult to accurately and objectively evaluate the cause or reason for the prolonged problem. In the past, this has required years of experience and/or a wide comprehensive knowledge of normal oral-pharyngeal development in order to adequately determine the range of dysfunction and outline an appropriate therapy program. With the current information available on assessment and treatment plus the availability of other disciplines, one need not be hesitant to assess and to make recommendations.

Problems Associated with Drooling

The reaction of family, relatives, and professionals toward the drooling child often produces a negative social attitude. Close physical contact is at a minimum because of the soaked clothing, which often gives off an unpleasant or foul aroma. The consistent presence of saliva increases the demand for nursing care from parents and staff because of the numerous changes of clothing and bibs. Bibs are generally associated with babies; thus the impression an older child gives, wearing a saliva-soaked bib, is one of low intellectual ability, and the expectations of that child are those of an infant.

The persistence of drooling has a high degree of influence, although unwarranted, on the child's future educational placement (Rapp, 1980; Rapp & Bowers, 1979). Problems associated with direct educational training include the additional expense and time to replace and/or protect instructional materials. The clarity of speech is also impaired since the muscles normally involved with pronunciation and articulation must instead deal with controlling lip closure to prevent the spillage of saliva.

Treatment of excessive drooling is important not only because of the social and educational implications it may have on the child and those who care for the child, but because of the improved physical condition the treatment may afford to the child. The continual presence of saliva on the chin, neck, and chest area can cause an irritation or sores that create a need for additional nursing care (Connor et al., 1978; Diamant & Kumlien, 1974).

Difficulties associated with dehydration have been discussed by Connor et al. (1978) and Guerin (1973), who pointed out the types of alterations that occur within the body as a result of the loss of fluid. Depending on the amount of saliva lost, how fast the body can replace it, and the suck/swallow problem, dehydration can occur. A decrease in water intake is accompanied by a decrease in tissue fluid. This loss is detected by the kidneys, which signal other organs to replenish the loss. Since the body's water reserves are not as stable as its food reserves, if the cycle is continually repeated the child's life may be endangered. To a lesser degree, dehydration causes a change in the quantity and quality of urine, which may be irritating to the skin and cause discomfort to the child when voiding (Connor et al., 1978).

Treatment Techniques

Numerous techniques to ameliorate a drooling problem have been advocated and studied, with very few receiving strong recommendations. As can be noted in the list below, many methods are either so ineffective as to result in little change or have side effects that create serious secondary problems.

Drugs

To be successful, large dosages must be administered, which increases such side effects as impaired vision or extreme dryness of the mouth (Guerin, 1973).

Radiotherapy

This approach is to be strongly avoided or, as viewed by Guerin (1973), "to be condemned." The effects on the mucous membranes and salivary tissue are unpredictable and unsatisfactory. The dosage required to control salivation reaches a hazardous level, possibly producing malignancy (Van de Heyning, Marquet, & Creten, 1980).

Surgery

A wide variety of surgical procedures includes rerouting the parotid duct posterior to the tonsillar fossa (Wilkie, 1967); retropositioning of the submandibular ducts with ligation and division of the sublingual ducts (Ekedahl, 1974); and a translocation of Stensen's duct to the pharynx (Van de Heyning et al., 1980). Unfortunately these procedures and others have been found to be only partially successful, with loss of taste, dry mouth, or occasional nerve regeneration noted.

Mechanical Apparatuses

Recent attempts to use battery-operated devices resulted in more disadvantages than advantages. P. R. Jones (1982), Rapp (1980), and Rapp and Bowers (1979) employed a small battery-operated box (called the Meldreth dribble control box) that, when activated by the examiner, would produce an auditory cue, thus signaling the child to swallow. Although Rapp and her colleagues reported a high rate of success, Jones was critical not only of their results but of the overall use of this technique. First, the original studies lacked appropriate control measures, which invalidated the high percentage of success. Second, control of drooling was not observed independent of wearing the "control box." Two further disadvantages of the box related to the malfunction problems encountered and the frequent changing of the box as clothes were changed. Finally, it was difficult to maintain staff interest in the project.

In another study (M. M. Harris & Dignam, 1980), several groups of children wore a chin cup attached to a head strap while attending a training class. Each training class consisted of exercises to increase lip closure and tongue mobility, such as blowing, sucking, and mirror games. During the 9-month training period, Group I wore the chin cup for 6 months, with an 88% improvement; Group II achieved an overall 75% level of success with 3 months of wearing the chin cup; Group III, who had not worn the strap, had an overall drooling decrease rate of 28%, and a fourth group who neither attended the class nor wore the chin cup had only an 8% reduction of drooling.

Behavior Management

The above four procedures essentially rely on external control, thus making the child a passive participant in controlling his or her drooling. The child has little opportunity to actively learn to develop normal lip closure, tongue control, or swallowing patterns. It is for these reasons that the following techniques are recommended.

Behavior management techniques implementing overcorrection procedures (Drabman, Cordua y Cruz, Ross, & Lynd, 1979) and the use of aware-ness-omission training (Barton & Madsen, 1980) have established positive results in controlling drooling. In the study by Drabman and his colleagues (1979), mentally retarded children were told to wipe their chin during the various timed interval settings during the day over a 20-week period (a 30-minute schedule, then every 15 minutes, and finally every 7.5 minutes). The results indicated that reminders every 7.5 minutes were most effective in elim-inating drooling in the highest functioning children. A reduction of drooling was noted in children who were physically impaired and profoundly retarded. It was hoped that overcorrection would make the children more aware of their drooling. Although the overcorrection techniques were effective, the authors questioned "whether the reduction in the level of wetness was a function of the increased frequency of wiping, rather than a reduction in drooling" (p. 55).

Barton and Madsen's (1980) study not only decreased drooling but also improved the subject's physical appearance, saved further destruction of educa-tional materials, and produced neater and drier finished academic work. This was accomplished through awareness-omission training. The training con-sisted of teaching the subject to discriminate when his or her face was wet or dry (awareness) and then to reinforce the child when his or her face was dry (omission). In addition to being made aware of drooling, the subject was also taught to wipe his or her mouth if it was wet. At the start of the study, the mean frequency of drooling was 43%; this was reduced to a mean of 9%. The per-centage of wipings started at a mean of 3% and ended with a mean high of 91%. The combination of awareness and wiping seems to have been more successful than was only wiping in the previous study.

Tongue Thrusting

Definition and Etiology

In order for a normal swallow to occur, the nasal cavity and the front of the vocal tract should be closed. In addition, the muscles of mastication will bring the teeth and jaws together, the tip of the tongue will press against the den-toalveolar ridge (back of the upper anterior teeth), the upper and lower back teeth will touch, and the lip and chin will be in a relaxed position (Ehrlich, 1970; Morris, 1982; Pierce, 1978; Straub, 1951). This process creates a negative pressure within the closed mouth. This negative pressure is necessary if the transfer of food or liquid is to be pushed by the tongue back toward the pharynx. Any deviation of the swallowing process as described, especially any attempt at pushing the tongue against or between the upper teeth during swallow or even at rest causes abnormal or positive pressure within the oral cavity and is known as tongue thrusting. Other terms associated with this motor action include infan-tile swallowing, reverse swallowing, atypical swallowing, oral myofunctional disorder, and deviant deglutition (Ehrlich, 1970; Pierce, 1978). Many investigators studying this problem are dissatisfied with the above definition. The basis for the disagreement lies in the fact that what has been described as a tongue thrust pattern has also been observed in individuals who have no speech problems or malocclusions. Tongue thrusting is generally agreed to be normal up through 6 months. A change in the tongue position during swallowing occurs with the eruption of the incisor teeth. A trial-and-error learning process is noted as the caregiver learns to place food farther back on the tongue and the infant learns to close the mouth during the swallowing process as well as developing a different placement for the tongue. Hanson (1976) advocated that if "tongue thrusting is to be studied objectively, it should be measurable" (p. 173). This holds true to the definition preferred by Hanson (1976) and by Mason and Proffit (1974), which determines the rate, quantity, and quality of tongue thrusting before identifying it as normal or abnormal. Campbell (1979) added that a true tongue thrust occurs only under specific conditions: when there is abnormal extensor tone, abnormal movement patterns, hyperextension of the jaw, retraction of the upper jaw, hypertonic tongue, and limited movement of the tongue (in a straight forward-backward direction).

The causes of tongue thrusting are as varied as the definitions. A few factors contributing to the development of tongue thrusting include mouth breathing, thumbsucking, improper infant feeding, retained infantile swallowing, and hereditary abnormalities (Ehrlich, 1970; Goldberger, 1975; Pierce, 1978).

Evaluation

A referral for an extensive evaluation should be made to a speech therapist, dentist, or orthodontist when a tongue thrust is suspected. An accurate evaluation is best achieved with knowledgeable information about normal swallowing. A basic guideline is present here to assist the casual examiner in distinguishing an abnormal swallow from a normal one. In normal swallowing movements the tip of the tongue rests on the alveolar ridge behind the front teeth, the upper and lower molars are touching, and there is no observable tension in the facial muscles (orbicularis oris and mentalis muscles). A child whose tongue is pushing outward between the front teeth (space is noted between the upper and lower molars and the muscles around the mouth and chin tighten) is probably displaying tongue thrust. This pattern should be considered normal in an infant up to the sixth month (Pierce, 1978).

Besides observing and recording what happens when the child swallows, there are a few other behaviors that a teacher or therapist can identify. Goldberger (1975) and Ehrlich (1970) have listed the following:

1. Child gulps when swallowing.
2. The tongue is positioned under the cup rim when drinking.

3. Speech problems exist, possibly including a lisp (lateral or frontal).
4. Up-and-down movements of the head and neck occur during swallowing.
5. There is excessive lip licking.
6. The child is a mouth breather.

Treatment Techniques

The activities included here are directed toward minimizing tongue thrusting during eating and drinking. These exercises may be only a part of the child's total oral program and caution must be taken not to overload the child and the family with too many exercises. A team agreement on the maximum number of exercises should help keep the child on a continuing line of progress.

During feeding, a tongue thrust can interfere with chewing and swallowing because the lips and mouth remain open (Ogg, 1975). If there is facial or oral hypersensitivity, creating an open mouth every time the child is touched, it is best to begin with a desensitizing program. Both Leibowtiz and Holcer (1974) and Morris (1977) recommended firm tactile pressure in an area that the child can tolerate best. This may often begin on the legs, trunk, or arms in the shape of roughhousing and then gradually work toward the face. First work on the outside, all around the mouth area, and as the individual is able to tolerate the stimulation without increased muscle tone, then provide stimulation to the inside of the mouth.

Applying jaw control to maintain a closed mouth during swallowing will prevent the food from being pushed out of the mouth. The jaw can be controlled from either of two positions, a side approach or a front approach. The most frequently used position is to sit to the side of the child and slip the nondominant arm around the child's shoulders. The thumb should be placed on the side of the face between the eye and ear. The index finger rests below the lower lip. Placing the middle finger underneath the chin will keep the tongue from pushing the food out.

When sitting in front of the child, place the thumb below the lower lip; the index finger goes near the jaw joint and the middle finger is positioned under the chin (Figure 4.2). An infant or toddler's head may be too small for the adult to use his or her entire hand to control jaw movement. The adult may find sufficient control is achieved just using the thumb and index finger. Initially the child may rebel by throwing his or her head or body backward, thus increasing the muscle tone. Control any backward head movement by supporting the head on top and angling the head in a downward position. Telling the child what is happening before or during the jaw control procedure oftentimes will lessen the child's fears and thus minimize the spasticity.

A shortened attention span and hyperactive and distractible behavior are frequently seen in children with mental retardation. Tactile perceptions are often underdeveloped. Many children with retardation have trouble identifying which finger has been touched or being able to handle more than one food tex-

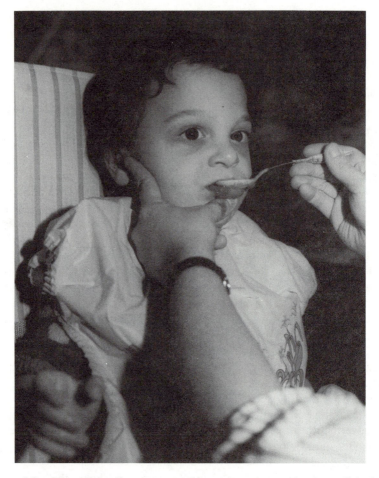

Figure 4.2. Normalizing lip, tongue, and jaw movements can be accomplished with finger placement alongside the jaw, below the lower lip, and under the chin.

ture inside the mouth. Many times tactile stimuli are perceived as being undesirable, and any contact with either internal or external tactile stimuli is avoided. However, "the therapy settings should present opportunities for tactile stimulation to occur in the normal course of events" (McCracken, 1975, p. 402). This can be accomplished by using different types of food or equipment. An excellent food selection resource can be found in the writings of Campbell (1976) and Morris (1982).

The thicker the food the less tendency there may be for the tongue to thrust forward. Also, presenting smaller portions on the spoon will encourage chewing movements as well as controlling tongue thrusting (Morris, 1977). An additional technique to decrease tongue thrusting is to give a firm downward pressure on the tongue with the spoon as it is being removed from the mouth. Another effective technique is placing an index finger across the child's "upper lip and nose, exercising firm and continuous pressure" (Finnie, 1975, p. 120).

Success has been achieved by holding an electric vibrator to the masseter muscle (jaw joint) and the digastric muscle (under the chin) for up to 2–3 minutes (McCracken, 1978). McCracken cautioned that although vibrating may be effective in increasing tongue movement, it may be contraindicated for some children. Since the vibration penetrates and extends beyond the immediate area stimulated, other muscle groups such as the pharyngeal muscles may be affected, which in children with spasticity may cause swallowing problems (McCracken, 1978). These children may still benefit from vibration but only when it is done manually. This is done using a swizzle stick and vibrating on either side of the frenulum (Farber, 1982). Farber described two other manual techniques that facilitate retrusion of the tongue. Applying upward thumb pressure under the chin is effective for those children who require minimal cues. Another procedure involves pulling the tongue out in a diagonal direction. Holding onto the tongue is best done by wrapping the adult's thumb and index finger with moist gauze.

Biting and Chewing

Normal Development

The normal process of biting and chewing is complex and requires coordinated as well as isolated movement of the jaw, lips, and tongue. Biting is viewed as the first stage of chewing and paves the way, through experimentation, for the development of jaw control. At birth, the phasic bite reflex is in control until 3–7 months, when it then becomes integrated with more voluntary control (Braun et al., 1983; Colangelo et al., 1976; Farber, 1982; Lederman, 1984; Morris, 1982). The phasic bite reflex is described as a rhythmical closing and opening of the jaw when the top or side surface of the gums receives tactile stimulation (Braun et al., 1983; Colangelo et al., 1976; Morris, 1982). When a child has difficulty opening his or her mouth (after responding to stimuli that have automatically closed the mouth) it is probably the tonic bite response eliciting the force. It is the tonic bite that interferes in the child's establishing independent chewing skills.

By 2 years of age, the child is able to visually interpret the size and shape of the food, open the mouth the right height, and bite using the correct amount of jaw force (Morris, 1982). Table 4.8 depicts a synopsis of the development of jaw control in biting and a summary of the various levels of chewing needed to arrive at a mature, complex pattern of chewing.

Gallender (1979) contends that chewing is a task that must be learned and that, in order for a child to learn this skill, several prerequisites should have

Table 4.8. Normal development of biting and chewing

Age (months)	Biting action	Chewing action
Birth	Onset of bite reflex	
3–5	Integration of bite reflex	
4–6	Sucks food instead of biting	Munching (or gumming)—tongue remains flat
5–7	Bite action should be under voluntary control	
6–9	Incisors erupt	
7–9	Separate movement of jaw, tongue, and lips when biting	Transfers food from side to center and back again using tongue. Beginning to control isolated movement of tongue, lips, jaw
10–12	Bites softs foods using well-graded opening and closing	Corner of lips and cheek are drawn inward during chewing. Can externally stabilize jaw while drinking by biting rim of cup
12–14	Molars erupt	
13–15	Bite more controlled with harder foods	Uses lip closure when chewing large mouthfuls of foods
16–18	Turns head toward side of biting food	Minimal loss of food and saliva during chewing. Side-to-side jaw movement
19–24		Firmer meats introduced into diet
24	Able to judge size of food and open mouth to correct distance	
25–36	Can maintain stationary head position while biting on food at side of mouth	Spontaneously transfers food smoothly from side to side. Can produce circular-rotary jaw movement when transferring food across mouth

Adapted from Bosley (1966), Braun et al. (1983), Farber (1982), J. A. Lewis (1982), Morris (1982), and Ogg (1975).

occurred. First, good head control and trunk stability should be established (Scherzer & Tscharnuter, 1982). Second, J. A. Lewis (1982) suggested that a mental age of 6–8 months is realistic to look for or to train chewing skills. By this time, the child can independently get to a sitting position, maintain sitting for long periods of time, shift to different positions through trunk rotation, and begin to finger feed and has progressed from strained (pureed) to semisolid (toddler) foods. Third, mobility and quickness of the tongue are needed to keep food between the molars while chewing. Lip closure is a fourth prerequisite that prevents the food from falling out of the mouth. Fifth, the jaw must be able to move up and down as well as sideways. This ability allows the upper and lower molars to slide across each other in a grinding fashion. Lederman (1984) stated that true rotary chewing will be established only when there is lateral tongue movement. Finally, the cheeks must be able to contract, thus assisting tongue and lips in keeping the bolus from falling into the outside space of the gums.

Biting and chewing require flexibility, control, and stability of the jaw, but these must be combined with assistance from the lips, tongue, and cheeks.

Abnormal Patterns

Children with neurological deficits lack the needed skills of both group and individual coordination within the oral cavity. Many of these children develop compensatory movements when trying to consume either food or liquid. Strained baby food often remains a child's sole diet long past the normal age of 6 months because oral hypersensitivity is affecting the child's overall performance. Children with tight muscle tone (spastic) will throw their head backward, arch their back, plantarflex (push downward) both feet, or display overflow movements throughout the entire body. Overflow is noted, for example, when an infant is holding onto a teething biscuit or rattle and increased tightness and the same type of movement is observed in the other hand. Increased tension may also be felt in the trunk and lower extremities.

Persistence of primitive oral reflexes such as the phasic bite reflex elicits a tonic response wherein release of the bite action is often difficult (Scherzer & Tscharnuter, 1982). The early munching pattern, when prolonged, will inhibit tongue lateralization and rotary chewing and encourage tongue thrusting.

McCracken (1978) believes that the open-mouth posture in children with retardation is probably due to too much muscle tone rather than a weakness of the muscles. Because of the overall spasticity, abnormal feeding responses are triggered by the slightest sensory stimulation anywhere on or near the body (Lederman, 1984).

Lip function may be limited because of: 1) hypotonicity, causing sluggish movement and drooling; 2) hypertonicity, resulting in lip retraction or jaw thrust; or 3) poor coordination with cheeks and tongue, making consuming solids and liquids difficult and thus causing gagging and choking.

Evaluation

First assess the individual's overall ability to handle food, then look at specific oral functions. Determine the effect positioning has on chewing skills. Does the child hyperextend the neck in order to compensate for poor lip control or severe bite reflex (Farber, 1982; Morris, 1982)? Is there gagging when solid food is presented? A child who is sensitive to touch or new textures inside the mouth may deal with this adverse stimulation by gagging and, if the sensation is severe, the child may even vomit. If the child's overall functional level is still below 6–8 months, physically and psychologically the child cannot manage chewing techniques.

When observing lip function, check to see if, while chewing, the lips remain closed. Mouth breathers find it difficult to chew with the lips together, resulting in dribbling food or a tongue thrust. Is there tightness around the mouth causing lip retraction, which in turn interferes with chewing? Or is there little to no active movement of the lips? Are the lips used to remove food from the spoon, or do the teeth scrape the food off? These types of questions will provide information on the amount of active control of feeding present in the lips. What the examiner is looking for is the drawing in of the lower lip in removing food from the spoon or when biting. Also, both the lips and cheeks tighten during chewing, even causing a dimple, which indicates the food is actively being contained inside the mouth (Morris, 1982).

Active tongue action should include movement in all directions in order to effectively transfer food back to the molars for grinding. Is there a tongue thrust and when does it occur?

Jaw control is essential for biting and chewing. Morris (1982) stated that some children may have control with biting and not during chewing or vice versa. Morris stressed that one should not assume that if a child has one ability the other is also functioning. Also, do not take for granted that if biting is not functioning properly the same will be true for chewing skills. What type of jaw movement is the child using: vertical? Circular/rotary? Bite and release? Is the jaw stable when needed, such as in biting?

Treatment Techniques

The normal chewing process requires active mastery of the following: tactile and food tolerance; jaw stability; and control of the tongue, lips, and cheeks. Campbell (1976) noted that, although chewing food is a complex process, if the evaluation time has been thorough and feeding problems well analyzed as to their cause, very few children will be found to have problems learning to chew. For example, too often the child has not been exposed to foods requiring chewing movements. Before any type of chewing techniques can be taught, Lederman (1984) believes there should be adequate jaw stability and tongue lateralization. The current authors' viewpoint is that each child's problem is unique and must be treated on an individual basis. There may be certain guidelines to recommend techniques that can help set up a treatment program, but in a given case one of the proscribed techniques may be just the method to help that child become more independent in chewing as well as improving the overall eating quality. The following techniques are only suggestions and it is up to the reader to expand on them. Extensive reading of Campbell (1976), Farber (1982), Farber and Huss (1974), Gallender (1979), and Morris (1978a, 1978b, 1982) will add to the reader's expertise. To assist the reader, the authors have selected the following activities to facilitate independent chewing.

Reducing oral hypersensitivity will be achieved by decreasing the number of times the spoon is used to wipe food off the face around and on the lips. If the face must be wiped, wait until the child has stopped chewing and then use a firm patting motion with a damp cloth. Other desensitization techniques include downward strokes above the upper lip and upward strokes between the chin and lower lip (Utley et al., 1977). Firm rubbing of the outer surface of the gums may help in decreasing sensitivity to food textures. A tonic bite reaction may develop when an infant has not had normal mouth exploration opportunity because of the oral hypersensitivity (J. A. Lewis, 1982).

Braun et al. (1983) and Mueller (1975) stressed the importance of *jaw control during biting and chewing.* Developing this control will help increase lateral movement of the tongue and control the vertical movements of the jaw. Jaw stability will automatically stimulate chewing, according to Farber (1982). Farber suggested that if poor jaw stability is interfering with chewing, quickly pull down on the chin after food has been placed in the mouth. Schmidt (1976) cautioned teachers/therapists not to facilitate jaw rotary movement because it is too subtle a motion to train and will generally develop spontaneously when side-to-side movement of the tongue is developed. Whereas Schmidt approved of up-and-down jaw motion training, Lederman (1984) disapproved of it because it will reinforce primitive pathological reflexive actions; Lederman suggested passively moving the jaw in a rotary fashion. It is up to the reader to try both techniques and carefully evaluate the results to determine which is more successful in developing the chewing skills of a given child.

In order to *release the jaw closure,* push up on the jaw (Farber, 1982) or press the area just in front of the ear (Bosley, 1966).

As has been stated previously, *active tongue movement* is crucial in developing a normal chewing pattern. In order for food to be chewed and swallowed, there must be vertical and horizontal as well as forward and backward tongue movement. To encourage lateral movement, push a swizzle stick against the side of the tongue. Releasing the pressure will cause the tongue to retract in the opposite direction (Bosley, 1966). Applying downward pressure on the tongue with a spoon toward the molar region of the mouth will also encourage tongue lateralization as well as inhibiting tongue thrusting. Schmidt (1976) and Zinkus (no date) provided further suggestions to stimulate up-and-down tongue movement, such as placing peanut butter on the roof of the mouth and having the child remove it with the tip of the tongue.

To *increase the muscle tone and strength of the lips,* Farber and Huss (1974) have recommended icing, vibrating, and quick stretching. Once minimal control has developed, the child can be required to actively increase the length of time the lips contract and hold that position. One technique Bosley (1966) has described as effective involves the child holding a tongue depressor (or popsicle stick) between the lips. The child is then told to open and close the jaw without dropping the stick.

The use of contrary or opposite direction techniques—for example, quickly pulling the chin down—has been effective with some children to *strengthen a weak bite* (Bosley, 1966). A bite reflex may be inhibited by vibrating the masseter muscles or by using a flat, narrow feeding spatula as described by Westmoreland and Burlingame (1977). Farber and Huss (1974) have indicated the masseters can be vibrated unless there is a strong bite reaction. Again, the reader is cautioned to carefully observe the individual child's responses to treatment.

The chances of developing chewing skills will be nil if the *food selected* remains pureed. Children need chewy and crisp types of food to provide both tactile and auditory cues to motivate independent chewing ability (Campbell, 1976). Table 4.9 lists a few foods recommended for specific problems teachers, therapists, and parents may have to deal with when working with the child with handicaps.

Self-Feeding

Staff members should not expect independent self-feeding skills unless the child has established the necessary prerequisites of head, trunk, and arm control. This includes the ability to move the head independent of trunk and arm motion, to sit unsupported, to bring the hand to the mouth, to maintain grasp on

Table 4.9. Feeding problems and suggested food solutions

Problem	Solution
Swallowing difficulties	Thicker foods, shakes, yogurt, thinned puddings, soft ice cream, creamed soups
Drooling	Avoid sweet foods and soft drinks
Chewing	Dried fruits, cheese, slightly cooked carrots, strips of rare beef, slices of liver sausage, orange slices
Tactile hypersensitivity	Larger pieces of food; be sensitive to temperature of food
Poor tongue movement	Grapenuts, chicken, roast beef
Poor nutrition	
Iron	Cream of Wheat, dried fruits: apricots, raisins, peaches, prunes
Calcium	Cottage cheese, yogurt, cheese slices
Difficulty handling foods with more than one consistency	Eat Jello separate from fruit or soup from vegetables
Excessive mucus secretion	Decrease amount of milk as a drink; increase intake of cheese and food containing milk, carbonated drinks

Adapted from Morris (1977).

the food or spoon handle, and to control the muscular action related to the lips, cheeks, jaw, and tongue (Banerdt & Bricker, 1978; Blanchard, 1966; Freeman et al., 1975; Lederman, 1984; Schmidt, 1976; Zinkus, no date). The kinesthetic awareness also has been identified by Blanchard and by Lederman as a prerequisite needed for total self-feeding control. Banerdt and Bricker (1978) agreed with Zinkus (no date) that not all of these skills need be mastered. Through the use of adaptations in positioning, behavioral management techniques, and adapting utensils, a child can learn to drink from a cup or to scoop food with a spoon without too much trouble.

The atmosphere during meals once a child can self-feed drastically changes for both parents and child. The child is much more comfortable because he or she is in control and not subject to the feeder's speed and style of presenting the food (Lederman, 1984). The parents are able to direct their attention to more social channels and not just to the physical mechanics of trying to feed their child within a given time period or keep the child from regurgitating.

Normal Development

Normally, children begin to self-feed with the fingers between 5 and 6 months of age and start using a spoon at 2 years, with moderate spillage expected (Scherzer & Tscharnuter, 1982). Table 4.10 (from Lederman, 1984) compares normal utensil achievement to the ages of children with mild and profound retardation. Parental expectations and attitudes can be altered through discussions and demonstrations pertaining to adaptations and manual techniques that will increase self-feeding skills.

Evaluation

When evaluating the functional level of an infant's or child's self-feeding skills, the teacher/therapist needs to assess the rate, quantity, and quality of the child's independent control. The difficulties many children with handicaps encounter include an inability to bring both hands to the midline, an inability to hold a spoon or food and bring the food to the mouth, a loss of balance when reaching for food, an inability to open a hand to hold onto a spoon, and an inability to maintain a grasp for any length of time.

Treatment Techniques

Cup Drinking

The introduction of independent cup drinking skills begins around 5–6 months. Generally, the infant has developed jaw stability, lip control (primarily lip closure), tongue elevation, and coordinated swallowing (J. A. Lewis, 1982). Initially, parents should expect the learning phase to be messy, with numerous spills, especially if the infant has any desire to hold onto the cup without assistance even when using both hands. The weighted bottom cup is helpful, but

Table 4.10. Age comparisons of feeding skills for normal versus retarded children

Skill	Normal Development	Mild Retardation ⁼ ⁼ ⁼ Retardation	Profound Retardation ⁼ ⁼ ⁼ Retardation
Holds and manages bottle independently	6–8 months	9 months	1.5 years or more
Finger feeds dry cracker, cereal	6–9 months	9–12 months	2.5 years or more
Holds spoon with pronated grasp	7–12 months	12–15 months	4 years or more
Attempts to feed self with spoon	9–12 months	14–18 months	4.5 years or more
Holds cup in two hands and drinks	12–15 months	16–22 months	5 years or more
Drinks from a straw	15–24 months	24–36 months	6 years or more
Drinks from a cup held in one hand	24 months	36 months	7 years or more
Spoon feeds self with supinated grasp and minimal spilling	3 years	4.5 years	9 years or more
Independently uses a fork	4 years	6 years	12 years or more
Uses knife to spread	5 years	7 years	12 years or more
Cuts meat with a knife and fork	7–8 years	9–12 years	Many profoundly retarded individuals never acquire this skill.

From Lederman, E. F. (1984). *Occupational therapy in mental retardation* (p. 348). Springfield, IL: Charles C Thomas; reprinted by permission.

the spouted lid is discouraged by most therapists for use by infants/children with handicaps. The lid encourages the abnormal primitive sucking pattern to continue long past the normal period.

To help a child achieve normal drinking patterns several guidelines should be followed. First, jaw control helps normalize weak lip closure, strong bite reflex, or abnormal swallowing. The best kind of cup to use while training is the pliable plastic glass with a narrow cut-out section that allows the cup to be tilted upward, thus avoiding hyperextensions of the head and upper torso (see Figure 4.3). The rim of the cup must be placed on the lower lip, not on or between the teeth, because this may stimulate the bite reflex. Mueller (1975) recommended not removing the cup between swallows in order to minimize abnormal reactions. Using jaw control, maintain lip closure while the child takes several sips and swallows before removing the cup and jaw support; then allow the child to

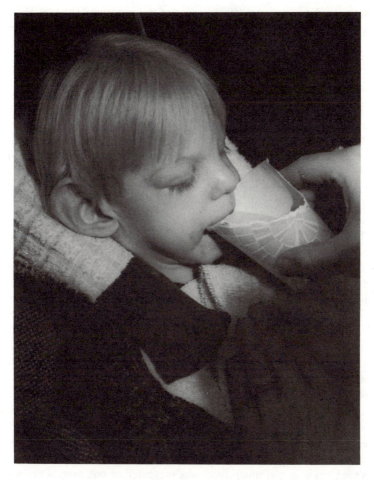

Figure 4.3. A cup with a cutout nose area minimizes hyperextension of the head, which can occur when a regular cup is used with a child with abnormal muscle tone.

rest (Utley et al., 1977). If the child is having trouble swallowing, it is better to use a single sip and swallow with the lip closure and swallow treatment techniques until more swallowing self-control is achieved.

Scherzer and Tscharnuter (1982) as well as J. A. Lewis (1982) suggested starting with thickened foods (yogurt, soft ice cream, milk shakes, or thinned puddings) until a tolerance and control of regular liquids can be managed. A sweet taste (milk) tends to increase salivation, which stimulates drooling and should be avoided. Scherzer and Tscharnuter (1982) indicated that extremes of temperature will increase hypotonicity in the oral area.

An effective cup drinking program depends upon doing a thorough task analysis of the problem, setting up a behavioral management program, and taking data. To determine the effectiveness of the program, Utley et al. (1977) suggested taking data one of two ways: either measure the number of ounces a child drinks within a given period of time, or note the amount of assistance required to consume two swallows.

Spoon Feeding

Incorporating behavioral management techniques of chaining and fading has proven the most effective way of establishing independent skills in spoon feeding. There is some controversy as to when spoon feeding should be introduced, but it is not uncommon to have it begin when the infant is 3 months old. However, even without the introduction of a new tactile sensation such as cereal, there is a lot of sensation in the oral cavity that the infant must deal with at this age. Pediatricians now seem to be stressing starting at a later age than they were 5 years ago.

Prior to learning to pick up a spoon, several prerequisites should have been achieved and/or adapted for. Head and jaw stability can be developed by adding neck and trunk supports to a wheelchair or by adding physical jaw control. Head hyperextension can also be controlled by pushing on the child's sternum. Built-up handles are helpful for those youngsters with weak or tight grasp. The bowl of the spoon can be turned toward the child who cannot supinate the arm. Staff must remember that the types of physical assists should be given at more removed keypoints of control. This means that, when helping a child learn to put food in his or her mouth, physical support should be given at the shoulder, elbow, or wrist instead of holding onto the hand or lower arm.

Connor et al. (1978) and Freeman et al. (1975) presented several useful suggestions when feeding a child with handicaps. First, present small amounts of food on the spoon. Letting the child know (visually and auditorily) of the presence of the spoon avoids an increase of muscular tone. Too often hypertension of the head and jaw results because the spoon was presented too fast or at the wrong angle or too much food was presented at one time. Prevention of hyperextension is primarily achieved through jaw control. If the problem develops it can be corrected by applying pressure or tapping on the child's chest (Mueller, 1975).

The next step in Connor et al.'s as well as Freeman et al.'s programs is to make sure to apply downward pressure on the tongue as the food is deposited on it. This technique also helps decrease tongue thrusting. Be sure to present and remove the spoon in a horizontal plane and in the center of the tongue. The author reminds the reader that this guideline may not be as easy to implement as it is to state. Finally, to avoid problems associated with poor swallowing and weak/tight lips or tongue, the adult should maintain jaw and lip control after the spoon has been removed. According to Scherzer and Tscharnuter (1982), the most effective means of minimizing exaggerated tongue action is to use jaw control. To minimize lip retraction or increased oral muscular tone, teach the child to remove the food with the lips and not scrape the food off with the teeth (Figure 4.4).

Training self-feeding with a spoon requires a thorough evaluation and a well-planned program. Aside from any adapted equipment (built-up handles, nonslide mats, plate guards, etc.), the program should include ways of using physical cues, graded chaining steps, fading procedures, and a variety of reinforcement tokens. Teaching independent spoon control cannot be done until the child can chew foods or achieves the eye-hand coordination of a 1-year-old. An example given by Lederman (1984) suggested starting out establishing independent eye-hand coordination by spreading small amounts of whipped cream, peanut butter, or chocolate syrup on the tray or table in front of the child. Encourage the child either verbally or physically to dip a finger into the food and bring the finger to the mouth. The next phase would be to introduce small, bite-size pieces of food such as cheese, fruit, cereal, or meat. When the ability to pick up small objects has been mastered, then introduce the spoon. If needed, begin physical support over the child's hand, gradually moving the physical assistance further away (wrist, elbow, shoulder) and fading the amount of pressure at each key point of control.

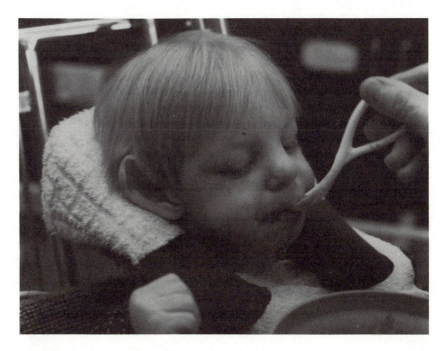

Figure 4.4. To avoid a bite reflex, food should be removed from the utensil with the lips and not the teeth.

Applied Behavior Analysis

The employment of behavior management procedures to establish independent feeding and eating skills is abundant in the literature and covers a variety of problems:

Examining the effects of various positions on an increase in self-feeding (Banerdt & Bricker, 1978).

Changing feeding habits from pureed to table foods (Holser-Buehler, 1973; S. Palmer, Thompson, & Linscheid, 1975).

Teaching independent spoon feeding (Berkowitz, Sherry, & Davis, 1971; Blanchard, 1966; Groves & Carroccio, 1971; O'Brien, Bugle, & Azrin, 1972; Song & Gandhi, 1974).

Using timeout procedures in order to decrease food spillage (Christian, Hollomon, & Lanier, 1973; Cipani, 1981).

Decreasing self-abusive behavior through a self-feeding program (Lemke & Mitchell, 1972).

Increasing food intake by improving staff performance (Korabek, Reid, & Ivancic, 1981).

Increasing food intake by using food as a reinforcer (Riordan, Iwata, Wohl, & Finney, 1980).

Teaching appropriate use of utensils through the use of numerous small meals (Azrin & Armstrong, 1973).

CHAPTER 5

Dressing and Toileting

Acquiring independence in self-help skills is dependent on more than just motor ability. The ability to voluntarily direct a movement to perform a functional task is not just a physical action but is also an integration of sensory stimuli, cognitive knowledge, and the development of a self-concept or the separation of one's self from the environment and other people (Coley, 1978).

Snell (1983) and Van Etten, Arkell, and Van Etten (1980) stated that three reasons why severely handicapped children have difficulty acquiring self-help skills are their poor fine motor skills, their associated handicaps, and their limited cognitive ability. First, many of the fine motor prerequisites needed for dressing and toileting skills have not been achieved. For example, the ability to control movements while reaching, grasping, and releasing are necessary components for pulling down pants and buttoning a coat. The child's muscular strength, flexibility, and endurance may not only determine the success of a program but may be an important factor in the child's motivation to learn and thus succeed. Specific dressing prerequisites that should be established but may need to be trained prior to developing a dressing program for the child with retardation are listed in Table 5.1. Until these basic skills are established, those involved with the program may become frustrated by the failure or poor quality of the child's performance. Williamson (1987) has identified similar basic skills needed by the child with spina bifida. A second reason for delays is the existence of concomitant physical handicaps (e.g., a visual impairment or cerebral palsy). Third, parents or staff may not have developed, implemented, or even thought about self-help programs because they believed the child's mental or physical impairment would drastically limit his or her ability to learn.

The staff must also assess the child's level of cognitive comprehension, which includes the length of attending skill, the level of motor imitation, and understanding of simple instructions. It may be more appropriate to work on these basic cognitive skills before expecting mastery of self-help skills such as dressing or toileting.

Table 5.1.   Prerequisite skills and abilities for dressing

NEUROMOTOR
- Adequate sitting balance without support so that both hands can be involved in dressing
- Sufficient upper extremity range of motion (i.e., elbow extension to reach the feet; shoulder flexion to raise the arms to put on a shirt; internal rotation to fasten a back-closing brassiere)
- Sufficient lower extremity range of motion (i.e., hip and knee flexion for putting on shoes and socks)
- Adequate upper extremity strength to handle heavy garments such as a winter coat
- Normal muscle tone to enable functional movement of the extremities
- Sufficient endurance to complete the dressing task
- Functional grasp for handling garments
- Functional pinch for manipulating fastenings
- Sufficient gross-motor coordination and fine-motor dexterity

PERCEPTUAL
- Adequate visual attention for focusing on the dressing task
- Sufficient form and space perception to determine the exact placement of the articles of clothing (i.e., tops from bottoms of shirts or socks)
- Adequate figure-ground perception to distinguish the foreground from the background (i.e., buttonholes on a patterned shirt)

BODY INTEGRATION
- Intact body awareness and body scheme for proper placement of clothing
- Adequate motor planning for the complicated movements involved in dressing
- Adequate bilateral coordination and dexterity so that both arms and hands can efficiently be involved in the task

COGNITIVE
- Sufficient ability to recognize clothes and their functions
- Adequate memory for remembering the necessary sequence of dressing
- Sufficient alertness and motivation to desire independence in dressing

---

From Lederman, E. F. (1984). *Occupational therapy in mental retardation* (p.366). Springfield, IL: Charles C Thomas; reprinted by permission.

Prerequisite Activities

Activities and games suggested by Williamson (1987) and Tingey-Michaelis (1983) focus on establishing and incorporating prerequisite skills that are practical, fun, and basic to dressing skills. To develop body awareness, a mother can incorporate games such as "Pat-a-Cake" or "Wheels on the Bus" into a toddler's daily schedule to teach body parts. Playing in front of a mirror before and after bathing or diapering is also an easy way to learn body parts. Auditory and visual stimulation are necessary sensory inputs for the emergence of body awareness.

Teaching fine motor prehension, used for grasping and holding onto clothing, can be developed by having the child hold onto a paper bag while putting in and taking out objects, or play with puzzles with a large knobbed handle. For learning to reach, a task that is needed when putting on a shirt, the adult can begin by popping bubbles above the child's head or playing the game "So Big."

For self-help skills (toileting, dressing, etc.) to be successful, training methods need to be carried over from the classroom or clinic to the daily home routine or vice versa. For this process to occur there must be an agreement from the parents that there is a need for special training. They also need to be willing in most situations to learn a new procedure for teaching their child a self-help skill. The staff member, in turn, must be willing to spend the time necessary to assess, interpret, and develop a program that can easily be incorporated into the family's schedule.

The collaboration between parent and teacher/therapist should include efforts to list priorities for training, an agreement of the training procedures, the establishment of tangible and social reinforcers, and a general consensus of the appropriateness of the teaching materials.

Because of the high priority and the complexity of training and establishing independent eating skills, a separate chapter (see Chapter 4) has been written on the problems with feeding and eating skills and possible solutions. Included in this chapter are descriptions of normal and abnormal development plus treatment techniques used to acquire basic dressing and toileting skills.

DRESSING

Dressing is not a life-sustaining skill in the same way that eating is; therefore, some parents and professionals assign less importance to this activity. The varying degrees of importance assigned to dressing depend upon the social, cultural, and religious rules followed by the individual parents. For some, the style and color of clothing is an important adjunct to the individual's self-esteem. Participation in learning to dress provides the child with the opportunity to learn the names of body parts and surfaces, the actions of the body parts, and the names of clothing. Dressing provides an excellent opportunity for speech, language, and communication between the caregiver and the child. Learning that the socks go on the feet before shoes enhances the cognitive development of prepositional concepts and sequencing. Dressing tasks help the child become aware of the different sides of the body (laterality) and require that the child use both sides of the body together in a coordinated manner. By participating in dressing and taking care of clothing, the child has the opportunity to learn more about the interrelationships between the body, clothing, and the environment.

Development of Dressing

The mastering of the complex skill of undressing and dressing takes the normal human approximately 5–6 years to accomplish. Table 5.2 lists a typical sequence of dressing development from simple assisted dressing skills to independent complex dressing tasks. Initially, the infant begins to cooperate during dressing by lying still while the caregiver takes off or puts clothing on the child. Around 12 months of age, the child is eager to help put clothes on by extending an arm to go into a sleeve. At this age, the child may not know which opening the arm goes through but does recognize what piece of clothing goes on what part of the body. At about 18 months of age, when the child has achieved independent sitting and no longer needs his or her hands for support, he or she will begin to assist with dressing by taking simple clothing off and helping the caregiver with more complex clothing. Finally, by the age of 5–6 years, the child can independently manage most dressing tasks. Children usually learn to undress before they master dressing. Undressing is easier because it requires less complex motor and cognitive skills. Pulling off a pair of socks requires gross grasp and simple arm maneuvers, whereas putting a sock on requires more re-

Table 5.2. Typical sequence of dressing development

- Cooperates with dressing (i.e., extends arm to put in sleeve)
- Removes socks
- Removes untied shoes
- Removes pants with assistance over hips
- Helps pull up or push down pants or panties
- Puts arms into armholes
- Attempts to put legs into pant legs (but may put both legs into one pant leg)
- Removes clothing completely except for small buttons and back fastenings
- Unlaces shoes
- Unfastens medium-sized buttons on shirt
- Puts on socks
- Puts on pants
- Puts on shoes
- Puts shirts on over head
- Puts on sweater or dress
- Tries to lace shoes
- Fastens large buttons on front-closing shirts
- Correctly laces shoes
- Fastens medium-sized buttons
- Completely dresses self except for bows and small buttons
- Tries to tie shoes
- Fastens small buttons
- Ties shoes
- Selects appropriate clothing
- Maintains clothing properly

From Lederman, E. F. (1984). *Occupational therapy in mental retardation* (p. 370). Springfield, IL: Charles C Thomas; reprinted by permission.

fined use of the thumb and fingers and more steps performed in the proper sequence. According to Schafer and Moersch (1981) and Snell (1983) mastery of unfastening (of zippers, buttons, buckles, snaps) is accomplished before mastery of fastening. Mastering unzipping is accomplished between 20 and 23 months, and unbuttoning and unsnapping are learned by 32–35 months. By 48 months, most children are able to pull on socks, buckle a belt, button front buttons, and lace shoes; most can tie shoe laces by 72 months (Sanford & Zelman, 1981). Table 5.3 lists undressing and dressing skills in the sequence in

Table 5.3.   Acquisition of undressing and dressing skills

Age	Undressing	Dressing
0–20 mos.	Cooperates with undressing	Cooperates with dressing, extending arm or leg
14 mos.	Names body parts	
5–18 mos.	Removes hat, mittens, sock	
6–18 mos.		Puts hat on head
18–24 mos.	Takes off untied shoes Helps pull down pants Unzips large zipper	Tries to put on socks
21–30 mos.		Puts on shoes with assistance
24–26 mos.	Pulls down pants with assistance Unbuttons large buttons	
26–32 mos.	Undresses with assistance	
30 mos.	Removes pants with elastic waist Can take off most "pull down" clothing	
30–36 mos.		Buttons large buttons Dresses with supervision Requires assistance with fasteners
3 years	Helps take off "pull-over" clothing	Puts on tube-socks independently
4 years	Undresses independently	Dresses with little assistance Can distinguish front and back Puts on socks with heel Laces shoes Buttons front buttons
5 years		Dresses completely except back buttons and tying shoes
5.5 years		Ties knot Buttons back buttons
6 years		Ties bow-knot

Data from Coley (1978), Copeland et al. (1976), Finnie (1975), and Furuno et al. (1985).

which they are usually acquired by normal children. This information can be used as a guide in planning a dressing training program.

Dressing Problems

Some of the problems children with mental or physical disabilities encounter in learning to dress or undress themselves center around sensorimotor deficits. The child with spina bifida has insufficient gross motor control, lacks sensory awareness, and is known to have delays in manipulative and perceptual skills (Williamson, 1987). Children with mental retardation may have short attention spans, low frustration level, limited communication skills, poor long-term memory, poor left-right discrimination, and inadequate fine motor dexterity (Coley & Procter, 1985). Similar problems are observed in the child with cerebral palsy. The child with jerky movements or limited range of motion will be easily frustrated because of the lack of muscular control and coordination.

Predressing Activities

Dressing is a complex task requiring the integration of many motor and cognitive skills. Dressing also requires from the child a desire to cooperate, participate, and eventually master all of these complex tasks. Some children who are physically, cognitively, and/or motivationally impaired may be more willing to participate in predressing activities rather than participating in the actual dressing program. This will help them experience success and develop self-esteem in a nonthreatening manner. Predressing activities are designed to enhance body awareness, gross and fine motor skills, and cognitive skills necessary for self-dressing. Predressing activities can include the use of games and toys that require the same motor and cognitive skill components that are required for dressing.

Developing Body Awareness

Associated skills necessary for self-dressing that need to be evaluated include the degree (or qualifying amount) of arm movements, eye-hand coordination, sitting and standing balance (this refers to the status of reflex integration), and social skills (Bailey & Wolery, 1984). This additional information will help the adult standing next to or behind the child know how much and what type of assistance to give the child. Shining a flashlight beam on a body part such as the knee and encouraging or assisting the child to touch that part is fun, but it also enhances body awareness and provides practice in reaching the body part with the hands (Finnie, 1975). Placing bracelets or ring-toss rings on body parts such as the ears, nose, arms or feet; placing poker chips or large buttons between the toes and fingers; or placing stickers on body parts not only draws the child's attention to that body part but usually results in an attempt to remove the item.

Any activity that allows the child to move about the room independently or with assistance helps the child learn more about his or her body and its relationship to the environment.

Developing Gross and Fine Motor Skills

Stability as well as mobility within the lying, sitting, or standing positions make self-dressing easier. For example, if undressing or dressing is performed in the sitting position, the child not only needs to be able to maintain a stable sitting position but also to shift weight when leaning forward or to the side to place an article of clothing on the arms or legs. A predressing activity designed to develop this ability can have the seated child lean forward to pick up toys placed near the feet. The child can be seated on the floor or in a chair, depending upon the abilities of the child. This stimulates some of the motor skills used in putting on or pulling off clothing. Pulling ring-toss rings off the feet requires more skill than picking up objects near the feet. As the skill develops, the difficulty of the task can be increased by having the child remove a scarf that has been loosely tied around one thigh by pushing the scarf down to the ankles, and under the heel and then pulling it off the foot. The same activity can be applied to the upper extremity. Putting on puppets and playing dressup can also be used to develop dressing skills.

Buttons, snaps, and zippers are often very difficult for children with physical limitations to master. There are many commercially made toys with different types of closures on them that provide the opportunity to practice as a by-product of playing with the toy. Prebuttoning activities can include pushing poker chips or large buttons through a slot cut in the plastic lid of a container such as a coffee can. Old purses with zippers, snaps, or other fasteners or dressup clothing may be appealing to some children. However, if mastering the closures on clothing is impractical for a child with limited movement it is wiser to purchase clothing without buttons, snaps, or zippers in order for the child to learn to complete this part independently or for the adult to do the undressing/dressing for the child.

Developing Cognitive Skills Necessary for Dressing

Throughout all of the previously described activities the parent or teacher can use the appropriate words describing the required action: on-off, push-pull, over-under, and front-back. Tactile awareness and discriminative ability can be taught when describing hard-soft, rough-smooth, and round-square.

The objectives of using predressing activities are to learn skills that can be generalized to actual undressing or dressing tasks, to experience success and enhanced self-esteem, and to have fun!

Assisted Dressing

Positioning and Handling for Dressing

Positioning for dressing will depend upon the child's age, type and severity of the movement disorder, level of functional ability, and the type of clothing to be taken off or put on. Prior to beginning dressing the caregiver needs to prepare the environment by gathering all of the required clothing, chairs, or positioning devices. The child needs to be prepared for the normalization of muscle tone and positioning.

Infants are usually dressed in the supine position, but too often this position increases extensor tone. If the infant has increased extensor muscle tone in supine, the infant's hips and knees can gently be flexed to reduce extensor tone (Figure 5.1). This will not only break up the extensor tone but also allow the child to see and touch the legs and feet. If excessive tone is still a problem, gentle shaking or rolling of the pelvis and lower extremities back and forth may help reduce muscle tone. Rolling the child from supine to side-lying will also reduce muscle tone as well as bringing the shoulders forward, and can be done while putting clothing such as pants on the lower extremities (Figure 5.2). Williamson (1987) recommends this position when teaching a child with spina bifida independent dressing skills. The placement of a pillow under the child's head will make it easier to bring both arms and hands together (Coley & Procter, 1985) because this position will lessen the strain on the neck muscles, allow for more comfortable viewing, and raise and relax the shoulders.

When dressing larger or older children in the supine position, it also may be necessary to place a firm pillow under the child's head and neck. The pillow will help flex the head and neck in the midline position and may aid in reducing extensor muscle tone (Coley & Procter, 1985). In addition to head flexion,

Figure 5.1. Infant positioned on adult's lap with hips, knees, and ankles flexed to reduce excessive extensor muscle tone.

Figure 5.2. Infant placed in side-lying position to reduce muscle tone while adult puts clothes on lower extremities.

bringing the arms forward and flexing the hip and knees in combination with handling techniques may reduce excessive extensor tone (Finnie, 1975).

If the supine position on the caregiver's lap, changing table, or floor does not reduce extensor tone, the infant or child can be placed prone over the caregiver's lap (Figure 5.3). The prone position will encourage hip flexion and may decrease extensor muscle tone. Lower and upper extremity dressing can be done in this position. The caregiver can also incorporate handling techniques to reduce excessive muscle tone.

The side-lying position has already been mentioned as a good neutral position for those children who exhibit excessive muscle tone in both supine and prone. Finnie (1975) suggested that by rolling the child from side to side, before and during dressing, the child will experience new positions, which results in excessive muscle tone being reduced or averted. Even softly talking to the child has helped in relaxing the child's tone prior to dressing. Since the child is less stiff in the side-lying position, there is greater opportunity for the child to

Figure 5.3. Child positioned prone over adult's lap to reduce excessive extensor muscle tone.

bring the hands and arms forward and establish eye contact with the hands and other body parts. This then may facilitate the process of developing visual and tactile body awareness and facilitate the beginnings of cooperation and assistance during dressing.

If the child has head and trunk control and can lift and use the hands without falling over, the sitting position may be appropriate for undressing and dressing. This position will encourage visual attention and participation in the dressing process (Williamson, 1987). The small child can be seated on the caregiver's lap or seated between the caregiver's legs while both are sitting on a couch or the floor. For the child with spasticity, sitting in the "valley" space created when the adult sits tailor-fashion enables the child to maintain flexion of the hips and knees (Connor et al., 1978). Other sitting positions include the child sitting on the corner of a large upholstered chair, in the corner of a room, on a corner seat or floor seat, or in a standard child's chair that provides whatever back, side, and foot support is necessary. Regardless of the means of supported seating, the caregiver should be sure that the child sits symmetrically. If muscle tone is excessive or increases as the child attempts to dress, the caregiver will need to develop positioning and handling techniques that reduce muscle tone. If muscle tone is inadequate, the caregiver can apply proprioceptive input to the top of the head, trunk and pelvis, and top of the knee while the child is seated. If muscle tone fluctuates, the caregiver can stabilize the child using the top of the head, back of the neck, lower back or hips, or top of the knees as key points of control. Another method of increasing stability is to provide a surface for the child to lean or push against or a handle to hold onto during dressing. For example, while pulling the pants up over the hips, the child can be supine on the floor with the hips and knees flexed and the feet pushing against the wall. In this position, using the wall as a stabilizer, the child can lift the hip and pull up the pants. This should not be used with the child who is tactually defensive or exhibits hyperextensive movements.

The child who has good head and trunk control and some mobility in the crawling, kneeling, and standing positions may be safer and more comfortable dressing while on the floor. Here the child can move freely from sitting for upper extremity dressing to supine, side-lying, or kneeling for lower extremity dressing.

Additional Suggestions for Dressing

Initially dressing the child in front of a mirror may enhance body image and concept. It is helpful to remember that the affected arm and leg should be dressed before the unaffected extremities (Payne & Reder, 1983). The adult must first straighten out the flexed arm before attempting to put it into a sleeve. If the toes curl up, making it difficult to put shoes on, flex the child's hip, knee, and ankle first. Flexing or bending the child's leg first will usually make it easier for the caregiver to straighten out the toes. Select clothing that is loose enough to be taken off or put on easily but not so large that the wrinkles and folds irritate the skin or the overall appearance is one of sloppiness.

Clothing Requirements

The physical characteristics of many conditions or syndromes may restrict the motoric and intellectual ability of the child to learn how to dress himself or herself with typical child's clothing. With minor alterations, the difficulties encountered by the child with spina bifida, cerebral palsy, or severe multiplehandicaps can attain various levels of independent dressing skills. Goldberry (1987) and Tingey-Michaelis (1983) have identified six components (physical limitations, design features, fasteners, fabric, wearing qualities, and fit) of appropriate clothing design for children with restricted movement. First, a few of the physical limtations can be dealt with by buying fuller cut clothing and making sure skirts and pants have elastic waistbands and tops have front openings. Second, clothes should be selected on the basis of simple lines, nonrestricting sleeves (e.g., raglan), or openings that are at the child's dexterity, strength, and prehension levels. A third component of appropriate clothing is that the fasteners should be easy for the child to manipulate, they should be adapted in such a fashion that a child with limited mental or physical abilities can be taught how to hold on to a large ring or leather strap attached to the zipper tab. Velcro strips or circles can be sewn on either side of the openings when the child cannot manipulate buttons or snaps. The fourth component is the comfort, easy care, and durability of the fabric. The wearing ability of the garment is the fifth component of appropriate clothes. The seams should be of the flat-fell type with double stitching under the arm and crotch area. The waistbands should include reinforced belt loops. Buttons need to be securely sewn. The sixth component requires that the fit be comfortable, allow for ease of movement, and provide a feeling of self-esteem. Williamson (1987) suggested that long zippers be constructed at the outside seams for those children wearing braces or a catheter bag.

In addition to the larger sized clothing, some children with limited movement (especially of fine motor functions) may need to have adaptations made to promote independent function. Simple changes to the child's clothes may be the determining factor of the success level of the child in functioning on his or her own. For example, pressure tape (also called Velcro tape) is easier to manage than snaps or buttons; elasticized waistbands on pants or skirts are handier than zippers and snaps; adding a metal ring through a zipper's tab makes it easier to grasp and pull; tube socks eliminate the problem of getting the heel positioned correctly; and slip-on shoes or pressure tape closures eliminate learning to lace and tie the shoe (Bailey & Wolery, 1984; Coley & Procter, 1985; Snell, 1983).

Other dressing considerations may be needed for the child who wears leg braces or arm splints, is confined most of the time in a wheelchair, or has a physical condition (scoliosis, kyphosis, or lordosis) that would alter the fit and comfort of the clothing. Other types of adaptations to increase range of motion are reaching tongs and long-handled shoehorns (Lederman, 1984).

Self-Dressing Program

Purpose

The purposes and reasons for establishing a self-dressing program, as listed by Whitman, Scibak, and Reid (1983b), are that it allows the child a chance to be self-sufficient and independent, allows the adult-in-charge (parent, teacher, or other staff members) to focus on preacademic or motor skills, and develops social acceptance when the dressing program includes a section on how to select appropriate clothes.

Prerequisites

Prerequisite skills for self-dressing, according to Snell (1983) and Bailey and Wolery (1984), are established attending skills, functional range of motion of the limbs, volitional arm movements, integrated postural and automatic reflex reactions, and social skills. The gross motor skills that are helpful in developing self-dressing skills include the ability to lean over and regain an upright posture, to raise one knee toward the chest while sitting on a bed or in a chair, and to stabilize and control trunk and arm movements while standing independently. The child should also be able to maintain a hand grasp (using thumb/finger opposition) needed to hold, pull, and push clothes on and off.

Snell (1983) suggested that if any of these skills are lacking they must be taught in lieu of the dressing skills. S. Henderson and McDonald (1973), on the other hand, indicated that it is not crucial that all basic tasks or concepts be learned prior to teaching dressing skills. They advocate teaching both the prerequisite and dressing skills together. It should be mentioned that the child with special needs may be slower in achieving both skills or may only learn one. Teachers and therapists must keep this fact in mind when setting up dressing programs, periodically reevaluate the child's progress, and be flexible enough to redesign the child's program when necessary. Van Etten and his coauthors (1980) stated that the training programs for children with profound handicaps will be more time consuming and more difficult to operate because of the short-term memory retention the children display when learning new skills. They also questioned the long-term effect, but did not rule out the inclusion of a dressing curriculum for this population.

Teaching Self-Dressing

Azrin, Schaeffer, and Wesolowski (1976) were able to train seven children with mental retardation to dress themselves within a 4-day period, averaging 5 hours of training sessions each day. Several guidelines suggested by Bailey and Wolery (1984), Coley and Procter (1985) and Snell (1983) all point to the fact that the success rate of self-dressing will greatly increase provided the following preliminary steps are included in the total program package. When at all possible, training should be done at appropriate times and in a natural setting. Training should also be done in the child's home and during times when dressing and undressing naturally occur. This infers active parent and staff participation in defining goals, teaching procedures, establishing several types and levels of reinforcers, and designing a functional and easy data system. If training within the home is not possible, specific dressing routines can be incorporated into the classroom or clinic schedule.

The Parsons Preschool Curriculum (Snyder-McLean, Sack, & Solomonson, 1985) stimulates and increases language development through a series of active play routines within the classroom. A 2-week routine usually employs a central theme, clearly identified roles that can be exchanged, and planned repetition and variation of roles (Snyder-McLean, Solomonson, McLean, & Sack, 1984). Going to the circus, a doctor's office, or the grocery store are examples of complex and detailed routines that easily can be designed and/or modified to fit the physical and mental limits of the children. These routines not only motivate language and communication but also provide opportunities to master motor, cognitive, and social skills. It's exciting to put on a ringmaster's outfit, a doctor's mask, or mom or dad's clothes. Learning to take turns entails taking off the clothes and switching roles. Many routines can be designed to include numerous dressing practices and to be a lot more fun than taking off and putting on one's own clothes over and over again.

Training programs should be initiated with the easiest garments and skills first, then later working on the refinement of skills necessary for garment closures. The success of the child with handicaps in independent dressing skills will be assured if training follows the normal sequential development of accomplishing undressing prior to learning to put on clothes. It also means that children find it easier to unzip, unbutton, or unbuckle than to secure these clothing fasteners. Clothes and fasteners should be enlarged during the first phases of training. The shirt, pants, socks, and buttons should be several sizes larger than the child's normal size for ease of position, control, and movement. Once the basic mechanics have been learned, the size of the clothing and closures can be reduced gradually. This method has proved to be more successful than using training boards or starting with the child's regular size, which may be too snug and restrictive of the child's movement.

A final self-dressing guideline is to train toward the establishment of generalization by using similar and different garments, in locations other than at home, and practicing with several other people besides the child's parents. This is best accomplished with active participation from the parents and child.

Training Techniques

The most effective way to train dressing skills is to use the principles of behavior management. Chapter 6 details and defines many of the procedures used to change behavior. The application of behavior management principles is reviewed in this section. In addition to selecting appropriate reinforcers, collecting baseline information, and setting a criterion level to measure progress, the task or garment to be taught should be broken into single teaching units (Copeland, Ford, & Solon, 1976). In other words, the teaching process of putting on a T-shirt needs to be broken into separate measureable steps. Each step is then *chained* together and comprises the training program. The number of identifiable steps may depend on the child's intellectual level, the amount of physical mobility, and the number of praises or rewards necessary for completion of a task. Putting on a T-shirt can be broken down into 7 (Copeland et al., 1976) or 17 (S. Henderson & McDonald, 1973) steps or even more depending on the child's needs. Table 5.4 shows the comparison between the 7- and 17-step methods.

Other aspects of behavioral management techniques useful for teaching a

Table 5.4. Comparison of two different forward chaining approaches to putting on a T-shirt

Procedure 1[a]	Procedure 2[b]
1. Reach toward shirt bottom opening.	1. Hold shirt bottom open with right hand.
2. Grasp bottom edge of opening.	2. Insert left hand into shirt.
3. Raise shirt opening.	3. With right hand, pull shirt over left hand so hand comes through sleeve.
4. Raise first arm to armhole.	
5. Flex arm.	
6. Put first arm into armhole.	4. Hold shirt bottom with left hand.
7. Raise second arm to armhole.	5. Insert right hand into shirt and through sleeve.
8. Flex arm.	
9. Put second arm into armhole.	6. Pull shirt over head.
10. Separate arms out.	7. Pull shirt down.
11. Slip T-shirt down arms.	
12. Position head opening on head.	
13. Lower elbows and arms.	
14. Pull hole over head.	
15. Grasp tail of shirt.	
16. Maintain hold.	
17. Pull shirt down to waist.	

[a]Adapted from Henderson and McDonald (1973).
[b]Adapted from Copeland et al. (1976).

child with special needs to dress or undress include forward versus backward chaining, shaping and fading, and prompting. Forward and backward chaining differ in regard to the point during training at which the child will be reinforced. If a reward is dependent on completion of the task, use of forward chaining delays the child's reward and makes reward contingent on learning to successfully complete all steps of the task. Backward chaining's advantage over forward chaining is that the child associates reinforcement with the completion of the dressing task from the beginning of training, which may help motivate the child to work toward completion when additional steps are added. Backward chaining is used in most cases to indicate what step will be reinforced first and at what step the training will be started (Fredericks et al., 1976; Snell, 1983), based on assessment of the child's existing skills and abilities. Whether to use forward or backward chaining is dependent on the particular skill taught and which way the child performs best (Copeland et al., 1976).

Shaping and fading procedures are two important techniques that give the adult constant feedback data as to whether the chaining steps are appropriate. Physical prompts can be faded when the adult can feel or see that the child is initiating or actively putting a leg into the pant leg. The status of the child's independent ability can be evaluated when the adult can start the movement with the child and notice that the child continues on with the remaining step. The child is trained by going through the entire chaining process with the heaviest emphasis on the step currently being trained. If training follows the natural dressing sequence, the adult will be able to shape any dressing skill.

TOILETING

Independent toileting skills are important self-help skills to learn and eventually enable a child to participate in educational, recreational, and social activities. The young mentally retarded child who has not attained toileting control is restricted from taking part in many of these functions, and the possibility for expanded self-help independence is significantly reduced. Failure to achieve toileting control may be the major barrier that separates the child with mental retardation from his or her normal peers. The older the child becomes without toileting skills, the more this self-toileting handicap will separate the child from society (Gallender, 1980).

There are many reasons why a child with mental or physical handicaps has not learned to control his or her toileting needs. Physical or neurological deficits may make the sensory awareness necessary to void or defecate difficult or impossible to learn. The child may have poor fine motor control, limited attending skills, numerous perceptual problems, or limited intellectual ability. In the past, this intellectual limitation has been interpreted as the main reason why individuals with mental retardation could not learn to toilet themselves.

Normal Development

The achievement of independent toileting skills signals a big accomplishment for all children and a great relief on the part of the parents or caregivers. Most children achieve bowel and daytime bladder control between the ages of 3 and 4 years (Adams, 1982; Copeland et al., 1976). This means the child is able to manipulate his clothing (provided the closures are easily manipulated), and can get to the bathroom with time to spare (minor accidents are expected), but may need help and reminders in wiping. Foxx and Azrin (1973b) developed a program that successfully trained 2-year-old children in less than a day. By the time the child reaches his or her sixth birthday, day and night control have been mastered (Adams, 1982; Bettison, 1982).

Problems and Concerns

For the child over 6 years and still in diapers, the lack of toileting control increases health problems. The child who is not toilet trained is subject to unsanitary conditions and other health problems such as skin rashes, sores, poor circulation, and a breakdown of skin tissues (Gallender, 1980; Semmel & Snell, 1980). According to Semmel and Snell (1980), the cause of skin breakdowns is the excessive pressure that occurs from a child remaining in one position over extended periods of time, poor circulation, or moisture remaining on the child's skin for long periods from elimination or sweating. Simple preventative techniques include frequent diapering and powdering, which will keep the genital and buttocks area dry and clean. Changing the child's position and increasing arm and leg movements by exercising on a regular basis would minimize sores and increase circulation.

Children with increased muscle tone have limited voluntary control over bladder and bowel movements and are often constipated. This in turn increases the muscle tone and discomfort these children normally have every day.

In the past, children still not toilet trained by the time they entered preschool or kindergarten programs were denied any type of formalized educational training. There has been a tendency to negatively judge a child's learning capability on the basis of the child's toileting skills (Whitman, Scibak, & Reid, 1983a). Fortunately this is no longer the case.

Children who need a specialized toilet training program may fall into one or several of the following categories: 1) mental retardation as the primary condition; 2) any number of mental, physical, or psychological components as a secondary factor; 3) an intelligence score of 20 or below; and 4) any type of physical limitation that may prevent complete independent gross and fine motor manipulation such as walking or pulling down pants (Gallender, 1980).

Prerequisite Skills

Just as there are an appropriate age and certain prerequisites for the nonhandicapped child before toilet training can be begun, the same conditions apply to the child with special needs. Prior to initiating a training program, it should be established that the child has numerous predictable dry periods (of at least 2 hours at a time and over several days) as well as regular patterns of elimination (Semmel & Snell, 1980; Van Etten et al., 1980). Sticking to a regular schedule of meals, exercise, and bedtime hours will help in regulating the bowel and bladder. A simple chart broken into half-hour slots over a 7-day period will document when the child is wet or dry and when a bowel movement has occurred.

Other useful established skills that speed the independent toileting control process are the ability to walk with or without assistance, the ability to indicate the need to use the toilet, the ability to remain in a sitting position for at least 5 minutes, and the ability to comprehend and follow through with basic instructions (Copeland et al., 1976; Snell, 1983). It is equally important to check to see if the child is consuming proper types and adequate amounts of solids and liquids to maintain a regular toileting schedule and if any prescribed medications would interfere with a toileting program by altering the child's mental or physical concentration or bowel and bladder function.

If the child is unable to maintain trunk control while sitting on a regular potty chair, adaptations can be made to the existing chair by adding back and side supports or hip and shoulder straps, or a commercial potty seat or chair that has these items as standard safety features can be obtained. A bar or knob can be attached to the front of the seat for the child to hold onto for support and a sense of security and to allow the abdominal muscles to relax (Finnie, 1975). The child's feet should always be supported either on the floor or with some type of foot rest. Adding grab bars on the wall next to the toilet will allow older children to get on or off the toilet by themselves.

Toileting Program

Bladder Management

A number of methods for training bladder independence have been tried with varying levels of success depending on the age of the child, the number of staff available, the degree of the child's physical or mental limitations, and the parents' commitment to use the program at home (Azrin & Foxx, 1971; Dayan, 1964; Ellis, 1963; Giles & Wolf, 1966; Lancioni, 1980; P. S. Smith & Smith, 1977). The two major types of toileting programs listed by Adams (1982) and Snell (1983) include the traditional (also called the schedule-based) method and the rapid training process. In addition, alternative bladder management necessitated by partial or complete loss of nerve innervention to the bladder or bowel is described.

Traditional Method

The traditional method requires extensive data recordings (up to 30 days) to ascertain when during the day the child is wet and the length of time the child stays dry. Over a period of time a pattern begins to emerge as to when the child wets or soils himself or herself. This is especially true when there is a regular meal and bedtime schedule that establishes a regular schedule for elimination. The program begins when the child is placed on the toilet or potty chair several minutes prior to the schedule of elimination. Praise is given for staying on the potty chair and for elimination.

Additional training skills such as pulling down or up underpants, walking independently to the bathroom, or learning to check if the pants are wet or dry can be emphasized as part of the general toileting program or separately at different times during the toileting program. It has been suggested by Fredericks, Baldwin, Grove, and Moore (1975) that initially the program be used only twice during the day and that the number of trials be increased gradually until the entire day is spent in toilet training. The program (20 minutes in length) consists of having the child go to the bathroom approximately 10 minutes prior to the usual time the child wets or soils himself or herself. If after 10 minutes the child has not eliminated, he or she is taken off the toilet. The next 10 minutes are broken into two equal periods where the child is taken to the bathroom and placed on the toilet during each 5-minute period. After a total of 20 minutes, the training is discontinued until the next scheduled training time. All successes are reinforced and any accidents or failures are essentially handled in a matter-of-fact manner. Although this method allows for a gradual concentration of toileting awareness and control, thus making for an easier transition into the daily classroom routine, it does mean a lengthy training period is required for a complete success and also carries a high probability of staff and parents losing interest in completing the program.

Rapid Training Method

The two versions of rapid toilet training most frequently used by classroom and institutional staff are the Azrin and Foxx (1971) and the Mahoney, Van Wagenen, and Meyerson (1971) methods. The Mahoney et al. method (and other variations) relies heavily on signal devices attached either to the child's training pants or to the toilet bowl that alert the child to the starting of urination. Once the association is made between the sound and the child urinating, the signal device can be faded and training proceeds to self-initiating control. The biggest difference between the traditional and rapid procedures is the amount of time required for the child to achieve complete toileting control. The rapid training procedure successfully trained individuals with retardation within 4–6 days and has been mastered by normal 2-year-olds in a matter of 4–5 hours (Bailey & Wolery, 1984).

Essentially, this intensive method requires the child and adult to commit themselves all day to the training program and nothing else. For the parent, this means no trips to the store, no washing or ironing clothes, no cleaning the house or visits to or from friends. The classroom staff must be sufficient for one adult to be assigned to train and maintain the data for the whole school day.

Baseline data are reduced to a minimum of 3 days or long enough to establish several 2–3-hour dry spells. This rapid technique employs continuous 30-minute training cycles that require the intake of as much fluid as possible (at least 8 ounces) at the start of every cycle. This increases the chance that the child will need to urinate as time passes. (It should be noted that during meals and naps, the training is temporarily postponed.) Ten minutes after drinking, the child is put on the toilet or potty seat for an established amount of time. This has varied from 5 minutes to the original 20-minute period that was used with male adults with retardation. Immediately after the child urinates, or at the end of the 5–10 minute period, he or she is taken off the potty, given assistance with clothing, and allowed to play. Every 5 minutes up to the end of the 30-minute cycle, the adult checks to see if the child has dry pants. If the child has dry pants, both verbal and physical praise are given. If an accident occurs, the child is helped into a pair of dry pants without negative commments but the child is told the reason the wet training pants are being removed. At the end of the 30-minute period, more liquids are given and the cycle is repeated.

Alternative Bladder Control Techniques

It is not uncommon for children with spina bifida to develop urinary tract infection (medically known as cystitis). This can happen when the muscles of the bladder do not fully contract or the sphincter muscle does not totally relax. The result is that some urine may remain in the bladder, causing a urinary infection. Urinary reflux occurs when urine backflows into the ureters, and, if not corrected, reflux can damage the kidneys.

Independent bladder control is difficult when there is partial or complete loss of nerve supply to that area causing a "neurogenic bladder," common with children with myelomeningocele (Orelove & Sobsey, 1987). The two types of neurogenic bladders (flaccid and spastic) both allow urine leakage. The flaccid muscles of the bladder wall cannot contract enough to eliminate all of the urine, resulting in leakage. Likewise, the spastic bladder causes dribbling because just a small amount of urine in the bladder causes involuntary contraction of the bladder. Therefore, the child will have frequent uncontrollable voiding. To correct the urinary problems of urinary backflow and involuntary leakage and at the same time assure full urinary evacuation, several bladder management techniques are taught to the parents and child. School personnel must become knowledgeable in the various techniques so continual care can be assured during school hours. Four methods are currently recommended depending on the child's needs and problems.

1. *Credé maneuver*—This is the first external manipulation the parents learn to do after each diaper change. The parent applies downward pressure on the abdomen over the bladder. This is not the ultimate technique in achieving continence, but it can be performed by the older child and it reduces the chance of infection by minimizing the amount of residual urine (Williamson, 1987).

2. *Internal catheter*—A small-diameter tube is inserted through the urethra and into the bladder. Urine then flows into a collecting bag that is strapped around the child's leg or waist.

3. *External catheter*—Used primarily by males, a condom-type covering is worn over the penis. A collection bag strapped to the child's leg allows easy removal when the child so chooses.

4. *Intermittent catheterization*—This technique has gained popularity over the past 10–15 years. The procedure is the same as for internal catheterization with the exception that when the bladder has emptied, the catheter is removed until the next scheduled emptying.

Recent Research

A 10-year study done by Uehling, Smith, Meyer, and Bruskewitz (1985) looked at the efficacy of an intermittent catheterization program (ICP) on 164 young children. The variables used to measure the efficacy of the ICP included the status of renal function, number of urinary tract infections, and degree of dryness. Fifty-two percent of the children (85) had been on the ICP over 5 years. Of these children, 81% were rated as dry with just an occasional accident (0% had numerous accidents), 92% had occasional urinary tract infections, and 70% had a stable renal status with only 13% listed as receiving a deteriorating renal level. Prior to the ICP, 40% of of the children were listed as having numerous urinary tract infections. Although the effect of the ICP did improve the quality of these children's daily lives, the authors pointed out that this technique does have its imperfections and limitations. Because of other interfering medications, urinary reflux, lack of sufficient dexterity to catheterize, and/or lack of privacy at school, the ICP did not prove to be a successful method for complete bladder elimination all the time.

The purpose of a study by Richmond (1983) was to modify the most frequently replicated toilet training method (Foxx & Azrin, 1973b) by reducing the time and effort required to toilet train young children. Four children with profound retardation between the ages of 32 and 46 months with limited expressive language skills were toilet trained during their preschool hours. The regular 30-minute cycle was reduced to 15 minutes during the first week, every

30 minutes the second week, every hour the third week, and every 2 hours during the fourth week the training was done. Simple correction procedures (the child was responsible for cleaning himself or herself and putting on dry pants) for accidents as well as rewards for dry pants were used as training methods. At the end of the fourth week, all of the children made substantial declines in toilet accidents and maintained similar rates even 7 weeks after training was terminated.

Bowel Management

Children with neural tube defects (spina bifida), tumors, cerebral palsy, severe multiple handicaps, and other similar central nervous problems have difficulty controlling their bowels. A common problem is either bowel incontinence or constipation. Chronic incontinence creates skin breakdown and odors. A bowel program both at home and at school gets the child moving about, changing positions and employing frequent toileting care, which is a good preventive program for the breakdown of skin tissue.

Long-term constipation has been identified as leading to "fecal impactions with leaking stool, distended bowel, hemorrhoids, foul breath, abdominal pain and vomiting" (Snell, 1983, p. 150). It has been noted that impacted stools in children with spina bifida can over time create damaging dilation of the colon (Williamson, 1987). Orelove and Sobsey (1987) explain that constipation occurs in part when children with varying handicaps are inactive, do not eat a high-fiber diet, consume only small amounts of fluids, and are in poor health. Constipation has been known as a common problem with children with cerebral palsy.

Similar problems previously mentioned with bladder incontinence are also noted when a child cannot control his or her bowel movements. When a child continues to wear diapers and is not changed regularly, skin irritations and a foul odor can develop. For a few children, bowel training has resulted in poor progress and frequent accidents. Sometimes this has occurred because the children did not understand some of the training techniques (e.g., verbalization of "grunting" sound to signal the child to begin intra-abdominal pressure) (Snell, 1983). A child's ability to manipulate and control his or her arm, hand, and fingers for "wiping, flushing, clothing arrangement and general cleanup . . . require finger dexterity and manipulation abilities to grasp, release, button and zip" (Gallender, 1980, p. 280). If these skills cannot be learned, the inability to maintain sanitary conditions can add to the child's health problems, and for an older child it may result in poor social acceptance.

A good bowel management program for any child with a central nervous system dysfunction centers on providing the child with a well-balanced diet that includes plenty of fluids (helps prevent constipation), raw fruit (skins included), a variety of vegetables, and whole grain products, and eliminates constipating foods such as bananas, milk products, or rice. An active exercise suited to the child's physical ability and interest also assists in bowel elimination.

Occasionally other means such as laxatives or glycerin suppositories are used to ease a child's discomfort due to constipation or impaction. Information needs to be shared among parents and school staff about the symptoms a child may exhibit that signal that the child is constipated or has an impacted stool. A decision must be agreed upon by the doctor and parents as to what type of medication to use, and the school staff should be supportive by recording the necessary information.

For those children requiring a surgical alternative for the evacuation of bowel contents, two procedures, a colostomy or an ileostomy, can be performed. In both procedures, a portion of the small intestine (ileum) or large intestine (colon) is brought out through the abdominal wall, allowing fecal matter to empty through the hole (stoma) and into an external collecting bag (Orelove & Sobsey, 1987). The external appliance consists of a faceplate with an opening in the center that fits around the stoma, a belt to hold the faceplate in position that goes around the child's abdomen, plus a collecting bag that fits over the stoma and faceplate.

Problems encountered with an ileostomy and colostomy include skin irritation around the stoma, such as an itching or burning sensation. This may be a sign that the appliance needs to be cleaned and changed because some of the fecal fluid is leaking around the stoma opening (M. Henderson & Mapel, 1984). Since the contents of the small intestine are liquid and known to be highly erosive to the skin, it is imperative that the appliance and surrounding area be checked and cleaned frequently. If the child is of school age, all adults involved with the child during school hours should be taught how to check, clean, and empty the collection bag and the surrounding area. M. Henderson and Mapel (1984) indicated that teachers and therapists need to contact the parents if they notice the following conditions:

1. Excessive bleeding from the stoma.
2. Copious watery diarrhea.
3. No passage of gas or fecal material from the stoma.
4. Pencil-thin feces.
5. Bloating (abdominal distention), pain, tenderness, fever, vomiting or increased irritability.
6. Redness and/or abrasion of the skin surrounding the stoma.
7. Any unusual out-pouching of the stoma. (p. 59)

New Research Approaches

A research study conducted by Whitehead et al. (1986) compared the effects of biofeedback and behavior modification in the treatment of 33 children (5 to 16 years old) who had bowel incontinence. During the biofeedback portion of the study, the children were instructed in sphincter muscle exercises while watching polygraph pen movements. In addition, each child was instructed to practice the exercises daily at home for the purpose of strengthening the sphincter muscles. Basically, behavior modification procedures included rewards and praise for successful bowel movements after every meal. Final results proved behavior modification combined with biofeedback could achieve bowel continence for a third of the children. Also, 64% of the group were able to reduce their frequent incontinency level to 50%. In the future, treatment programs may be based on this and similar studies. Therefore, the cooperation and involvement of the school staff need to be closely allied with the parents.

Conclusions

Teachers, parents, therapists, and caregivers need to approach toilet (bladder and bowel) training as a team effort. The establishment of any type of toileting routine, be it for bladder or bowel control, requires patience, perseverance, and motivation (Snell, 1983). It is critical to know the child's personality, to establish a rapport with the child and the parents, and to really work as a team. Not only do decisions need to be made about which method (traditional or rapid) or what type of variations will be used, but it must also be decided who will do the training, if the parents are willing to spend the time at home and if there is agreememt about the reinforcers that will be used. The team should ask themselves, in each individual case, if a reduced training time is used will the long-term effectiveness decrease? An in-depth study on the pros and cons of each method is recommended by the team prior to discussing and designing an extensive program. Readers are directed to the works of Adams (1982), Bailey and Wolery (1984), Bettison (1982), Orelove and Sobsey (1987), Semmel and Snell (1980), Snell (1983), and Williamson (1987) as well as the developers of the traditional (Fredericks et al., 1975) and the rapid (Azrin & Foxx, 1971; Foxx & Azrin, 1973b) training methods. Until the child can control his or her toileting needs at a socially acceptable level, the high stress level for adults and children will remain and learning opportunities will be limited.

_____ CHAPTER 6 _____
Behavior Management

Behavior management is defined as a way of changing the frequency of a response through the use of reinforcement after the response has been given (Kolderie, 1971). It is also defined as "a method of changing observable behavior through systematic application of appropriate reinforcers" (Chandler & Adams, 1972, p. 400). Therapists and teachers have used behavior management (also called behavior modification) techniques to change many types of behavior, from eye tracking (Mayberry & Gilligan, 1985) to self-injurious behavior (Lancioni, Smeets, Ceccarani, Capodaglio, & Campanari, 1984) to walking (Chandler & Adams, 1972; Hester 1981; Westervelt & Luiselli, 1975), dressing (Ford, 1975), and feeding (Leibowtiz & Holcer, 1974; Mann & Sobsey, 1975; Sobsey & Orelove, 1984) problems.

During the late 1960s and early 1970s professionals began applying behavior management techniques to the problems created by the numerous physical limitations exhibited by children with cerebral palsy and severe/profound retarded children (Forness & MacMillan, 1970; Lovitt, 1970; J. E. Martin & Epstein, 1976; Rice, McDaniel & Denney, 1968). Brain damage and abnormal muscle tone and the concomitant physical, mental, cognitive, and social problems of handicapped children interfere with everyday self-help skills; therefore they are referred to and treated by therapists and teachers instead of behavioral psychologists (Rapport & Bailey, 1985). Because of this, the basic terms and procedures of behavior management techniques must be explained and understood by therapists and teachers so that they can be incorporated into their repertoire as a regular treatment routine.

Goetz (1982) has stated that children with mental and/or physical handicaps do not learn effectively through trial-and-error methods, nor do such methods have long-lasting effects. If these children do try this method on their own, it is generally a slow, tiring process and does not last very long, because of either cognitive or physical limitations. This can explain why many children do not even attempt to try different approaches or why they are not reinforced for their initial attempts. In order for a behavioral change to occur, several procedures must be applied in a consistent and exacting fashion. First, data on behavior must be recorded and a behavioral baseline established so that both the need for modification and the relative success of a given intervention can be determined. Then an intervention based on one of the many behavior management techniques is employed to effect the desired behavioral change. Data recording, baseline, and intervention phases are discussed below, followed by definitions and descriptions of the various behavior management techniques that can be used to motivate the desired behavior change. Finally, examples are given of the use of various behavior management techniques in selected research studies.

TYPES OF DATA RECORDING

The success of behavior management programs depends on consistent observation and measurement of behavior. Numerous methods have been developed to look at and record responses, and they can be used on either a formal or an informal basis. R. V. Hall (1974) categorized measurement techniques into three different types: automatic recordings, permanent products, and observational recordings. *Automatic recordings* are used primarily in a controlled laboratory environment with animals or birds operating an electrical device that automatically records a response. A number of activities in the classroom can be measured by a *permanent product*. Teachers measure a child's knowledge in various subjects through tests, daily practice papers, or crafts projects.

The professional whose primary duty during the working hours is interaction with infants and young children finds *observational recording* the most appropriate way of measuring progress on individualized educational plan (IEP) goals. Many therapists and teachers use behavioral management techniques, specifically observational data recordings, in a haphazard and uninformed manner. They are then confused when they do not see the child making progress on a continual basis. Part of the problem stems from the errors made in observing and interpreting the targeted behavior. When asked to write down a child's preference during a free-choice play session, the three errors most frequently made are omission, commission, and transmission (Bell & Low, 1977). Information left out that should have been included is an *error of omission*. Incorrect information that should have been left out but has been included is an *error of commission*. *Errors of transmission* include correct information used incorrectly because the events are out of order as to when they really occurred.

It is very difficult to observe everything that is going on without the aid of systematic approach. One of the best ways to check the accuracy of an observational recording is through intrarater and interrater reliability checks. Reliability refers to the consistency of the observation. Intrarater reliability determines if a person can obtain the same results over two or more observational sessions. Interrater reliability measures the degree of consistency of two people observing the same behavior at the same time. Interrater reliability has a higher degree of objectivity than does intrarater reliability. Prior to performing a reliability check, the two observers should agree upon a definition and understand how the behavior is to be observed. This will avoid any unnecessary disagreements. Once all the definitions and instructions are worked out, a percentage agreement can be calculated. Count the number of agreed behaviors, divide the total number of behaviors into the agreed number and multiply by 100 to arrive at a percentage:

$$\frac{\text{No. in agreement}}{\text{Total possible}} \times 100 = \% \text{ agreement}$$

The type of data recording used during a reliability check (as well as during the training sessions) depends on the type of behavior to be observed.

Continuous Recording

Also called ancedotal recording, a continuous recording is usually written in a narrative style. The observer writes down everything the child does, including the target behavior. Any related event or events that occur before, during, or after the target behavior is performed should be included. This means some of the information is taken from memory and is susceptible to subjectivity (Bell & Low, 1977). Continuous recording takes a lot of time, and most people find it very difficult to write down everything that occurs. However, it may be beneficial in identifying a pattern for the cause of the behavior (e.g., the child who appears to start to fight when he is touched from behind later is determined to have a sensory integrative or tactually defensive problem). This type of recording can give clues for the use of a specific test or for the observer to record another behavior. The written report must be free from interpretative comments.

Event Recording

Instead of recording everything a child does, it may be more practical and convenient to record a specific behavior whenever it occurs. This can be done over a short period of time of minutes or extended over several hours. Event recording is easy because only a simple check or tally mark on a piece of paper is necessary. Some people find it more convenient to wear a golfer's wrist-counter or to make a simple bead counter that is attached to a belt (see Figure 6.1). This type of recording provides a general indication over a prescribed amount of time of how many times a behavior occurs.

Interval Recording

It may be more important for a teacher or therapist to know exactly when a child misbehaves during a specified time. For example, a 30-minute therapy session

Figure 6.1. The bead counter can be used as an easy way to record the successful completion of a task without relying on paper and pencil. For every correct response of the child's, the adult pulls a bead down on the string and charts the total after the session is over.

can be broken into five equal time periods. During each time period, the observer can indicate the number of times the child exhibits the target behavior or just mark whether or not the behavior was observed (see Figure 6.2). The information gained by the counting (Figure 6.2A) versus the indication (Figure 6.2B) style assists the therapist or teacher in redesigning the program so as to minimize any "down" time or the appearance of inappropriate behavior. In (Figure 6.2B) one does not know if in any of the squares marked "Y" there was a greater number of instances of inappropriate behavior because, as indicated, all squares receive the same value. R. V. Hall (1974) favored counted interval

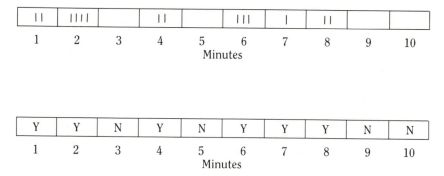

Figure 6.2. Recording number of times a behavior was observed during a 10-minute interval. *A,* Counting method. *B,* Indication method.

recording since it reflects both the frequency and a general duration of the behavior. It is also a good way of observing several behaviors at one time and assessing if there is a relationship between the behaviors. To be effective, there should be an additional person recording the behavior, not the adult working with the child.

Time-Sampling Recording

This approach, although similar to interval recordings, differs as to when the recording is done. Only at the end of each time interval does the observer check to see if the child is exhibiting the behavior. For example, at the end of every 10 seconds the adult would look to see if the child is attending to a task, or staying at the table, or doing the assigned exercises, and so on. Thus the recording is done only when each time period is over. The most convenient attribute of either interval or time-sampling recording is that the periods can be broken down into very small intervals. R. V. Hall (1974) indicated that time samplings are best for ongoing behaviors and that other behavior (e.g., intermittent) should be recorded using one of the other recording types. Also, Bell and Low (1977) suggested using time-sampling to determine the percentage of time spent engaging in the behavior or to determine reliability between two or more observers.

Duration Recording

The length of occurrence of a behavior may be more important to know than how often if occurs (R. V. Hall, 1974). This requires having a stopwatch on hand if one is recording to the nearest second. Otherwise, a clock or a watch can be sufficient for taking data when less precise measurements are needed.

Latency Recording

When instructions are given to a child, many times the complaint from the parents or staff is that it takes forever for the child to respond. Also, it may take repeated instructions before the child begins the behavior. This latency can be measured by starting a stopwatch once the instructions are given and stopped when the child starts the activity.

ESTABLISHING THE BASELINE

In order to design a behavioral management program, one must first determine whether there is a need for a behavioral change. This is usually done by establishing a baseline, recording the behavior without any kind of intervention procedure. Until there is information about the frequency of the behavior it is difficult to ascertain if the intervention phase is really affecting the desired change or if the behavior itself is really a disturbing factor or not.

Several sessions or days are needed to establish an average picture of the behavior. The exact number may depend on the targeted behavior and can be anywhere from 3 to 7 days. In order to rule out any interfering variables, which may drastically affect the behavior being observed, the baseline data should be collected, insofar as possible, at the same time, in the same room, and with the same person. Panyan (1975) suggested taking an interrater reliability check during the baseline phase to see if there is agreement as to the rate of occurrence of the behavior or skill and also to see if there is an agreement as to where to begin the first training step.

INTERVENTION

The intervention phase (also known as treatment or the experimental condition) refers to the period during which the intervention procedure used to change a behavior or skill is implemented. A mechanism to evaluate the treatment procedure can be used with many behaviors or skills. The consequence of that treatment modality is then observed and recorded as it affects the inappropriate behavior or poorly performed skill.

The treatment procedures are discontinued at some later point and there is a return to baseline observation. This measures the effectiveness of the intervention program and also is a way of checking to see if the criterion level needs to be changed. This second baseline check lasts only for a short time. Two or three days appears enough time to obtain an objective picture of the effect the intervention has had on the behavior. Generally, the intensity of the behavior will return toward the original level during second baseline procedure. An intensity very close to the original level may be an indication that the treatment procedure needs to be continued or changed. A pictorial graph can help determine the next approach (see below). A second intervention period begins once a decision has been made to continue the previous procedures or to make changes.

When the skill has been learned or the behavior is under control, the criterion level probably has been reached. This means that the reinforcements themselves have been successful, the rate and type of reinforcement do not need to be as intensive, the prompts and fading cues have been effective, and the child does not have to be reminded (verbally or physically) to perform the task or to behave appropriately. With many programs, researchers will go back several weeks or months later and recheck the level of the skill or behavior. This re-evaluation is known as a postcheck, and the primary aim is to observe whether the criterion level is where it was at the conclusion of the program or the responses have returned toward the original baseline readings. This type of program is called a *reversal design* (R. V. Hall, 1974) and helps to establish a checks-and-balances system of baselines, experimental conditions, and postchecks that can easily be learned by professionals and parents.

GRAPHING DATA

Line Graphs

Recording any type of behavior is done on individual data sheets using tally marks or numbers that are later averaged and then transferred to an easier and more readable profile sheet. Using graph paper, two lines are drawn that intersect at a 90-degree angle, and the point where the two lines meet is labeled "0" (see Figure 6.3). The vertical line is called the *y* or vertical axis or the ordinate, and the horizontal line is known as the *x* or horizontal axis or the abscissa. The label for the ordinate line is reserved for frequency, duration, rate, or percentage information. The abscissa labels the time or length of the program in minutes, hours, days, or sessions (Bell & Low, 1977; R. V. Hall, 1974). The raw data are placed on the graph using symbols such as a dot or an "X" or a small square on the intersecting point of the time and frequency lines (see Figure 6.3). Each added symbol is connected to the previous one by a narrow straight line. Lines should not be used between one phase of the program and another (e.g., from baseline to treatment or from treatment to the second baseline). Instead, a heavy vertical line is drawn between each phase of the reversal design. Also, if postcheck data are taken more than once, there are no connecting lines used between each postcheck session.

More than one behavior, skill, or step can be charted on the same sheet, which is known as *multiple baseline design*. For example, several children's

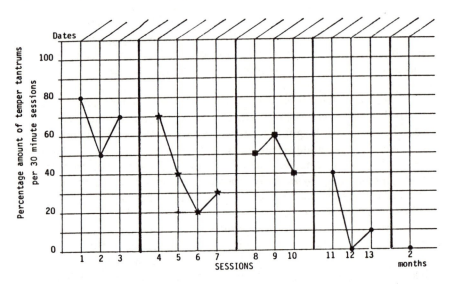

Figure 6.3. Example of a line graph representing temper tantrums per session over time.

responses to the same intervention program can be plotted on the same paper, which provides the examiner an overall visual picture of their progress.

Bar Graphs

Line graphs as described above are one of several ways of viewing the data. Another commonly used method is the bar graph. The horizontal version typically displays pretest and posttest results as well as baseline, treatment, and postcheck comparisons (see Figure 6.4). The vertical bar graph can be used to depict the number of items or percent correct.

BEHAVIOR MANAGEMENT TECHNIQUES

The following are a few of the behavioral management techniques used to reinforce behavior, change behavior, or teach new behavior.

Techniques to Reinforce Behavior

When a child is rewarded or praised immediately following a response to a stimulus this is known as reinforcement. Use of effective reinforcers increases the probability that the response will be repeated in the near future. In order for the reinforcer to make an effective change, it must be used right after the be-

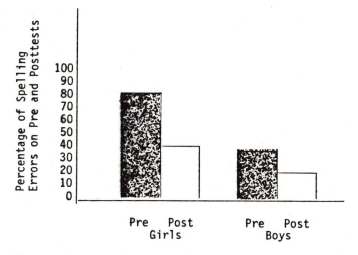

Figure 6.4. Example of bar graph representing pre- and posttest results on spelling tests.

havior is performed. For example, when a child with mental retardation imitates a circular stroke of a pencil on paper he is immediately praised for making the right shape ("Yes, you made a circle"), and the child makes another that results in more praise. Over time the child learns to associate the word "circle" with the shape and learns how to draw the desired shape.

No cookbook approach should ever be used when it comes to "dispensing" reinforcements for one simple reason. What is reinforcing for one individual may be extremely disliked by another. Each reinforcer must be individually chosen and varied on an intermittent schedule. Another point to remember is that effective reinforcers for a child may lose their initial impact if consistently presented too late or too soon, or if used too often.

According to Krumboltz and Krumboltz (1972), several myths have led the way to an aversive reaction to reinforcement as a behavior management technique. Reinforcement procedures are thought to be a way of coaxing the individual to perform the desired behavior. Coaxing is more appropriately defined as an attempt to persuade or flatter an individual into performing the behavior; "it is flattering attention following refusal, not praise following performance" (Krumboltz & Krumboltz, 1972, p. 25). Others consider reinforcement to be a type of bribe ("You do this and I'll give you that"). Although bribery does denote promise of reward for performing a task or behavior, the control of that behavior is dependent upon an external force to make the change, not a force from within the individual. Bribery as described by Krumboltz and Krumboltz is a misuse of reinforcement. Reinforcement procedures are not a panacea for behavioral problems or teaching new skills; there are limitations to the use of reinforcements. A lack of progress may result because the child is either psychologically or neurologically immature, the child cannot comprehend the instructions, the chaining steps are too complicated, or the child has no interest or desire in learning the targeted behavior.

Reinforcement Types

The type of reinforcement described above is known as *positive reinforcement,* as opposed to punishment (see below), which is a form of negative reinforcement. Either of these types of reinforcement will assure that there will be a response. Positive reinforcements are pleasing to the individual because they are either socially (primary type) or tangibly (secondary type) rewarding (Goetz, 1982). Socially, the person is receiving direct attention in the form of a smile, a hug, or a verbal compliment. The social praise can be either a general or descriptive response. *General praise* is telling the child that he is doing a good job but does not specify what part of a task was performed the best. There is nothing wrong in telling a child he is good or the job was well done, but the clinician should not forget to vary the general verbal praise. It is great to see a Down syndrome child smile and physically respond to "Give me five!" However, if the same general social praise is given over and over again, the child soon will not attend to the request at all. When this occurs, a behavior phenomenon called *satiation* develops wherein the reinforcement overloads the system and the child does not perform the skill as frequently. A repetitive verbal comment can have the same effect as putting the child on extinction (see below). Generalities are difficult for many handicapped children to interpret. Therefore, *descriptive praise* given in words that are understood by the child is more direct and to the point of what is being correctly performed. Chances that the child will retain the behavior are greater with descriptive than general praise. If the child knows he is doing a good job of putting the puzzle shapes in the right spot, the child knows exactly why the adult is pleased with his behavior.

Tangible reinforcers can be combined with or used in place of social reinforcers. For older children who may tire of continual verbal comments and who may need more concrete evidence that they are "doing a good job," something concrete will have more meaning. It will also have a stronger effect on changing the desired behavior. Tangible reinforcers are justified when a complex task needs more attention directed toward it or if the child learns better with concrete feedback (Goetz, 1982). Food is the basic and primary form of a secondary reinforcer. Therapists and teachers must remember even a child's favorite food will lose its effectiveness if that is the only type of reward used. It is for that reason that the examiner would be wise to evaluate what other foods are also a favorite of the child. Parents can be a valuable source of obtaining information about favorite foods at home. Also, it is a good idea to set up a special session where the child is given the opportunity to choose from several primary and secondary reinforcers. This can be done by watching what the child does, what the child plays with, and what the child verbally says he likes (Panyan, 1975). It is important to remember that a new skill will require more attention and should be frequently reinforced. This means reinforcements will be given often and in small amounts (i.e., small sips of juice every time a close approximation is achieved). To maintain a high level of interest several different types of reinforcers could be paired together.

Another type of tangible reward in the classroom or the therapy room, called *token reinforcement,* involves the use of poker chips, stickers, happy faces on a chart of paper, punched holes on a card, or plastic token tags. The advantages of tokens over edibles are that they are easy to administer, they are tangible, they allow the reward to be sectioned into smaller portions, and the child does not become satiated with them as quickly as happens with food (R. V. Hall, 1975). A set number of tokens are required prior to receiving a material reward (toy, book, etc.) or special privileges (favorite TV program, blow bubbles, eating out, ride tricycle, etc.). Once the desired behavior is on the way to being established or learned, the token system can be paired with verbal praise and gradually faded until just intermittent verbal praise maintains the acquired skill.

Reinforcements can also be applied with the knowledge of both the adult and the child. *Contingency contracting* is a written and signed agreement between the two designated individuals stating who will do what for how long and what will happen when the agreed behavior is completed. Older children, even those with physical or mental limitations, can understand the consequence of what happens when, for example, their toys and clothes get put away in the proper places, when the trash is taken outside when requested, or when five blocks are stacked. In order to maintain prolonged interest, a weekly record can be posted on the refrigerator at home or on a bulletin board in the clinic where colorful stars, shapes, or amusing stickers can be pasted on the chart. Acknowledgment on the part of the child of how many stickers are required at the end of the week in order to receive a reward will help motivate and maintain the child's interest.

Techniques to Change Behavior

Punishment

As a result of the use of rewarding a child for desirable behavior, punishment is very seldom necessary, but inevitably there will be times when the child will test the rules or will resist the commands of others and punishment of a particular design is needed. The most important parts of any punishment procedure are consistency and immediacy. Punishment is an important behavioral control, but in order to be effective, it has to be used very carefully. Once a behavior has been selected for punishment, if the punishment is not given each time the behavior occurs it will not work. Also, if the punishment is not given immediately or is delayed, the child will not know why he is being reprimanded. Two forms of punishment most likely to be used by therapists and teachers are timeout and overcorrection. Both procedures deal with the inappropriate behavior children with verbal and/or physical handicaps use to express their feelings of frustration, boredom, or anger, their desires, or their need for attention. What is important to remember is that the punishment or behavioral management procedures should fit the child and not the "crime." Also, this form of control or correction should not be used when a child is unable to understand what the punishment is for.

Timeouts

There may be times in the classroom or during a therapy session when a child may not want to do the assigned work and responds by acting out in a noncompliant manner (throwing toys, kicking adult under the table, spitting out food, looking away from the activity). Attending to the inappropriate behavior only reinforces the idea to the child that that behavior is a good way to get attention or avoid doing a task. Not attending to the behavior or removing the child from the stimulating environment effectively teaches appropriate behaviors. A simple timeout procedure is the adult turning his head away from the child or turning the child in his chair away from the activity. If the head- or chair-turning method is not effective, another technique physically removes the child from the area for a specified amount of time (usually just a matter of several seconds or a few minutes). Haphazard or inconsistent application of this procedure often makes the matter worse. This is because parents do not see any immediate positive end results and often discontinue the whole process much too soon. Timeout has been identified as a mild form of punishment (Goetz, 1982).

Before anyone tries timeout techniques it would be best to follow some of the guidelines of Creer and Cristian (1976) and R. V. Hall (1975).

1. Identify the target behavior.
2. Tell the child ahead of time what will happen if the inappropriate behavior occurs again.
3. Decide the length of timeout for the target behavior. The duration should be brief (no more than a few minutes). In the case of temper tantrums, for example, the child should be told that when he can stop crying or control himself, he can return to the activity or to the group.
4. If at the end of the timeout the behavior still exists, tell the child that the timeout will begin again.
5. When applying timeout, avoid unnecessary attention and be matter of fact about placing the child in timeout.

6. Every time the targeted behavior occurs, follow it with timeout procedures.
7. Do not leave the child unattended during timeout.
8. After the timeout period is over, praise the child for his appropriate behavior; attention should not be paid to the timeout period.

Neisworth and Smith (1973) stated that it is a good idea to let the child perform a positive task before returning to the prior activity. They also caution not to depend on timeout as a normal, everyday practice. Since timeout is more related to punishment, it is better to employ positive reinforcement for those behaviors and skills that are currently in the child's repertoire. Not all children or all types of behaviors benefit from timeout procedures. Teenagers respond to brief timeouts from television or telephone usage, but its effectiveness is greatly reduced if used as a regular control factor. Timeout for autistic-like behavior (self-stimulating activities such as twirling around or hand flapping) only provides an opportunity for those children to engage in more self-stimulating behavior (R. V. Hall & Hall, 1980).

Overcorrection

An overcorrection procedure is used to reduce inappropriate behavior. The procedure requires the adult to instruct the child to perform a task related to the inappropriate behavior over and over again. This is another procedure of punishment not used often by therapists and teachers, but studies have proved the procedure effective in controlling a high rate of self-stimulation (Foxx & Azrin, 1973a), self-injurious behavior (Agosta, Close, Hops, & Rusch, 1980) and aggressive-destructive behavior (Altman & Krupsaw, 1983). Relating to motor problems, Barrett and Linn (1981) used overcorrection to reduce stereotyped toe-walking in a 9-year-old mentally retarded boy. The youngster was required to sit in a chair while he tapped the toes of the one foot that was observed in the forefoot (tip-toe) position. The boy was instructed to tap his toe on three footprints (a left-center-right-center-left pattern) for 30 seconds with the heel held against the floor by the therapist. Baseline data indicated the rate of toe-walking was between 40% and 60% during physical therapy sessions and 100% during generalization probes after each therapy session. Postintervention data recorded in both situations indicate near 0% toe-walking using the positive practice overcorrection procedures. Those wishing more information on how to use the overcorrection procedures are directed to the works of Azrin and Besalel (1980).

Extinction

Behavior that has increased through the application of social or tangible reinforcements will decrease in rate and eventually cease if the reinforcing consequence no longer exists. This procedure is known as extinction and can be used as a forceful tool in changing behavior if used correctly. If a child has been getting attention for inappropriate behavior such as throwing a temper tantrum and his actions are no longer spotlighted (in fact, they are ignored), the tendency to repeat the tantrum behavior is diminished or eliminated, especially if the child is praised for other appropriate actions. R. V. Hall (1975) and Reynolds (1975) remind readers that it is common for behavior to increase in rate and intensity before it shows signs of decreasing. Therefore, when a child is deliberately put on extinction (e.g., for whiney behavior), and when that behavior then fails to get the desired results (attention, food, etc.), the behavior's rate then drastically drops. Aiken and Salzberg (1984) used a sensory extinction procedure (white noise through earphones) to substantially reduce stereotypic and inappropriate vocalizations (snorting sound and a high-pitched musical sound called "aria"). The procedure had little effect on hand-clapping noise.

Techniques to Teach New Behavior

Teaching any new skill to a child with mental or physical impairment requires careful planning. Additional time is required in setting up a systematic program that will assure successful independent completion of a task. Several procedures used to achieve independence in new skills or behaviors include chaining, shaping, prompting, and fading. Panyan (1972) described the relationship and effect each procedure has on the others. The chaining process combines steps previously learned with related new steps. Shaping involves reinforcing one step at a time and not expecting the other steps to be praised as intensely. Fading helps the child learn the task without extensive external cues (not as many physical prompts or as many social or tangible rewards). Reinforcements are the means by which the child learns more and more steps.

Chaining

Basically, chaining divides a skill (e.g., brushing teeth) into a series of behaviors that are "linked together in sequences where one behavior produces a reinforcer for a preceding and a cue for a subsequent behavior" (Neisworth & Smith, 1973, p. 69).

With any new skill one ventures to learn, it takes time. It is best mastered by going slowly and repeating portions of the entire task either cognitively or motorically until the task is learned. Learning a new musical piece on the piano is best done by concentrating or repeating smaller portions more often rather than practicing the entire piece all the time. The same principle can be applied to the child with handicaps by breaking a skill into several sections and concentrating on each section one at a time. There are some skills best taught as forward chaining, where the child receives the reinforcement upon completion of step 1. Next, the reward is given only when steps 1 and 2 are completed. This continues until all the steps are learned. Examples of skills best taught with forward chaining are bathing (Panyan, 1975); cognitive skills such as learning the alphabet, music, or poetry (R. V. Hall, 1975); and learning to walk and toilet training (Goetz, 1982).

Backward chaining reverses the emphasis of reinforcements to the last step being rewarded first. Activities of daily living (ADLs), also called self-help skills, which have a high level of motor movement involvement, require less learning time using backward chaining than if taught as a forward chaining method (Weber, 1978). Skills required in teaching a child to be independent in handwashing, using utensils, tying shoelaces, and dressing can be remembered sooner if, for example, after the child puts on a polo shirt, the first reward is given after the child pulls the shirt down to his waist. Ford (1975) used backward chaining to teach an 8-year-old boy with severe retardation to take off his shirt using five chaining steps in 16 sessions. Copeland and her coworkers (1975) as well as S. Henderson and McDonald (1973) have divided dressing with many types of apparel (trouser, sweaters, coats, belts, snaps) into basic chaining steps. Depending upon the physical and mental abilities of a child, the staff may wish to expand or combine these steps. Table 6.1 shows an example of a dressing chaining process.

Shaping

Shaping as defined by Panyan (1975) begins with the child's current level of ability and slowly increases until all steps are accomplished. The guidelines for achieving a high level of accomplishment are as follows:

1. Define the desired terminal behavior and measure the operant level.
2. Find a beginning behavior that the person can perform and which resembles the desired terminal behavior.
3. Break the target behavior into graduated steps, beginning with the easiest and ending with the terminal behavior.
4. Have the person perform each step, reinforcing each one as it is successfully accomplished.
5. If a step is not performed, go back to an easier step or divide the step into smaller steps.
6. Continue the procedure until the person is performing the terminal behavior before being reinforced. (R. V. Hall, 1975, p. 26)

Guiding the child toward the terminal behavior can be done by the use of physical prompts (physically guiding the child's arm or hand through the movement), verbal prompts (the use of specific words that evoke a response with each trial), or gestural prompts (often paired with verbal prompts) using hand motions such as sign language (R. V. Hall, 1974).

Table 6.1. Forward chaining process for putting on a polo shirt

Trainer		Child
Step A:		
1.	May assist	1. Holds shirt bottom with right hand on cue
2.	Helps child insert left hand and arm into shirt bottom	2.
3.	Helps child pull shirt so left hand comes through left opening	3.
4.	Helps child bring left hand to cue	4.
5.	Helps child insert right hand into shirt bottom and up through right sleeve opening	5.
6.	Assists child in putting shirt over head	6.
7.	Assists in pulling shirt to waist	7.
Step B:		
1.		1. Holds shirt bottom with right hand on cue
2.	May assist	2. Inserts left hand and arm in shirt bottom
3.	Helps child pull shirt so left hand comes through left sleeve opening	3.
4.	Helps child bring left hand to cue	4.
5.	Helps child insert right hand into shirt bottom and up through right sleeve opening	5.
6.	Assists child in putting shirt over head	6.
7.	Assists in pulling shirt to waist	7.
Step C:		
1.		1. Holds shirt bottom with right hand on cue
2.		2. Inserts left hand and arm into shirt bottom
3.	May assist	3. Pulls shirt so left hand comes through left sleeve opening
4.	Helps child bring left hand to cue	4.
5.	Helps child insert right hand into shirt bottom and up through right sleeve opening	5.
6.	Assists child in putting shirt over head	6.
7.	Assists in pulling shirt to waist	7.
Step D:		
1.		1. Holds shirt bottom with right hand on cue

continued

Table 6.1. *continued*

Trainer		Child	
2.		2.	Inserts left hand and arm into shirt bottom
3.		3.	Pulls shirt so left hand comes through left sleeve opening
4.	May assist	4.	Brings left hand to cue
5.	Helps child insert right hand into shirt bottom and up through right sleeve opening	5.	
6.	Assists child in putting shirt over head	6.	
7.	Assists in pulling shirt to waist	7.	
Step E:			
1.		1.	Holds shirt bottom with right hand on cue
2.		2.	Inserts left hand and arm into shirt bottom
3.		3.	Pulls shirt so left hand comes through left sleeve opening
4.		4.	Brings left hand to cue
5.	May assist	5.	Inserts right hand into shirt bottom and up through right sleeve opening
6.	Assists child in putting shirt over head	6.	
7.	Assists in pulling shirt to waist		
Step F:			
1.		1.	Holds shirt bottom with right hand on cue
2.		2.	Inserts left hand and arm into shirt bottom
3.		3.	Pulls shirt so left hand comes through left sleeve opening
4.		4.	Brings left hand to cue
5.		5.	Inserts right hand into shirt bottom and up through right sleeve opening
6.	May assist	6.	Puts shirt over head
7.	Assists in pulling shirt to waist	7.	
Step G:			
1.		1.	Holds shirt bottom with right hand on cue
2.		2.	Inserts left hand and arm into shirt bottom
3.		3.	Pulls shirt so left hand comes through left sleeve opening

continued

Table 6.1. *continued*

Trainer	Child
4.	4. Brings left hand to cue
5.	5. Inserts right hand into shirt bottom and up through right sleeve opening
6.	6. Puts shirt over head
7. May assist	7. Pulls shirt down to waist

From Copeland, M., Ford, L., Solon, N. (1976). *Occupational therapy for mentally retarded children* (p. 100). Rockville, MD: Aspen Publishers, Inc.; reprinted by permission.

Fading

As the child shows signs of learning a new skill or developing more appropriate behavior, as shown from the data sheets, the amount of physical or verbal prompting can be phased out. This means the amount of assistance can be gradually removed. This also means that obtaining any type of reward requires more work on the part of the child. Copeland and others (1976) designed a series of training programs for dressing and eating skills (see Table 6.2) that depicts how physical prompts help develop independent skills.

EXAMPLES OF USE OF BEHAVIOR MANAGEMENT TECHNIQUES: SELECTED RESEARCH STUDIES

Behavior management techniques have been used successfully in a program with patients who complained about wearing leg braces (Gouvier et al., 1985). The program, carried out by the physical therapist with assistance from the occupational therapist and psychologist, resulted in a more consistent wearing program for longer periods of time throughout the day.

Westervelt and Luiselli (1975) used primary and secondary reinforcement

Table 6.2. Physical prompts used to achieve independent spoon usage

Trainer		Child
Step A:		
1.	Places child's hand around spoon handle	1.
2.	Assists to fill spoon	2.
3.	Guides child's hand to mouth	3.
4.	Inserts food into mouth	4.
5.	May assist	5. Removes food with lips
6.	Returns spoon to plate	6.
Step B:		
1.	Places child's hand around spoon handle	1.
2.	Assists to fill spoon	2.
3.	Brings food to 3″ of mouth	3.
4.	May assist	4. Inserts food into mouth
5.		5. Removes food with lips
6.	Returns spoon to plate	6.
Step C:		
1.	Places child's hand around spoon handle	1.
2.	Assists to fill spoon	2.
3.	Brings food ½ way to 3″ from mouth	3.
4.	May assist	4. Brings food 3″ from mouth
5.		5. Inserts food into mouth
6.		6. Removes food with lips
7.	Returns spoon to plate	7.
Step D:		
1.	Place child's hand around spoon handle	1.
2.	Assists to fill spoon	2.
3.	Brings food ½ way from plate	3.
4.	May assist	4. Brings food ½ way to mouth
5.		5. Inserts food into mouth
6.		6. Removes food from lips
7.	Returns spoon to plate	7.
Step E:		
1.	Places child's hand around spoon handle	1.
2.	Assists to fill spoon	2.
3.	May assist	3. Brings food from plate to mouth
4.		4. Inserts food into mouth
5.		5. Removes food with lips
6.	Returns spoon to plate	6.

continued

Table 6.2. *continued*

Trainer	Child
Step F:	
1. Places child's hand around spoon handle	1.
2. May assist	2. Fills spoon with food
3.	3. Brings food from plate to mouth
4.	4. Inserts food into mouth
5.	5. Removes food with lips
6. Returns spoon to plate half way	6.
7.	7. Returns spoon rest of way
Step G:	
1. May assist	1. Places hand around spoon handle
2.	2. Fills spoon with food
3.	3. Brings food from plate to mouth
4.	4. Inserts food into mouth
5.	5. Removes food with lips
6. May assist	6. Returns spoon to plate all the way
Step H:	
1.	1. Places hand around spoon handle
2.	2. Fills spoon with food
3.	3. Brings food from plate to mouth
4.	4. Inserts food into mouth
5.	5. Removes food with lips
6. Touch wrist lightly with downward tap	6.
7.	7. Returns spoon to plate

From Copeland, M., Ford, L., Solon, N. (1976). *Occupational therapy for mentally retarded children* (p. 148). Rockville, MD: Aspen Publishers, Inc.; reprinted by permission.

procedures to successfully get a child with physical handicaps to pull to stand and then push off to walk. Both shaping and fading procedures were employed to change the reinforcements from edibles to both verbal praise and physical contact whenever the chaining step was achieved. The authors also used inter-rater reliability to collaborate the employment of reinforcers to increase motor independence.

Hester (1981) was successful in increasing standing and walking behavior of a 14-year-old female with profound retardation with 30-minute individual sessions over 24 days. Positive reinforcement included physical (pat on the back), social ("Good, Mary"), and edible (candy divided into quarters to avoid satiation) reinforcers. Fading procedures were used to diminish the physical prompting used from firmly holding on to the girl's arm as they walked to just an initial light touch on the elbow. Unfortunately, a postcheck 2 months after the program ended revealed the child's responses had returned to the baseline level. The behavior management procedures were correct; inconsistent staff employment appeared to be the cause of the breakdown of the reinforcement procedures.

Six children with cerebral palsy who had a strong reverse tailor sitting pattern (also called W-sitting) were trained to increase the frequency and duration of long-sitting with proper anterior pelvis tilt (Bragg, House, & Schumaker, 1975). This was accomplished through the use of positive social praise and prompting.

Chandler and Adams (1972) were able to increase the number of independent steps taken by a 7-year-old boy with multiple handicaps by turning on a radio when walking began and turning it off when the boy stopped taking steps. This produced erratic results so a second reinforcer was introduced, which increased the number of independent steps with a more consistent rate. A positive side effect from this study was an increase in the child's social interaction among staff and peers.

Horner (1971) developed a 10-step procedure to teach a child with mental retardation and spina bifida to use crutches independently. The child was first taught, as a prerequisite to crutch training, to hold on to both sides of parallel bars, next to pull to a standing position, and then to walk the length of the parallel bars. After the six steps of parallel walking were mastered, the crutches were introduced. Reinforcement (root beer drink) was contingent upon completion of the previous step or steps plus the present chaining step. Although the child did learn to walk with the aid of crutches, it was not without difficulty. Problems consisted of decreasing motivation and fatigue, which resulted in temper tantrums or crying spells. The study provides a good example of the steps to include and some of the expected behaviors that must be dealt with prior to replicating these procedures.

Another study done by Manella and Varni (1981) with similar behavioral reactions was with a 4-year-old child who had a repaired myelomeningocele. In this study the authors taught the child to stand up from a horizontal position using the aid of the crutches, by first rolling over to the prone position and then to the four-point position. If training is to be done in the home by the parents, this chaining procedure appears to be more practical than that used in the previous study. Tangible reinforcers in the form of stuffed toys as well as social reinforcement from the therapist were used as a motivating factor. Inappropriate behavior (crying, tantrums, deliberately falling, or refusing to move) was essentially ignored. Increasing self-motivation was the primary factor in getting this child to walk with crutches independently. Results indicated the home and clinic intervention program helped increase the child's motivation to ambulate on her own. It was noted that muscular strength had also increased flexibility and endurance while performing tasks.

Hill (1985) reviewed studies that applied behavior modification techniques to motoric problems associated with cerebral palsy. Using a developmental approach, the author looked at those studies that used specific behavioral techniques to gain head control, perioral movements, fine motor manipulation, balance, and relaxation skills. Head control was gained through aversive conditioning in one study, but most researchers used social reinforcement. Mechanical devices used to teach head control included head-position trainers (helmets) to electronically measure the head position and electromyographic biofeedback. A common oral problem with children with cerebral palsy is drooling. Hill found numerous methods used to control mouth, jaw, and throat movement, ranging from shaping procedures to aversive auditory consequences, food, tokens, social reinforcement, and visual graphs. To increase arm and hand movements, researchers have employed various electronic and electrical equipment to provide visual and auditory feedback for both the therapist and child. Independent walking has been trained by reinforcing successive approximations as well as praise and attention. To increase leg or ankle movement, several studies researched by Hill (1985) found either an electrogoniometer or an electromygraphic biofeedback machine gave the necessary stimulus to improve range of motion.

The persistence of primitive reflexes is a common diagnostic sign of severe/profound levels of mental retardation and cerebral palsy. The most frequently exhibited primitive reflex is the asymmetric tonic neck reflex (ATNR). The motor response of extending one arm (on the face side) and flexing the other arm (on the skull side) when the head is actively or passively turned sideways interferes in many self-help (eating, dressing) and academic activities. Lee, Mahler, and Westling (1985) constructed a foam rubber headpiece that was attached to a commercial feeder seat in order to reduce the high incidence of the ATNR during lunch time. Portions of the foam rubber apparatus were cut out to make room for the child's head, neck, shoulders, and upper trunk area, and it did not restrict movement or alter the response of the tonic labyrinthine reflex. The height of the foam was "approximately 2.54 cm behind both eyes" (Lee et al., 1985, p. 619). Physical fading procedures were used with 12 separate reductions of no more than 1.58 cm with each cutback. Not only were the number of ATNR incidents eliminated to zero, but the average percentage of correct bites in the midline position rose to 100 for most of the study's duration. The authors stated that the reason for the success of the intervention is only speculative. First, the headpiece reduced a high percentage of peripheral visual distractions, which tend to elicit the ATNR. Second, the headpiece maintained the child's head in the midline position and was reinforced by the presentation of food. Continued food ingestion reinforced head control even without the headpiece in position. Third, the verbal praise, physical prompting, and additional attention given when the child's head was in midline may have been socially reinforcing more appropriate eating habits. In any event, the procedures designed proved beneficial to this 11.5-year-old girl with multiple handicaps. The authors recommend similar investigations to further analyze the procedures.

Riordan, Iwata, Finney, Wohl, and Stanley (1984) looked at the the problem of food refusal of four children with handicaps and the ineffectiveness of currently practiced methods of forced feeding, intravenous feeding, and various types of gastric tube feedings. The primary reasons these methods are viewed as ineffective are that they do not reinforce normal feeding behavior, they are themselves associated with health risks, and they are not conducive to a positive parent-child relationship. Contingencies through the use of social praise, access to preferred foods, brief periods of playing with toys, and forced feedings brought about on the child's part an acceptance of food ingestion and a general reduction of food expulsion in all four subjects. The authors believe the presentation of a preferred food after accepting the target food might have influenced the reduction of further food refusal and reinforced swallowing. One of the subjects made better progress when praise and the opportunity to play with toys was offered. A side effect of this study was that the subjects would also accept foods that were not a part of the food selection that was given to them during the study.

CONCLUSIONS

In the areas of motor development and self-help skills (whose achievement is primarily dependent upon motor ability) the behaviorists have been successful in expanding knowledge of how to effectively train a child with developmental disability in skills pertaining to independent motor function. This does not mean that teachers, therapists, parents, or other allied health personnel have all their questions answered or concerns solved. The understanding of how to use behavioral management techniques is just now in its infancy. More research needs to be done by teachers and therapists to show how the behavioral approach will or will not benefit the child with handicaps, and his or her parents and siblings.

CHAPTER 7

Health/Safety Procedures and Physical Transfers

HEALTH/SAFETY PROCEDURES

Between the legislative enactment of Public Law 94-142 in 1975 and Public Law 99-457 in 1986, physically and medically fragile infants and children have been: 1) surviving earlier life-threatening situations, 2) remaining in the home environment, and 3) involving the entire family in infant and early childhood intervention programs. As infants, toddlers, and preschoolers, these children still will require frequent medical check-ups or perhaps will need to be scheduled for specific therapy intervention sessions. Many of the children will be dealing with poor motor control, seizures, and susceptibility to upper respiratory illness. It is for these reasons and others that a child may develop frequent colds, contract a number of the common communicable illnesses, or require care for accidents. This means teachers, therapists, and parents must be knowledgeable in first-aid techniques and be able to recognize and deal with medical emergencies. A few of these children will have limited means of communicating to their parents and others when and where they feel discomfort, which is an important reason that parents, teachers and therapists be knowledgeable in safety techniques.

Any person employed by a program that enrolls children with disabilities should be familiar with both the symptoms and the treatment procedures of the physical and medical problems associated with this population. Children with mental, medical, and physical handicaps are at high risk for further complications if certain precautions are not taken in advance. These children are just as susceptible to getting childhood illnesses such as measles, chicken pox, colds, or strep throat as nonhandicapped children. Because of the children's tendency toward more frequent upper respiratory infections, however, they may take longer to recover. Because of these factors, state regulations are designed not

239

only for licensing purposes but to assure parents that their child will be receiving high-quality care. Each center should have a listing of the phone numbers of parents, hospital, poison control center, ambulance, police, and fire station. In a separate file and in each child's folder should be release forms signed by the parent authorizing emergency medical treatment. The staff must also be familiar with the various medications (their effects and side effects) and basic safety precautions with regard to lifting and transferring children.

First Aid Principles

Programs affected by state licensing regulations must adhere to specific requirements, one of which is that all personnel must pass a first aid course. Everyone should be familiar with were the first aid supplies are kept and also of the contents of the first aid kit. The first aid kit should be kept in the same place, fully stocked, and items should be replaced as they are used. Among the most widely used supplies included in the kit are sterile gauze pads and bandages, scissors, tweezers, and safety pins, plus assorted items for insect bites, fainting, or to induce vomiting. First aid principles to remember that will help lessen unnecessary confusion about what to do in order that teachers and therapists can respond quickly, efficiently, and effectively are listed below:

1. Stay calm and in control of the situation.
2. Always remain with the child. If necessary, send another adult or child for help.
3. Don't move the child until the extent of injuries or illness can be determined.
4. Quickly evaluate the child's condition, paying special attention to an open airway, breathing, and circulation.
5. Carefully plan and administer appropriate emergency care. Improper treatment can lead to other injuries.
6. Don't give any medications unless they are prescribed for certain lifesaving conditions.
7. Don't offer diagnoses or medical advice. Refer the child's parents to health professionals.
8. Summon emergency medical assistance if the injury or illness is too difficult to handle alone.
9. Always inform the child's parents of the injury and first aid care that has been administered.
10. Record all the facts concerning the accident and treatment administered; file in the child's permanent folder. (Marotz, Rush, & Cross, 1985, p. 218)

Some of the more familiar first aid conditions and the treatment procedures for those injuries or illnesses that may affect children with handicaps are discussed in this chapter. Readers wishing an in-depth description of first aid and emergency management techniques are directed to the excellent work of Marotz and her colleagues (1985).

Childhood Illnesses and Injuries

Communicable illnesses (e.g., chicken pox, colds, dysentery, encephalitis, measles) can be spread from child to child if a pathogen (bacteria or virus) is present in one child and is transmitted to other children. The pathogen leaves the host individual via the respiratory (nose, throat, lungs) and intestinal tract and enters another child by means of the skin, respiratory, or digestive tract (Marotz et al., 1985). There are both direct (touching, coughing, sneezing) and indirect (toys, water, utensils, animals) methods of transmitting communicable illnesses from one person to another person.

Once the pathogen has entered the child's system, there are, according to Marotz and her colleagues (1985), several stages of progression (incubation, prodromat, acute, and convalescence) that the illness takes, and each stage will vary in duration depending on the specific illness. The incubation stage varies with each illness but it is the period of rapid growth of the organism. This is the time when most communicable illnesses are in the contagious stage, even before any of the symptoms appear.

The next stage, prodromat, is when the beginning symptoms are apparent, such as a slight sore throat, headache, or a general feeling of restlessness or irritability. Because these symptoms may be of low intensity, the parent or teacher may not be aware that the child is highly contagious and will still send their child to the day care center or preschool classroom.

The stage when the symptoms are definitly apparent and easily recognized is called the acute stage. For example, the chicken pox blisters are rapidly erupting or the cold symptoms of runny nose, cough, and watery eyes are in full bloom. The child continues to be highly contagious during this time.

The last stage of an illness is the convalescent or recovery stage, during which the symptoms gradually disappear. The child is on the road of recovery when the chicken pox blisters are dry and scabbed over or the child's cold no longer keeps him or her coughing all day or night and the runny nose no long requires constant tissue care.

Parents and teachers/therapists need to work together in knowing and reporting to each other the early signs of an illness. The center's or school's policy on when and why children should remain home should not only be in writing but be discussed with the parents individually and if possible at a parent's meeting.

Any time children are gathered under one roof for any length of time, communicable illnesses are inevitable. With an awareness of the various symptoms, careful planning, and established guidelines, the severity of the illness and number of children who contract the illness can be kept to a low level. There is a tendency for the parents to bring their child back to school too soon. The teacher should communicate to the parents the importance of keeping the child home until he or she is fully recovered to avoid infecting the other children in the classroom.

Descriptions of the more common injuries or illnesses and the treatment procedures that pertain to children with handicaps are given below.

Abrasion

An abrasion is a rubbing away of an area of skin caused by friction of two surfaces. When moving on a carpeted floor, children with spasticity tend to hyperextend their entire body and pull or drag themselves across the surface, creating friction between the carpet and the skin. This abnormal movement pattern can develop floor or carpet burns, which should be treated like any minor injury.

Bleeding

If a child is bleeding from the nose, arm, leg, trunk, or face area, apply direct pressure over the area using a clean cloth or gauze pad. If direct pressure alone does not control the bleeding, apply pressure on the nearest pressure point (Table 7.1) while continuing direct pressure. Elevating the extremity may help stop the flow of blood. After the bleeding has stopped, apply a bandage of the appropriate size. A tourniquet band applied to an arm or leg should be used only in an extreme emergency and only after direct pressure and pressure point procedures have been tried. A narrow band of cloth or a tie can be wrapped around the limb just above the wound and tied in a knot. Insert a stick or peg just under the knot and twist it until the bleeding stops; secure the stick or peg in place. Mark somewhere on the child what time the tourniquet was applied, do not loosen the band, and seek medical help immediately.

Table 7.1.   Pressure points

Area	Technique
Scalp	Place the thumb on side of face in front of the child's ear (near the temple).
Face	Apply pressure over the hollow area of the cheek.
Neck	Press the fingers on side of the neck and apply pressure toward the back of the neck. This will avoid applying pressure near or on the windpipe (larynx).
Chest	Place the thumb in the hollow space behind the child's collarbone.
Arm	Place the thumb on the outside of the arm and position the fingers between the biceps and triceps muscles. Apply pressure toward the bone.
Hand	Hold the child's hand palm up in your own hand with the thumb over the wrist area. Apply pressure downward.
Leg	Position the heel of the hand on the inner side of the affected leg near the crease of the groin. Pressure is applied downward toward the femur bone.

Adapted from Green (1977).

In the case of a nosebleed, have the child sit down and lean forward, then apply direct pressure to the affected nostril or pinch the nose for about 5 minutes. Leaning forward "allows the blood to exit through the mouth so that it does not choke the youngster or obstruct the airway" (Johnson, 1981, p. 40). If the bleeding continues, roll up a small gauze pad and pack it into the nose, then pinch the nose up to 10 minutes (M. I. Green, 1977). If after careful checking the bleeding has stopped, carefully remove the gauze pad.

Blisters

The braces worn by children with cerebral palsy, spina bifida, or those children who have multiple handicaps are generally attached to high-top, hard-soled shoes. If new, these shoes can cause blisters on the back of the heels of the children's feet. Because of the loss of nerve innervation to the lower extremities or inadequate communication skills, a number of children lack the ability or knowledge to be able to inform anybody that their heel hurts. Parents should be reminded to check carefully when they remove the braces and shoes for any blisters or beginning signs of blistering, such as redness of the skin. Treatment of blisters should be directed toward protecting the area from infection. This may mean not wearing the shoes while the healing process takes place. Do not break the blister; if it is broken, wash the area with soap and water before covering the blister with a bandage (Marotz et al., 1985).

Breaks and Sprains

Broken bones, sprains, or strains can occur to children with uncoordinated movements due to hypertonia, hypotonia, or seizures. If a child should fall and fracture or dislocate an arm or leg, the staff member should immobilize the extremity. Depending upon the severity of the fracture, the extremity can be immobilized using a splint made of pillows, magazines, broomstick, boards, tongue depressors, or even pencils. The temporary splint can be secured with a belt, string, yarn, tape, or any type of fastener that will hold the splint in place. Splinting in this case is simply used to immobilize the break until the child can be moved to the hospital or to the doctor's office.

Burns

Knowledge of the classification of burns will aid the adult in quickly deciding on the treatment procedure. The classification system is based on how deeply the skin is burned. There are three levels of burns (first, second, and third degree) that parents and school personnel should be able to recognize.

With a first-degree burn, the skin is red. Apply a cold compress to the area or immerse (if on the hand, arm or leg) in cold water. Cover afterward with a sterile bandage. Children with spina bifida may get first- or even second-degree burns on their legs and not know it because of the loss of sensory input. It is important to check any child with a handicap for their response to positioning or movement as well as not exposing them to the sun for long periods of time.

Second-degree burns entail blistering of the skin. Do not break the blisters or apply home remedies of butter, lard, ointments, or sprays because dirt can accumulate on top of the skin surface, increasing the chance of infection. Instead immerse the area in cold water for 15–30 minutes and then cover the area with a sterile gauze pad or bandage.

When the skin and underlying tissues are brown or white or charred, a third-degree burn has occurred (Marotz et al., 1985) and the child requires emergency care. This requires calling an ambulance and the parents, and performing cardiopulmonary resuscitation (CPR) if the child is unconscious. A person trained in CPR must remember with a child not to pinch the nostrils but instead to cover both the mouth and nose with his or her mouth, use small puffs of air, and lighty place their hand on the child's chest to help check for lung movement.

Choking

Choking can appear during meal time with children who have difficulty with chewing and swallowing. Also, children have a tendency to place nonedible objects in their mouth that can block the air pathway and cause choking. Quickly see if the child has stopped breathing, is not coughing, or cannot speak. Then check to see if the bite of food or the object can be removed. This must be done with caution: the child may bite down on the adult's fingers, and, of more concern, the food or object may become more firmly lodged or be pushed further into the throat. If the object or food cannot be removed or is pushed in further in an attempt to remove it, the Heimlich maneuver should be performed immediately.

The Heimlich maneuver can be used with all ages, from infants through adults, and has proved successful in dislodging food and other objects. If possible, lower the child's head, then wrap both arms around the child's waist from behind. Make a fist with one hand, placing the thumb next to the child's body over the breastbone (between the nipples or only slightly lower). The top portion of the fist will form a knot that, when forced against the breastbone, will result in sufficient exhalation force to dislodge the object from the child's throat. To dislodge the object, give a rapid, forceful thrust to compress the chest. This is done by pressing inward and upward against the fisted hand with the other hand (preferrably the dominant one). The adult should not squeeze with the arms but rather do the thrusting with the hands. If the first thrust is not successful, the procedure should be repeated as long as the child is conscious; coughing or resumption of breathing by the child indicates that the food or object has been dislodged. If the child loses consciousness and still is not breathing, mouth-to-mouth breathing (CPR) may be required. The technique varies slightly for infants and children from adults. Personnel not familiar with this technique should learn it or quickly be able to locate other staff members that are certified in this life-saving procedure.

An alternative technique with a small child is to dangle the child head down over one arm with the arm supporting the body from underneath and the hand over the lower part of the child's breastbone. Place the other hand on the child's back just below the shoulder blades. Forceful downward pressure with the hand on the child's back should dislodge the food or object obstructing the airway.

Colds

Many children with handicaps are susceptible to colds, and if they are enrolled in a group program (nursery, day care, preschool) they may develop numerous colds during the school year. Children should be excluded from coming to school during the highly contagious period (the day symptoms develop to 2–3 days afterward). The common cold symptoms will vary from child to child, so they may include a few or many of the following (Marotz et al., 1985):

Slight fever	Coughing
Sneezing	A red or sore throat
"Glassy" or watery eyes	Listlessness

Parents are encouraged to keep the child in bed and to give plenty of liquids and nonaspirin anti-inflammatory or cold remedy products. Steam inhalation can help soothe stuffed-up nasal passages.

Shock

Shock often accompanies serious injuries resulting from fractures, burns, bleeding, heat exhaustion, and poisoning. If the child shows signs of shock (irregular shallow or deep breathing; pale or mottled, cold, clammy, skin; nausea; rapid and weak pulse; increased perspiration; or confusion, anxiety or restlessness) lay the child down and cover him or her lightly with a blanket or coat. It is necessary to maintain a normal body temperature, and covering the child will avoid further body heat loss. If a child with known seizures or who has poor muscle tone falls without wearing a protective helmet, serious head injuries could occur. Check for any additional problems of shallow breathing, unconsciousness, bumps or bruises, or dilated pupils. This information should be relayed to the physician before moving the child. Try to assess the cause of the shock and administer to that problem first. If there are no fractures, elevate the legs 8–12 inches. If breathing is difficult for the child, place a pillow or article of clothing underneath the head to help raise the neck and shoulders.

Vomiting/Diarrhea

Vomiting or diarrhea may be an indication of a medical problem such as a virus or flu or, in the case of vomiting, a delayed reaction to too much vestibular stimulation. Vomiting in the child who has a shunt to relieve excessive cerebrospinal fluid within the brain may be an indication that the shunt or tubing needs to be surgically repaired. Food poisoning, dietary changes, food allergies, or illnesses (earaches, colds, or strep throat) may be other causes of the sudden watery or soft consistency of diarrhea (Marotz et al., 1985). Vomiting can also be a sign of indigestion, an emotional problem, meningitis, salmonellosis, Reye's syndrome, or a drug reaction.

Medication

The classification of medicine or drugs used for improving a child's behavior, development, or physical discomfort falls, according to Orelove and Sobsey (1987), into four categories: anticonvulsants, tranquilizers, stimulants, and muscle relaxants. Numerous anticonvulsants have been used to reduce many types of seizures known to occur in infants and young children. A description of these medications and their side effects are discussed in more detail later in this chapter. A major percentage (approximately 85%) of the children taking anticonvulsants have had their seizure behavior significantly reduced. School personnel must be knowledgeable of any particular drug's side effects and help parents keep data on the change in the child's behavior when there is a change in the type or dosage of those drugs.

Tranquilizers and stimulants can alter the child's behavior drastically. Both should be used only in rare circumstances and under close medical supervision. Some of the serious reactions can include an increased incidence of seizures, headaches, vomiting, diarrhea, and uncontrolled movement due to confusion, depression, nervousness, or hallucinations (Orelove & Sobsey, 1987).

Muscle relaxants have been prescribed for children with cerebral palsy who have spastic or tight muscle tone. Of the several tranquilizers used as a muscle relaxant (Diazepam, Dantrium, Meprobamate, and Valium), Valium appears to be the most effective and to have the least side effects (Batshaw & Perret, 1981). Initially, the child becomes drowsy and drools excessively, but after a few days these behaviors diminish.

Overall, the less desired reactions to medicine (drowsiness, uncontrolled movements, health problems) may have their toll on the rate, quality, and quantity of the child's performance. This change in behavior may become noticeable some time after a change in the medication. Therefore, parents and school staff must be notified not only of when the new drug (or an increase or decrease in the current drug) has been given but also approximately when a change in behavior could be observed. An inservice on the side effects of medications and what and how to observe for adverse reactions would be a great benefit for the inter- or transdisciplinary team members.

Seizures

Children with central nervous system damage are highly prone to exhibit one or more types of seizure disorders during their lifetime. Although many individuals use terms such as "convulsions," "fits," or "spells" interchangeably, the term used now is either "epileptic syndrome" or "seizure disorder." The Commission on Classification and Terminology of the International League Against Epilepsy (1985) has defined an epileptic syndrome as a group of behaviors and symptoms often occurring together. These characteristics may include a case history, the seizure type, the frequency of the seizure, and a record and result of psychological information and medical testing (electroencephalogram, x-ray, computed tomography). Gadow (1986) has indicated that in order for seizures to be classified as a seizure disorder they must be recurring.

In 1969, the International League Against Epilepsy (ILAE) proposed the adoption of the International Classification of Epilepsies and Epileptic Syndromes (ICE); this classification was revised in 1981 (Dreifuss, 1985). This classification not only categorizes similar seizure behaviors that were previously unclassified but also provides definitions and descriptions of the generalized and specific types of seizure syndromes. Basically, there are two main classification groups (partial and generalized) with a third group (unclassified) that, although similiar in appearance, are not in fact associated with any epileptic syndrome or seizure disorder (see Table 7.2). Readers wishing more detailed information on the current classification categories are directed to the Commission on Classification and Terminology of the International League Against Epilepsy (1985), Dreifuss (1985), or Jan, Ziegler, and Erba (1983).

Prevalence

The percentage of children identified with seizure disorders varies from study to study, but in general has been accepted as between 0.5% and 1% for preschool children; for school-age children in regular classrooms it has been reported to be between 0.3% and 0.6% (Gadow, 1986).

Causes and Descriptions

There are a multitude of reasons and possible causes for the occurrence of seizures in infants and young children, ranging from infection, fever, or head trauma to metabolic disorders (Snell, 1983). Just a few of those causes can explain the reason for the sudden abnormal excessive discharge of electrical impulses in certain nerve cells in the brain. Depending on the type of seizure, this causes a loss of control of one or more of the following behaviors: muscle movement, consciousness, senses, and thoughts (Gearheart & Weishahn, 1976). This in turn results in behavior that may be so subtle and brief in duration that numerous seizures may occur undetected. In the case of *absence* (petit mal)

Table 7.2. Childhood seizures and medications

		Medications	
Type of seizure	Characteristics	Frequently used drugs	Common side effects
Primary generalized seizures			
Absence (petit mal); 6%–12% of identified cases	Occurs more often between ages of 4 and 14 years; appears to stare, may blink eyes or smack lips. Last 5–25 seconds and occurs as often as 100 times (average 25–50) a day. Loss of consciousness without falling down. Described as daydreaming.	Clonopin Zarontin Sodium valproate Diamox	Drowsiness, slurred speech, drooling, ataxia, irritability, tolerance to drugs develops Vomiting, dizziness, stomach upset, hiccups Occasional nausea and vomiting, gastric irritation Produces temporary control in many cases
Myoclonic/akinetic (lightning seizures)	Sudden uncontrolled jerking of head, eyes, and arms (or whole body) with or without loss of consciousness.	ACTH Valium Depakene	Elevated blood pressure, muscle weakness, intestinal bleeding Drowsiness, incoordination, vertigo, irritability Weight gain, drowsiness, loss of appetite, abdominal pain, vomiting
Infantile spasms (infantile myoclonic)	Onset 3–9 months of age; normal development prior to episodes, which are sudden, brief, and flexor in nature. After several weeks of onset child becomes inert, unresponsive, behavior regresses.	Clonopin ACTH	Same as absence seizures Same as myoclonic seizures
Tonic-clonic (grand mal); 80% of all identified cases	Overall electrical discharge with loss of consciousness during tonic-clonic phase. Prewarning or aura takes on many forms. Afterwards (postictal state) may be sleepy, irritable, confused, tired, and have a headache.	Phenobarbital Mebaral Mysoline	Aggressiveness, drowsiness, irritability, hyperactivity Same as phenobarbital Dizziness, ataxia, dysarthria, nystagmus, headaches
Partial seizures			
Simple (focal)	Characteristic behaviors are governed by the specific brain area that is affected. Generally, there is no loss of consciousness. Includes motor, sensory and/or automatic behavior.	Tegretal Dilantin	Impairs cognition, drowsiness, ataxia; dosage may have to be increased over long-term use Growth of gum tissue, excessive body hair, thickening of skin around face
Complex	Includes psychomotor, confusion or behavioral symptoms. There is a loss of consciousness.	Mysoline	Same as tonic-clonic seizures

Adapted from Gadow (1986) and Jan et al. (1983).

248

seizures, the child may be thought to be daydreaming because of the so-called staring-off-in-space behavior. Upon closer observation, one may note the twitching or blinking of the eyelids, slight jerking of the arms, or slight smacking of the lips. The behavior may last from 5 to 30 seconds and may occur as many as 50 to 100 times a day with loss of consciousness but not loss of muscle control or any drowsy aftereffects (Gearheart & Weishahn, 1976; Jan et al. 1983; Wolraich, 1984c).

Myoclonic seizures in infants are sudden flexor spasms with forward head flexion, extended tension of the arms, and upward bending of the legs toward the stomach. This describes *infantile spasms,* which can occur as often as 100 times a day and are hard to differentiate from colic behavior. Unfortunately, many infants with infantile spasms develop other types of seizures between 3 and 4 years of age. Another type of myoclonic seizure is *Lennox-Gastaut,* which develops between 3 and 7 years. There is similar quick jerking of the head forward and arm extension. If this happens in a standing position, the child usually has recovered by the time he or she hits the floor, but not without receiving a bump or cut on the face. Since these episodes can occur on a daily basis, a helmet should be worn as a protective measure.

In contrast to absence seizures, *tonic-clonic* (grand mal) seizures exhibit a more severe form of behavioral response. Most children and adults have an initial warning or aura that is characterized by an unusual sensory sensation. This may be described later by the child has a feeling of "extreme uneasyness or danger," smelling unpleasant odors, hearing strange sounds, seeing spots dancing in front of his or her eyes, or feeling a tingling sensation on the surface of the skin. Grand mal seizures are generalized throughout the body and occur in two main stages.

The first stage of the seizure (tonic) occurs when the child loses consciousness, falls to the ground, the entire body stiffens, breathing is interrupted, and the face may become pale. The clonic or second stage is characterized by the jerking motion (rapid contraction and relaxation of the muscles) of the entire body. Additional responses may be a loss of bladder control, drooling, heavy and noisy breathing, and pale or bluish skin color.

Partial seizures are those seizure disorders originating in one hemisphere or part of the brain and that may or may not spread to other sections of the brain. There is no loss of consciousness and, depending on the area of the brain that is involved, motor, sensory, autonomic, or psychic symptoms may be present. Reactions difficult for the child to describe to others are flashing lights, odd noises, vomiting, flashbacks, illusions, or hallucinations. Partial seizures are known to be inherited; occur during sleep; also involve the jerking movement of the tongue, arm, and leg; and occur between the ages of 5 and 10 years (Gadow, 1986).

Complex partial seizures are more commonly known as psychomotor or temporal lobe seizures. The properties of a complex partial seizure consist of a longer staring period than an absence seizure (up to 5 minutes) followed by minor atypical behavior (smacking the lips, chewing motion, drooling or mumbling) and possibly continued to more unusual behaviors (starting to undress, looking for objects, or hitting oneself). Sometimes a turning of the head or body and extending the arm on the side of the turn occurs, and other types of psychic behavior are seen (changes in sensations, distorted thoughts, or changes in moods) (Gadow, 1986). These types of seizures are not often seen in children under the age of 6 years.

Most seizure episodes are controlled or minimized with medication (see Table 7.2). Once the medication and dosage are regulated, the child may never have another seizure for years. For others, regulating the type and amount of medication is difficult, and there may be repeated seizure attacks. The most frequently prescribed antiepileptic drugs for children between the ages of 3 and 5 years for tonic-clonic seizures are phenobarbital, Dilantin, and Mysoline. Children with absence seizures are given Depakene or Zarontin (Gadow, 1986). It is not uncommon for children to be taking two or more drugs to control the frequency and severity of the seizures. A combination of drugs may be necessary to control a seizure as well as to prevent the development of a tonic-clonic seizure, or because a child may have more than one type of seizure.

Management

Although an epileptic seizure (grand mal) lasts but a few minutes, it can seem like an eternity to someone who has never witnessed one, let alone knows what a person should or should not do to help the child. Most importantly, one should remain calm. Once a seizure begins, there is nothing that can stop it but time; therefore let the seizure run its course and do not try to restrain the child's involuntary movements. If the child has fallen, clear any nearby furniture, loosen any tight clothing (around the neck in particular), turn the child's body or his or her head toward one side to allow excessive saliva to drain out and avoid placing anything in the mouth. Because of the increased breathing and contracted muscles, there is a buildup of saliva that is not automatically swallowed and gives the appearance that the child is "frothing at the mouth." For this reason, it is important to make sure the head position allows the saliva to flow out of the mouth.

Because of the intense amount of energy exerted during the seizure, the child needs to rest and sleep afterward. This is called the postictal state and is not considered part of the actual seizure but rather part of the recovery period. After sleeping, some children may feel disoriented or may be drowsy, tired, cranky, or lethargic and/or have a throbbing headache. It is important for the child's parents, teachers, and therapists to be aware of these possible behaviors.

General information about a child's seizure behavior should be kept on file, with an individual seizure data sheet for recording each seizure in as much detail as possible, including what went on prior to the seizure, length of time of the seizure, description of the movements, description of the behavior of the child afterward. This information can be relayed to the parents at the end of the school day or immediately depending if the child has already been identified as having seizures or if the behavior is unusual for the child.

TRANSFERS AND BODY MECHANICS

The purposes in learning and becoming familiar with transfer techniques and proper body mechanics are: 1) to be able to move a child safely and comfortably; 2) to provide better body alignment for the child; 3) to allow the child to develop independent movements through normal handling; 4) to allow the child to assist as much as possible; 5) to normalize muscle tone through proper handling, which also prevents secondary muscular and structural problems (Campbell, 1987); and 6) to help the child to develop self-confidence about his or her own ability despite physical limitations. Table 7.3 lists general guidelines to help maintain good adult body mechanics. Children with varying types and degrees of neurological damage that would affect lower or upper extremity movement may be able to ambulate with the use of braces, crutches, or walkers or may be limited to a wheelchair as a means of independent locomotion. Getting into or up next to a walker or wheelchair may require adult physical assistance. The process used to help a child get from one place to another is called transferring, and involves four stages: preparation, lifting, carrying, and the actual transfer itself.

Preparation

Assessing what type of equipment (belt, wheelchair) or obstacles (toys on the floor, chairs) need to be within reach or removed prior to the actual transfer

Table 7.3. Basic guidelines in adult body mechanics and transfers

1. Squat or bend the knees, then straighten up.
2. Use the thigh muscles when standing, not the back muscles.
3. Keep the chest up and forward; this will avoid bending at the waist.
4. Keep the spine straight as possible.
5. Get as close to the child as possible when lifting and carrying.
6. Stand with both feet apart with one foot forward to establish a broader base of support, balance, and natural footing.
7. Stabilize the pelvis position by contracting the abdominal muscles.
8. Bring the child's weight up next to the adult's body.
9. Use the arm and hand muscles to maintain a good grasp and hold onto the child.
10. Plan where and how to transfer the child before doing the actual movement.
11. Tell the child what is going to be done and what the child should do to help.
12. Praise the child for his or her help.

process will eliminate unnecessary movements, time, and injuries. The following list should be used as a general guideline that can be adapted to fit a specific child or problem.

1. Assess the child's weight and size to help determine if the transfer can be accomplished by one or two people. Orelove and Sobsey (1987) suggested that if the child's weight is more than one quarter of the adult's weight then it is safer to use a two-person lift and carry.
2. The child should be evaluated as to the amount of independent assistance he or she can provide during the transfer. If the task is to get from one part of the classroom to another, the child should be encouraged to do as much as possible. If this means rolling across the room, using both arms to pull him or herself across the floor, or creeping on all four extremities, then be sure enough time is allowed for this task. It may mean that the child begins to start toward the new activity several minutes prior to the other children or, depending on the new activity, the child can join the task already in progress.
3. For the child who needs to be lifted and carried, the adult should still determine what the child can do (move an arm, remain relaxed, etc.) and reinforce the child for any level of participation (Orelove & Sobsey, 1987).
4. Because each type of muscle tone requires a different lifting or holding pattern the child should be evaluated to see if his or her tone is spastic (extensor or flexor) or hypotonic. Also, will the child be assisting or will the adult be picking up essentially dead weight?
5. It is best to plan ahead of time what and how movements are to be done. This means having all equipment, materials, and toys within easy reach. Be sure to explain to the child (at the child's comprehension level) what is being done and why.

Lifting

Lifting can be accomplished by one or two people. In a two-person lift, the person supporting the head, neck, and shoulders is bearing the heaviest portion of the child's weight. This responsibility should be equally shared between the two lifters or given to the stronger of the two lifters. The following guidelines will make the moving transition from one surface to another (e.g., floor to chair) more comfortable, safe, and secure for the child and will avoid painful back injuries for the adult.

1. Be sure when bending down that the adult's knees and hips are bent and the back is straight. Remember to tighten the abdominal and buttock muscles and take a deep breath before lifting the child. The leg muscles need to be providing most of the upward motion (Fraser & Hensinger, 1983).
2. The adult's legs should be placed at least as far apart as the width of the

adult's shoulders and the feet should be placed in a stepping posture with one foot slightly ahead of the other foot. This will give a better base of support while shifting the adult's weight in any one direction when lifting or carrying a child (Williamson, 1987).

3. Make the lifting or transferring movements slowly and smoothly. Be sure to tell the child what is going to occur. Quick or jerky movements may tend to increase already spastic muscle tone. For the child with spastic muscle tone, movement that is too rapid will increase the spastic muscle tone and restrict the child's range of motion. In the case of hypotonic muscle tone, rapid successive movement does not allow the child enough time to stabilize body posture. It is important to continually evaluate the child's muscle tone while shifting the child's body and to alter the rate of movement accordingly.

4. In order for the adult to maintain proper control, it is essential to keep the child close to the adult's center of gravity. In this way the child will feel secure and the adult can control his or her own movements as well as the child's movements.

5. The child should be handled with a firm, confident grasp, using proximal control (shoulders, elbows, hips). Never pull or force an extremity distally because this will only increase the chance that the child will pull the extremity (fingers, arm, leg) opposite to the desired direction.

6. Allow the child to assist as much as possible in all phases of the transfer process. The child should be given time to respond to the broad spectrum of sensorimotor stimulation, such as tactile, vestibular, visual, auditory, and proprioceptive inputs.

7. The child should be in as relaxed a mood and position as possible. Then the adult should bring the child into a sitting position with head in midline and supported at the head/neck, shoulders, and hips.

8. Remember, one of the primary goals is to reduce the adult's support and assistance as soon and as much as possible. The amount or degree of muscle strength, independent mobility, cognitive comprehension, equilibrium response, protective reaction, and motivation, and the child's age will determine the particpation level one can expect initially from a child (Copeland et al., 1976; Williamson, 1987).

Carrying

The primary carrying position to avoid is holding the child as one would carry an infant. This fully supported position does not permit the child to develop his or her own muscular or postural control nor does it give the child a good visual picture of what is going on in his or her immediate surroundings (Finnie, 1975). Proper carrying methods can help normalize muscle tone, maintain body alignment, and provide an opportunity for self-directed movement (Campbell, 1987) of the head, neck, trunk, and extremities. In taking small steps while moving the child, the adult will avoid twisting his or her own body, thus avoiding possible lower back injury, muscle spasms, or loss of control (Williamson, 1987).

The type of muscle tone and postural control will determine how a young child should be carried. For the child displaying tight muscles and extended extremities, Finnie (1975) recommended the following procedures be performed. Start by pulling the child into a symmetrical sitting position by flexing the hips and knees. Next provide support under the arms and at the back of the shoulders as the child is brought up and forward in the direction of the adult. This will help maintain the arms in internal rotation and close to midline as the child's arms are placed or requested to go around the adult's neck and shoulders. Finally, the legs are positioned in flexion and external rotation by straddling the adult's hip on the nondominant side. The adult's dominant hand supports the child's arm and hand while the other hand supports the buttocks and lower back area.

When a child has predominantly flexed extremities but is still influenced by spastic muscle tone, it is important to carry this child with the arms and legs in extension. Start the child in the supine position and roll him or her to one side. The adult should kneel behind the child's back. Relaxation techniques (slow rolling) may be necessary to position the legs in flexion. Slide one hand between the legs and the other hand under the child's arm, holding onto the child's upper arm. Once a firm hold is obtained, the child can be lifted and held close to the adult's body.

The fluctuating tone of other children requires handling that is firm and steady, which gives the child the stability needed for smoothly controlled movements. The best posture while carrying this child is in flexion. Depending on the amount of uncontrolled movement, both arms and legs can be stabilized while facing the child away from the adult's body. This can be done by straddling the child across the adult's hip or holding the child in a sitting or horizontal position in front of the adult at or above lap height. This will mean that both of the adult's hands are supporting and controlling both arms and legs or just both legs or possibly one arm and one leg. Adult hand placement will vary depending on the child's changing tone.

The child with low or hypotonic tone, such as those with Down syndrome, cerebral palsy, or cri du chat syndrome, is in need of firm, steady support at the shoulders and arms so better head control can be facilitated. Again, do not carry the "floppy" child as one would an infant. Instead, give good flexion and support at the hips while carrying the child facing away from the adult's body. Any additional upper trunk or head support can be obtained by pulling the child closer to the adult's chest.

The teachers and therapists working with infants exhibiting abnormal muscle tone can provide appropriate carrying support in several ways. Swaddling, once a common technique used with nonhandicapped infants, now is being used with premature infants to provide security and to facilitate flexor posture. The infant is placed diagonally on a blanket with three corners snuggly wrapped around the feet, legs, chest, arms, and hands. The infant can then be held and carried resting on the adult's shoulder, in one arm (sometimes called the football carry), in the feeding position (referred to as the tucked carry), or the "comfort" carry, where the infant is resting in the middle of the adult's chest with one hand supporting the infant's neck and shoulders while the other arm gives support under the infant's bottom.

A child with spina bifida or cerebral palsy wearing braces must be given support around the legs while being carried to avoid losing control as a result of the added weight around the legs. The adult carrying a child with spina bifida without braces must make sure the child's legs are kept in a "neutral, well-aligned posture" (Williamson, 1987, p. 184).

Transfers

Copeland et al. (1976) and Williamson (1987) have identified two types of transfers: active (independent) and passive (dependent). In passive transfer most of the work will be done by the parent, teacher, or therapist. An active transfer implies that the child has sufficient muscular strength, coordination, and balance to take an active role in moving from one surface to another. Depending on the surface, the child may require some degree of assistance. The main piece of equipment used in a transfer is the wheelchair. The surfaces the child generally is being transferred to are a bed, toilet, floor mat, or chair, and then return to the wheelchair. To determine what type of transfer (active or passive) should be used with any particular child, one must assess the child's strength, mobility, balance, motivation, cognitive comprehension, physiological condition, and age (Copeland et al., 1976). Campbell (1987) stressed that whatever transfer method is used, it should be "as motorically efficient as possible for the student" (p. 176). The child's weight, the degree of the child's active participation, and the combination of the direction and height of the transfer usually determine whether the transfer can be done by one, two, or three people.

The transfer methods used are side-to-side (transfer board to a bed or wheelchair), forward (wheelchair to standing position), backward (bed to wheelchair), standing/pivot (moving from standing to chair), and upward/downward (floor to chair or bed and the reverse direction). Copeland et al. (1976) recommended that the following guidelines be used when transferring a child from a wheelchair to any other surface:

1. If the child seems to have more involvement on one side of his body than on the other, make the transfer in the direction toward the stronger side.

2. Securely lock the wheelchair in a stable position before a transfer is made.
3. Push the wheelchair foot rests and leg rests up out of the way or remove them entirely so that the child can easily place his feet on the floor.
4. When making a sitting transfer, remove the wheelchair arm nearest the surface to which the child is transferring. If possible, use a transfer board to ensure safety.
5. Stand in front of the child to offer maximum support and protection.
6. Grasp the child firmly around the waist or use a transfer belt, which eliminates slipping of clothing upon lifting.
7. Stand with feet apart, one foot slightly in front of the other, to give a wide base of support.
8. Avoid back strain in lifting a child by bending at the hips and knees, not at the waist. (p. 57)
9. Anytime a child is removed from a wheelchair be sure the foot straps (usually Velcro) are unfastened before placing your arms around the back and under the knees of the child. The time spent securing a good hold on the child as well as verbally preparing the child for the lift is wasted if the lift is prevented from happening because the feet are still strapped down onto the foot rests.
10. After placing the child in the wheelchair, prioritize which additional supports (neck collar, belts, straps, etc.) should be secured first. For some children, the seat belt (at the hips) should be attached before the feet straps in order that the child does not slide off the seat. For a child with poor neck control, the cervical collar should first be secured, then the seat belt. The child's security and comfort should be an important factor in selecting what fasteners to use and which one to begin with.

The following transfer descriptions will aid the parent or teacher/therapist in establishing good body mechanics and better body handling and facilitating normal body alignment for the child.

Side-to-Side Transfer

The purpose of a side-to-side transfer using a rectangular board (which usually has receding or tapering ends) is to allow more independence for the child with upper extremity mobility and poor lower leg movement or strength. The ability to push up on extended arms allows ease in moving the entire body sideways.

1. Position the wheelchair next to the furniture.
2. Remove the arm support next to the edge of the furniture.
3. Lock the wheels, and lift or have the child remove both feet from the footrests. The footrests are then lifted and swung out of the way.
4. One end of the transfer board is placed on the furniture surface and the other end is placed on the wheelchair seat. The distance between the two

surfaces should not be more than two-thirds the length of the board (Williamson, 1987).

5. If the child has sufficient mobility, strength, and balance, he or she should be encouraged to slide across the board using both arms for support and movement.

6. For a passive transfer, the adult stands in front of the child and supports the child's body with the arm on the side of the transfer direction. With the adult bent down even with the child, any loss of the child's balance can be stopped while he or she is sliding across the transfer board.

Forward Transfer

The forward transfer is a good method of moving from a wheelchair to the toilet, bed, or chair, or into a car. It requires the child be an active participant, meaning there must be sufficient upper arm strength to help move the buttocks forward or to be able to push the child upward into a standing position. The child must also have sufficient sitting and standing balance and equilibrium response to react when his or her center of gravity is suddenly shifted.

Option 1

1. The wheelchair faces the surface to which the child will transfer. The brakes must be locked, and the footrests are swung over to each side of the chair's wheels.

2. The child uses his or her arm strength to help pull or lift the buttocks forward to the edge of the wheelchair seat. The child then pulls to a standing position.

3. Procedures used in a stand/pivot transfer listed below should then be employed.

Option 2

This option is for children who cannot independently support their full weight in a standing position.

1. After completing step #1 in Option 1, the child's legs are extended onto the other surface (this primarily will be a bed).

2. The child continues to use the arms to move his or her body from the wheelchair seat to the bed. Once on the bed, the child can pivot in the sitting position until he or she is parallel to the bed's length.

Stand/Pivot Transfer

For an active transfer, some independent body movement is required with or without braces. A passive transfer still requires a fair amount of trunk control and arm strength.

Active Transfer

1. Place the wheelchair next to the furniture, preferably at a 90-degree angle.
2. Push the wheelchair footrests up out of the way or remove them so the child's feet can be placed on the floor without any interference.
3. Using the armrests, the child pushes his or her body into a standing position.
4. The child pivots his or her back toward the transfer surface, using one hand to hold onto the furniture and the other on the armrest closest to the child.
5. The child is now facing the wheelchair and lowers him or herself onto the chair, toilet seat, or the bed. Assistance may be needed afterward to remove the wheelchair if it restricts the child's movement or interferes with other furniture.

Passive Transfer

This is a specific example for a child with limited upper and lower strength transferring from a bed to a chair (or vice versa).

1. Position the wheelchair at right angles to the other surface. Remember to lock the brakes and lift the footrests.
2. With the child sitting on the edge of the bed (it is assumed that the horizontal to sitting procedure has already been done by the child or an adult) the adult bends his or her legs so the child and adult are at the same level. The adult's foot farthest from the wheelchair is on the outside of the child's foot (which is also the foot furthest away from the chair). This is to prevent the child from slipping to the floor as the adult pulls the child into a standing position.
3. Supporting the child's waist, the adult straightens up, giving any additional support with his or her legs next to the child's legs.
4. The child is then turned until his or her back is in front of the wheelchair. The adult then slowly bends his or her knees and hips, lowering the child into the wheelchair.

Floor or Bed to Wheelchair Transfer

There will be many times when activities (individual or group) are easier to teach and perform when done on the floor or a mat. The example given describes getting the child back into the chair from the floor. To get down to the floor, the steps are done in reverse order.

1. The wheelchair seat should be near the child's head. Lift the footrests out of the way and lock the wheels.
2. Place the child in the side-lying position facing toward the chair.
3. Slide one arm under the child's neck and support the upper back with the

hand. With the other arm bend the hips and legs and bring the child into a sitting position.

4. From a kneeling position, raise one leg into a half-kneeling position while maintaining the support of the child around his or her trunk and under the legs.
5. Slowly lift the child onto the adult's kneeling leg.
6. Slowly rise to a standing position, keeping the back straight and pushing upward and slightly forward using leg muscles.

Two-Person Transfer

Two people can safely lift and transfer an older or heavier child easier and with less back strain than one person attempting it.

Option 1

1. Bring the child to a long-sitting position.
2. One adult supports the head, neck, and shoulders, with the right arm reaching between the child's arm and trunk, grasping onto the top of the child's left forearm. The same movement is done with the adult's left hand holding onto the child's right hand. This helps bring the child's arms toward his or her midline. It also provides a good lifting leverage.
3. The adult kneeling at the other end (near the child's feet) places both forearms under the child's knees and locks hands.
4. The lift and transfer should be done in unison and preplanned as to the verbal cues (e.g., "One, two, three, lift") and where the child will be moved. The commands are usually given by the person supporting the trunk area.
5. Be sure each adult steps forward (toward the child) during the lifting so the child's body will be closer to each adult.

Option 2

1. Both adults begin by facing each other in a kneeling position on either side of the child's chest.
2. Assist the child into a sitting position. Each adult will support the child by grasping hold of each other's forearm closest to the child's back. Another version is for each adult to bring "one arm diagonally behind the student's shoulders from the point of the near shoulder to below the far armpit (aides arms cross on the student's back)" (Fraser & Hensinger, 1983, p. 195).
3. Then both adults half-kneel their leg nearest the child's trunk and on command, both lift the child onto the adult's thighs.
4. After the child and both adults have adjusted to this position, another com-

mand is given to stand. The weight of the adults is shifted forward in order to keep the child close to their bodies. The advantage to Option 2 over the first option, according to Fraser and Hensinger (1983), is that the child's weight is equally divided between the two lifters.

PART II

Special Considerations for Specific Developmental Disabilities

___CHAPTER 8___

At-Risk Infants

RISK FACTORS AND CATEGORIES
OF ABNORMAL DEVELOPMENT

Any complication occurring before, during, or after birth becomes a risk factor that predicts a greater probability of developmental delays. The greater the number of abnormal medical and environmental variables existing in an infant's family history, the more likelihood there is of long-term dysfunctions (Denhoff, 1981; Honig, 1984; Murphy et al., 1982). Honig (1984) noted that not all risk factors develop into conditions that affect later development. There are only a few problems that by themselves or when associated with other complications will predict a higher risk factor for the future outcome of the infant. Thus several terms are used to describe the infant's current condition depending upon the occurrence of certain factors.

The terms "at risk" and "high risk" have been commonly used in the literature without clear-cut distinctions, and, in general, they are used interchangeably. Scheiner and Abrams (1980), however, have attempted to distinguish the terms by listing specific conditions for each category. Subsequent authors have either added or deleted certain conditions, which in turn has created new categories. There appears to be no consensus as to whether one, two, or more levels of risk should be identified and, if so, what and how many factors should be placed in each category (see Table 8.1). As stated by Rostetter and Hamilton (1982), the exact terminology (at risk, high risk, biological risk, environmental risk) used is inconsequential compared to the overwhelming effects any combination of factors may have on the infant's developmental progress.

Murphy et al. (1982) proposed identifying infants with abnormal development within three categories (delay, disorder, and deficit) that would describe various problems according to the severity level and prognosis. A developmental *delay* is an indication that a skill has not been achieved or mastered within the normal age range but the infant has displayed evidence of a gradual progression toward the final task. For example, a child may not have mastered walking by 17 months (Frankenberg & Dodds, 1969) but all other prerequisite developmental steps (crawling, creeping, kneeling, half-kneeling, standing) have been

Table 8.1. Risk factors

Author(s)	Category	Risk factors
Bricker (1985)	Medically at risk	1. Prematurity 2. Low birth weight Associated conditions: 1. Respiratory conditions 2. Regulation of body temperature 3. Toxemia 4. Asphyxia 5. Respiratory problems
Campbell and Wilhelm (1985)	Very high risk	1. Apgar score of 5 or less at 5 minutes 2. Asphyxia 3. Persistant cyanosis 4. Seizures 5. Resuscitation at birth 6. Central nervous system hemorrhage/infarction 7. Skull fracture
Denhoff (1981)	At risk	1. Poverty 2. Deprivation of nutrition, senses, and emotions 3. Family instability 4. Developmental disability
	High risk	Prediction of adverse outcome when the infant's history contains a higher than normal number of abnormal conditions relating to maternal gestational, obstetric, neonatal, and early infant data
Farber and Williams (1982, p. 182)	At risk (brain damage)	1. Abnormal muscle tone 2. Abnormal reflex development 3. Abnormal sleep-wake cycle 4. Abnormal skull size 5. Anoxia, hypoxia 6. Asymmetrical neurological findings 7. Extended respiratory assistance 8. Extreme irritability or abnormal cry 9. Feeding dysfunction/weak or absent sucking 10. Apgar score less than 5 at 5 minutes 11. Jerky or myoclonic movement patterns 12. Meconium staining 13. Nonmetabolic seizure activity 14. Nystagmus 15. Severe birth trauma 16. Severe infection

continued

Table 8.1. *continued*

Author(s)	Category	Risk factors
Morrison, Pothier, and Horr (1978, p. 106)	Risk factors	1. Maternal (poor nutrition, history of mental deficiency, miscarriage, age under 16 or over 40, physical condition of mother) 2. Related factors (low family income, no or late prenatal care, unwanted pregnancy, alcoholism, drug addiction) 3. Labor/delivery (long labor, abnormal delivery process, anesthetic depression, cesarean section, fetal distress signs) 4. Neonatal (birth weight under 2,500 grams or over 4,000 grams; poor sucking, gagging, or swallowing; poor asymmetrical muscle tone; excess lethargy; hyperbilirubinemia in first 48 hours) 5. Postnatal (illness or accident; inattention to visual and auditory stimuli; abuse from parents; unpredictable patterns of behavior/crying, sleeping; failure to thrive)
Pelletier and Palmeri (1985)	At risk	Complications during prenatal or perinatal time that greatly influence future developmental delays or deficits
Scheiner and Abrams (1980)	At risk	1. Respiratory distress 2. Asphyxia 3. Less than 33 weeks of gestation 4. Weight less than 1,800 grams 5. Cyanosis 6. Surgery for congenital malformations 7. Convulsions 8. Meconium aspiration 9. Central nervous system disturbance causing abnormal behavior

achieved at an equally slow pace. In other words, the rate at which skills are achieved is slower than normally expected.

A *disorder* differs from a delay in the quality of performance that is accomplished if the skill is left unattended. Murphy et al. (1982) explained that, without corrective glasses, myopic vision will always remain blurred. Corrective lenses will help the child attain normal sight. Similarly, because of a neurological impairment a toddler may not be able to pull to stand and walk independently. With the aid of a walker or braces a whole new vista presents itself to the child.

The third category Murphy and his colleagues advocated is the developmental *deficit,* which implies a more permanent disability such as blindness or a congenital hearing loss. The condition cannot be corrected but as the infant grows he or she can be taught to adjust to the disability and become more independent with the use of adapted equipment (walkers, braces, canes, etc).

Whatever category is preferred in describing the cause of developmentalproblems or the functional level of the infant, therapists and teachers must equip themselves with the necessary skills that are uniquely special to the infant population.

CATEGORIZATION OF RISK FACTORS

Whereas the definitions for high risk or at risk vary from author to author, a categorization of risk factors by developmental stage makes it easier to comprehend them and to draw useful conclusions. As depicted in Table 8.2, the different stages of early development (prenatal, perinatal, and postnatal) include a number of preventable conditions. Important contributing factors during the *prenatal stage* are in many cases unknown to a prospective mother but nonetheless can be avoided with proper prenatal care. Maintaining proper weight, an adequate diet, and regular physical check-ups are three simple ways of assuring a positive beginning for the unborn infant. Early and continued medical care during the pregnancy can also evaluate the potential effect on the unborn child of a mother who has had previous premature infants, current maternal health, and/or any maternal emotional problems. Attending to these factors can greatly minimize risks to the overall health and future development of the infant.

To some extent, the preventive measures taken during the prenatal stage can diminish a number of possible problems that can develop during the *perinatal stage.* Many of the psychological factors such as financial worries, addictions, or an unwanted pregnancy can be dealt with during the months prior to the birth of the child. Other factors relating to prematurity (placenta previa, toxemia, anoxia, or multiple fetuses) must be handled at the time of delivery. Advanced obstetrical procedures and neonatal intensive care techniques have given many infants a chance for a healthy life not known 20 years ago.

The cause of *postnatal-stage* problems can be physical trauma resulting from a fall, an illness, a neurological injury, or physical abuse. Additional difficulties can arise from stress factors (see Chapter 1). For example, Murphy and his coworkers (1982) have found that parents exhibit shock reactions upon learning their newborn may be handicapped or that the infant's survival is questionable. Family stress factors develop as financial demands for hospital and

Table 8.2. Factors contributing to high-risk conditions

Developmental stage	Precipitating factors
Prenatal (occurring before birth with reference to the fetus)	High-risk maternal history 1. History of stillbirths or premature infants 2. Chronic pulmonary or metabolic disease 3. Excessive (over 36 lbs.) or inadequate (less than 10 lbs.) weight gain 4. Virus infection (rubella or cytomegalovirus) 5. Diabetes 6. Severe renal or heart disease 7. Previous children with congenital malformations 8. Psychological disorders 9. Cardiovascular disease 10. Age less than 15 or over 35 11. Lower socioeconomic status 12. Late or no medical prenatal care 13. Poor nutrition 14. Separation of placenta 15. Miscarriage 16. Drug, alcohol, smoking addiction

Perinatal
(28 wks. gestation to 1–4
wks. after birth)
	Labor and delivery
	1. Long labor
	2. Anesthetic depression
	3. Cesarean section
	4. Fetal distress signs
	Gestational weight and age
	1. Small for gestational age
	  a. Weighing 1,500–2,000 grams or less
	  b. Weight, height, and head circumference are at or below 10th percentile
	  c. Intrauterine growth retardation
	  d. Congenital abnormalities
	  e. Psychological-social factors: teenage motherhood, drugs, alcohol, etc.
	2. Large for gestational age
	  a. Head, weight, and height above the 90th percentile
	  b. Diabetic mother
	  c. Seizures
	Breech delivery problems
	1. Risk of central nervous system damage when cervix and birth canal are less than adequate

continued

Table 8.2. *continued*

Developmental stage	Precipitating factors
	2. Possible bronchial plexus palsy
	3. Cesarean section may produce hyaline membrane ("wet lung") disease (amniotic fluid remains in the lungs)
	Prematurity
	1. Born at less than 38 weeks gestational age (7%–10% of live births)
	2. Immature, underdeveloped organs
	3. Inability of cervix to remain tightly closed
	4. Insufficient placental circulation to fetus
	5. Maternal hypertension
	6. Multiple fetuses
	7. Overall poor maternal health and nutrition
	8. Poor suck, swallow, gag, cough reflexes
	9. Lack of prenatal care
	10. Placenta previa
	11. Toxemia
	12. Low birth weight
	Postmaturity
	1. Gestational age over 41–42 weeks
	2. Characterized by thickened, peeling skin and long thin body
	Social/psychological contributors
	1. "Mourning" syndromes: guilt, denial that child is not normal
	2. Low family income
	3. Unwanted pregnancy
	4. Maternal and/or paternal psychiatric disorder (abusive parent)
	5. Alcoholism and/or drug addiction
	6. Increasing financial burdens
Postnatal (occurring after birth)	**General contributors**
	1. Prolonged illness or serious accident
	2. Unpredictable behavior
	3. Parental abuse
	4. Does not respond to visual or auditory stimuli

Adapted from Denhoff (1981), *Dorland's Illustrated Medical Dictionary* (1974), Goldberg (1975), Gorski (1984), Honig (1984), Michelsson, Ylinen, and Donner (1981), Morrison et al. (1978), Murphy et al. (1982), Nelson and Ellenberg (1979), and Scheiner and Abrams (1980).

doctor bills increase as well as when siblings feel left out and begin to evidence behavioral problems.

PROFESSIONAL AND PARENT ROLES

Seven to ten years ago very few therapists were counting the high-risk infant in their end-of-the-year or quarterly report. A survey done by Pringle, Kaninski, and Raymond (1978) indicated that 58.5% of physical therapists nationwide did not evaluate or treat infants under the age of 3 months. Although many occupational and physical therapists were quite familiar with the various techniques used with toddlers and older children, not many had had the opportunity to use the same type of methods with infants. Encouragingly, 5 years later Redditi 91983) reported on a survey that looked at the quality of treatment given by physical and occupational therapists working in the state of Iowa. Of the 57 therapists returning the questionnaire, 39 (42%) were actively working with infants (birth to 2 years). A high percentage of therapists (82%–97%) had strong feelings about parental involvement during the therapy session, and 64% taught specific treatment techniques to the parents. The questionnaire revealed that those therapists with a master's degree in education attended more continuing education courses and incorporated this knowledge into their daily practice.

Working in a neonatal intensive care unit (NICU), in an infant intervention clinic, or in the home requires the following prerequisites of a professional, according to Farber and Williams (1982) and Goldberg (1975). First, the therapist must have a good knowledge of normal and abnormal infant development even at the prenatal stage. Second, an effective therapist should be able to evaluate the normal full-term infant in the areas of reflex responses, muscle tone, and general body activity. Third, he or she should be familiar with the concepts of normal neuromuscular maturation and function. Finally, therapists should keep abreast of current research studies and the results pertaining to medical conditions, diagnostic assessments, and intervention techniques. It is not crucial that all four prerequisites be satisfied, but any combination of two or more will aid the therapist in effectively assessing the infant's assets and deficits, in developing an appropriate program, and in communicating comfortably with parents. This additional knowledge will be useful when coordinating an infant's program with other team members.

One of the team objectives should stress combining common goals across disciplines. This will help avoid overloading parents with too many activities to possibly carry out in a daily family routine. Also, the team should look very carefully at the type of data recording requested from parents. The process involved in measuring behavior is generally a natural part of a staff's professional repertoire. For a parent, however, this is like learning a new language. Some parents will acquire the basic concept and follow through with practical applications quite readily. Others will have difficulty even with the reason for taking data, let alone learning the various components of the process. The staff should carefully evaluate and compare staff and parent priorities before designing the infant's home program. Flexibility should be woven into everyone's language and schedule. This may mean scheduling therapy sessions around the infant's feeding cycles or sleeping pattern, or around the parent's visits if the infant is in an NICU.

The importance of communication among and across disciplines cannot be stressed too strongly. Bricker and Dow (1980) described the staff frustration amid persistent efforts during the development of a measurement system for a population of infants with severe multiple handicaps that hoped to provide both valid and practical indices of progress. Although it took 2 years to develop an effective program, the outcome resulted in only 2 out of 50 children being placed in a residential facility. The staff consensus that the longer the infants were receiving intervention training the better they would perform on the post-test was borne out.

Pringle and her coworkers (1978) recommended further research to: 1) find or develop an assessment tool for infants that the majority of therapists would agree upon, 2) confirm the validity and reliability of such a test, and 3) substantiate the effectiveness of the treatment procedures being used based on the test results.

One of the most important roles of the professional, which should be of concern to all allied health personnel, is establishing a comfortable and respectful working relationship with the parents. It is a major responsibility of the staff to inform and acquaint parents with the types of assessment used and the reason the test was chosen, and to help the parents understand the overall interpretations based on the subtest results (Figure 8.1). Erickson (1976) encouraged the presence of parents during testing (even stressing an active participation role) because this provides the examiner time to observe parent-infant interaction and to develop a therapist-parent rapport in a less threatening atmosphere. By having the parent get down on the floor with his or her baby and the therapist, everyone will be more relaxed; the "across-the-desk" barrier is eliminated (Figure 8.2). Experience has shown Pelletier and Palmeri (1985) and the current authors that most parents not only want to know the cause of the problem and test results but are also eager to learn what they can do at home.

Bricker (1985) found parental educational and income level to be the most accurate predictors to date of the infant's overall future development. Any educational gains attained at the center would inevitably decrease unless reinforced through home experiences (Pines, 1982). Parents should not be expected to know what type of therapeutic activities are best suited for their baby; it is the professional's duty to design the appropriate program. When programs are not available, the parents have the right to demand and to seek out programs that provide more therapeutic input than just babysitting.

There is general agreement that all staff members can and should help parents understand their infant's condition, develop realistic goals and routines based on their baby's personality, develop an organized approach to treatment

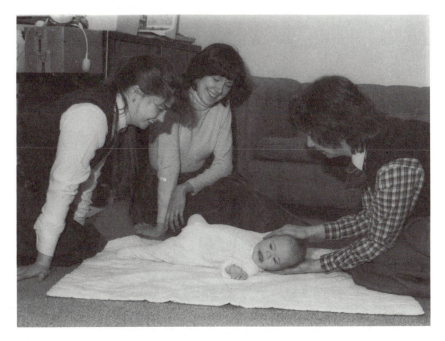

Figure 8.1. A good working relationship with parents begins with a discussion of the test results and the establishment of an individual family service plan (IFSP).

that will lead to progress, learn the history and effects of specific high-risk conditions, and foster a healthy and positive attitude about their child's condition and potential progress (S. K. Campbell & Wilson, 1976; Ferry, 1981; Pines, 1982).

It has taken years to close the communication gap between the parents and professional staff that Pines (1982) indicated stems from the "rigidity of professionals and their fear that parents might demand too much from their children" (p. 50). Since the infant's sensory inputs and developmental environment are to a large extent controlled by their parents, the infant's responses and ultimate physical growth and emotional development need to be carefully and accurately evaluated by staff and parents together.

PUBLIC LAW 99-457

Of particular interest to personnel working with infants with disabilities is one of the sections of the latest amendment (PL 99-457) to the Education of the Handicapped Act Amendments of 1986. Public Law 99-457 provides an opportunity for each state to plan, develop, and implement programs that would ad-

Figure 8.2. An effective infant intervention program includes active parent participation both in the clinic and at home.

dress the needs of at-risk and handicapped infants, toddlers, and their families. As an incentive for state participation, grant funding will be available by 1991. In order to be in compliance with the new act and eligible for federal funding, an interagency coordinating council, appointed by the governor of the state, will advise and help the state agency plan and operate the 14 law requirements:

1. A state definition of "developmentally delayed."
2. A timetable for services to all infants in need.
3. A comprehensive multidisciplinary evaluation of needs of children and families.
4. Individualized family service plan (IFSP) and case management services.
5. A child find and referral system.
6. A public awareness program.
7. A central directory of services, resources, experts, and research and demonstration projects.
8. A comprehensive system of personnel development.
9. A single line of authority in a lead agency to carry out general administration and supervision, identify and coordinate all available resources, as-

sign financial responsibility, develop procedures to ensure services are provided, resolve intra- and interagency disputes, and enter into formal interagency agreements.

10. A policy regarding contracts or arrangements with local service providers.
11. Procedures for timely reimbursements of funds.
12. Procedural safeguards.
13. Policies and procedures for personnel standards.
14. A system for compiling data regarding the early intervention programs.

Another part of the new amendment provides incentives for states to develop and document programs to 3–5-year-old children with handicaps and their family on an IFSP.

Because each state will develop and define their own programs, some of the requirements listed above will vary from state to state. How this will affect the daily operation of the local centers may depend on the involvement of the parents and professionals with their state lead agency. Toole (1987) mentioned that "some programs will have to report to a state agency with which they have had no previous contact" (medical instead of education) (p. 1). This may mean major changes in areas ranging from the way services are delivered to how the infant's progress is reported. It is therefore imperative that professionals and parents are aware of the direction the state agency chooses and support that directional emphasis. The total impact of PL 99-457 upon existing infant programs and the ease of developing future programs will have to wait until each state's regulations have been designed and implemented for several years.

ACQUIRING INFORMATION ON THE AT-RISK INFANT

The process of obtaining information about an infant's abilities across a number of developmental domains (motor, language, cognitive, social, self-help) is best accomplished through an assessment test. Bailey and Wolery (1984) described three ways of acquiring the information: direct testing, observation, and parental interview (see Table 8.3).

Direct Testing

There are a number of ways of gathering information from the direct testing method, depending upon the extent or depth of information desired. *Screenings* may be given to large numbers of infants easily and quickly by professional and

Table 8.3. Advantages and disadvantages of various assessment strategies

Procedure	Advantages	Disadvantages
Testing	Standard procedures allow meaningful comparisons of children Necessary for diagnostic needs Facilitates transfer of information	Alternate procedures for children with sensory or motor impairments are not generally allowed Some tests require considerable training Lack of validated measures for educational planning Skills sampled are limited to those included as the test
Observation	Measures what children do in real world settings Sensitive to changes over time Can be done during regular classroom activities	Time-consuming Requires a certain amount of skill to design a good observation system Lack of guidelines to interpret data gathered
Interview	Information comes from another's perspective Efficent use of time	Not direct measure of child behavior The interviewee may not accurately report skills

From Bailey, D.B., & Wolery, M. (1984). Determining instructional targets. In *Teaching infants and preschoolers with handicaps*. Columbus, OH: Charles E. Merrill; reprinted by permission.

paraprofessionals. Information procured from screenings is also based on observations and parental interviews. The Denver Developmental Screening Test (DDST) developed by Frankenburg and Dodds (1969) encompasses all these procedures. The screening process of looking at an infant's abilities merely focuses on a skill or skills in one or more domains that are not performed and does not indicate a diagnosis or curriculum strategy. Screenings can be used as a precursor for further extensive diagnostic testing. A *diagnostic test* will verify that a particular problem does or does not exist. More items at each age group and within each domain are found with this type of test. It requires a longer administration time as well as a thorough training period. The examiner must be qualified either through a licensed examination or with extensive testing experience. The Bayley Scales of Infant Development (Bayley, 1969) serve as an example of a standardized diagnostic measure. A third type of test, referred to as an *educational assessment,* is used primarily but not exclusively by teachers for the purpose of instructional planning (Bailey & Wolery, 1984). Examples include the Hawaii Early Learning Profile, also known as HELP (Furuno et al., 1985), the Portage Project Checklist (Bluma, Shearer, Frohman, & Hilliard, 1976), and The Carolina Curriculum for Handicapped Infants and Infants At Risk (Johnson-Martin et al., 1986).

To further assist therapists and teachers in selecting the appropriate assessment tool, a taxonomy of assessment measures has been developed for the purposes of identification and programming. *Norm-referenced* measurements determine an infant's performance in relationship to the average behavior of other infants of similar ages (Bailey & Wolery, 1984; Fewell & Sandall, 1983). Normative tests are useful in documenting the extent of deviation from a sampling of skills within a number of developmental domains. These types of tests, according to Sheehan and Gallagher (1984), should not be used for curriculum development because they have "few teachable items and therefore provide little guidance for instructional planning" (p. 98). Standardized norm-referenced tests include the DDST, the Bayley, and the Milani-Comparetti tests.

   Criterion-referenced tests provide an overall level of performance and the mastery of a skill on a pass/fail rating, instead of comparing the infant's ability to perform to that of other infants of the same age, as do the norm-referenced tests. Various skills are grouped into similar domains and ranked on a sequential scale. For example, the ability to coordinate alternating movements up and down stairs begins with creeping on hands and knees. This is one subskill within the gross motor domain. Assessing a child's ability in this manner serves to determine the quantity and quality level of performance. It also serves in the intervention decision. Criterion-referenced tests have been used as pre-post test comparisons, especially when the Brigance Diagnostic Inventory of Early Development (Brigance, 1978) is used as both an evaluation and program (individualized education program) tool. A few authors contend that since there is a greater emphasis on the achievement of skills within domains, the criterion is used primarily as a means of measuring the performance within these domains. These tests should more accurately be labeled as *domain-referenced* measures (Fewell & Sandall, 1983; Sheehan & Gallagher, 1984). There is difficulty in establishing a consistent criterion cutoff level for all domains or even different skills within a domain. This only serves to confuse the evaluator, in addition to requiring a substantial amount of time to assess each area. Putting less emphasis on the criterion factor and stressing the mastery process can help therapists and teachers design a more efficient and practical program. A measureable system is still needed but the focus will be centered on developing the most to least restrictive program.

Observation

Another way of gathering information about an infant's ability to perform is through observation. Observing when, what, and how an infant performs a particular activity enlightens the observer as to the type of sibling interaction, appropriateness of behavior, and level of communication and independence (Bailey & Wolery, 1984). Many therapists and teachers include observation as part of the testing process because of the valuable information obtained that generally is not covered in any testing format. There are a number of ways of recording behavior that produce different results depending on which one is selected. Information accumulated from observation data needs to be taken over a period of time (days or even weeks) in order to get an accurate record of the average behavior. The process, advantages, and disadvantages for each type of recording are described in detail in Chapter 2.

Parental Interview

Parental interviews are a valuable tool for the staff to use not only at the initial session but as an ongoing procedure even during the intervention sessions (Figure 8.3). Those tests falling under the parent interview category include the Carey Infant Temperament Questionnaire (Carey & McDevitt, 1978), the DDST (Frankenberg & Dodds, 1969), and the Developmental Profile II (Alpern, Boll, & Shearer, 1980). The parents know the infant best with regard to what skills he or she has and how well those skills are performed, and without good interviewing skills on the part of the examiner this useful information will not be passed on to the staff. It is recommended that the examiner ask the parents how their baby achieves a task rather than asking if the skill is performed. This can be done, for example, by asking the parent how his/her infant gets from a sitting to a standing position rather than asking if the infant can get to

Figure 8.3. Ongoing parental feedback in the form of verbal or written interviews can be helpful when evaluating the results of an infant's program.

standing from a sitting position on the floor. The latter will elicit a negative or positive one-word response; a descriptive explanation will usually accompany the former inquiry. There are several guidelines discussed in Chapter 1 that may help the therapist or teacher develop professional interviewing and test selection tools.

ASSESSING INFANTS

Identifying those infants who require special services may be done through a multistep process. Cross and Goin (1977) have outlined and described a systematic process that assures that each individual infant can receive the best and most effective program possible within his or her geographical area.

Initially, there must be some way of knowing how many infants within a given area are in need of services. This process is known as *casefinding*. By using various community resources (newspapers, radio and television stations, civic groups, prediatricians, public health agencies), information can be made available about the type of special services being offered. Feedback from surveys sent to the community agencies will help answer questions such as the age range of the infants with handicapping conditions (and the type of problems) plus the geographical boundaries needing to be served.

The next step in the identification process is called *screening*. In some areas, both the casefinding and screening steps are done at the same time. Often called "Child Find Screenings," this is done semi-annually or annually. Screenings are conducted quickly by a number of professionals or trained paraprofessionals to decide if the infant is in need of further evaluations or if a particular behavior is still within normal limits.

A few communities have reevaluated their annual screening schedule and have instigated monthly screenings. Instead of having to wait for several months or perhaps a whole year, the infant can be screened and referred to an appropriate program or for further testing within weeks. Thus early intervention can lessen possible extensive deficits.

If the screening results do indicate that a problem exists, it will be the *diagnostic* process that will determine the cause of the problem. Professionals with a specialty closely related to the infant's symptoms will be called upon to give an in-depth analysis and interpretation as to why the infant may not, for example, be vocalizing or independently getting to a sitting position. Four reasons for a diagnostic examination, according to Cross and Goin (1977), are: 1) to identify physical abilities and deficits, 2) to rule out or detect an organic condition, 3) to obtain an in-depth family and infant history, and 4) to observe the infant's interaction with his or her parents, environment, and objects.

It is during this stage of investigation that the parents play an important role. Parents can provide past and current detailed information about how their infant responds to various sensorimotor stimuli or if their infant's behavior in the clinic is typical or not.

The purpose of the last step, *assessment,* is "to develop a comprehensive and specific educational plan that provides the information that is necessary in planning a day-to-day program for the child" (Harbin, 1977, p. 35). The outcome of an assessment will give rise to the infant's strengths and weaknesses plus functional ability.

TYPES OF INFANT INTERVENTION PROGRAMS

There are basically three types of infant intervention programs (homebased, center based, and a combination of home and center based), with variations added (such as parent group sessions) depending on the needs of the parents and infant and the expertise of the staff (Filler, 1983; Heward & Orlansky, 1984; Ramey, Sparling, Byrant, & Wasik, 1982). A *home-based program* requires the staff to travel to the parents' home, providing services using a transdisciplinary model. One or two staff members are responsible for coordinating multi-disciplinary activities on a one-to-one basis. The key person in this type of intervention is the parent. Any skill needing to be learned by the infant is trained by a parent who was taught by the staff member. Cost-effectiveness in terms of time and finances is very poor with this type of system, and only a limited number of infants can be scheduled during the day. However, this type of program allows the infant to remain within the home environment while making it more convenient for other family members to actively participate during the session. Other advantages are that there is less tension between parent and infant in their own home, so that everyone will perform at a higher level. Since the health of the infant is better controlled within the home atmosphere, the number of attended sessions is greater. The materials and equipment available in the home may be more functional and financially efficient for a family's needs. Numerous toys can be made from throw-away materials (orange juice cans, paper plates, strings, ribbon, etc.) usually used in the home.

A measurement used to evaluate the effectiveness of a home-based intervention is the Home Observation for Measurement of the Environment (HOME) for infants ages birth to 3 years (Caldwell & Bradley, 1978). Behavioral test items in five areas (parent verbal and physical contact with the child, acceptance of the child's behavior, opportunities for daily stimulation with adequate play materials, and organization of physical environment) provide information for teachers/therapists to help lessen those factors within the home setting that could delay developmental progress.

The *center-based program* has been housed within a multipurpose facility such as a hospital, public school, university building, or day care center. This program style allows more staff members to be directly involved on a regular basis both in interacting directly with the infant and in providing consulting services to the parents. The total operating cost for a center-based program is less since more families are being served at any one given time. Care must be taken that there is not an overload of sensory stimuli to the infant and an over-abundance of requests for the parents to perform. There must be a built-in monitoring system to assure a well-balanced curriculum that generally emphasizes cognitive, social, and language skills (Filler, 1983). A center-based program offers informal and formal social exchanges among parents who have children with similar problems. Even at a very young age, infants have a chance in a group setting to develop social skills. In the center-based program, therapists and parents often find themselves exchanging roles as teacher/student. The therapist can teach proper positioning and handling. Parents can help therapists understand the infant's personality.

The third type of infant intervention program combines the contact with clients in both settings, *home and center.* Bryant and Ramey (1985) reviewed 12 studies dealing with preventive education for disadvantaged at-risk infants. The authors' conclusion suggests that the increased contact made with both parents and infant in a combination-based program resulted in more positive and effective data being obtained on the infants and an improvement in parent behavior and attitudes.

The type of service model available to parents has usually been determined by the center's philosophy toward intervention education, the boundaries of a federal/state grant, or a decision made by the staff. Final selection should be based on obtaining the maximum individual end results plus being able to serve the community effectively. Serving a larger population may be accomplished through outreach dissemination packets, workshops, or seminars.

INTERVENTION TECHNIQUES

The controversy over the effectiveness of early childhood intervention programs continues to receive positive and negative press. Those in favor of infant stimulation (Bricker, 1985; S. K. Campbell & Wilson, 1976; Farber & Williams, 1982; Gorski, 1984; Levine & McColoum, 1983; Pines, 1982) far outnumber those opposed (Ferry, 1981). Ferry contended that many intervention studies are invalid because there were too few subjects, a matched control group was not used, only one or two aspects of development were evaluated, poorly standardized measures of the outcome were used, and sufficient longitudinal follow-up was not included. Even with what appears to be strong evidence in favor of stimulation, Pelletier and Palmeri (1985) stated that there are still no hard data to prove or disprove any early infant intervention study's conclusion.

Soboloff (1981) followed 50 children with cerebral palsy from 1952 to

1965 who had no previous intervention input and another similar group of 50 children between 1965 and 1978 who did have early intervention services. The study was to determine what the effects of early intervention were on future surgical requests. The results indicated that although early intervention did not pevent surgical operations, it did make their study team more aware of the need for early surgery. In addition, the study revealed that age-related motor skills (ability to sit, stand, and ambulate) were attained sooner with the early intervention group than with the control group.

INTERVENTION GUIDELINES

Staff members who first begin working with infants by using a basic set of guidelines will not only find specific techniques easier to assign to the infant's needs but will also find parental rapport and support quicker to establish. Although it has been slow in evolving, professionals are now acknowledging the importance of taking the time to instruct parents in basic handling mechanics or behavioral management techniques. Evidence gathered from a few research studies points to the fact that a center-based program alone will not produce long-term effects. Parental input within the home is necessary to facilitate the desired results provided the parents are given the appropriate support and training.

This also means staff members must be prepared with up-to-date information about handicapping conditions and treatment approaches. Those who work with the infant population must develop the skills of a generalist, being able to apply procedures from several disciplines effectively using their understanding of the sensorimotor, cognitive, and communicative systems (Sweet, Vanden-Berg, & Flushman, 1982). Several authors stress the importance of being aware of the effect on the infant of quantity, quality, and especially rate of a sensory input. Gorski (1984) believes "timing may be as important as the content of an intervention" (p. 70).

Just as too much stimulation has a negative reaction on the infant, so does a lack of adequate sensory stimulation. Infants with Down syndrome tend to demand from their parents very little in the way of communication or handling. The infants with spastic cerebral palsy may not be able to move toward or away from any stimuli, and the communicative skills of the infant with mental retardation or developmental disability may not be interpreted correctly. What therapists and teachers need to do is to instruct the parents to reach out and encourage some type of feedback from their infant. This in turn builds up an exchange of verbal and/or nonverbal communication that, because of the increased amount of handling and positioning, encourages normal tone, active movement, and parent-infant bonding (Farber & Williams, 1982; Fetters, 1981). The overall goals of any professional working with infants should contain some of Pelletier and Palmeri's (1985) goals, which include: 1) developing a strong parent-infant bond, 2) increasing the infant's awareness of the immediate surroundings, 3) developing normal tone, and 4) encouraging normal movement.

According to Anderson (1986) and Farber and Williams (1982), while still in the NICU, infants need normalization of the automatic nervous system via the vestibular and tactile systems. This can be accomplished by rocking the swaddled infant, using the forward and backward motion not just for tactile input but also to prevent loss of body heat. Case (1985) encouraged proper positioning of the NICU premature or at-risk infant because of the positive end results. First, positioning not just with swaddling but with placement of rolled towels around the head and trunk and under the knees provides a sense of security. Another positioning goal is to provide vestibular stimulation as both a calming influence and a facilitator of movement; this is accomplished when the infant is placed on a heated oscillating waterbed. Frequent position changes will prevent skin breakdown and maintain skin integrity. The use of lamb's wool pads under and around the infant can have a calming effect, providing a comfortable flexed position as well as preventing skin breakdown. Older infants need more time in a semiflexed position to increase the visual field (either supine or prone), to aid in digestion, to increase upper extremity movement, to develop neck and trunk control and stability, and to encourage symmetrical response. Close monitoring is needed to avoid overstimulation, which would satiate the sensory inputs when the infant is left in any one position for a long time.

A variety of therapeutic approaches are available to the physical and occupational therapist, who then can delegate activities to the parents and other staff members. Depending on the stimulus used, the following suggestions can be incorporated into the program of a premature infant in an NICU or full-term infants who are identified as at risk because of a possibility for later developmental problems.

For the infant with hypertonic muscle tone the therapeutic goals and techniques may have to be directed initially toward maintaining and/or increasing range of motion and joint mobility through passive exercise, positioning, and handling. The possible need for adaptive equipment ought to be assessed and discussed as a team-parent project in order for the infant to obtain normal muscle tone and maximum range of motion no matter where he or she is during the day and who has charge of caring for him or her.

Tactile Stimulation

Both the premature and Down syndrome infant display hypotonic or reduced muscle tone. The main goal for these infants is to facilitate the development of normal muscle tone, which in turn will increase flexor tone and prevent overstretching of joints (Pelletier & Palmeri, 1985). One mechanism by which muscle tone can be increased is massaging the infant all over his or her body. If the room is warm enough, completely undress the baby; otherwise undress only the extremity that is being massaged. Lotion, powder, or even bare hands can be an effective medium. One must remember that the manner in which the massage is applied (firm versus light touch; fast versus slow speed) will determine if the effect will inhibit or facilitate alertness. Massaging also enhances body awareness, heightens tactile sensitivity, and even encourages respiration. The massage should start with the head by stroking from the forehead to the nape of the neck, going around the eyes and mouth and from the chin down the neck. From there move to the front and then back of the chest, to the arms (shoulder to the fingers), and down the back of the legs, concluding with massaging the top and bottom of each foot.

A prolonged tactile hypersensitivity could explain why, for example, a 12-month-old infant has not yet crawled on hands and knees or likes to stand while in an infant walker. The tolerance of tactile stimulation can also be promoted by stroking the infant with various textured materials like terrycloth, soft sponges, velveteen, or sheepskin. These are generally thought to elicit a pleasing response when firmly applied to the body. It is a good idea to rotate the type of materials used from day to day and to observe the infant's increased or decreased tactile acceptance.

It is generally a good idea to approach the infant with slow movements, talking in a soft soothing voice, and learn to wait for the infant to respond. Do not touch the baby without first alerting him or her to the impending contact. Otherwise, the infant may startle, tighten the whole body, and even attempt to move away from the tactile stimulus.

Vestibular Stimulation

The vestibular system has receptors in the inner ear (three semicircular canals) that respond to the slightest movement of the head and body. It is also responsible for detecting the degree of balance, muscle tone, and eye movement and is associated with the various levels of alertness. Elaborate equipment is not necessary to assess or treat vestibular deficits; a blanket, waterbed, regular bed, rocker, swing, cradle, and an adult's own body are all that is needed. Providing movement in all directions will include back and forth in a rocker, up and down on a bed, side to side in a blanket or cradle, and circular movement in an adult's arms. A sure way to increase the alertness level, quiet crying, or gain an infant's attention is to hold the baby securely with both hands away from the adult's body. Quickly repeat down and up movements while talking to the infant until the behavior comes under the adult's control. Movement then can be slowed and the infant can be cuddled against the adult's body. No matter what type of movement is used, include auditory and visual stimulation. Let the baby see and hear the adult so no drastic surprises occur.

A number of infant studies have related the effect of vestibular stimulation to increasing muscle tone and calming irritable behavior. A number of studies have used vestibular stimulation to soothe neonates (Korner & Thoman, 1972), to increase motor performance in infants with Down syndrome (Kantner, Clark, Allen, & Chase, 1976; Lydic et al., 1985), and to enhance visual pursuit in neonates (Gregg, Haffner, & Korner, 1976). Results of these studies are varied but do reflect the need to investigate new areas of comparisons as well as repeating or expanding previous efforts. Those studies with significant results indicate that this treatment modality does show results in improving eye contact, postural control, frequency of vocalization, and head/trunk control, and decreasing overactivity, self-stimulation, and self-abusive behavior (Urbanik, 1986).

Visual Stimulation

The rationale for attending to visual stimulation is that it will help encourage head movements of flexion, extension, and rotation in various positions as well as developing eye tracking and eye fixation. Visual stimulation also will help develop the necessary developmental skills needed to attend to and concentrate on tasks in the classroom.

It has been known for years that infants attend best to pictures and design patterns that are colored black and white or bright red. Shiny objects such as aluminum (pie plates) or mirrors also attract and hold the infant's attention.

While the infant is in the crib, mobiles (commercial or home-made types) provide good visual stimulation (Figure 8.4). Too many times commercial mobiles are designed and positioned on the crib so as to attract the adult's eye while the infant rarely gets to fully view or attend to the entire mobile. Fisher Price produces a mobile that slants toward the infant. Simple designs of black and white circles or stripes on a card can be glued to a pie plate. This in turn can be suspended above the infant's face with a string that is attached from the plate to another string or ribbon that is tied across the crib. A narrow piece of clear plastic securely attached (using Velcro strips for easy removal when not needed) across the top of the crib can be used to lay various colored pictures on top for the infant's attention.

When the infant is lying on the parent's lap, on the floor, on the couch, or on the changing table, one can introduce visual stimulation at close range. Let the infant attend to a small toy (especially one that provides noise) for about 3 seconds. Then slowly move it to the right until the infant loses interest. Return the toy to the midline position (the adult may need to reposition the infant's head forward) and repeat the procedure in the opposite direction. Each time this activity is done, try to increase the angle or range that the infant follows as he or she watches the toy with his or her eyes and/or head. Varying the toy will help maintain interest and determine what toys, designs, or pictures the infant pre-

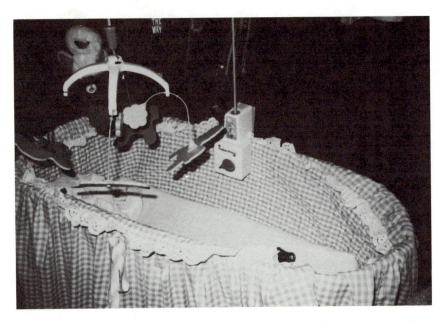

Figure 8.4. Hand-made and commercial toys should be positioned over the crib so they can be seen best by the infant, not the adult.

fers. Change the position of the infant in the crib and even the crib position in the room to give a different view of the infant's limited environment.

Placing the infant in the prone position develops head extension and shoulder stability and encourages visual attending and tracking while watching a moving toy.

Auditory Stimulation

In combination with visual, tactile, or vestibular stimulations, auditory input assists in informing the infant what must be done or what has just happened. If properly implemented, auditory stimulation (the adult's voice) can tell an infant with tight muscle tone that his or her position will be changed, thus minimizing an increase in overall muscle tightness.

There is evidence that not only does the normal neonate hear different sounds but also that he or she heard sounds in the uterus (Segal, 1983). A newborn baby can discriminate between a human voice and other sounds. It is not known if a high-risk infant without handicaps develops the same reactions at the same rate, or what type of retarded responses the infant may experience.

By listening to the sounds around him or her, the infant is developing a foundation for receptive and expressive language. Since language comes from an interaction with people and various experiences, the infant needs and wants to hear sounds. In order for language to develop, the infant needs to be praised with words as well as visual and tactile reinforcements.

An easy way to assess an infant's auditory skills is to observe arm and leg movement when a noise (adult's voice or toy) is first presented. Generally, motion of arms and legs ceases until the infant habituates to the sound, then movement resumes. Changing the rhythm, volume, or type of sound will repeat cessation of limb movement. Over several months the infant's auditory discrimination of position and volume of sounds gradually develops so the infant can tell where the sound originates and who is making the sound. Visual and motor responses can then be directed toward the sound (e.g., a parent enters the room and the baby begins to "talk" and turn toward the parent).

Segal (1983) suggested auditory activities keyed to the age of the infant in 1-month increments beginning at birth. Sound should be varied in the type, volume, rhythm, and speed presented in order to stimulate the infant's developing motor, language, cognitive, and social skills. Singing nursery rhymes while moving legs and arms can be entertaining and is a motivating reason for moving. Hiding a wind-up toy under a washcloth and seeing if the baby can find it (a skill normally acquired between 6 and 9 months) can be used to develop object permanence (Furuno et al., 1979). Tying a ribbon around two similar rattles about 3 inches apart will encourage the infant's interest in retrieving one while grasping the other and thus increase bilateral hand use.

AROUSAL STATE

Normally, infants go through various states of arousal during the day: quiet or active sleep, a quiet-alert state, and an active state. Many high-risk infants are in need of sensory inputs to change a repeating arousal state. The infant with Down syndrome or the premature infant who spends too much time sleeping or remaining quiet for long periods of time needs to increase his or her active state of arousal through tactile and auditory stimulation and passive or active movement. Other infants need to be wrapped firmly in a blanket (swaddled) and rocked in a dimly lit room to increase the quiet-alert state or to encourage the sleep state. Pelletier and Palmeri (1985) advocated the self-quieting techniques of reducing the brightness of a room or allowing the infant to suck on a pacifier or fingers.

EFFECTS OF INFANT INTERVENTION

A search of efficacy studies on infant stimulation programs has resulted in several interesting findings. It is generally agreed that early intervention programs (infants younger than 12 months) have not necessarily proved to have long-lasting effects (Gentry & Adams, 1978; Gorski, 1984; Strauss & Brownell, 1985), and the short-term gains have been rated as only moderate (Strauss & Brownell, 1985).

The cause of such negative comments on infant intervention programs stems in part from the way the research was conducted. In the studies done by Gentry and Adams (1978), S. R. Harris (1981b), and Hourcade and Parette (1984), the conclusions were that the problem of achieving validity and reliability was typical of similar studies. The number of subjects were too few to make a significant difference one way or the other. Too often a control group was not used, thus making the evaluation procedures subjective. The measurement tool used to evaluate progress may not be comparable or have sufficient data on reliability or validity. S. K. Campbell and Wilhelm (1985) found that the usual screening tests used as a follow-up with high-risk infants were not picking up those infants in need of special services. This may not be totally the fault of the test content; it may also have a bearing on the competency of the examiner. Many of the studies lacked a follow-up or postcheck on the level of performance that was the target of intervention.

Although these comments may draw a bleak picture for infant intervention programs, the literature is still shedding some light on the reasons and rationale for continuing to operate and fund these programs. Most interventionists agree with Bricker and Dow (1980) and Matthews (1985) that intervening early with a systematic approach using a combined home- and center-based program works best up to the age of 2 years. Attending to desired behaviors or establishing normal movement patterns at an early age helps minimize the development of related disabilities.

Although specific gains or isolated skills have been difficult to assess or have not proved to have significant results, many of the benefits for early infant training far outweigh the disadvantages (Denhoff, 1981; Matthews, 1985). To aid the experienced or neophyte therapist/teacher working with the high-risk or handicapped infant, a number of guidelines have been formed based on research results, professional opinions, and parental requests. The program's foundation should be based on an educational and medical model. Active parental involvement should be a primary goal of any program (Vincent, Dodd, & Henner, 1978). The progress of the infant, family, and program should be assessed by a checks-and-balances procedure on a routine basis. The specific schedule will vary, and there should be enough time to incorporate both formal and informal evaluations. Behavioral management training that starts when the infant/family enters the program will establish positive developmental patterns across all domains. Effective reinforcers for this age range change rapidly; therefore a backlog of the infant's preferences needs to be established. To assure involving the parents and maintaining their participation in the program, the schedule of evaluations, training, and conferences needs to be flexible enough to continue the initial interest and support from the family. An infant intervention program cannot be an entity of its own if the efforts of staff and parents are to pay off. These programs need to be just one link in the developmental continuum of independence for the child.

CHAPTER 9

Cerebral Palsy

This chapter discusses the basic problem and the etiology of cerebral palsy. Handling and positioning techniques designed to normalize abnormal muscle tone and maximize the child's functional abilities in play, self-care, and school work are described.

Cerebral palsy, in some form, affects 2 children per 1,000 live births each year. (Some sources report from 0.6 to 5 per 1,000 live births.) Thus, in a city of 1 million there would be approximately 500 children in the age range of 3 to 16 years with some form of cerebral palsy (Keele, 1983; Piper, 1983; Scherzer & Tscharnuter, 1982).

DEFINITION AND DESCRIPTION

Cerebral palsy is a nonprogressive disorder of movement and posture resulting from a defect or lesion occurring in an immature brain. A nonprogressive or fixed disorder is one that does not change from bad to worse. In cerebral palsy the brain lesion does not get larger, nor does the damage spread to other areas of the brain. However, since the damage has occurred in an immature brain that will mature, at least to some extent, there may be changes in the kind of movement or postural disorders as the child gets older.

The disorders of movement and posture are characterized by the child's ability to maintain a symmetrical, stable posture in many positions, especially when the child is attempting to hold a posture or move against the pull of gravity. For example, children with cerebral palsy may have difficulty lying supine in a symmetrical, relaxed posture; lifting the head up while prone; or maintaining a symmetrical, stable sitting position. Balance or equilibrium mechanisms are absent, delayed, or incomplete and therefore safe and easy movement is difficult. These movement and postural problems are caused, in part, by a predominance of some primitive reflexes and the presence of abnormal muscle tone.

A primitive reflex is present before birth, at the time of birth, or soon after birth but becomes integrated within more complex movement patterns by the time the infant is 4–6 months old. When a primitive reflex becomes integrated it has been modified by higher centers of the brain and usually cannot be elicited after the age of 4–6 months unless the individual sustains brain damage or is under extreme stress. The grasp reflex is a primitive reflex. Automatic grasping or closing of the fingers is the response to the stimulus of touch pressure applied to the infant's palm.

Abnormal muscle tone and a predominance of primitive reflexes are related to brainstem malfunction. The brainstem is the area of the brain that is initially affected by malformation or damage in the neonate (Scherzer & Tscharnuter, 1982). Muscle tone in the child with cerebral palsy can be excessive, insufficient, or fluctuating between the two.

Normal muscle tone is a quality of muscle characterized by a natural tenseness and elasticity allowing the muscle to respond appropriately to stimuli. A muscle with normal tone is in a steady state of contraction and can resist outside force (Thomas, 1985). Brazelton (1984) described muscle tone in the neonate as a measure of consistency and extensibility of the muscle in reaction to passive stretching of the limb, as well as the amount (degree) of recoil of the limb after extension.

Muscle tone and muscle strength are two different characteristics of muscle. Muscle tone is an automatic quality based on an intact proprioceptive system and automatic central nervous system function. B. Bobath (1985) described tonus as an ongoing (automatic) physiological adaption and organization of the periphery and a condition of readiness. Muscle strength is the muscle's ability to move a body part against the pull of gravity and other outside forces such as a heavy object. Muscle strength is usually tested by having the individual voluntarily move the body part away from the pull of gravity against the resistance of an outside force (e.g., lifting weights).

In cerebral palsy, the movement and postural disorder is primarily related to abnormal muscle tone rather than inadequate muscle strnegth. Without normal muscle tone the individual cannot maintain automatic, stable postures and cannot move voluntarily in a coordinated manner.

Normal infants initially function at a brainstem level. This means that their posture and movements are often, but not always, influenced more by flexor muscle tone than extensor muscle tone, and by some primitive reflexes. As the normal infant's central nervous system matures, the balance between flexor and extensor muscle tone evens out and the primitive reflexes are gradually inhibited and become integrated within more complex movement patterns (Molnar, 1979).

The infant with cerebral palsy will exhibit not only abnormal muscle tone but also a more persistent pattern of primitive reflexes than observed in the normal infant. Primitive reflexes are often present in an exaggerated form in the child with cerebral palsy and last longer than the 30 seconds observed in normal infants. For example, a child with cerebral palsy exhibiting the asymmetric tonic neck reflex is stuck in the "fencer" position, often for more than 30 seconds (Figure 9.1*B*).

Primitive reflexes may appear to be obligate (i.e., they last more than 30 seconds each time elicited and can be elicited each time the stimulus is present) in the child with cerebral palsy but are never obligate in the normal infant. A primitive reflex cannot always be elicited in a normal infant. For example, if a normal infant is full the sucking reflex probably cannot be elicited. However the sucking reflex can probably be elicited in a child with severe involvement with cerebral palsy each time the appropriate stimulus is applied. In other words, the suck reflex is obligate.

The lesion causing cerebral palsy occurs in an immature brain, which means that the damage occurs in a brain that has not yet completely developed. Myelination of the nerves in the brain is not completed until the age of 2 years (Scherzer & Tscharnuter, 1982). Equilibrium or balance reactions, which emerge as a result of central nervous sytem maturation, are not completely developed until 4–6 years of age. The damage can occur anytime before birth (prenatally), during the birth process (perinatally), and during infancy (postnatally). Acquired cerebral palsy can be caused by brain damage occurring after birth up to 2–4 years of age.

ASSOCIATED PROBLEMS

Approximately one-third of the children with cerebral palsy have only motor problems; the remaining two thirds have additional disorders (Prensky &

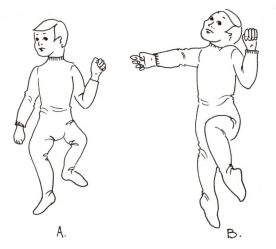

A.   B.

Figure 9.1. Asymmetric tonic neck reflex. *A*, Normal child—may last no longer than 30 seconds at any one time. *B*, Cerebral palsied child—reflex will be exaggerated and last longer than 30 seconds at any one time.

Palkes, 1982). These additional problems are associated with the brain damage or disorder causing cerebral palsy or are secondary to the primary problems of abnormal muscle tone, predominant primitive reflexes, and delayed or absent development of higher level motor skills. Associated problems may include mental retardation, seizures, visual and auditory impairment, dental problems, poor nutrition, speech and language dysfunction, upper respiratory difficulty, urinary tract infections, perceptual and learning disabilities, and emotional and behavioral problems.

Excessive muscle tone can cause the child's body to be positioned in one static position (i.e., flexed or extended) for long periods of time and result in a shortening of muscle and tendon tissue. Eventually, contracture or a permanent shortening of muscle and tendon occur. Contractures will further limit the child's ability to move and will interfere with the caretaker's attempts to properly position, feed, bathe, and dress the child. The child who is in an asymmetrical position for long periods of time is in danger of developing contractures not only in the joints of the extremities but in the spine as well. Spinal deformities such as scoliosis (Figure 9.2) and kyphosis (Figure 9.3) can interfere with the function of the internal organs such as the heart, lungs, and kidneys.

Excessive, insufficient, or fluctuating muscle tone can affect not only the muscles that control the extremities but also those muscles that control eye movements, the lips and tongue, and respiration. This can cause dysfunction in visual tracking, eye-hand coordination, speech production, eating, and breath control. A child with abnormal muscle tone may have difficulty coughing. Adequate cough is necessary for getting rid of unwanted matter in the trachea. Abnormal muscle tone may contribute to upper respiratory infections; bowel and bladder problems may also be related to abnormal muscle tone.

A predominance of the primitive reflexes, especially those that result in asymmetrical posture, can also cause spinal deformities, joint contractures,

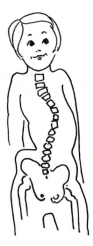

Figure 9.2. Scoliosis—medial to lateral curve of the spinal column.

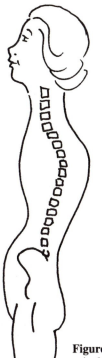

Figure 9.3. Kyphosis—anterior to posterior curve of the spinal column.

and even dislocation of joints. A child who is trapped in these static positions not only does not develop more mature movement patterns, but may have the additional problem of skin breakdown. The child who is stuck in a sitting or lying position for long periods of time and cannot adequately shift weight in these positions will have reduced blood circulation to those parts of the body bearing most of the body's weight. This inadequate blood circulation can cause pressure sores or skin breakown.

The statically positioned child is also unable to voluntarily explore and learn from the environment. This child is deprived of new sensory, cognitive, and social stimulation. Studies designed to determine the kinesthetic, or movement and position, sense in children with cerebral palsy have demonstrated that this type of sensory awareness is impaired (B. Jones, 1976; Opila-Lehman, Short, & Trombly, 1985). Children with the athetoid type of cerebral palsy appear to have better sensory discrimination than children with spastic cerebral palsy (Kenny, 1963). Sensory deficits such as impaired kinesthesis may be related to the abnormal muscle tone as well as the lack of normal movement experiences. Impaired awareness of where the body parts are makes it difficult to perform efficient or appropriate movements.

The delayed or absent development of higher level reactions, such as the head righting, protective extension, and equilibrium reactions means that the child will not develop normal head control or stability and balance in sitting and standing, let alone learn to walk or run normally and safely. Without stability and balance in sitting and standing, there are consequent delays in the development of fine hand skills, independent play, self-care, and schoolwork.

CAUSES OF CEREBRAL PALSY

Many factors can interfere with the normal development of the human brain between the time of conception and the age of 2–4 years. Only the most frequently listed factors are mentioned here. Of all the cases diagnosed as cerebral palsy only 60% can be associated with an identifiable cause (Batshaw & Perret, 1981). Choreoathetosis is the only form of cerebral palsy in which the cause, severe jaundice in the first few days of life, has been clearly established (Batshaw & Perret, 1981; Piper, 1983).

Approximately 85% of the cases are related to congenital factors (40% prenatal and 45% perinatal) and 10%–15% of the cases are acquired postnatally in the neonatal period or early childhood. For as many as 15% of the cases multiple etiologies may exist (Batshaw & Perret, 1981; Bleck & Nagel, 1983; O'Reilly & Walentynowicz, 1981; Piper, 1983; Scherzer & Tscharnuter, 1982).

Prenatal Factors

During the first trimester it is believed that cerebral palsy is related to maternal infections such as rubella, maternal malnutrition, and maternal ingestion of teratogens such as drugs and alcohol. Exposure to radiation, chromosomal abnormalities, and central nervous system malformations are other causes. During later pregnancy brain damage can be related to abruptio placenta and anoxia. Multiple pregnancies and prematurity are also related to a higher incidence of cerebral palsy (P. N. Clark & Allen, 1985). Monreal (1985) found that 60%–70% of the children with cerebral palsy in one population had a family background of neurological features that were possibly indicative of a genetic origin.

Perinatal and Neonatal Factors

During the birth process, prolonged labor and conditions such as the umbilical cord wrapped around the infant's neck can cause anoxia. A precipitate delivery can cause head trauma and intracranial hemorrhage.

One of the frequently cited etiological factors related to cerebral palsy is prematurity along with its postnatal complications such as infection or sepsis, metabolic problems, respiratory distress, and intracranial hemorrhage.

Anoxia, or a lack of oxygen and a deficient blood supply during the newborn period (neonatal hypoxic-ischemic encephalopathy), has been cited as the most common cause of nonprogressive neurological deficits in infants and children. Hyperbilirubinemia related to the Rh factor is also cited (Adsett, Fitz, & Hill, 1985; Batshaw & Perret, 1981; P. N. Clark & Allen, 1985; Largo, Molinari, Weber, Pinto, & Duc, 1985; O'Reilly & Walentynowicz, 1981; Piper, 1983; Scherzer & Tscharnuter, 1982).

Infancy and Early Childhood

Head trauma related to accidents and child abuse; infections such as Reye's syndrome, meningitis, and encephalitis; ingestion of toxic substances such as lead; intracranial hemorrhage caused by stroke; and neoplasms are some of the known causes of cerebral palsy or cerebral palsy–like symptoms in older children.

CLASSIFICATION, DISTRIBUTION, AND SEVERITY OF CEREBRAL PALSY

The motor deficit of each child with cerebral palsy is usually described by the physician according to the types of movement disorder (classification) and the parts of the body that are involved (distribution) (Figure 9.4). Batshaw and Perret (1981) described three basic types of cerebral palsy. Pyramidal-type ce-

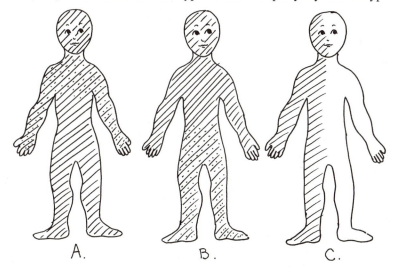

Figure 9.4. Topographical distribution of cerebral palsy: *A,* Quadriplegia; *B,* Diplegia; *C,* Hemiplegia.

rebral palsy is more commonly called spastic cerebral palsy. Extrapyramidal cerebral palsy includes choreoathetosis, rigidity, and atonia. The third type is referred to as mixed-type cerebral palsy. The severity of the disorder is also assessed according to the strength or predominance of the abnormal muscle tone. Refer to Tables 9.1, 9.2, and 9.3 for examples of classification, distribution, and severity, respectively.

The information about an individual child's classification, distribution, and level of severity is useful in providing clues as to what kind of movement or control can be realistically expected of the child, and is one basis for selecting the most appropriate management approaches. Children classified as severely involved are less likely to be independent ambulators. Therefore, future management will include the purchase of an appropriate wheelchair for mobility. Children who are involved on the right side of the body have sustained an injury or a developmental delay in the left hemisphere of the brain. It is in the left hemisphere that the speech and language centers are located. This child is more likely to have special needs related to speech and language training.

DEVELOPMENTAL CHANGES IN
CHILDREN WITH CONGENITAL CEREBRAL PALSY

Parents and students frequently ask why, as the child gets older, does the condition appear to get worse—if, indeed cerebral palsy is a nonprogressive disorder.

It is important to remember that there are muscle tone changes in the normal infant as well as in the infant born with cerebral palsy. Even the damaged central nervous system of an infant with cerebral palsy will mature to some extent. For example, if brain hemorrhage is the cause of the damage, scar tissue will probably form at the site of the damage. When scar tissue forms, it may cause normal surrounding tissue to be pulled or puckered. Even though the hemorrhage does not recur and new scar tissue does not form, there can be effects on the surrounding normal tissue as it grows. It is also believed that the uneven maturation of the damaged and undamaged portion of the child's brain causes some of the puzzling changes in muscle tone. For example, the infant who is initially hypotonic at birth may appear to be spastic or hypertonic by the age of 7 or 9 months. In another child, athetosis may not evolve until the child is 18 or 24 months of age (Haynes, 1983; Prensky & Palkes, 1982; Scherzer & Tscharnuter, 1982).

In the normal, full-term infant, the primitive reflex activity and the predominance of flexor muscle tone is a reflection of the infant's immature central nervous system (Molnar, 1979). The normal, full-term infant is functioning at the brainstem level because nerves in higher levels of the brain have not yet myelinated, or matured. As the normal infant's central nervous system ma-

Table 9.1. Classification of cerebral palsy

Type	Incidence	Location of lesion	Characteristics
Pyramidal (spastic)	50%– 75%	Motor cortex or pyramidal tract of brain	Hypertonicity Increased stretch reflex Exaggerated deep tendon reflexes Voluntary movement is difficult or impossible because of stereotypical positioning and movement (i.e., flexor or extensor synergies) Contractures are a possibility As a newborn may initially appear to be floppy Common distribution: hemiplegia, 60%; diplegia, 20%; and quadriplegia, 20%
Extrapyramidal choreoathetosis (athetosis, dystonia)	20%– 25%	Extrapyramidal pathways, basal ganglia of brain	Fluctuating muscle tone Difficulty maintaining a fixed or stable position and difficulty controlling movement since damage has occurred in nerve tracts that regulate movement, not in tracts that initiate movement Athetosis: slow, writhing, involuntary movements, especially in distal parts; extensor tone predominates Chorea (choriform): irregular, spasmodic contraction of individual muscle or in small groups of muscles; fluctuates between hypotonicity, normal tone, and hypertonicity Dystonic: involuntary twisting and distortion and change in muscle tone between hypotonic and hypertonic, especially in the trunk and proximal parts of limbs Contractures less likely As infant, more likely to be hypotonic
Rigidity	1%		Lead pipe or malleable rigidity Floppy or hypotonic Muscle tone May develop into hypertonicity later
Mixed	15%– 25%	Pyramidal and extrapyramidal tracts	Characteristics of both spasticity and athetosis or dystonia with one type usually predominating

Adapted from Abroms and Panagakos (1980), Batshaw and Perret (1981), B. Bobath (1985), Keele (1983), O'Reilly and Walentynowicz (1981), and Scherzer and Tscharnuter (1982).

Table 9.2. Topographical distribution (see Figure 9.4)

Quadriplegia	Whole body, including the trunk and all four extremities, often with the arms more involved than the legs Severity of distribution often asymmetrical because of predominance of asymmetric primitive reflexes such as the asymmetric tonic neck reflex Often the mixed type of cerebral palsy
Diplegia	Whole body with the legs more affected than the arms Often spastic with some dystonia in the distal parts of the limbs
Hemiplegia	One side of body (arm, leg, and trunk on same side) Right spastic hemiplegia is more common than left
Paraplegia	Lower extremities only Very rare in cerebral palsy Usually really a diplegia with very mild involvement in the upper extremities
Monoplegia	Only one extremity Very rare in cerebral palsy Usually really a hemiplegia
Triplegia	Only three extremities are involved Usually really a diplegia with mild to minimal involvement in one arm

tures, flexor muscle tone becomes less dominant and increased extensor tone allows the infant to develop better head control as well as other motor skills. The primitive reflexes are integrated and become part of more mature motor patterns. The damaged brain of the infant with cerebral palsy will also mature. However, the maturation will take place upon a foundation of abnormal muscle tone and possibly obligate primitive reflexes.

Because there may be changes in the pattern or type of abnormal movement during the first 2 or 3 years of life, it is often difficult for a physician to assign a specific diagnosis (i.e., spasticity, athetoid, or mixed) to a child until he or she is older. Myelination of nerves takes up to 2 years for completion in a normal child. As long as myelination is occurring there will be observable changes in the child's pattern of muscle tone and movement. Spasticity may not emerge until 7–9 months, athetosis at about 18–24 months, and ataxia at about 30–36 months, and the mixed motor pattern may be even further delayed in emerging (Scherzer & Tscharnuter, 1982).

Predicting how much a child with cerebral palsy will progress in later years is difficult because so many factors influence development and progress. Molnar (1979) suggests that prognosis can be based on the following criteria:

1. Clinical type, distribution, and level of severity:
   a. Hemiparetics usually eventually walk unless there is severe intellectual dysfunction.

Table 9.3. Designation of level of severity in cerebral palsy

Level of severity	Functional level
Mild	
Only traces of primitive, tonic reflex activity can be observed, usually when the child attempts a difficult voluntary movement such as running or scissor cutting	Attains a gross motor age of 12 months or above
	Good head control and trunk control; kneeling and standing present
Tonic reflexes are not evident when simple, more automatic movements are attempted	Righting and equilibrium reaction are present but may be delayed or incomplete in more advanced and complex skills such as standing and walking
	Some voluntary use of arms, hands, and legs
Moderate	
Tonic reflexes are seen in certain positions that elicit their occurrence (i.e., supine increases extensor tone) or when the child is excited or exerts great effort	Attains a gross motor age of approximately 5–12 months
	Good head control and incomplete trunk control for sitting
Tonic reflexes may not be constantly present	May be able to move into and out of sitting but will use abnormal movement patterns to do so
	May be able to creep on all four extremities but not in the normal manner (i.e., will use asymmetric tonic neck reflex to creep or "bunny hop")
Severe	
Primitive tonic reflexes occur regularly, instantaneously, and in their unmodified or exaggerated form (the primitive reflexes are often obligate, occurring each time the stimulus is present)	May attain a gross motor age of approximately 1–4 months
	Poor head control and little or no trunk control
	Primitive form of rolling may be only means of mobility
No normal automatic or voluntary movement	Probably unable to manage self-care, independent play, or schoolwork without a great deal of assistance

Adapted from Sommerfeld, Fraser, Hensinger, and Beresford (1981).

 b. Severe, permanent hypotonia and rigidity have a poor prognosis for independent function.

 c. Spastic and athetoid quadriplegics demonstrate varied outcome depending on level of severity and intellectual abilities.

 d. More than half of the diplegics walk by the age of 3 years.

2. Rate of motor development or the length of the delay in achieving gross motor milestones. There appears to be a significant correlation between the ability to sit independently by the age of 2–4 years and the potential for

walking. A lack of ability to sit by the age of 4 years usually means the child has little potential for walking.

3. Evolution of primitive relexes. If the integration of the primitive reflexes and the emergence of the higher level motor reactions is significantly delayed and if the primitive reflexes are obligate and their influence cannot be reduced, the potential for advanced motor development is reduced.

4. Other factors such as intellectual dysfunction, sensory impairment, and emotional-social maladjustment, which can also have a negative effect upon the child's ability and motivation to attain a maximal level of development.

MANAGEMENT AND TREATMENT

The management or treatment plan is based upon the information gathered in an assessment or evaluation. This information can also be an important tool used in the education of the parents and others who are responsible for the daily care of the child. The assessment should delineate not only the problems but the child's strengths as well. A management program will be more effective if it addresses problems that interfere with development as well as utilizing and enhancing the child's strengths.

The specific purpose of the assessment of the young cerebral palsied child is to identify the early patterns of postural maladjustment (abnormal muscle tone, etc.) so that they can be corrected or reduced before more serious deformities occur and so more normal development can be encouraged (Scherzer & Tscharnuter, 1982).

The general areas of function that are assessed by an occupational therapist or a physical therapist are the child's overall present level of development and the pathology or problems that have interfered with development. The evaluation of the overall developmental level may include gross and fine motor skills, adaptive or cognitive skills, visual-perceptual skills, general speech and language skills, self-care and play skills, social skills, and emotional status. The evaluation of the problems specific to cerebral palsy will include an assessment of muscle tone; the status of the reflexes and higher level motor reactions; positioning and handling needs; the status of the tactile, kinesthetic, proprioceptive, and vestibular systems; and the presence of contractures or other deformities. The therapist and teacher should also assess the effect of the child's motor and sensory impairment on the child's ability to play, interact with, and learn from the environment. The reader is referred to Chapter 2 for further discussion and a sample assessment outline.

The presence of abnormal muscle tone or contractures that limit joint movement will interfere with the development of normal motor skills. Therefore, the child with cerebral palsy who may have normal cognitive skills may be functioning at a motor skill level that is several months to several years below the cognitive level. As a result of significant motor delays, it may be difficult or impossible for the child to respond to standard assessments designed to evaluate cognitive, visual-perceptual, or language skills. It may be necessary to carefully adapt standard assessments or select assessments designed specifically for children with motor impairment.

Management Concerns

Management includes helping the child's caretaker to provide optimal care of the child and to provide an environment that will promote maximal development in all areas. Thus, comprehensive management will also include the instruction and training of the child's parents, teachers, and other caregivers in appropriate handling and positioning techniques for lifting and carrying, feeding, dressing, schoolwork, and play activities.

Besides extending therapeutic intervention to the home, use of proper handling and positioning techniques will assist the parents in their role of providing optimal care for their child. The positioning and handling techniques must always be adapted to the needs of the individual child as well as to the skills of the parents or other caregivers. As shown in Figure 9.5, proper positioning may require a specially adapted or designed wheelchair. Parents must not only understand how to correctly place the child in the chair but should also be aware of the reasons for the specific adaptations. This will make it easier for the parent to evaluate when the child needs to be repositioned for better body alignment or when the child has been positioned incorrectly.

Keele (1983) suggested that the following areas of instruction should be provided to the parents: techniques of positioning and handling to reduce effects of abnormal muscle tone, posture, and movement; training in feeding, bathing, dressing, and toileting; techniques to improve gross motor skills such as walking; techniques to improve fine motor skills; instructions in play and other modalities designed to provide a variety of sensory experiences; speech and language training; and instruction in the use of adapted equipment such as special chairs, walkers, and standing supports.

Initiation of early parent instruction and early treatment will help establish effective parenting of the child with special needs (Molnar, 1979). Some studies of child abuse indicate that defective parent-child bonding and ineffective parenting have contibuted to that problem. Therefore, therapists and teachers are obligated to do whatever is possible in helping to prevent abuse of children with special needs.

Treatment Concerns

The general aims of treatment are to correct already existing deformities such as those caused by poor positioning and contractures; to stimulate more normal

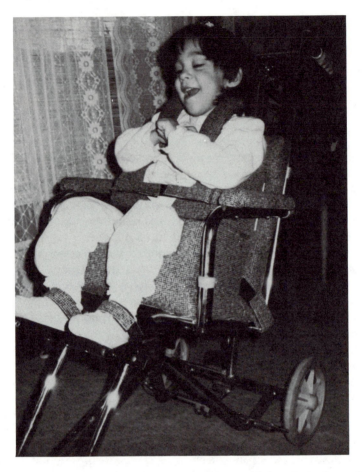

Figure 9.5. This young girl has a better view of her world since the neck, trunk, leg, and foot adaptations allow for better body alignment, arm movement, breathing ability; increased communication skills; and an expanded visual field.

development of neuromotor patterns of movement and interactions with the environment; and to prevent further delays in development. Specific treatment goals include:

1. Normalization of abnormal muscle tone
2. Reduction of the negative effects of primitive reflex patterns that have persisted beyond the time that their influence should have diminished
3. Promotion of the development of stability and flexibility in certain positions
4. Improvement of functional use of the arms and hands

5. Development of as much independence as possible in play, self-care, and work

In many cases, the accomplishment of these goals will have a positive effect on cognitive and psychosocial development. The child's motor development should always be addressed in conjunction with the development of cognitive, emotional, and social skills since this is how development normally occurs.

The treatment techniques described will be those that are usually carried out by an occupational therapist, physical therapist, or a parent with a therapist's supervision. Other treatment team members may include individuals from speech and hearing, education, psychology, nutrition, social welfare, and medicine. The treatment team may be coordinated by a member from one of these disciplines. Occupational therapy and physical therapy will primarily address the problems of abnormal muscle tone, persisting primitive postures, and movements that can interfere with normal development and can lead to permanent deformity. The occupational therapist will also address feeding problems. This is done through nonmedical methods such as specific handling techniques and careful positioning. The handling techniques and positioning are based on normal principles of development when appropriate. For example, normal development proceeds in a cephalocaudal (head to foot) sequence; therefore, head control would be emphasized before sitting in early treatment (Molnar, 1979).

Among the many different professionals who address the needs of the child with cerebral palsy and the family, there are many different theoretical approaches to treatment. Surgery, bracing and splinting, careful positioning and handling or manual manipulation of body parts, and sensory stimulation are just a few of the therapeutic modalities included in the different treatment approaches. According to Molnar (1979) treatment should be eclectic. Carefully selected and well-timed combinations of therapeutic exercise, orthodotics, surgical procedures, and other methods of intervention should be designed for each individual child's unique set of problems and strengths. This writer agrees with Molnar's premise; however, due to the limitations of this book, the treatment techniques described in Chapter 3 are primarily those based on the neurodevelopmental treatment (NDT) approach developed by Berta and Karel Bobath (B. Bobath, 1985; K. Bobath & Bobath, 1972).

CHAPTER 10

Mental Retardation

The American Association on Mental Deficiency's (AAMD)[1] 1983 definition of mental retardation reflects the latest thinking about defining and classifying an individual's functional abilities. This is the eighth revision and represents a consensus that previously has not been noted from professionals associated directly and indirectly with the Association (H. J. Grossman, 1983). The definition states that "mental retardation refers to significantly subaverage general intellectual functioning existing concurrently with deficits in adaptive behavior and manifested during the developmental period" (H. J. Grossman, 1983, p. 1).

Within this definition can be found further explanations to help the reader develop a better understanding of who does and does not fall within this category. The term "mental retardation" in itself should not imply a stagnate level of ability but should imply a level of "behavioral performance without reference to etiology" (H. J. Grossman, 1973, p. 11). *Significantly subaverage general intellectual functioning* refers to an intelligence score that is 70–75 or below as measured on one or more standardized tests designed to assess an individual's intellectual ability. *Deficits in adaptive behavior* describes the level of delay in several domains (independent functioning, physical, communication, and social) according to what is expected within a particular cultural group for any particular age group. Table 10.1 describes the various levels of adaptive behavior. *Developmental period* usually refers to the time from conception through the 18th birthday.

Although the definition is a broad description of an individual who has physical and/or cognitive limitations, the greatest emphasis is placed on how that person is able to effectively adapt to the demands of his or her environment (Hallahan & Kauffman, 1982; M. J. Martin, 1985). Kidd's (1983) comments, as the representative of the Council of Exceptional Children–Mental Retardation Committee (CEC-MR), about the latest revisions are important inputs that reflect society's development. The CEC-MR committee approves of the new ceiling of intelligence (ranging from 0 to 5) and flexibility within each level of

---

[1]In 1987, the membership voted to change the organization's name to the American Association on Mental Retardation (AAMR).

Table 10.1. AAMD adaptive behavior levels

Adaptive behavior level		Skills		
	Independent functioning	Physical	Communication	Social
3 years and above —Profound	Drinks from cup with help "Cooperates" in eating	Sits unsupported Pulls self upright momentarily Reaches for objects	Imitates sounds: "ba-ba," "ma-ma" May use simple gestures Responds to gestures	Indicates in nonverbal way knowing familiar persons
3 years—Severe	Finger feeds self	Stands by self	One or two words	Uses gestures to indicate needs
6 years—Profound	Helps with dressing and bathing	May walk with help or unsteadily on own	Generally uses gestures or vocalizing	Engages in simple games— "Patty-cake"
3 years—Moderate 6 years—Severe 9 years—Profound	Tries to use a spoon but lots of spilling May indicate wet pants	Walks alone with confidence Able to run and climb steps with help	Uses 4–10 words Still uses gestures to indicate needs	Parallel play May prefer some people over others
3 years—Mild 6 years—Moderate 9 years—Severe 12 years—Profound	Uses spoon but still messy Pulls off clothes and puts on some clothing More independent in toileting skills	Climbs stairs but not alternating Runs and jumps and briefly stands on one foot Completes puzzle of four to six pieces on own	Speaks in sentences of two to three words Names common objects like ball, hat, car Knows people by name	Interacts with others in simple play activities Definite preference for certain persons over others
6 years—Mild 9 years—Moderate 12 years—Severe	Uses spoon and fork—few spills Needs help with buttons	Hops, skips and alternates on steps Rides tricycle	Uses 300–400 words in correct sentences Understands simple directions and questions	Participates in simple group games—"Store"
15 years—Profound	Tries to wash and dry hands Toilet trained—few accidents	Throws ball and may hit target	May recognize advertising signs—STOP, EXIT	

Age—Level	Self-Care	Motor	Communication	Social
9 years—Mild	Needs help in cutting meat	Can run, skip, hop, dance	Uses complex sentences	Is part of competitive exercise games
12 years—Moderate 15 years—Severe	Can button and zip Washes face and hands on own	Can alternate feet on stairs Throws ball and does hit target	Speech is clear and distinct Recognizes words but does not read with comprehension	
12 years—Mild	Feeds, bathes, dresses self	Coordination in gross and fine motor skills is good	Carries on simple conversation	Interacts cooperatively and/or competitively with others
15 years—Moderate	Chooses own clothes Combs, shampoos, rolls up hair Washes and iron clothes		Recognizes words and reads sentences with comprehension	Interacts cooperatively and/or competitively with others
15 years and above—Mild	Does well in personal care May need reminders in health and personal care Needs help in selecting clothes	Has no trouble going around own town Does well on equipment requiring good coordination	Can communicate in everyday conversation but cannot discuss abstract concepts Uses telephone and writes simple letters	Initiates group activities for social or recreational purposes

Selected items from Grossman (1983).

mental retardation. Without this type of feedback toward society's changing attitude, the lives of retarded individuals would forever be limited.

INCIDENCE AND PREVALENCE

Incidence represents the number of new mentally retarded cases reported within a given period, such as 1 year. Blackman (1984c) has found a very small percentage (0.5) of the preschool population having a mentally retarded label. The number generally increases when children enter the public school system. Figures reported by Peterson (1986) indicate that of the 3.4 million live births each year, those reflecting a genetic, physical, or biological defect represent 7%.

The *prevalence* of mental retardation is the number or percentage of cases present in the whole population at any given time (Bruininks, Warfield, & Stealey, 1982). The percentage of the population considered to have mental retardation ranges from 2.3 to 3.5 depending upon the source. Hallahan and Kauffman (1982) believe that if an adaptive behavior criterion was considered, only around 1% of the total population would be identified as mentally retarded. However, until the use of such a criterion gains popularity, most professionals will use a prevalence of 3% to identify a wide range and several levels of retardation. Actual prevalence numbers are difficult to determine, and estimates have been used for program planning and funding. Based on the latest United States population census, the number of persons classified as mentally retarded is 6.5 million. This covers all age ranges and levels of retardation from mild to profound categories. The 1983 U.S. Bureau of the Census report also noted that around 2 million infants, toddlers, and preschoolers with handicaps are in need of special services now (Peterson, 1986) and not when they are old enough to enter the public school curriculum. Information on the number or percentage within this group that are mentally retarded is not available, but, taking into account the various handicaps associated with mental retardation, there will no doubt be a higher number of mentally retarded conditions in this group.

CLASSIFICATION

Numerous classifications are used to plan programs, to identify levels of mental and physical functional ability, to determine eligibility for services, and to assess the etiological factors. Depending on what purpose is required, either a medical, educational, or adaptive behavior classification is generally used.

Medical Classification

Only a small number of mental retardation conditions can be attributed to a specific medical cause. The 1983 AAMD medical classification (Grossman,

1983) lists the known causes (see Table 10.2 for the major medical classification scheme). Descriptions of the physical characteristics that depict syndromes or disorders of children that both authors have assessed and worked with in occupational therapy clinics are included in this chapter. Only a small sample of medical causes are described here, and the reader is referred to Blackman (1984a), Menolascino and Egger (1978), and Robinson and Robinson (1976) for more in-depth information.

Infections and Intoxications

Congenital Rubella

Congenital rubella, also known as German measles or three-day measles, can produce severe visual, auditory, and heart damage as well as mental retardation in newborn children. This happens when a pregnant woman contracts the usually harmless disease during the first trimester of her pregnancy (Apgar & Beck, 1974). The chances are 15%–20% that the infant will be born with some type of defect such as deafness, cataracts, microcephaly with mental reatardation, heart anomalies, and low birth weight (Blackman, 1984a; Menolascino & Egger, 1978). Some of the infants will later develop problems associated with seizures, diabetes, central nervous system dysfunctions, bone anomalies, or a thyroid condition. Blackman (1984a) warned that the infected infant may still be contagious for up to 12 months and cautions any female adult who is pregnant or planning to be in the near future to avoid contact with the infant.

Congenital Toxoplasmosis

Congenital toxoplasmosis results from a maternal infection caused by a parasitic organism called *Toxoplasma gondii*. The incidence ranges from 1 to 6 infections per 1,000 pregnancies in the United States (Blackman, 1984a; Sikes, 1982; C. B. Wilson & Remington, 1980). Stagno (1980) has found reports that have estimated 3,300 women give birth to congenitally infected infants each

Table 10.2.   AAMD medical classification

---

1. Infections and Intoxications
2. Trauma or Physical Agent
3. Metabolism or Nutrition
4. Gross Brain Disease (Postnatal)
5. Unknown Prenatal Influence
6. Chromosomal Anomalies
7. Other Conditions Originating in the Prenatal Period
8. Following Psychiatric Disorder
9. Environmental Influences
10. Other Conditions

Adapted from Grossman, H.J. (Ed.). (1983). *Classification in mental retardation.* Washington, D C : American Association on Mental Deficiency.

year. It is reported that 30%–40% of the human population have an immunity to the disease, indicating previous exposure (Sikes, 1982). In the adult, the symptoms resemble a mild flu or infectious mononucleosis, with a cough, swollen glands, or a brief rash. If the first exposure occurs while the female is pregnant then transplacental infection occurs, with severe side effects directed toward the unborn child.

One way of transmitting this parasite to humans is by eating raw or uncooked meat (pork, beef, mutton or veal) that contains the parasite. The most widely recognized means of contracting the infection is by handling cats who have become infected with *T. gondii* after they have ingested rodents or birds. The parasite produces fertilized eggs called oocysts in the intestinal lining of cats. Although harmless when first excreted, the oocysts become infective 1–4 days later. They then can contaminate the soil or litter box for as long as 52 weeks. If the pregnant woman is in charge of cleaning the cat's litter box she may become infected herself.

The earlier the contact is made in the pregnancy the more severe will be the effects on the fetus. In some cases a spontaneous abortion will result (Menolscino & Egger, 1978). The clinical picture of the affected infant includes hydrocephaly, microcephaly, and blindness, and later on the child may show evidence of mental retardation or seizures (Blackman, 1984a; Frenkel, 1985). The most effective means of preventing further cases from occurring is through careful preventive measures. People working out in the garden, especially when handling soil or sand, should wear gloves. Litter boxes should be changed daily since it takes several days for the oocysts to become infective; preferably, someone other than the pregnant woman should change them. Meat should be cooked to 140° F and, when preparing meals, the pregnant woman should follow these guidelines: avoid touching herself around the mouth and eyes while handling raw meat, wash hands and countertops thoroughly after preparing the meat, and keep flies and cockroaches from coming in contact with fruit and vegetables (C. B. Wilson & Remington, 1980).

Herpes Simplex

Herpes is the common cause of sores on the mouth (Type I or HSV-I) and on the genitals (Type 2 or HSV-2). Blackman (1984a) and Leo (1982) reminded readers that the viral infection should be listed as neonatal rather than congenital. This statement relays several bits of information. First, the virus affects the unborn infant during delivery while the baby passes through the birth canal only when the mother has an active case of genital herpes ("Confusion over," 1984). Second, the disastrous effects on the baby can be prevented by performing a cesarean section before or soon after the mother's water bag ruptures (Blackman, 1984a). The number of infants infected with herpes who were born the natural way has increased drastically over the past 20 years from 2.6 cases per 100,000 live births in 1969 to 17.2 in 1982 ("Confusion over," 1984). The infected infant could develop either the mild form, which involves a rash on the skin and mucous membranes of the mouth and eyes, or the severe type, which may involve all the organs of the body and can cause blindness, mental retardation, and neurological disorders. Therapists and teachers must deal with spastic muscle tone, limited voluntary movement, possible contractures, feeding difficulties, and low cognitive abilities.

Trauma or Physical Agent

Prenatal Injury

"Prenatal injury" is a generic term that denotes possible brain damage as a result of prenatal irradiation or hypoxia.

Mechanical Injury at Birth

Any difficulty of malposition, malpresentation, or other complications requiring the use of special tools increases the probable damage of the infant's brain.

Perinatal and Postnatal Hypoxia

Extended periods of anoxia caused by premature placental separation, a knotted umbilical cord, or other perinatal problems can result in mentally retarded abilities. Postnatal anoxia can develop from convulsions, shock, or poisoning and can create mental deficits.

Metabolism or Nutrition

Phenylketonuria

Phenylketonuria (PKU), which if left untreated, causes severe mental retardation, is an inborn error of metabolism. When food containing the protein phenylalanine is consumed, an important enzyme called phenylalanine hydroxylase is released. Phenylalanine is then converted into another amino acid (tyrosine) in another step in the digestive process. The infant with PKU inherits a recessive gene from each parent that prevents the infant's body from forming phenylalanine hydroxylase; thus the infant cannot change phenylalanine into tyrosine (Menolascino & Egger, 1978; Schultz, 1984). This causes a high blood concentration of phenylalanine to develop after the infant begins to ingest foods high in protein, resulting in brain injury and other associated handicaps. The level of phenylalanine was originally tested with a urine test when the infant was 3 weeks old (Hawcroft, 1976). A blood analysis (Guthrie blood test) has been developed that detects the level of phenylalanine; it can be done within 48–72 hours after birth (S. R. Harris & Tada, 1985; Meryash et al., 1981). However, according to Meryash and his coworkers (1981), there is still a concern about the reliability of doing screenings so soon. Many children end up with false-negative results and by the time retardation has been identified, treatment procedures are ineffective. The testing error rate in the United States is about 8% (Koch & Friedman, 1981) and as many as 20% of infants born are never screened (Meryash et al., 1981).

There are two types of PKU, classic and variant (Berry, 1981). *Classic* PKU is associated with a serum phenylalanine level of 20–30 mg/dl; the *variant* cases have levels lower than 15 mg/dl and are labeled as mild hyperphenylalaninemia (MHPA). In the review done by O'Flynn, Holzman, Blaskovics, Azen, and Williamson (1980) the recommended PKU diet could be hazardous to the variant cases in view of the anorexic, anemic, hypoproteinemic, and hypoglycemic complications that develop because there is not enough of the phenylalanine level for normal growth and development. Suspected variant PKU can be identified when there is a more rapid decline of the serum phenylalanine level than is usually expected once the special diet is begun. The powdered formula diet provides the correct amount of nutrients for normal growth. Side effects of the diet are the unpleasant taste and smell and the general monotony, which can present serious discipline problems (McBean, 1982). Close monitoring of the diet by parents and the clinical team (physician, nutritionist) is necessary to check on the serum phenylalanine level. When the serum level increases it may be because the child is eating regular food, and behavior management techniques might prove beneficial to the child and family.

By the time the child is ready for public school, the diet is generally no longer necessary nor as effective. Controversy still exists as to whether to eliminate the diet all at once or to gradually introduce the child to more and more normal menus. A lot depends on how the child reacts to a normal diet and if the serum phenylalanine level is maintained within the normal range. Koff, Boyle, and Pueschel (1977) found that although the dietary treatment is effective in mitigating intellectual retardation, perceptual-motor dysfunctions are present. Unfortunately, they do not list or discuss specific areas of dysfunction. Therapists and teachers working with treated PKU children should be aware of their limited performance ability and investigate specific problem areas.

Gross Brain Disease

Tuberous Sclerosis

Tuberous sclerosis, caused by a dominant gene, is characterized by tuberous skin lesions in a butterfly distribution across the cheeks and nostril area as well as on internal organs, by epilepsy (grand mal), and by mental retardation. The research of Cassidy (1984) reveals the mental retardation range to be from borderline to profound, with a number of tuberous sclerosis patients having normal intelligence. The lesions generally do not occur prior to the fourth or fifth year of age. In addition to medical care for the seizures, early intervention stimulation is recommended to attempt to minimize the severity of mental retardation.

This is an infrequent disorder (1:30,000), but because of the retardation level and increased muscle tone, these children need to be referred for early childhood intervention programs (S. R. Harris & Tada, 1985).

Unknown Prenatal Influence

Cornelia de Lange Syndrome

No cause has been identified for this condition of severe mental retardation (although there is a case study of one girl who had an IQ score of 78 at 12 years of age); small stature, hirsutism (abnormal growth of hair) on and between the eyebrows, on the forearms, and on the back; and skeletal deformities of the arms and hands (Brylewski, 1978; Grossman, 1983; Menolascino & Egger, 1978). Figure 10.1 shows the small stature of a toddler of 2 years. These children are known to be hyperactive and self-mutilating. Therefore teachers and therapists need to know how to use behavior management techniques to minimize self-injurious behavior.

Figure 10.1. This 2-year-old girl with Cornelia de Lange syndrome displays some of the common features, such as small features and stature, hearing impairment, and delayed motor skills. She was beginning to understand and use some gestures to communicate her needs.

Hydrocephalus

Hydrocephalus is characterized by an overabundance of cerebrospinal fluid (CSF) within the brain cavities (see Figure 10.2). This increased CSF can be caused by brain tumors, pre- or postnatal bleeding, inflammation from infections, lead poisoning, or a combination of other factors (Menolascino & Egger, 1978). It is not uncommon for children with spina bifida to be born with hydrocephalus. In external or communicating hydrocephalus there is more fluid (situated between the skull and the brain) being produced than can be absorbed. In obstructive or internal hydrocephalus there is blockage in one of the channels (i.e., aqueduct of Sylvius) that allows the fluid, as it builds up, to cause pressure inside the brain and against the skull (Apgar & Beck, 1974). The intellectual ability of hydrocephalic children will vary depending on the severity of the condition and can range from above normal to profoundly retarded. The lower

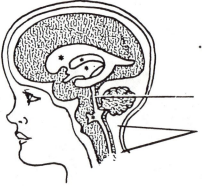

*60 percent of the cerebrospinal fluid (CSF) is produced and flows within the 4 ventricles.

It also travels through the aqueduct of Sylvius . . . and then . . . down the spinal cord and up into the subarachnoid spaces of the brain. From these two areas the CSF is absorbed into the bloodstream.

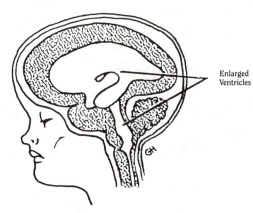

Enlarged Ventricles

Figure 10.2. Cross-sectional view of the normal and abnormal size of the four ventricles.

IQ range may be found in untreated or delayed treatment cases. Thus, it is essential that a plastic drainage tube (shunt) with an attached one-way valve or pump be surgically implanted from one of the ventricles down to the jugular vein, where the fluid can eventually become absorbed into the bloodstream. Intracranial pressure may begin to build up even in the presence of a shunt because of blockage or inflammation, possibly due to an infection. The common signs indicating an increase in cranial pressure are vomiting, headaches, and abnormally quiet or irritable behavior (Wolraich, 1984a). These are signs the professional staff member must keep in mind when working with the hydrocephalic child.

Macrocephaly/Microcephaly

Two other conditions that often are mistaken for hydrocephalus, or for one another, are microcephaly and macrocephaly. Basically, macrocephaly refers to an increase in the size and weight of the brain, which may be a familial condition, associated with mental retardation, epilepsy, and poor vision. Microcephaly is characterized by a head circumference of 17 inches or less. The lower portion of the skull is of normal size, which means the chin, mouth, nose, and ears also will be of normal portions. The forehead becomes angled, slanting backward in almost a straight line to the top of the head.

Chromosomal Anomalies

Down Syndrome

Down syndrome is the most common of all the chromosome abnormalities, affecting 1 out of 600–800 live births (Blackman, 1984b; Menolascino & Egger, 1978). Confirming the diagnosis of Down syndrome can be done by a karyotype count of individual chromosomes, which will reveal a count of 47 instead of the normal 46 chromosomes. In 1959 it was discovered that there were three ways for this anomaly to occur (Lejeune, Gautier, & Turpin, 1959). *Nondisjunction* occurs spontaneously as a result of a sorting error during meiosis prior to ovulation when chromosome #21 fails to separate, resulting in an abnormal ovum (24 chromosomes). The union with a normal sperm (23 chromosomes) then produces a count of 47. Nondisjunction represents the highest percentage (95%) of Down cases, with a recurrence rate (subsequent Down syndrome children born to the same woman) of 0.50% to 1.0% (Blackman, 1984b). It has been suspected that nondisjunction happens with greater frequency in older pregnant women. A less frequent form (only 4% of all cases) is caused when the attachment of a part of the #21 chromosome is translocated to another chromosome, usually #15 but sometimes #22 or #14 (Blackman, 1984b; Robinson & Robinson, 1976). In *translocation*, one of the child's parents (mother or father) is a normal carrier, which means for each succeeding pregnancy there is a high risk for another child to be born with Down syndrome. *Mosaicism,* 1% of Down syndrome cases, occurs after conception and during the early embryonic cell development. This means there are some cells that have 47 chromosomes and others that have the normal 46 count. Therefore, the effect on the individual's physical characteristics is less, which minimizes the overall physical appearance. Several studies have shown that in a 19-year period (1961–1979) there has been a decrease in the number of children born with Down syndrome (Fryers & Mackay, 1979; Owens, Harris, Walker, McAllister & West, 1983). Both articles point out that more women of older ages (35 +) are having amniocentesis performed and if the results indicate the presence of the extra chromosome, they then have the option of an abortion.

Many of the features prevalent in Down syndrome are easily recognizable in young children but until recently were not that easy to identify in the newborn (Figure 10.3). A number of attempts have been made to choose a few of the over 100 identifiable characteristic signs as being most characteristic in both age groups (Table 10.3). Preus (1977) expanded on previous assessments that looked at the digit patterns and creases of the hands and feet to diagnose Down syndrome. This was found to be too restrictive, and a quick, easy, reliable diag-

Figure 10.3. Infants with Down syndrome now receive early intervention services, due to the support and advocacy of parents.

Table 10.3. Commonly known Down syndrome characteristics

Newborn	Young Children
1. Muscle hypotonia	1. Muscle hypotonia
2. Epicanthal folds of eyes	2. Epicanthal folds of eyes
3. Gap between first and second toes	3. Wide gap between first and second toes
4. Protruding tongue	
5. Flat facial profile	4. Small oral cavity—protruding tongue
6. Dysplastic ear	
7. Corners of mouth turned down	5. Congenital heart defect
8. Excess skin at back of neck	6. Small stature
9. Lack of Moro reflex	7. Mentally retarded
10. Oblique palpebral fissures	8. Speckling of iris (Brushfield spots)
11. Dysplastic pelvis	9. Simian crease in middle of palm
12. Simian crease in middle of palm	10. Hyperflexibility of joints
13. Hyperflexibility of joints	11. Upward slant of eyes (questionable)
14. Dysplastic middle phalanx of fifth finger	

Adapted from Blackman (1984b), Fried (1980), and National Down Syndrome Society (1984).

nostic tool was developed by Fried (1980) using eight common signs. For scoring purposes, each sign was given a point value of 1. The results are divided into three scoring groups: confirmed (6–8), suspect (3–5), and disproved (0–2). The suspect category would require a cytogenetic investigation to establish or disprove the diagnosis of Down syndrome. The eight features of Fried's test are listed as the first eight signs in Table 10.3 under "Newborn." Use of this diagnostic tool has shown that 70% of the infants can be clinically identified, 20% need further investigation, and 10% do not have Down syndrome.

Additional signs and problems in the older infant and young child are susceptibility to upper respiratory infections, small head size with a flat shape to the front and back, short and wide neck, immature digestive tract, and a tongue furrowed on the dorsal surface. In addition to the shortness of the hands and fingers, the fifth digit is curved inward. Strabismus, nystagmus, and refractive errors (myopia) are common visual problems (Pesch, Nagy, & Caden, 1978), and mild to moderate hearing defects are also found. Lederman (1984) explained that the restricted movement of a child with Down syndrome is caused by lack of trunk rotation. The child with Down syndrome has a very characteristic prone-to-sit movement pattern. The hips are externally rotated as the child pushes upward using both hands. At the same time, the child spreads his or her legs outward until they are 180 degrees from each other, making the child hyperextend the back to maintain sitting balance. Understanding this movement pattern is important for teaching correct maneuvers. The delayed myelinization of the nervous system is believed by S. R. Harris and Tada (1985) to be the reason for the persistence of generalized hypotonic muscle tone as well as the persistence of numerous primitive reflexes (palmer, plantar grasp, stepping, and Moro). This in turn delays the protective equilibrium reactions.

A number of studies have compared the development of institutionalized children versus children raised in the home and have come to the same general conclusions. Motor milestones are achieved sooner (Melyn & White, 1973) and social skills are higher than cognitive abilities (J. A. Connolly, 1978; Cullen, Cronk, Pueschel, Schnell, & Reed, 1981) in children raised at home.

Those studies of the last 10 years pertaining to the Down syndrome population of interest to therapists and teachers include studies on motor deficits (S. E. Henderson, Morris, & Frith, 1981); feeding problems (Gisel, Lange, Niman, 1984a, 1984b); sensorimotor development (Dunst & Rheingrover, 1983; Greenwald & Leonard, 1979); physical growth (Chen & Woolley, 1978; Cronk, 1978); gait patterns (Lydic & Steele, 1979; Parker & Bronks, 1980); temperament (Gunn, Berry, & Andrews, 1983); postrotary nystagmus (Ling-Fong & Hardman, 1983); proprioceptive input (Esenther, 1984); primitive reflexes (Sand, Mellgren, & Hestnes, 1983); comparison of assessment tools (Eipper & Azen, 1978; Ramsay & Piper, 1980); and efficacy of early intervention programs (B. H. Connolly, Morgan, & Russell, 1984; B. Connolly, Morgan, Russell, & Richardson, 1980; S. R. Harris, 1981b; Ludlow & Allen, 1979; Oelwein, Fewell, & Pruess, 1985). Lydic's (1982) extensive annotated bibliography on motor development should be used as a guide in planning efficient and effective individualized education programs (IEPs) that can be shared with the family and team and members.

Cri-du-Chat Syndrome

Cri-du-chat syndrome is a relatively rare syndrome but one that causes not only severe cognitive deficits but also motor delays. S. R. Harris and Tada's (1985) literature search found 150 identified cases as of 1977. The syndrome is caused by the deletion of the short arms of chromosome #5, and the name is taken from the French term for cat cry, representing the familiar sound the infant makes when crying (S. R. Harris & Tada, 1985; Menolascino & Egger, 1978). This characteristic apparently dissipates by the time the child reaches school age. These children are microcephalic, have unusual low-set ears, and an abnormal shiny, translucent appearance to the skin. Of primary concern for therapists is developing gross and fine motor skills by increasing muscle tone and developing muscle strength. Teachers will be concerned with improving functional levels in self-help and cognitive domains.

Turner Syndrome

Instead of the normal XX female sex chromosome, individuals with Turner syndrome have only one sex chromosome (XO); the incidence is estimated to be between 1 and 2 per 2500–5000 live births (S. R. Harris & Tada, 1985; Menolascino & Egger, 1978; D. P. Wilson, Carpenter, & Holcombe, 1985). Physical characteristics include heart abnormalities, webbed neck, short stature, droopy upper eyelids, low hairline on the back of the neck, edema of the hands and feet (usually disappears as the infant grows older), and low-set, elongated ears. Wilson et al. (1985) found 75% of the individuals they studied had conductive hearing deficits, which they felt would result in impaired speech and general learning disabilities. Failure of the development of secondary sex characteristics is evident as the youngster reaches puberty. The breasts do not develop, menstruation does not begin, there is scant pubic and auxiliary hair and ovarian development is severely deficient, being replaced by fibrous tissue (Apgar & Beck, 1974; S. R. Harris & Tada, 1985). Intellectual ability is within normal limits, but incidences of mental retardation has been reported. Of concern to therapists and teachers are the difficulties relating to spatial perception and orientation as well as hearing losses and insensitivity to taste and smell (S. R. Harris & Tada, 1985).

Other Conditions Originating in the Prenatal Period

Disorders Relating to Short Gestation and Unknown Low Birth Weight

Conditions in this category that may result in mentally retarded behavior can be caused by the following factors:

1. Birth weight of less than 1,000 grams
2. Gestation age of 28 weeks or less
3. Slow fetal growth and fetal malnutrition (shows signs of dry peeling skin)
4. Long gestational period and high birth weight (4,500 grams or more)

Following Psychiatric Disorder

Psychosis, according to the AAMD medical classification manual, is the category "for retardation following psychosis or other psychiatric disorder when there is no evidence of cerebral pathology" (Grossman, 1983, p. 149).

Environmental Influences

Psychosocial Disadvantage

A child is considered to be psychosocially disadvantaged when one parent and one or more siblings are functioning at a subnormal intellectual level. A poor environmental picture may include inadequate diet, poor housing, and infrequent medical care. These children may have been born prematurely, have had a history of infectious diseases, or a combination of these and other environmental problems.

Sensory Deprivation

Sensory deprivation occurs when there is a long history of tactile or social deprivation in the infant and early childhood years. A child who is not provided adequate stimulation as a baby and toddler will be slow in achieving many of the developmental milestones (areas such as walking, talking, dressing, eating, and comprehension of abstract ideas).

Other Conditions

Defects of Special Senses

In order to classify a child as having defects of special senses, there must be evidence that the visual or auditory defect is the only factor contributing to the slow development of the child. Generally, there are no other physical problems, no psychosocial difficulties, or no signs of mental retardation in the immediate family.

Educational Classifications

Mildly Retarded

Eighty-nine percent of the total retarded population are classified as mildly retarded. All the causes of retardation for the majority of mildly retarded persons are not known. This level of retardation is often referred to as "familial" retardation because of the contibuting factors of nutritional deficits, poor environmental stimulation, lack of early intervention stimulation, and limited communication feedback (Lederman, 1984). Detection of mildly retarded abilities is not easy during infancy, but once these children are in school (although sometimes not until the second or third grade) the lack of certain abilities is recognized. Grasp of academic subjects is confined to the second- to fourth-grade level by the time the 16th birthday is reached (Keele, 1983), and poor memory retention and shorter attention span are noted. There is an absence of physical anomalies; thus very few individuals have a neurological impairment that would affect their movement ability. However, there are limitations in sensorimotor skills; specific examples include eye-hand and or eye-foot coordination, bilateral integration, apraxia, fine motor dexterity, and visual and auditory perception (Lederman, 1984). As adults, many individuals with mild retardation manage independently in the community and can manage semi-skilled or unskilled jobs, and some are able to take care of household and family responsibilities.

Moderately Retarded

With moderate retardation the limitations are more pronounced and the causes are more identifiable: included are maternal infection and chromosomal disorders as well as metabolic errors. As with the mild category, there are both specific and nonspecific causes in the moderate cases. There are significant delays that are evident during the preschool years. These individuals have an IQ of 35 to 49, with limited speech and language, demonstrating a level of mental ability about half that of the average population (Keele, 1983). Even though the individual with moderate retardation will require some assistance in everyday self-care skills and economic supervision in managing a budget and household chores, he or she is able to learn to read certain words and to participate in group activities.

Severely Retarded (Severely Multihandicapped)

Numerous causes of severe retardation can be identified at birth or shortly afterward, ranging from infections and intoxications, chromosomal anomolies, and metabolic disorders to postnatal head traumas. Associated with these etiologies are medical and/or physical problems that add to the severity of the condition. Seizures are a common problem, as are visual, auditory, circulatory, and ambulatory functional problems that require some type of therapeutic remediation. Language capabilities may be limited to a few words or phrases expressed vocally or with the use of a communication board.

Profoundly Retarded (Severely Multihandicapped)

Persons with profound retardation need full assistance in taking care of their self-help skills (dressing, toileting, feeding, and bathing). Mental and physical complications abound with these individuals because of the overwhelming central nervous system impairment (primitive reflexes dominate) and organic pathology (Keele, 1983). Extreme retardation is noted as early as infancy and continues into adulthood. Expectations for this population were almost nonexistent until the passage of the Public Law 94-142, which mandated a free public education to all handicapped individuals up to the age of 21. Since then, classroom programs have incorporated a multidisciplinary approach (occupational therapy, physical therapy, speech therapy, nutrition, and psychology) in addition to special education.

For years the severely and profoundly retarded groups were lumped together, and it was very difficult to define either one or to obtain federal/state funding for one without including the other. Several attempts have been made at defining each level (Geiger & Justen, 1983; Switzky, Haywood, & Rotatori, 1982), but at this writing there has been no agreement from those educators involved.

In both the severe and the profound retardation classification, one of the most frequently observed characteristics is deviant behavior. The concept of deviant behavior is based on a value judgment; it is considered to be any behavior not in the best interest of the child or any type of behavior that interferes with an opportunity for the child to learn. Two examples of deviant behavior are stereotypic and self-injurious behavior. Stereotypic behavior, or self-stimulation, is any type of rhythmic repetitive movement that does not cause any personal injury and is observed as body rocking, head rolling, hand waving, and twirling or spinning toys or objects. The most common examples of self-injurious behavior are head banging, biting lips or arms, scratching the body, gouging at the eyes, and pulling out chunks of hair (Schroeder, Mulick, & Rojahn, 1980). According to Bright, Bittick, and Fleeman (1981), such behavior is due to a lack of exploration and interaction with the environment since birth. Generally, the more severe the retardation, the greater the frequency and severity of the self-injurious behavior (Schroeder et al., 1980).

Adaptative Behavior Classification

As indicated from the AAMD's definition, a person cannot be classified within the mental retardation category without the inclusion of a delay or deficit in their adaptive behavior abilities. This means that an individual is evaluated according to his or her ability to function within certain standards for his or her age or cultural group in social responsibility, communication skills, physical ability, and independent functioning (Grossman, 1983). During infancy and the early childhood years, there is a greater emphasis and expectation on mastering the basic sensorimotor skills, coe mental retardation category without the inclusion of a delay or deficit in their adaptive behavior abilities. This means that an individual is evaluated according to his or her ability to function within certain standards for his or her age or cultural group in social responsibility, communication skills, physical ability, and independent functioning (Grossman, 1983). During infancy and the early childhood years, there is a greater emphasis and expectation on mastering the basic sensorimotor skills, communication skills, self-help skills, and social skills. The training for the older child and adolescent centers on applying many of these beginning skills to basic academic skills in daily life, appropriate reasoning and judgment in mastery of the environment, and appropriate interaction within group activities and with interpersonal relationships (Grossman, 1983).

The person's age and functional or adaptive ability may determine the mental retardation classification for that person. The Adaptive Behavioral Scales (Nihira, Foster, Shellhaas, & Leland, 1974) can be completed by a person (parent, caregiver) who is familiar with the child's functional ability. Three phases of adaptive behavior (maturation, learning, and social adjustment) play varying degrees of importance for different age groups.

ASSESSMENT

Assessing children with mental retardation requires the cooperation and interaction of many people in order to design the most appropriate and complete program that will achieve the highest function level possible for each individual child. More and more the responsibility of evaluating a child within one's own area of expertise is becoming a thing of the past. As the focus of a transdisciplinary approach of treatment becomes accepted, so is the change being made in assessment. Concrete evidence of this can be seen in the IEP process. Therapists are becoming immersed in the educational environment and are no longer the sole proprietors of positioning and handling techniques (Sears, 1981). Therapeutic sessions are being carried out by the school staff (therapists, teachers, aides) within the classroom setting. The extent of the motor assessment performed by teachers or other therapists usually is determined by their knowledge and expertise and by the specific assessment tool used. Most teachers feel confident in administering a developmental checklist dealing with motor skills but will shy away from a sensory integrative or reflex test. This is as it should be; the technical administering and interpreting should be left to those who are qualified or certified in a particular area or with a specific test.

According to Sears (1981) the advantages of a transdisciplinary assessment and treatment for the team include: 1) the ability to expand one's competencies, 2) the development of or increased communication among team members, and 3) the combination of a program representing both the medical and educational viewpoint. Inge and Snell (1985) have proved the effectiveness of inservice training in teaching proper positioning and handling across disciplines. The one to derive the most from this transdisciplinary approach is the child. In addition, the child also benefits from a continuity and consistency in the development of skills, increased services from related disciplines, and the "total child" treatment approach rather than treatment of isolated deficits such as hearing loss.

Upon completion of all the various assessments there are four reasons for therapeutic referrals: habilitation, prevention, maintenance, or rehabilitation (Prensky & Palkes, 1982). Under these headings come the goals such as to develop the highest level of potential, to minimize or prevent deformities, to teach self-help skills, to help control head and trunk movements, and to improve balance in all positions. The function of a therapist within the public school system is to provide an evaluation that is appropriate for the child, be a part in planning an education that is appropriate for the child, be a part in planning an educational program based on the evaluation results, implement an intervention program designed to achieve an optimal learning level, be responsible for managing a therapy program, and assume the role of consultant to teachers and parents (Gilfoyle & Hays, 1979). When working as a consultant, L. McCormick and Lee (1979) reminded readers, therapists have an opportunity to have an effect on programming and "subsequent behavior change for a substantially larger number of children" than with the direct service programs (p. 588). Especially in the case of children with severe multiple handicaps with limited mobility, therapists may be called upon to give an inservice program on correct techniques in lifting, handling, and carrying these children (S. R. Harris & Tada, 1985). Readers needing an in-depth description of the duties of the therapist can find it in the works of Gilfoyle and Hays (no date) and Langdon and Langdon (1983).

CHAPTER 11

Neural Tube Defects

Crain (1984) reported that each year in the United States there are 6,000–8,000 children born with some form of neural tube defect. Neural tube defects include a number of syndromes consisting of structural abnormalities that may involve the brain and spinal cord as well as surrounding structures such as the spinal nerves and vertebrae (Badell-Ribera, 1985). These abnormalities as a group are called myelodysplasia and include spina bifida occulta, spina bifida cystica (which includes meningocele and myelomeningocele), and anencephaly. The abnormal development occurs during embryonic development in the first trimester of pregnancy and results in problems requiring lifelong management (Crain, 1984; Ensher & Clark, 1986). It has been reported that 90% of the mothers who bear an infant with a neural tube defect have had no other affected child (Crain, 1984).

DEFINITION

To understand abnormal spinal development and thus be able to describe to others what has happened, it would be helpful to define some of the terms used in referring to neural tube defects. Figure 11.1 provides a visual description of the different types of neural tube defects. *Occulta* refers to a condition that is not physically apparent other than the patch of hair over the section of the defective spine. *Meningo-* means the covering of the spinal cord and brain. *Myelo-* refers to the spinal cord. *Cele-* means the sac or cavity that is filled with fluid that protects the spinal cord and brain.

Meningocele means that the meninges and cele extend through the unfused vertebral arches but without protrusion of the spinal cord into the sac. This also means there will be no neurological impairment of the lower extremities after surgery. *Myelo*meningocele does mean neurological problems because the spinal cord along with the meninges is contained within the sac. This condition may be just an open area without a skin covering over the defect. Anencephaly is a severe condition where there is an absence of the cerebrum and cerebellum and the area is not covered by skin or bone.

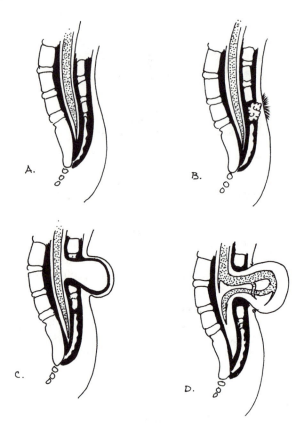

Figure 11.1. *A,* Normal spinal structure. *B,* Spina bifida occulta—failure of posterior vertebral arches to fuse without herniation of the spinal cord or meninges. Tuft of hair may be only external sign. *C,* Meningocele—cyst contains meninges and cerebrospinal fluid. *D,* Myelomeningocele—cyst contains meninges, part of spinal cord and spinal nerves, and cerebrospinal fluid. May or may not have skin coverage.

DEVELOPMENT

Neural tube defects can occur anywhere from the brain to the base of the spinal cord and can be described as a midline defect of the skin, brain or spinal cord, and skull or spinal column (vertebrae). In normal human development the neural tube is initially like a flat ribbon of tissue running in a straight line down the center of the developing embryo. The flat ribbon of tissue develops a groove that becomes deeper while the sides grow up and form a tube. The neural tube, which forms at about 3–4 weeks of gestational development, eventually evolves into the brain and spinal cord. The neural tube closes in two directions, from the center toward the cephalic (head) end and from the center toward the caudal (tail) end. The spinal cord is surrounded first by membranes called meninges and then by the bony spine, called vertebrae (Williamson, 1987; Wolraich, 1984b). Incomplete segmental closing of the neural tube can occur on the posterior or anterior side and result in a cleft or opening in the spinal cord and surrounding structures. If the anterior neural tube fails to close, the lesion is usually in the cephalic end and may result in a condition called Arnold-Chiari malformation. This interferes with the flow and absorption of the cerebrospinal fluid, which subsequently results in the development of hydrocephalus. This condition occurs in 80%–90% of the children with neural tube defects. If the lesion occurs in the posterior part of the neural tube, the result is usually spina bifida cystica, with corresponding levels of paralysis, or spina bifida occulta (Badell-Ribera, 1985; Ensher & Clark, 1986). Refer to Table 11.1 for a description of the different types of neural tube defects.

INCIDENCE

The number of children born with neural tube defects varies greatly depending upon the geographical area in which the studies have been conducted. In the United States, the incidence of neural tube defects varies from 0.1 to 4.13 per 1,000 live births (Batshaw & Perret, 1986; Bricker, 1986; Feldman, Manella, Apocada, & Varni, 1982; Peterson, 1987). On average, the incidence is higher in British Columbia (3.07:1,000) and in the British Isles (4.5:1,000) (Akins, Davidson, & Hopkins, 1980; Badell-Ribera, 1985). Meningocele and myelomeningocele are the second most common birth defects after Down syndrome. The myelomeningocele form of spina bifida is four to five times more common than meningocele (Bleck & Nagel, 1983; Peterson, 1987).

Survival rates have improved significantly with the development of earlier and more effective medical and surgical techniques of spinal defect closures, shunting, and antibiotics. Badell-Ribera (1985) reported that in 1918, 80%–90% of the infants with meningomyelocele died within the first year of life. In 1971, 40% of the children survived past the age of 7 years, primarily as a result of early surgical treatment. By 1981, the survival rate past the 10th year of life was 60% (Crowe et al., 1985; A. H. Hayden & Beck, 1982; Hunt, 1981; Williamson, 1987). The chance of future siblings being born with a neural tube defect is thought to increase to 1 out of every 20–25 births. This is because of complex inheritance patterns. How many genes need to be involved to cause neural tube defects is not known and may be proved to be a false assumption with the recommendation that future studies be conducted with larger family samples.

Table 11.1. Types of neural tube defects (see Figure 11.1)

Type of defect	Description
Spina bifida occulta	Most common type of spina bifida and the least serious.
	The back arches of one or more vertebrae do not fuse; however, the spinal cord and meninges usually do not protrude out of the opening and there is usually good external skin covering.
	Externally the only sign may be tufts of hair and a skin dimple in the midline of the lower back.
	Twenty-five percent of the general population has this condition and most experience no neurological problems.
Spina bifida cystica	
Meningocele	The meninges (covering or membrane of the spinal cord) protrude out through the openings in the vertebra.
	The sac, which is called a meningocele, will contain meninges and cerebrospinal fluid.
	The spinal cord may be intact.
	Generally produces no neurological disability.
	When it occurs on the high back or neck, the nerve tissue is not affected.
Myelomeningocele	Second most common and most serious type of spina bifida.
	The posterior neural tube failed to close and resulted in a herniation of the spinal cord and meninges into the sac along with cerebrospinal fluid.
	The protruding spinal cord and spinal nerve tissue may have developed abnormally.
	Ninety percent of children with myelomeningocele also develop hydrocephalus.
	All children with myelomeningocele have sensory and motor dysfunction below the site of the lesion.
	Most frequent level is the lumbosacral region.
Anencephaly	Any or all of the brain may fail to develop when the anterior surface of the neural tube fails to close.
	Death occurs within the first several days after birth.

Adapted from Akins et al. (1980), Badell-Ribera (1985), Ensher and Clark (1986), and Williamson (1987).

ETIOLOGY

The cause of neural tube defects in any given case is usually unknown. The condition is most likely related to multiple causes, including the cumulative effect of genetic abnormalities interacting with unknown environmental factors. There is a belief that "parents may carry genes which make them susceptible to various nongenetic (environmental) factors known to be associated with it" (Wolraich, 1984b, p. 161). Although it is not clearly understood nor has it been proved that any chemical or other agent is the cause of neural tube defect, it is believed that there may be a relationship to the genetic susceptibility and environmental factors (Myers, Cerone, & Olson, 1981). Each parent must be a carrier for spina bifida to occur. At present there is no way of testing the parents prior to their baby's birth to verify if either one is a genetic carrier.

Studies have pointed to a higher incidence of neural tube defects with advanced maternal age, poverty, urban settings, season of birth (autumn and winter), multiple pregnancies, and the use of oral contraceptives in the month prior to conception (Crain, 1984; Crowe et al., 1985).

DETECTION

Diagnosis of a neural tube defect is generally made at birth, but such a defect can be detected in the fetus in one of three ways. First, the alpha-fetoprotein (AFP) manufactured by the fetal liver and gastrointestinal tract is normally present in the fetal blood, spinal fluid, and the amniotic fluid. The presence of an open spinal lesion allows a high level of AFP to then leak into the amniotic fluid, which can be detected during the 16th to 18th week of gestation. A less accurate means of detection is by testing the mother's blood level of AFP, but this must be done between the 12th and 14th week of gestation. It has been reported that only 12% of women with a high level of AFP have delivered a child with spina bifida. Also, this test misses 1 out of 5 fetuses with spina bifida that later are diagnosed as a less serious type. A third test can be accomplished with ultrasound waves but it is usually done in conjunction with either amniocentesis or blood tests. Normally, movement of the legs can be observed; with the more severe types of spina bifida this action will be absent. As the technology of this technique improves so will the reliability of identifying neural tube defects.

MEDICAL TREATMENT

The spinal cord and meningeal lesions require surgery, usually within the first 24–48 hours after birth. This is performed to place the myelomeningocele mass back into the spinal canal, to graft bone in order to close the incomplete vertebrae, and/or to close the external lesion by suturing the skin or applying skin grafts. The surgeon will attempt to save as much of the neurological tissue as possible in order that as many of the nerves as possible below the lesion will be intact. Early closure is also important for reducing the risk of infection, such as meningitis, and any further damage to the child's central nervous system (spinal cord, brain, and meninges).

If the infection spreads to the ventricles (ventriculitis) and is left untreated, death can occur. If the open spine is not closed, death occurs within the first year of life as a result of infections. The attitude of the physician is an influencing factor in the parents' decision whether or not to approve of the corrective surgery.

If hydrocephalus develops, the excess cerebrospinal fluid must be drained by surgically implanting a drainage system called a shunt (Figure 11.2). The shunt drains the excess fluid from the cerebral ventricle to the atrium of the heart or to the peritoneal cavity of the abdomen via a plastic tubing. This tube is generally inserted through the skull to a ventricle and is attached to a pumping valve located just underneath the skin behind the right ear. Another tube is attached from the lower portion of the valve for drainage either into the heart or into the abdomen. The valve assures that the fluid can only flow in one direction, and only opens when the pressure within the ventricles reaches a certain level (Myers et al., 1981). The functionality of the valve can be monitored by pushing down on the valve. On the one hand, if it fails to collapse, there is probably an obstruction below the level of the valve. On the other hand, if the valve fails to refill or inflate, there may be a blockage above the valve. Signs of shunt malfunction include irritability, headaches, stridor (a harsh-sounding respiration), vomiting, drowsiness, ocular motor incoordination, sudden periods of total rigidity, periods of confusion, and hyperreflexia in the arms. The signs indicate brain malfunction related to increased pressure caused by excessive cerebrospinal fluid.

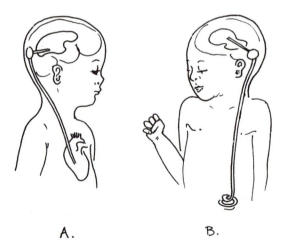

A.   B.

Figure 11.2.   *A,* Ventriculoatrial shunt. *B,* Ventriculoperitoneal shunt.

CLINICAL FEATURES

In children with neural tube defects such as myelomeningocele, there are two major factors used in classifying the disorder. First is the primary lesion of the spinal cord, meninges, and the vertebra, which usually results in sensory and motor dysfunction below the site of the lesion. Second, there are a number of secondary features that may evolve during the child's developing years and may decrease the child's functional abilities (Badell-Ribera, 1985; Best, 1978; Shepherd, 1986). Refer to Table 11.2 for a list of primary and secondary clinical features. The secondary problems that interfere the most with the child's cognitive, social, and emotional development are reduced mobility, kidney disease, and defects in mental development, primarily seen in children with hydrocephalus.

Visual Impairment

Another secondary characteristic associated with a child with spina bifida is visual impairments. Some of the visual problems include strabismus, visual focusing, eye tracking and visual scanning problems related to increased cere-

Table 11.2. Clinical features in myelomeningocele

Primary features	Flaccid paralysis below the site of the lesion
	Muscle weakness
	Muscle wasting
	Decreased or absent tendon reflexes
	Decreased or absent exteroceptive and proprioceptive sensation
	Rectal and bladder incontinence
	Paralytic and congenital deformities of the spine and lower extremities, especially the ankles and feet
	Hydrocephalus
Secondary features	Pressure ulcerations of the skin due to absent sensation and poor nutrition
	Severe vasomotor changes
	Osteoporosis with increased probability of fractures
	Soft tissue contractures and eventual skeletal deformity due to unopposed muscle action, gravity, and poor aligned posture
	Urinary tract infections
	Delayed mental, physical, and emotional development due to the child's inability to move about and explore the environment, to play normally, and to interact with other children
	Spasticity, impaired sensation and impaired fine motor skills in the upper extremities in children with hydrocephalus

Adapted from Badell-Ribera (1985), Best (1978), Garwood (1983), and Shepherd (1986).

brospinal pressure, refractive errors, and nystagmus. Strabismus occurs when one eye is turned inward or outward while the other eye is looking forward. The eyes may alternate turning in or out or only one eye will be able to focus correctly. In the first example, the child may not be aware there is a visual problem since this shifting occurs constantly within a split second. In the latter example, the child is still not aware of any trouble because the brain ignores the incoming messages from the shifting eye. Eventually, vision in that eye is lost even though the optic nerve function is still intact. For this reason, it is important that the child's eyes be checked to determine if suppression (amblyopia) or blindness is developing so corrective therapy can begin.

The most frequently used method of strabismus correction is to place an eye patch on the good eye in order to force the affected eye to develop normal control and vision. The patching process may take months before normal eye movement is achieved. In the meantime, parents, teachers, and therapists must be aware of the child's resistive behavior. This stems from the fact that the child's vision is probably reduced to one quarter to one tenth of what normal vision usually can produce. Adults need to be firm and consistent with the child when establishing the amount of time for wearing the eye patch. Spain (1974) has identified strabismus as a contributing factor to poor manipulative ability. In cases when surgery on the eye muscles is needed there is generally a high rate of success.

Other visual problems (focusing, tracking, and scanning) are prerequisites for school-related activities that require the child to shift visual gaze from the blackboard down to the table, read in a book, or maintain visual attention on someone or something for a period of time. Treatment may be dependent on the outcome of visual testing to determine whether the cause is a perceptual or refractive (near- or far-sighted) problem. The Erhardt Developmental Vision Assessment (Erhardt, 1986) can be used to check both reflexive and voluntary eye movements in infants and other children with all types of visual problems. Although it is not a test specifically for children with spina bifida, it will give valuable information on the child's ability to fixate, localize, track, and gaze shift. Reflexive responses include pupillary reactions, response to passive rotation of the head, and response to eyelid stimuli (blinking). Other visual perceptual tests include the Developmental Test of Visual Motor Integration (Berry & Berktencia, 1967) and the Motor-Free Visual Perception Test (Colarusso & Hammill, 1972).

Bowel and Bladder Incontinence

Bowel and bladder incontinence are managed by the application of external collection devices and surgical diversion of the feces and urine to the external collection devices. Lesions occurring within the lumbar area will have a loss of bladder control. When the site occurs at the sacral region (vertebrae S2, S3, or

S4) there will be a lack of bladder control with constant dribbling of urine, resulting in an inability to completely empty the bladder. When the child has no feeling or control of the urinary sphincter it is known as a neurogenic bladder. This can lead to infections of the kidneys and ureters because of poor urinary drainage. A neurogenic bowel can result in constipation and/or incontinence (Wolraich, 1984). More detailed bladder and bowel problems and management techniques are described in Chapter 8.

Bony Deformities

Spinal deformities such as kyphosis, lordosis, and scoliosis are managed through careful positioning, therapeutic exercises, bracing, and surgery. Hip dislocation and ankle and foot deformities are managed in the same manner.

Sensory Problems

The absence of sensation below the lesion increases the risk of damage of the soft tissue over weight-bearing areas such as the buttocks and heels. The child will not feel pain, pressure, or dangerously high temperatures. The child must eventually learn to take responsibility in checking for signs of skin damage and learn to change body positions to relieve pressure and enhance circulation for tissue nourishment. Impaired proprioception and equilibrium responses must be compensated for by teaching the child to use visual cues in order to develop body awareness.

Other sensory problems apparent in some of these children when first mastering tasks are in self-help (dressing), recreational activities (catching a ball), or academic concepts (reading or writing). These difficulties may stem from poor sensory processing of visual-motor perception or tactile discriminative ability. Grimm's (1976) study identified 14 out of 17 children with high-lesion myelomeningocele and hydrocephalus as having impaired hand function and in specific, tactual identifying skills. In order to perform a motor task (e.g., writing) one must be able to discriminate, process, and interpret the tactile messages into a meaningful planned motor response. It requires that the child is able to plan and implement a motor action based upon discriminative tactile response. Deficits in this area are known as apraxia. Grimm's study suggests that children with high-level myelomeningocele would benefit from therapy if they were treated as having a motor planning problem or developmental apraxia.

Gluckman and Barling (1980) found visual-motor remedial sessions over a 6-month period (with 30-minute individual sessions twice weekly) did reduce a visual-motor perceptual dysfunction in a group of children with myelomeningocele and associated hydrocephalus. Thirty-six boys and girls (mean age of 82.87 months) were randomly placed in one of three groups (control, attention-placebo, and experimental). Using the Frostig Program for the Development of Visual Perception (Frostig & Horne, 1964), the experimental group who received the individual training program made the most significant progress compared to the control (received no special training) or the attention-placebo (received attention but it was not directed to specific visual-motor activities) group. It is suggested that similar studies be administered to determine which type of assessment tool (sensorimotor or perceptual-motor) can best identify motor problems of the child with spina bifida.

Language Deficits

One of the more typical language deficits of children with spina bifida and hydrocephalus is known as the "cocktail party" syndrome or displaying hyperverbal behavior. Although the development of language takes on the form of good sentence and grammatical structure, there appears to be difficulty with the content or meaning and direction of what is being discussed (Williamson, 1987). This type of language comprehension has been noted more in children with below-average intelligence or with hydrocephalus (regardless of having a shunt or not). Some of the characteristics of the cocktail party syndrome listed by Williamson (1987, pp. 32, 149, 150) include:

1. Distractibility to auditory stimuli
2. Continuous talking
3. Poor comprehension of vocabulary despite ability to use words in conversation
4. Inability to establish or maintain a topic in conversation
5. Excessive use of social phrases
6. Difficulty terminating or changing topics within a conversation
7. Difficulty comprehending stories and answering questions related to details, main ideas, and the sequence of events.

MOVEMENT PATTERNS

Delayed development of independent movement resulting from immobility related to paralysis, casting of body parts, or frequent hospitalization for surgeries can be compensated for with careful and varied positioning to facilitate the development of head control, upper body control, and upper extremity skills. Upright positioning and mobility can be enhanced through the application of therapeutic exercises, bracing, wheelchairs, and other mobility aids.

The amount of voluntary movement a child will have depends upon the level of the primary lesion and the subsequent development of hydrocephalus and associated motor and cognitive dysfunction. Additional soft-tissue contractures in the trunk and limbs develop: 1) as a result of muscle imbalance resulting in paralytic deformities that are consistent with unopposed action of stronger muscles, 2) in response to the effect of gravity and positioning; and 3) as a result of spinal reflex activity (Badell-Ribera, 1985).

Where the open spine defect is located will determine the degree of paralysis below that lesion and the amount of mobility that can be expected. Ninety-eight percent of all spinal bifida cases will occur within the low-thoracic to sacral region. Within that area, 42% of the cases are located between the third and fifth lumbar vertebrae (Myers et al., 1981). The number of vertebrae involved can be from 1 to 4, and the lesion may be 2–4 inches in length.

If the primary lesion is at the *thoracic* level (vertebrae T1 through T12), the legs, hips, and lower trunk will be predominantly flaccid. When placed in the supine position, the hips will be externally rotated. The knees will be semiflexed with external tibial rotation and the feet will be in plantar flexion (Badell-Ribera, 1985). The positions described above will be the more likely positions of soft-tissue contractures unless routine range of motion exercises are provided and good positioning is employed using specially designed chairs or other positioning devices. There will be little or no spontaneous movement below the site of the lesion; however, it may be possible to elicit partial or total flexor withdrawal of the legs in response to a pin prick on the bottom of the foot, since this is a spinal reflex and does not require an intact pathway to the brain (Badell-Ribera, 1985). Ambulation, using a parapodium or bracing from trunk to heel and crutches, at best will be a drag or swing gait. Ambulation will be functional only for short distances, and a wheelchair will be necessary for long distances (Badell-Ribera, 1985). Typical deformities of the spine and the legs may be scoliosis or lordosis, coxa valga (angle formed by the head and neck of the femur and the axis of the shaft of the femur is increased), and occasionally hip subluxation.

With the lesion at the *high or midlumbar* level (vertebrae L1 to L3), a baby will typically show hip flexion and adduction in the supine position. If the third lumbar segment is intact, a restless baby may demonstrate some kicking movements with intermittent knee extension and flexion (Badell-Ribera, 1985). Ambulation with bracing and crutches will be with a four-point gait for household mobility and some travel in the community. Hip extensors and abductors and foot evertors and invertors will be paralyzed. With lesions between levels L3 and L4, there will be normal function of the hip flexors and good to normal function of the hip adductors. High lumbar deformities include scoliosis or lordosis, flexor and adductor contractures of the hip with subluxation of the hip, and occasionally dislocation of the hip.

Babies with *low lumbar* lesions (vertebrae L4 or L5) will demonstrate, in the supine position, kicking movements using hip flexion and adduction and possibly feeble hip abduction and extension. The ankle will characteristically be dorsiflexed. Ambulation with some bracing and crutches will be accomplished with a four-point gait with good endurance for household and community mobility (Badell-Ribera, 1985). Lordosis and scoliosis are still problems that may need surgical correction. Contractures and subluxation and dislocation of the hips will also be problems at this level.

When the lesion is at the *sacral* (vertebrae S1 or S2) level, there will be normal hip movement with hip extensors functioning at a fair to good rating. Knee, foot, and ankle function will be from good to normal. Subluxation of the hip may occur occasionally but scoliosis and lordosis remain a concern even at this low level of neural tube defect. Table 11.3 lists some of the sitting skills a child can be expected to master with lesions at various spinal levels.

As described, the prognosis for walking varies according to the level of the primary lesion and subsequent medical complications as well as intellectual and emotional factors. According to Badell-Ribera (1985), the prerequisites for ambulation are head control, ability to maintain erect posture with bracing,

Table 11.3. Transitional sitting skills

Level of Lesion	Horizontal to Sitting	Sitting to Standing
Sacral	Can obtain sitting position in normal manner from prone to supine.	Minimal problem getting to standing.
Lumbar	Some problems getting to sitting position. Not many children can obtain sitting position from a straight supine position.	Uses a series of developmental steps to achieve an upright posture. Begins in prone, then four-point, kneeling, then the vertical position. This is usually accomplished with long-leg braces and forearm (Loftstrand) crutches.
Thoracic	Cannot get to sit from four-point because the ability to use hip flexors (innvervation) getting to sitting position is gone. Must use side-lying position to push or walk up with extended arms If hip flexors are present, children from four-point position end up in a side-lying position which then requires putting their legs in long- or ring-sitting position.	With no innervation of the hip flexors, the child cannot use the four-point and kneeling process. Must start in prone (locking knee joint and unlocking hip joint of brace) by pushing with hands and crutches into "bear-walk" stance (extended arms with head near floor, legs with buttocks the highest part of the body) and then pushing up with the crutches into a standing position.

Adapted from Williamson (1987).

adequate muscle strength, and coordination of the shoulder girdle and arm muscles if crutch walking is planned. Ability to ambulate may regress during the growth years, especially if obesity or progressive postural malalignment occurs. Ambulation for many children with myelomeningocele is possible only at a high energy cost. Even if a child cannot be ambulatory for more than a very short distance it is still important for the child to receive ambulation training for the purpose of making transfers from the wheelchair to toilet or other surfaces easier as well as for health reasons. In a study conducted by Mazur (1987), 70% of the patients with upper lumbar and thoracic level myelomeningocele became wheelchair users by adolescence. However, those children who were encouraged to walk during preschool years had only one fracture and 1.3 skin sores per child, whereas childhood chair users had 2.1 fractures and 5.0 skin pressure sores. Children who walk with aids before going into a wheelchair tend to be more mobile in the wheelchair than those who do not walk first. Other advantages of early ambulation training include a decrease in osteoporosis and neuropathic fractures resulting from weight bearing. Walking also aids in the development of self-image and provides a means of meeting the child's need to establish some mastery of the body and the environment (Badell-Ribera, 1985).

MANAGEMENT

Management of the child with spina bifida begins with the assessment of the physical, mental, communicative, and social skills. Then comes the development of specific goals and objectives based on the outcome of the child's performance in several areas of early development. The general management goals for the child with a neural tube defect such as myelomeningocele will be the development of head control, sitting balance, and prone mobility and the maintenance of an upright stance and upright ambulation. The purposes for developing home and clinic objectives for these developmental motor stages are listed in Table 11.4. Numerous management techniques (exercises, equipment, positioning, sensorimotor input, and health preventative measures) are employed to develop and increase independent motor and self-help skills.

The type of positioning and handling used to promote developmental and reflex maturation, to develop an awareness and tolerance of sensorimotor input, to minimize development of skeletal abnormalities, and to motivate learning should be discussed by the therapist with the team and the parents. The pros and cons for any particular position or equipment should be known by the staff and parents. The staff should also work with the parents in preventing, correcting or minimizing health problems that can occur to the child with spinal neural defects.

The child's social and psychological development will be enhanced through parent education and training, the facilitation of the child's mobility,

Table 11.4. Management goals for children with spina bifida

Management goal	Primary purpose
Head control	To avoid contractures of the hip adductors To correct deformities To promote developmental stimulation To increase head extension in all positions
Sitting balance	To avoid contractures of tight hamstrings by stretching the knees with the hips in abduction To encourage eye-hand control and coordination To protect anesthetic skin of the buttocks and lower extremities
Prone mobility	To avoid contractures of the hip flexors To encourage upper arm strength To encourage bilateral hand use To increase child's independent mobility and expand child's environmental opportunities
Upright stance	To evaluate and avoid weight-bearing contractures To expand child's social contact with peers and the community resources
Upright ambulation	To increase and encourage independent mobility of the child regardless of the type of apparatus needed (crutches, braces, wheelchairs)

and the provision of social-educational programs (Badell-Ribera, 1985; Best, 1978; Shepherd, 1986; Williamson, 1987).

Exercises

Exercises (passive, active, and developmental) should be an essential part of the family's daily routine from the day the infant is brought home from the hospital. The most beneficial type of exercise for an infant or toddler is the holding, swinging, lifting, tilting, and rolling that a parent normally would do with an infant. The infant with myelomeningocele will require specific exercises and equipment in order to gain the maximum level of upright static and dynamic motor independence. Positioning and movement should follow one another and not always be independent of each other. Passive exercises in the form of hand massage or gentle patting and mechanical vibration to the lower extremities can help improve body awareness, stimulate active movement, and increase postural reactions.

Many of the passive exercises described in Chapter 3 can be applied or modified for the child with myelomeningocele. It is crucial that during the first year, the parents and therapists work on developing head and trunk control, strengthening arm skills in weight-bearing positions, developing motoric transition stages (prone to sit, sit to kneel, kneel to prone, etc.), and improving balance ability in both sitting and standing positions. Head and trunk extension and control can be developed by placing the infant over the adult's lap, a cylinder, or a wedge while encouraging weight bearing on the arms. In the supine position, a game that requires the adult to hold onto the infant's hand, then employ a resistive push and pull movement, can help develop muscular strength and assist in weight-bearing tasks. The parent can hold onto the infant's legs and flex, extend, abduct, adduct, or rotate them so the infant can see what is being done. In addition to these activities, tying bells or a fabric-covered rattle around the ankles will help develop body awareness, leg movement, and foot play (Williamson, 1987).

Independent rolling can be achieved once scapular control and weight-bearing stability of the upper extremities have been mastered. To reach this stage of control, the infant should be placed either on his or her back and encouraged to reach above the chest for a toy or placed on the elbows in the prone position and encouraged to shift his or her weight from side to side. Providing support at the trunk and thighs will allow the child to support himself or herself on extended arms and move forward like a wheelbarrow. Rolling movements can be facilitated from prone to supine and supine to prone using both passive and active exercises. Going from supine to prone, the infant's side movements can be stimulated by the sound or movement of a toy. This then encourages eye contact, head and trunk rotation toward one side, and an upward and then sideways movement of the opposite arm across the body, which helps to increase head and trunk extension. Rolling over is completed when the legs also flop or roll from the prone to supine. In order to go from prone to supine the child must be able to push his or her trunk up with one arm with enough force to start the backward roll.

The ability to change from the rolling to four-point position is dependent first on achieving upper extremity weight-bearing skills that help push the upper body up off the floor. Then the child must be able to shift his or her weight in both a forward/backward and side-to-side direction. This step, in addition to a pulling motion of the upper arms, will position the child in a functional hands-and-knees position (also called a four-point or quadripedal position). To maintain the four-point position, the child must have good active use of the upper extremities and hip flexors (Williamson, 1987). Most of the children with higher level lesions will have difficulty controlling the side-to-side movement necessary in a creeping movement. Instead, the child will pull forward using the hands in front of the body and the legs (locked in a flexed position) are pulled forward as a unit. Other children, using a modified "bunny hop," sit either on the backs of both legs or on the floor between the legs. Forward movement is completed by pushing or swinging the legs and hips between and in front of the extended arms (Williamson, 1987).

The skills needed to achieve and maintain independent sitting posture are head control, abdominal and hip extensor co-contraction, arm and trunk coordination, and normal postural reflexes (equilibrium responses and protective reactions). The typical sitting posture of a child with spina bifida, as shown in Figure 11.3, is a forward tilt of the pelvis and extreme flexion of the hips. This will bring the upper trunk into extension to avoid falling forward and may tilt the head backward to maintain the sitting posture. This restricts head movement and visual tracking and is done because the child is afraid of falling and not being able to protect himself or herself. Many children who have poor abdominal and hip extensor muscles are initially fearful of getting on their own from sitting to a horizontal position. In addition to strengthening muscles and responding to weight shifting, parents and therapists need to build up the child's self-confidence. The objectives for improving sitting balance are: 1) to extend the arms up and to the side (caution: extension too high up causes the child to revert to hyperextension of the neck and trunk); 2) to facilitate flexion of the head and trunk in a forward and side direction; 3) to develop co-contraction of the abdominal and trunk extensor muscles; and 4) to develop trunk rotation. These objectives can be worked on while the child is sitting on the floor, on an adult's tap, straddling a bolster, or on a small stool or chair. This is the position in which one should use behavior management techniques. This is done to develop self-confidence, to strengthen weak muscles, and to avoid compensatory postures.

While the child is working and mastering belly-crawling and creeping, kneeling and knee-walking can be encouraged. This is begun while the child is on his or her hands and knees. The adult should sit next to the child on the floor and have the child pull up on the adult's leg. Vary the height of the leg or use other equipment until the child can pull himself or herself up next to the couch or coffee table. This is a good place to play with toys and to learn to get back down on the floor. Protective reflex reactions can be facilitated in this position.

Figure 11.3.   Typical sitting posture of a child with myelomeningocele. The hips are in excessive flexion.

As balancing skills improve, knee-walking as another means of mobility can be encouraged.

A daily practice of getting to and maintaining a standing position should be started when the child is around 1 year of age. Prior to gait training, the child should be taught how to get from a horizontal or a sitting position while wearing braces and using crutches. Williamson's (1987) pictures and instructions are helpful for parents to teach their child how to get to a standing position from the floor or a wheelchair. Payne and Reder (1983) provide step-by-step instructions in using the proper gait pattern with different braces.

Equipment

There are different types of equipment used by the child with spina bifida that will provide trunk support, develop and maintain symmetrical skeletal alignment, and allow a means of independent movement.

A long-leg brace with a pelvic band assists the child in maintaining a standing position and necessitates a rotation gait pattern. This requires holding on to a walker or crutches while the child rotates or turns his or her body forward on one side. This will shift the body weight to the opposite leg, which then rotates the leg forward. The child then shifts his or her weight to the opposite side and repeats the procedure.

Long-leg braces without a pelvic band are used when the child can maintain an upright position but needs support for the lower extremities. The type of ambulation with braces or on parallel bars is a swing-to-gait pattern. This requires the child to push down on the bars of the walker and pull or swing his or her body forward.

Short-leg braces are used when the child can control his or her movements above the knee but needs ankle support (Figure 11.4). Moving one leg at a time (a reciprocal gait) is the mode of ambulation with this type of brace. The use of crutches or a walker is still probably a needed walking aide (Figure 11.5). Helping the child develop a positive attitude toward learning to use crutches or a walker with braces can help ease the child's fear of not being able to always control his or her movements.

Some type of walking pattern should be expected of children with spina bifida, regardless of the level of lesion. For some, the amount of independent walking will be limited and later on may prove to be more than the child can physically handle. The child may eventually have to depend on a wheelchair as the major means of ambulation.

Positioning

Ward (1984) has stated the goals of positioning are threefold: 1) to promote normal development; 2) to promote compensation; and 3) to prevent, mini-

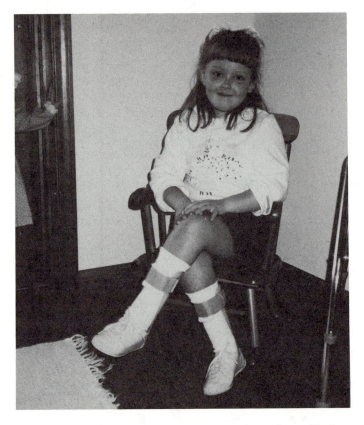

Figure 11.4. Short-leg brace variations can be in the form of an ankle-foot orthosis (AFO) to provide foot and ankle stability for some children with lower lesions. The AFO is plastic material molded to the child's foot and worn inside regular shoes.

mize, or delay physical deformity. It is important to remember that any position or equipment used must be closely monitored to assure maximum body symmetry, joint mobility, joint stability, skin integrity, and respiration and pulse (Ward, 1984).

Giving a child a chance to use crutches (axillary or Lofstrand), braces (parapodium, long leg with pelvic band, short leg, ankle-foot orthosis, or a reciprocating hip extension brace), walkers (four wheel, two wheel, ring seat, or trunk supported), prone scooter board (padded with carpet or plastic), hand-propelled tricycles (low to the ground), and low to the ground wheelchairs (brand names such as Flex, Viveka, Playwagon Rolly Royce) can help the child attain these goals. Figure 11.6 shows how a wheelchair of this type or one that has been adapted can help the child become independent in mobility. Payne and Reder (1983), Ward (1984), and Williamson (1987) provide excellent rationale

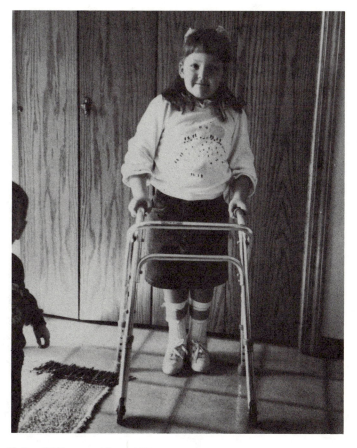

Figure 11.5.   Walkers enable a child to move about faster and with a smoother gait pattern but are not always preferred by the child.

and guidelines in the selection of appropriate positions, activities, and various types of equipment.

PARENTAL AND FAMILY CONCERNS

The birth of a child with a neural tube defect may periodically create financial and emotional stress on the entire family as the child grows up. A telephone survey conducted by M. C. McCormick, Charney, and Stemmler (1986) examined what factors might be sources for parental stress. The survey covered acute and chronic health problems, the child's limited participation in activities of daily living, the quality and quantity of health care expenses, the availability of

344 / Special Considerations

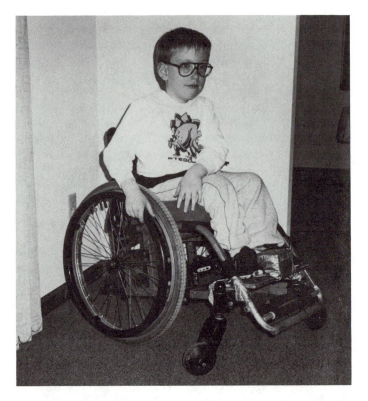

Figure 11.6. This wheelchair with the adapted foot support enables this young man to maneuver around furniture safely and get in and out of the wheelchair independently.

educational and therapeutic services, and the parents' perception of the child's problems. The results pointed to the number of activities the child was unable to do independently (which requires more nursing care from a parent) as the major contributing factor toward the development of stress. Other factors causing stress but with less importance was the parental perception of the child's health and the amount of medical care the child requires. Other related variables (social supports, environmental stress, and educational, recreational, and respite care) were not included, but the results reinforce the need for both financial and social support for the continuing medical care for the child and the personal resources of the family.

A study done by Spaulding and Morgan (1986) questioned whether parents of nonretarded children with spina bifida differed from parents of matched nonhandicapped children in approaches in parental attitudes, perception of their child's behavior, and stress. A home visit followed an introductory letter and phone interview with 19 children and their parents in both the disabled and nondisabled groups. This study indicated that the families in the disabled group showed no special psychological difficulties that distinguished them from the nondisabled children and their parents.

No matter what the socioeconomic level of the parents or their perception of their child's condition, there will be times when the family is going to be faced with high stress levels. The cost of surgery and hospitalization plus the doctor's bills is seldom financed 100% by health insurance companies. Most families will have to pay a portion of the bills out of their own pockets or perhaps consume a good portion if not all of the family's savings. The child's need for braces, a walker, or a wheelchair for ambulation may add to the family's expenses. The daily health care (e.g., infections from pressure sores, bowel and bladder management, and infections) and educational adjustments required of the child and family need not be undertaken alone.

The professional staff can develop home training programs, provide psychological and educational support, and be an influence on the child's overall development. To develop the most beneficial educational and home program for the child with spina bifida, there must be a close two-way open communication channel between the professional staff and the parents. The IEPs and IFSPs are good mechanisms in establishing practical and functional goals. They also provide an excellent way for the staff to maintain a close working relationship with the child and the family.

HEALTH PROBLEMS

All children with a spinal neural tube defect, as they grow older, need to be checked for spinal, hip, and leg (primarily knee and ankle) deformities and for possible skin breakdown. Difficulty in getting to a sitting or standing position, the transitional process in achieving different positions, and the ability to ambulate (rolling, scooting, or walking) may be the result of muscle paralysis due to the spinal neural defect. The loss of movement below the site of the lesion, due to poor or absent innervation, affects the child's ability to distinguish touch, heat, and pain, which are stimuli normally used in identifying and protecting a child from discomfort, a fracture, or an injury. This lack of sensory awareness can cause spinal deformities and pressure sores, especially if the right kind of feedback information is missing. It is vital to vary the child's positions and get the child moving about his or her environment. In addition to preventing possible surgical procedures, active movement will also aid in normal urinary function, better respiratory function, and increase bone and muscle development.

Muscle and Bone Problems

Curvatures of the spine can occur because of the loss of innervation to the muscle groups used for both stability and movement of the upper extremity, or from deformed or absent vertebrae. Treatment to prevent or correct spinal curvatures (scoliosis, kyphosis, or lordosis) ranges from using passive and active physical exercises to wearing a thoracolumbar body brace (most effective when worn both during the day and night but sometimes it is prescribed to be worn just during the night) to surgical procedures that correct the curvature. Surgical procedures, done in the more severely involved cases, fuse several vertebrae together, which maintains straight alignment of the spine. The outcome of the surgery, although limiting the child's flexibility (rotation, flexion, and extension of the trunk area), is viewed as more acceptable than allowing the spinal curvature to continue and to further decrease the child's mobility. Therapeutic exercises and activities should be part of the child's daily routine done by therapists, teachers, and parents who are working together to: "1) maintain or increase the range of motion of the trunk, 2) promote symmetry of the trunk, and 3) strengthen weak musculature" (Williamson, 1987, p. 86). The following activities and positions can be used to aid the goals of both trunk mobility and strength:

1. With the child in the supine position, support his or her head and shoulders with a pillow. Have the child reach toward and above the midline of the body for a toy that is attached to a horizontal bar supported by four legs approximately 12 inches above the child.
2. With the child straddling a bolster, support his or her hips or trunk area while rolling the bolster from side to side. The establishment of protective responses and equilibrium reactions are encouraged as well as trunk rotation.
3. Reaching for attractive toys sewn on socks or those set near the child's feet can be one way to encourage trunk elongation.
4. Activities such as sitting on the floor with the legs extended, or in a corner or straight back chair, or maintaining standing positions (supported via braces, walkers, etc.) can be part of a trunk rotation objective when the activity (ball playing, puzzles, shape sorters, or stacking blocks) is presented to the child's side. Flexion and extension of the trunk can be included as a part of this activity when the child has to reach down to the floor for a block on the right side, return to a standing position, and then turn to stack the block on a table slightly to the child's left side and above the child's waist.

The primary hip difficulties can be contractures, dislocations, or subluxations. Contractures can develop when there is an imbalance of muscle control between the extensors and flexors or adductors and the abductors because of paralysis of one of the groups of opposing muscles. This can lead to tightness of the flexors and/or adductors because they are pulling, and thus stretching, the extensors and/or the abductors. Since there is no back-and-forth movement of the muscle groups contractures may develop. This also increases the chances for hip dislocation or subluxation. Williamson's (1987) definition of *dislocation* is the condition when the femoral head lies completely outside of the hip socket. When the femur head is partially outside the socket it is known as a *subluxation* of the hip. This can occur with hip flexion and adduction, and is also known as a partial dislocation. Surgical procedures consist of muscle transfers and/or releases when conservative or therapeutic techniques are no longer effective or appropriate. The child's doctor, therapist, and parents should work together to establish activities and exercises that will minimize the hip dislocation or subluxation condition.

Deformities of the knee, ankle, and foot are the result of weakness or paralysis of opposing muscle groups. A condition called "back knee" occurs when there are stronger knee extensors than flexors, forcing the knee to push back (or hyperextend). This creates instability in the knee, a joint in which stability is necessary for good upright weight bearing and active mobility. Internal tibial rotation or external torsion is caused by weakness of opposing muscle groups and can be corrected at night time when the child wears a splint composed of a metal bar attached to shoes.

Dorsiflexion, plantar flexion. inversion, and eversion are normal movements of the ankle joint that allow for proper movement and stability in the upright position. A lack of or weakness in achieving these positions can create foot deformities. The foot needs surgical correction for the abnormal up, down, or side muscular pull of the foot. This is seen more often with children who have lower lesions because only a few muscles are weakened, thus making the normal muscle group pull the foot position out of normal alignment. Casting, bracing, and physical exercises are also used to support and stretch tight muscles, ligaments, and tendons. The following type of exercises and activities used for lower extremity (hip, knee, or ankle) stretching can be employed by the parents after careful training and supervision by the therapist:

1. In the supine position, heel cord stretching can be done by supporting the heel in one hand and the bottom of the foot with the other hand. Gradually push the child's foot toward the leg, hold for a second or two, and relax; repeat the procedure several times.
2. Encourage the young child to reach for his or her feet and bring them up near the chest, or play games such as "London Bridge," lifting his or her buttocks off the floor.
3. Passive exercises as well as active resistive exercises of the hip adbuctors, flexors, and extensors and knee extensors will help develop and maintain proper alignment when the child is on his or her back.

4. Initially, prone mobility can be accomplished with the child pushing or pulling with the hands while on a padded scooter board or rolling down a large wedge. The latter activity will encourage trunk rotation and hip adduction. Limitation of leg movement in accomplishing these activities need not prohibit the chance to roll around the floor with other children. The child needs to learn to compensate for his or her weaknesses by strengthening and actively using the arms and upper torso.

Skin Problems

Proper skin care is essential for children who have total or partial loss of skin sensation. The feedback a child normally receives from the skin receptors indicate the amount of pressure, pain, and temperature being applied to a specific area of the body. Without the proper incoming messages from the nervous system, a child cannot tell if he or she should change positions, that the bath water is hot enough to cause pain or blisters, if a bone has been broken, or if the plastic or metal parts of the car seat will cause burns because they are too hot for exposed skin to be touching.

Skin problems can develop with prolonged periods of sitting or lying in one position, or with the consistent rubbing of clothing or bedding against the child's skin, or the constant pressure from equipment (braces or wheelchairs). Because of limited movement, poor circulation tends to be an important reason for examining those pressure areas of the back, elbow, hip, sacral area, heel, and ankle susceptible to pressure sores. Since blood is necessary in keeping the skin healthy, anytime circulation is slowed (as happens with a lack of movement with these children) skin breakdown is a possibility. The following suggestions should help alert the parent or therapist to the safety precautions to be used when sensations are absent or decreased:

1. Be sensitive to various types of clothing that when rubbed on the skin may develop skin irritation, causing reddishness.
2. Check for wrinkles in clothing, chair covers, or bedding; tight socks (especially at the top edge); or tight underwear. This can cause increased pressure and can decrease the already minimal circulation the child has.
3. If the child is scooting on his or her buttocks, or using the hands and arms to pull across the floor, or when on all fours the legs are pulled across the rug, be sure to keep long pants on during this time.
4. Be sure to check for pressure sores after removing braces, shoes, or socks.
5. Since moisture and warmth are the prime ingredients for bacterial growth and thus encourage ammonia burns or the development of skin sores, be

sure to cleanse the area with soap and water. After each diapering procedure, protect the skin with lotion or powder.

6. If bed sores or decubitus ulcers are *beginning* to occur, one can rub the area to increase circulation, or change the child's position to relieve the pressure. One should be sure to keep the area clean and dry.

III

Appendices

Appendix A. Assessment Tools for At-Risk Infants

Name (reference) and source	Age range	Content areas	Description
Apgar Scoring System (Apgar, 1960)	Birth	Pulse, grimace, respiration, activity, appearance	Administered at 1, 5, and/or 15 minutes after birth. Each item is scored as 0, 1, or 2. Normal range is between 7 and 10. Assesses current status; not predictive. Criterion-referenced measure.
Bayley Scales of Infant Development (Bayley, 1969) The Psychological Corp. 1372 Peachtree St. NE Atlanta, GA 30309	2 months to 30 months	Mental, motor, and infant behavior record	Scored as a pass or fail and results give a developmental index score with 100 as the mean performance at any given age. Norm-referenced measure.
Brigance Diagnostic Inventory of Early Development (Brigance, 1978) Curriculum Associates, Inc. 5 Esquire Rd. North Billerica, MA 01862	Birth to 72 months	Psychomotor, self-help, speech and language, general knowledge and comprehension, early academic skills	Determines developmental or performance level, identifies areas of strengths and weaknesses, identifies instructional objectives. Contributes data for referral or diagnosis. Criterion- and domain-referenced measure.
Callier-Azuza Scale (Stillman, 1978) Callier Center for Communication Disorders University of Texas/Dallas 1966 Inwood Road Dallas, TX 75235	Birth to 9 years	Gross motor, fine motor, cognitive, language, social, self-help	Completed by observation in structured or unstructured environments. Provides a rough developmental age profile. Criterion-referenced measure. Designed for deaf-blind and severely handicapped.

The Carey Infant Temperament Questionnaire
(Carey & McDevitt, 1977)
William B. Carey, M.D.
319 West Front Street
Media, PA 19063

	4 months to 8 months	Activity level, rhythmicity, adaptability to change, approach threshold to stimulation, intensity of mood, distractibility from interesting stimuli, and crying and persistence	Contains 70 multiple choice items to be answered by parent or primary caregiver. Takes 20 minutes to complete and 10 minutes to score; results in a high, medium, or low score. Can be used in dealing with an infant's behavior.
The Carolina Curriculum for Handicapped Infants and Infants At Risk (Johnson-Martin, Jens, & Attermeier, 1986)	Birth to 24 months	Twenty-four content areas: tactile integration, auditory localization, object permanence, reach and grasp, object manipulation, bilateral hand activity, space localization, functional use of objects, control of physical environment, gestural communication, gestural imitation, feeding, dressing, grooming, vocal imitation, vocal communication, responses to communication from others, social, gross motor—prone, gross motor—supine, gross motor—upright, auditory localization, readiness concepts, self-directed	Developed in response to the need for curricular materials for the severely handicapped, deaf-blind infants and toddlers. Criterion- and curriculum-based measure.
Denver Developmental Screening Test (Frankenburg & Dodds, 1969) Ladoca Project & Publishing Foundation East 51st Street & Lincoln Denver, CO 80216	Birth to 6 years	Personal-social, fine motor-adaptive, language, gross motor	Items are scored as pass, fail, refusal, or no opportunity. Interpretation of normal, abnormal, questionable, or untestable. Norm-referenced measure.

continued

353

Appendix A. *continued*

Name (reference) and source	Age range	Content areas	Description
Developmental Profile II (rev. ed.) (Alpern, Boll, Shearer, 1980) Western Psychological Services 12031 Wilshire Blvd. Los Angeles, CA 90025	Birth to 9.6 years	Physical, self-help, social, academic, communication	186-item inventory designed to assess a child's function, developmental age level. Can be given as an interview or as a direct test. Provides an overall profile. Criterion-referenced measure.
Early Intervention Developmental Profile & Developmental Screening of Handicapped Infants (D'Eugenio & Rogers, 1975) The University of Michigan Publications Distribution Service 615 East University Ann Arbor, MI 48109	Birth to 36 months	Language, social, self-care, cognition, perceptual-fine motor, gross motor	Helps in screening a child's skills, selecting appropriate objectives for treatment of developmental delays, and designing an appropriate, individual curriculum. Given 4 times a year; reflects the child's highest levels.
Early Learning Accomplishment Profile for Developmentally Young Children (LAP) (Glover & Preminger, 1978) Kaplan School Supply Corp. 600 Jonestown Rd. Winston Salem, NC 27103	Birth to 36 months	Gross motor, cognitive, fine motor, language, self-help, social-emotional	Determines an appropriate developmental age; designed to generate developmental-appropriate instructional objectives and task analysis programming. Domain- and norm-referenced measure.

Hawaii Early Learning Profile (HELP) (rev. ed.) (Furuno et al., 1985) VORT Corporation P.O. Box 60880 Palo Alto, CA 94306	Birth to 36 months	Cognitive, expressive language, gross motor, fine motor, social-emotional, self-help	Results provide developmental sequence in small incremental steps, and suggestions for activities to teach developmental skills. Curriculum-based measure.
Koontz Child Developmental Program (Koontz, 1974) Western Psychological Services 12031 Wilshire Blvd. Los Angeles, CA 90025	Birth to 48 months	Gross motor, fine motor, social, language—receptive, language—expressive	Provides a method for assessing, for plotting progress, and for planning suitable activities.
Milani-Comparetti Motor Development Screening Test (Pearson, 1973)	Birth to 24 months	Primitive reflexes, postural responses	Identifies reflexes that remain beyond normal age and identifies those that have not emerged. Can be used to identify problems such as cerebral palsy or motor delays.
Neonatal Behavioral Assessment Scale (Brazelton, 1984)	Birth to 1 month	Reflexes and movements, habituation, orientation, motor maturity, variation, self-quieting abilities, social behavior	Rated on best performance in neurological items (4-point scale) and behavioral items (9-point scale). Assesses current status; not predictive.
Peabody Developmental Motor Scales (Folio & Fewell, 1983) Teaching Resources Corp. 50 Pond Park Rd. Hingham, MA 02043	Birth to 83 months	*Gross motor* Reflexes, balance, nonlocomotion, locomotion, receipt and propulsion of objects. *Fine motor* Grasping, hand use, eye-hand coordination, manual dexterity	Identifies motor skills that are delayed or abnormal. Gives a comparison between gross and fine motor. Provides assessment and programming information. Criterion-referenced measure.

continued

355

Appendix A. *continued*

Name (reference) and source	Age range	Content areas	Description
Portage Guide to Early Education (Bluma, Shearer, Frohman & Hilliard, 1976) CESA 12 Portage Project Box 564 Portage, WI 53901	Birth to 6 years	Infant stimulation, socialization, motor, language, self-help, cognitive	Includes a checklist and a card file to aid in assessing present behavior, targeting emerging behavior and providing suggested techniques to teach each behavior. Domain- and curriculum-referenced measure.
Uzgiris-Hunt Scales of Infant Psychological Development (Uzgiris & Hunt, 1978) University of Illinois Press Urbana, IL 61801	Birth to 24 months	Visual pursuit and the permanence of objects, means for obtaining desired environmental events, vocal imitation, gestural imitation, operational causality, object relations in space, schemes for relating to objects	Evaluates seven sensorimotor domains using five stages of development based on Piagetian theory of development. Norm-referenced measure.

Appendix B. Tests Used to Assess Children with Cerebral Palsy

Name (reference)	Age range	Content	Description
A Cerebral Palsy Assessment Chart (Semans, Phillips, Romanoli, Miller, & Skillea, 1965)	No age specific	Assesses gross motor control in the supine, prone, sitting, kneeling, squatting, and standing positions. All of these positions are considered necessary for various functional activities.	First the child is placed in various test positions. Second, the child is asked to maintain the positions. Finally, the child is asked to move into the test positions independently.
Development Hand Dysfunction (Erhardt, 1982)	Newborn to 15 months and 1 to 6 years	Assesses hand function, including involuntary arm-hand patterns, cognitively directed voluntary movements, and prewriting skills.	Specific stimuli are presented to the child and the child's responses are recorded on the protocol sheets.
Milani-Comparetti Motor Development Screening Test (Kliewer, Bruce, & Trembath, 1977)	Birth to 12 months	Assesses the status of head control, primitive reflexes, and higher level reactions, which include equilibrium reactions.	A specific stimuli is presented or the child is placed in a specific position. The child's response is recorded on the scoring chart.
Norton's Basic Motor Evaluation (Norton 1972)	No age specific	Assesses movement and posture in supine, prone, sitting, kneeling, crawling, standing, and components of walking. This assessment is based on the cerebral palsy assessment by Semans et al. (1965) and is for less severely involved children.	The child assumes and holds specific positions after a verbal command is given. Demonstration is given only if the child has difficulty following directions.
Reflex Evaluation (Barnes, Crutchfield, & Heriza, 1977)	No age specific	Assesses the status of the primitive reflexes, prehensile reactions, righting reactions, and equilibrium reactions.	A specific stimulus is presented or the child is placed in a specific position. The child's responses are observed and the responses are recorded on the recording form.
Reflex Testing Methods for Evaluating CNS Dysfunction (2nd ed.) (Fiorentino, 1973)	No age specific	Assesses the status of the spinal brainstem, and midbrain reflexes; automatic reactions and equilibrim reactions, and the effect of different positions on the status of movements and arm and hand development.	Specific stimuli are presented and the child's responses are recorded on the recording form.

Appendix C. Assessment Tools for Children with Mental Retardation

Name (reference) and source	Age range	Content areas	Description
AAMD Adaptive Behavior Scales (Nihira, Foster, Shellaas, & Leland, 1974) American Association on Mental Deficiency 1719 Kalorama Rd. N.W. Washington, D.C. 20009	3 years to 16 years	Independent functioning, physical and language development, socialization, antisocial behavior, time and number concepts, domestic activity, self-direction, maladaptive behaviors, unacceptable vocal habits, use of medication	Measured some of the ways individuals act in a number of different situations. It is a measure of how a person is able to adapt to his/her surroundings and is not an intellectual measure.
Balthazar Scales of Adaptive Behavior (I and II) (Balthazar, 1971) Consulting Psychologists Press, Inc. 577 College Ave. Palo Alto, CA 94306	3 to 57 years	Measures functional independence (eating, dressing, toileting), play activities, verbal communication, unadaptive self-directed behaviors, unadaptive interpersonal behavior, response to instructors	Derived from direct observation; then performance levels can be determined and remedial programs can be developed.
Bayley Scales of Infant Development (Bayley, 1969) The Psychological Corp. 7500 Old Oak Blvd. Cleveland, OH 44130	2 months to 30 months	Mental, motor, and infant behavior record	Scored as a pass or fail and results give a developmental index score with 100 as the mean performance at any given age. Norm-referenced measure.

Test	Age Range	Areas	Description
Brigance Diagnostic Inventory of Early Development (Brigance, 1978) Curriculum Associates, Inc. 5 Esquire Rd. Borth Billerica, MA 01862	Birth to 72 months	Psychomotor, self-help speech and language, general knowledge and comprehension, early academic skills	Determines developmental or performance level, identifies areas of strengths and weaknesses, identifies instructional objectives. Contributes data for referral or diagnosis. Criterion- and domain-referenced measure.
Bruininks-Oseretsky Test of Motor Proficiency (Bruininks, 1978) American Guidance Service, Inc. Circle Pines, MN 55014	4.6 years to 14.6 years	*Gross motor* Running speed and agility, balance, bilateral coordination, strength *Gross & fine motor development* Upper limb coordination *Fine motor* response speed, visual-motor control, upper limb speed & dexterity	In addition to evaluating general gross and fine motor skills, neurological development is also assessed in this test of validity and reliability.
Callier-Azuaz Scale (Stillman, 1978) Callier Center for Communication Disorders University of Texas/Dallas 1966 Inwood Rd. Dallas, TX 75235	Birth to 9 years	Gross motor, fine motor, cognitive, language, social, self-help	Completed by observation in structured or unstructured environments. Provides a rough developmental age profile. Criterion referenced measure designed for deaf-blind and severely handicapped.
Camelot Behavioral Checklist (Foster & Tucker, 1974) PRO-ED 5341 Industrial Blvd. Austin, TX 78735	Adolescents and adults	Self-help, physical development, home duties, vocational behavior, independent travel, numerical skills, communication skills, social behavior and responsibility	Intended for trainable-level children and completed by observation or knowledge of child. Skills are arranged in order of difficulty.

continued

359

Name (reference) and source	Age range	Content areas	Description
The Carolina Curriculum for Handicapped Infants and Infants At Risk (Johnson-Martin, Jens, & Attermeier, 1986) Paul H. Brookes Publishing Co. P.O. Box 10624 Baltimore, MD 21285-0624	Birth to 24 months	Twenty-four content areas: tactile integration, auditory localization, object permanence, reach and grasp, hand-watching, space localization, functional use of objects, control of physical environment, gestural communication, gestural imitation, feeding, vocal imitation, vocal communication, response to communication from others, social, gross motor—prone, gross motor—supine, gross motor—upright	Developed in response to the need for curricular materials for the severely handicapped, deaf-blind infants and toddlers. Criterion- and curriculum-based measure.
Developmental Test of Visual-Motor Integration (Beery & Berktencia, 1967)	Form A: 2–8 years Form B: 2–15 years	Visual-motor skills	Tests child's integration of visual and motor ability when asked to copy different shapes and designs. Becomes more complex with each succeeding design.
Gross Motor Management of Severely Multiply Impaired Students (Fraser, Galka, & Hensinger, 1980)	All ages	Range of motion, reflexes, gross motor	Can be administered by therapist or a special education teacher. Provides information on normal range of motion positions for neophyte staff member. Also has numerous pictures and descriptions of equipment used by severely multiply handicapped persons. Volume II includes treatment techniques.

Test	Age range	Areas assessed	Description
Hawaii Early Learning Profile (HELP) (rev. ed.) (Furuno et al., 1985) VORT Corporation P.O. Box 60880 Palo Alto, CA 94306	Birth to 36 months	Cognitive, expressive language, gross motor, fine motor, social-emotional, self-help	Results provide developmental sequence in small incremental steps, and suggestions for activities to teach developmental skills. Curriculum-based measure.
Learning Accomplishment Profile (LAP) (rev. ed.) (Sanford & Zelman, 1981) Kaplan School Supply 600 Jamestown Rd. Winston Salem, NC 27103	12–36 months	Gross-motor, fine-motor, self-help, language, cognitive skills, pre-writing	Criterion-referenced test designed to identify skills for developing objectives and assessing progress. Can be used with young handicapped children.
Milani-Comparetti Motor Development Screening Test (Pearson, 1973)	Birth to 24 months	Primitive reflexes, postural responses	Identifies reflexes that remain beyond normal age and identifies those that have not emerged. Can be used to identify problems such as cerebral palsy or motor delays.
Peabody Developmental Motor Scales (Folio & Fewell, 1983) Teaching Resources Corp. 50 Pond Park Rd. Hingham, MA 02043	Birth to 83 months	*Gross motor* reflexes, balance, nonlocomotion, locomotion, receipt and propulsion of objects *Fine motor* grasping, hand use, eye-hand coordination, and manual dexterity	Identifies motor skills that are delayed or abnormal. Gives a comparison between gross and fine motor. Provides assessment and programming information. Criterion-referenced measure.
Pennsylvania Training Model (Somerton Fair & Turner, 1979)	Birth to 36 months	Curriculum assessment guide, competency checklists, individual prescriptive planning and data sheet	Intended for person with physical impairments.

continued

Appendix C. *continued*

Name (reference) and source	Age range	Content areas	Description
Prescriptive Behavior Check list for the Severely and Pro-foundly Retarded (Popovich, 1977)	All ages	*Motor development* head and trunk control, sitting, hand-knee position, standing *Eye-hand coordination* *Language development* attending, physical imitation, auditory training, object discrimination, concept development, sound imitation *Physical eating problems*	Not standardized but reliability was taken on all but motor development and physical eating problems. Information also given on parent training and writing behavior objectives and task analysis.

References

Abell, M. K. (1978). Movement. In F. P. Connor, G. G. Williamson, & J. M. Siepp (Eds.), *Program guide for infants and toddlers with neuromotor and other developmental disabilities.* New York: Teacher's College Press.

Abroms, I. F., & Panagakos, P. G. (1980). The child with significant developmental motor disability (cerebral palsy). In A. P. Scheiner & I. F. Abrams (Eds.), *The practical management of the developmentally disabled child.* St. Louis: C. V. Mosby Co.

Adams, G. L. (1982). Independent living skills. In L. Sternberg & G. L. Adams (Eds.), *Educating severely and profoundly handicapped students.* Rockville: Aspen Publishers, Inc.

Adsett, D. B., Fitz, C. R., & Hill, A. (1985). Hypoxic-ischaemic cerebral injury in the term newborn: Correlations of CT findings with neurological outcome. *Developmental Medicine and Child Neurology, 27,* 155–160.

Agosta, J. M., Close, D. W., Hops, H., & Rusch, F. R. (1980). Treatment of self-injurious behavior through overcorrection procedures. *Journal of The Association for the Severely Handicapped, 5*(1), 5–12.

Aiken, J. M., & Salzberg, C. L. (1984). The effects of a sensory extinction procedure on stereotypic sounds of two autistic children. *Journal of Autism and Developmental Disorders, 14*(3), 291–299.

Akins, C., Davidson, R., & Hopkins, T. (1980). The child with myelodysplasia. In A. P. Sceiner & I. F. Adroms (Eds.), *The practical management of the developmentally disabled child.* St. Louis: C. V. Mosby Co.

Ali, Z., & Lowry, M. (1981). Early maternal-child contact: Effects on later behavior. *Developmental Medicine and Child Neurology, 23,* 337–345.

Alpern, G., Boll, T., & Shearer, M. (1980). *Developmental Profile II: Manual (revised edition).* Aspen, CO: Psychological Development Publications.

Altman, K., & Krupsaw, R. (1983). Suppressing aggressive-destructive behavior by delayed overcorrection. *Journal of Behavioral Therapy & Experimental Psychiatry, 14*(4), 359–362.

Anderson, J. (1986). Sensory intervention with the preterm infant in the neonatal intensive care unit. *The American Journal of Occupational Therapy, 40*(1), 19–26.

Anthony, E. J. (1979). The child's discovering of his body. In C. B. Kopp (Ed.), *Readings in early development for occupational and physical therapists.* Springfield, IL: Charles C Thomas.

Apgar, V. (1960). The newborn (Apgar) scoring system: Reflections and advice. *Pediatric Clinics of North America, 13,* 645.

Apgar, V., & Beck, J. (1974). *Is my baby all right?* New York: Pocket Books.

Arnold, L. E. (1978). *Helping parents help their children.* New York: Brunner/Mazel.

Atwater, E. (1983). *Adolescence.* Englewood Cliffs, NJ: Prentice-Hall.

Ayres, A. J. (1972). *Sensory integration and learning disorders.* Los Angeles: Western Psychological Services.

Ayres, A. J. (1975). *Southern California postrotary nystagmus test.* Los Angeles: Western Psychological Services.

Ayres, A. J. (1979). *Sensory integration and the child.* Los Angeles: Western Psychological Services.

Ayres, A. J. (1980). *Southern California sensory integration tests manual.* Los Angeles: Western Psychological Services.

Azrin, N. H., & Armstrong, P. M. (1973). The "mini-meal"—A method of teaching eating skills to the profoundly retarded. *Mental Retardation, 11*(1), 9–13.

Azrin, N. H., & Besalel, V. A. (1980). *How to use overcorrection.* Austin: PRO-ED.

Azrin, N. H., & Foxx, R. M. (1971). A rapid method of eliminating bedwetting (enuresis) of the retarded. *Behavior Research and Therapy, 11,* 427–434.

Azrin, N. H., Schaeffer, R. M., & Wesolowski, M. D. (1976). A rapid method of teaching profoundly retarded persons to dress by a reinforcement-guidance method. *Mental Retardation, 14*(6), 29–33.

Badell-Ribera, A. (1985). Myelodysplasia. In G. D. Molnar (Ed.), *Pediatric Rehabilitation.* Baltimore: Williams & Wilkins.

Bailey, D. B., & Wolery, M. (1984). *Teaching infants and preschoolers with handicaps.* Columbus, OH: Charles E. Merrill Publishing Company.

Balthazar, E. E. (1971). *Balthazar scales of adaptive behavior (I and II).* Palo Alto: Consulting Psychologist Press, Inc.

Banerdt, B., & Bricker, D. (1978). A training program for selected self-feeding skills for the motorically impaired. *American Association for the Education of Severely/Profoundly Handicapped (AAESPH) Review, 3*(4), 222–229.

Banus, B. S., Kent, C. A., Norton, V., Sukiennicki, D. R., & Becker, M. L. (1979). *The developmental therapist* (2nd ed.). Thorofare, NJ: Charles B. Slack, Inc.

Barnes, M. R., Crutchfield, C. A., & Heriza, C. B. (1978). *The neurological basis of patient treatment—Volume II: Reflexes in motor development.* Atlanta: Stokesville Publishing Co.

Barrett, R. P., & Linn, D. M. (1981). Treatment of stereotyped toe-walking overcorrection and physical therapy. *Applied Research in Mental Retardation, 2,* 13–21.

Barton, E. J., & Madsen, J. J. (1980). The use of awareness and omission training to control excessive drooling in severely retarded. *Child Behavior Therapy, 2*(1), 55–63.

Batshaw, M. L., & Perret, Y. M. (1986). *Children with handicaps: A medical primer* (2nd ed.). Baltimore: Paul H. Brookes Publishing Company.

Bayley, N. (1969). *Bayley scales of infant development.* New York: Psychological Corporation.

Beckman, P. J. (1983). Influences of selected child characteristics on stress in families of handicapped infants. *American Journal of Mental Deficiency, 88,* 150–156.

Beery, K. E., & Berktencia, N. A. (1967). *Developmental test of visual motor integration.* Chicago: Follett Publishing Company.

Bell, D. R., & Low, R. M. (1977). *Observing and recording children's behavior.* Spokane, WA: Performance Associates.

Bennett, F. C. (1982). The pediatrician and the interdisciplinary process. *Exceptional Children, 48*(4), 306–314.

Bergen, A. (1974). *Selected equipment for pediatric rehabilitation.* Valhalla, NY: Blythedale Children's Hospital.

Berkowitz, S., Sherry, P. J., & Davis, B. A. (1971). Teaching self-feeding skills to profound retardates using reinforcement and fading procedures. *Behavior Therapy, 2*(1), 62–67.

Berry, H. K. (1981). The diagnosis of phenylketonuria. *American Journal of Disabled Children, 135,* 211–213.

Best, G. A. (1978). *Musculoskeletal disabilities and other health impairments: Individuals with physical disabilities.* St. Louis: C. V. Mosby Co.

Bettison, S. (1982). *Toilet training to independence for the handicapped.* Springfield, IL: Charles C Thomas.

Blackman, J. A. (1984a). Congenital infections. In J. A. Blackman (Ed.), *Medical aspects of developmental disabilities in children birth to three.* Rockville, MD: Aspen Publishers, Inc.

Blackman, J. A. (1984b). Down syndrome. In J. A. Blackman (Ed.), *Medical aspects of developmental disabilities in children birth to three.* Rockville, MD: Aspen Publishers, Inc.

Blackman, J. A. (1984c). Mental retardation. In J. A. Blackman (Ed.), *Medical aspects of developmental disabilities in children birth to three.* Rockville, MD: Aspen Publishers, Inc.

Blanchard, I. (1966). Developing motor control for self-feeding. *The Cerebral Palsy Journal, 27*(5), 9.

Bleck, E. E., & Nagel, D. A. (1983). *Physically handicapped children: A medical atlas for teachers* (2nd ed.). New York: Grune & Stratton.

Blockey, N. J. (1975). *Children's orthopedics—Practical problems.* London: Butterworths.

Bluma, S. M., Shearer, M. S., Frohman, A. H., & Hilliard, J. M. (1976). *Portage guide to early education.* Portage, WI: Cooperative Educational Agency.

Bobath, B. (1985). *Abnormal postural reflex activity caused by brain lesions* (3rd ed.). Rockville, MD: Aspen Publishers, Inc.

Bobath, K., & Bobath, B. (1972). Cerebral palsy. In P. H. Pearson & C. E. Williams (Eds.), *Physical therapy services in the developmental disabilities.* Springfield, IL: Charles C Thomas.

Bonadonna, P. (1981). Effects of a vestibular stimulation program on stereotypic rocking behavior. *The American Journal of Occupational Therapy, 35*(12), 775–781.

Bosley, E. (1965). Development of sucking and swallowing. *The Cerebral Palsy Journal, 26*(6), 14–16.

Bosley, E. (1966). Teaching the cerebral palsied to chew. *The Cerebral Palsy Journal, 27*(4), 8–9.

Bragg, J. H., House, C., & Schumaker, J. (1975). Effects on reverse tailor sitting in children with cerebral palsy. *Physical Therapy, 55*(8), 860–868.

Braun, M. A., Palmer, M. M., & Salek, B. (1983). *Early detection and treatment of the infant and young children with neuromuscular disorders.* New York: Therapeutic Media, Inc.

Brazelton, T. B. (1984). *Neonatal behavioral assessment scale, Second edition.* Philadelphia: J. B. Lippincott Company.

Brazelton, T. B., & Als, H. (1979). Four early stages in development of mother-infant interaction. *Psychoanalytic Studies of the Child, 34,* 85–117.

Brewster, A. B. (1982). Chronically ill hospitalized children's concepts of their illness. *Pediatrics, 69,* 355–362.

Bricker, D. (1985). The effectiveness of early intervention with handicapped and medically at-risk infants. In M. Frank (Ed.), *Infant intervention programs: Truths and untruths.* New York: The Haworth Press.

Bricker, D. D. (1986). Population description. In *Early education of at-risk and handicapped infants, toddlers and preschool children.* Glenview, IL: Scott, Foresman and Co.

Bricker, D. D., & Dow, M. G. (1980). Early intervention with the young severely handicapped child. *Journal of The Association of the Severely Handicapped, 5*(2), 130–142.

Brigance, A. H. (1978). *Brigance diagnostic inventory of early development.* North Billerica, MA: Curriculum Associates, Inc.

Bright, T., Bittick, K., & Fleeman, B. (1981). Reduction of self-injurious behavior using sensory integrative techniques. *The American Journal of Occupational Therapy, 35*(3), 167–172.

Broman, S., Nichols, P., & Kennedy, W. A. (1975). *Preschools: Prenatal and early developmental correlates.* Hillsdale, NJ: Lawrence Erlbaum Associates.

Bruinincks, R. H. (1978). *Bruininks-Oseretsky test of motor proficiency.* Circle Pines, MN: American Guidance Service, Inc.

Bruinincks, R. H., Warfield, G., & Stealey, S. (1982). The mentally retarded. In E. Meyen (Ed.), *Exceptional children and youth.* Denver: Love Publishing Company.

Bryant, D. M., & Ramey, C. T. (1985). Prevention-oriented infant education programs. In M. Frank (Ed.), *Infant intervention program: Truths and untruths.* New York: The Haworth Press.

Brylewski, J. (1978). A typical case of Cornelia de Lange's syndrome. *British Medical Journal, 1*(6114), 756.

Buckley, J. J. (1983). Roles of the professional. In R. K. Mulliken & J. J. Buckley (Eds.), *Assessment of multihandicapped children.* Rockville, MD: Aspen Publishers, Inc.

Cadman, D., Chambers, L. W., Walter, S. D., Feldman, W., Smith, K., & Ferguson, R. (1984). The usefulness of the Denver Developmental Screening Test to predict kindergarten problems in a general community population. *American Journal of Public Health, 74*(10), 1093–1097.

Caldwell, B., & Bradley, R. (1978). *Home observation for measurement of the environment.* Little Rock: Center for Child Development and Education, University of Arkansas.

Campbell, P. H. (1976). *Problem-oriented approaches to feeding the handicapped child* (first draft copy). Akron, OH: The Children's Hospital of Akron.

Campbell, P. H. (1979). Assessing oral-motor skills in severely handicapped persons: An analysis of normal and abnormal patterns of movement. In R. L. York & E. Edgar (Eds.), *Teaching the severely handicapped: Vol. IV.* Seattle: American Association for the Education of Severely/Profoundly Handicapped.

Campbell, P. H. (1987) Physical management and handling procedures with students with movement dysfunction. In M. E. Snell (Ed.) *Systematic instruction of persons with severe handicaps* (pp. 174–187). Columbus, OH: Charles E. Merrill.

Campbell, S. K., & Wilhelm, I. J. (1985). Development from birth to 3 years of age of 15 children at high risk for central nervous system dysfunction. *Physical Therapy, 65*(4), 463–469.

Campbell, S. K., & Wilson, J. M. (1976). Planning infant learning programs. *Physical Therapy, 56*(12), 1347–1357.

Caplan, F. (1973). *The first twelve months of life: Your baby's growth month by month.* New York: Crosset & Dulays.

Capute, A. J., Accardo, P. J., Vining, E. P. G., Rubenstein, J. E., Walcher, J. R., Harryman, S., & Ross, A. (1978). Primitive reflex profile. *Physical Therapy, 58*(9), 1061–1065.

Carey, W. B., & Mcdevitt, S. C. (1977). *The Carey infant temperament questionnaire.* Media, PA: William B. Carey, M.D.

Carey, W. B., & McDevitt, S. C. (1978). Ability and change in individual temperament diagnoses from infancy to early childhood. *Journal of Child Psychiatry, 17,* 331–337.

Case, J. (1985). Positioning guidelines for the premature infant. *Developmental Disabilities—Special Interest Section Newsletter* (The American Occupational Therapy Association), *8*(3), 1–2.

Cassidy, S. B.(1984). Tuberous sclerosis in children: Diagnosis and course. *Comprehensive Therapy, 10*(11), 43–51.

Chandler, L. S., & Adams, M. A. (1972). Multiply handicapped child motivated for ambulation through behavior modification. *Physical Therapy, 52*(4), 399–401.

Chen, H., & Woolley, P. V. (1978). A developmental assessment chart for non-institutionalized Down syndrome children. *Growth, 42,* 157–165.

Christian, W. P., Holloman, S. W., & Lanier, C. L. (1973). An attendant operated feeding program for severely and profoundly retarded females. *Mental Retardation, 11*(5), 35–37.

Cipani, E. (1981). Modifying food spillage behavior in an institutionalized retarded client. *Behavioral Therapy & Experimental Psychiatry, 12*(3), 261–265.

Clark, F. A., & Shuer, J. (1978). A clarification of sensory integrative therapy and its application to programming with retarded people. *Mental Retardation, 6*(3), 227–232.

Clark, P. N., & Allen, A. S. (1985). *Occupational therapy for children.* St. Louis: C. V. Mosby Company.

Cliff, S. (1979). *The development of reach and grasp.* El Paso: Guynes Printing.

Colangelo, C., Bergen, A., & Gottlieb, L. (1976). *A normal baby—The sensory-motor process of the first year.* New York: Blythedale Children's Hospital.

Colarusso, R. P., & Hammill, D. D. (1972). *Motor-free visual perception test.* San Rafael, CA: Academic Therapy Publications.

Colber, E., & Koegler, R. (1958). Toewalking in childhood schizophrenia. *Journal of Pediatrics, 53,* 219–220.

Coley. I. L. (1978). *Pediatric assessment of self-care activities.* St. Louis: C. V. Mosby Company.

Coley, I. L., & Procter, S. A. (1985). Self-maintenance activities. In P. N. Clark & A. S. Allen (Eds.), *Occupational therapy for children.* St. Louis: C. V. Mosby Company.

Collingwood, J., & Alberman, E. (1979). Separation at birth and the mother-child relationship. *Developmental Medicine and Child Neurology, 21,* 608–618.

Commission on Classification and Terminology of the International League Against Epilepsy. (1985). Proposal for classification of epilepsies and epileptic syndromes. *Epilepsia, 26*(3), 268–278.

Confusion over infant herpes. (1984, January 16). *Time,* 73.

Connolly, B. H., Morgan, S., & Russell, F. F. (1984). Evaluation of children with Down syndrome who participated in an early intervention program. *Physical Therapy, 64*(10), 1515–1519.

Connolly, B., Morgan, S., Russell, F. F., & Richardson, B. (1980). Early intervention with Down syndrome children. *Physical Therapy, 50*(11), 1405–1408.

Connolly, J. A. (1978). Intelligence levels of Down's syndrome children. *American Journal of Mental Deficiency, 83*(2), 193–196.

Connor, F. P., Williamson, G. G., & Siepp, J. M. (1978). *Program guide for infants and toddlers with neuromotor and other developmental disabilities.* New York: Teachers College Press.

Coopersmith, J. (1967). *The antecedents of self-esteem.* San Francisco: Witt & Freeman.

Coopersmith, S. (1959). A method for determining types of self-esteem. *Journal of Abnormal and Social Psychology, 59,* 87–94.

Copeland, M. (1982). Development of motor skills and the management of common problems. In K. E. Allen & E. M. Goetz (Eds.), *Early childhood education—Special problems, special solutions*. Rockville, MD: Aspen Publishers, Inc.

Copeland, M., Ford, L., & Solon, N. (1976). *Occupational therapy for mentally retarded children*. Baltimore: University Park Press.

Crain, L. S. (1984). Prenatal causes of atypical development. In M. S. Hanson (Ed.), *Atypical infant development*. Baltimore: University Park Press.

Cratty, B. J. (1979). *Perceptual and motor development in infants and children*. Englewood Cliffs, NJ: Prentice-Hall.

Creer, T. L., & Cristian, W. P. (1976). Behavior modification. In *Chronically ill and handicapped children*. Champaign, IL: Research Press Co.

Crnic, K. A., Friedrich, W. N., & Greenberg, M. T. (1983). Adaptation of families with mentally retarded children: A model of stress, coping, and family ecology. *American Journal of Mental Deficiency, 88*, 125–138.

Cronk, C. E. (1978). Growth of children with Down syndrome: Birth to age 3 years. *Pediatrics, 61*(4), 564–568.

Cross, L., & Goin, K. (Eds.), (1977). *Identifying handicapped children: A guide to casefinding, screening, diagnosis, assessment, and evaluation*. New York: Walker and Company.

Crowe, C. A., Heuther, C. A., Oppenheimer, S. G., Barth, L. D., Jeffrey, E., & Reinhart, S. (1985). The epidemiology of spinal bifida in southwestern Ohio, 1970–1979. *Developmental Medicine and Child Neurology, 27*, 176–182.

Crysdale, W. S. (1980). The drooling patient: Evaluation and current options. *Laryngoscope, 90*(5), 775–783.

Cullen, S. M., Cronk, C. E., Pueschel, S. M., Schnell, R. R., & Reed, R. B. (1981). Social development and feeding milestones of young Down syndrome children. *American Journal of Mental Deficiency, 85*(4), 410–415.

Danella, E. A. (1973). A study of tactile preference in multiply-handicapped children. *American Journal of Occupational Therapy, 27*(8), 457–463.

Dayan, M. (1964). Toilet training retarded children in a state residential institution. *Mental Retardation, 2*, 116–117.

de Chateau, P. (1979). Parent-infant relationship after immediate post-partum contact. *Child Abuse & Neglect, 3*, 279–283.

DeGangi, G. A., Berk, R. A., & Valvano, J. (1983). Test of motor and neurological functions in high-risk infants: Preliminary findings. *Developmental and Behavioral Pediatrics, 4*(3), 182–189.

Denhoff, E. (1981). Current status of infant stimulation or enrichment programs for children with developmental disabilities. *Pediatrics, 67*(1), 32–37.

Dennis, R., Reichle, J., Williams, W., & Vogelsberg, R. T. (1982). Motoric factors influencing the selection of vocabulary for sign production programs. *The Journal of the Association for the Severely Handicapped, 7*(1), 20–32.

de Quiros, J. B., & Schrager, O. L. (1978). *Neuropsychological fundamentals in learning disabilities*. San Rafael, CA: Academic Therapy Publications.

D'Eugenio, D., & Rogers, S. (1975). *Early intervention developmental profile & developmental screening of handicapped infants*. Ann Arbor: The University of Michigan Publications Distribution Service.

Diamant, H., & Kumlien, A. (1974). A treatment for drooling in children with cerebral palsy. *Journal of Laryngology and Otology, 88*(1), 61–64.

Dorland's illustrated medical dictionary (25th ed.). (1974). Philadelphia: W. B. Saunders.

Douglas, J. W. B. (1975). Early hospital admission and fate disturbance of behavior and learning. *Developmental Medicine and Child Neurology. 17*, 456–480.

Drabman, R. S., Cordua Y Cruz, G., Ross, J., & Lynd, S. (1979). Suppression of chronic drooling in mentally retarded children and adolescents: Effectiveness of a behavioral treatment package. *Behavior Therapy, 10*(1), 46–56.

Dreifuss, F. E. (1985). Classification and recognition of seizures. *Clinical Therapeutics, 7*(2), 240–245.

Drotar, D., Baskiewicz, A., Irvin, N., Kennell, J., & Klaus, M. (1975). The adaptation of parents to the birth of an infant with a congenital malformation: A hypothetical model. *Pediatrics, 56,* 710–717.

Dunst, C. J., & Rheingrover, R. M. (1983). Structural characteristics of sensorimotor development among Down's syndrome infants. *Journal of Mental Deficiency Research, 27,* 11–22.

Duvall, E. M. (1971). *Family development* (4th ed.). New York: J. B. Lippincott.

Edwards, N. (1968). The relationships between physical condition immediately after birth and mental and motor performance at age four. *Genetic Psychology Monographs, 78,* 27–289.

Ehrlich, A. B. (1970). *Training therapists for tongue thrust correction.* Springfield, IL: Charles C Thomas.

Eipper, D. S., & Azen, S. P. (1978). A comparison of two developmental instruments in evaluating children with Down's syndrome. *Physical Therapy, 58*(9), 1066–1069.

Ekedahl, C. (1974). Surgical treatment of drooling. *Acta Oto-laryngologica 77,* 215–220.

Ekedahl, C., Mansson, I., & Sandberg, N. (1974). Swallowing dysfunction in the brain damaged with drooling. *Acta Oto-laryngologica, 78*(1-2), 141–149.

Ellis, N. R. (1963). Toilet training the severely defective patient: An S-R reinforcement analysis. *American Journal of Mental Deficiency, 68,* 98–103.

Ensher, G. L., & Clark, D. A. (1986). Neurology of the newborn. *Newborn at risk: Medical care and psychoeducational intervention.* Rockville, MD: Aspen Publishers, Inc.

Erhardt, R. (1982). *Development hand dysfunction.* Laurel, MD: Ramoco Publishing Company.

Erhardt, R. P. (1986). *Erhardt developmental vision assessment.* Fargo, ND: Rhoda P. Erhardt, 2109 3rd Street North.

Erickson, M. L. (1976). *Assessment and management of developmental changes in children.* St. Louis: C. V. Mosby Company.

Esenther, S. E. (1984). Developmental coaching of the Down syndrome infant. *The American Journal of Occupational Therapy, 38*(7), 440–445.

Farber, S. D. (1982). *Neurorehabilitation—A multisensory approach.* Philadelphia: W. B. Saunders Company.

Farber, S. D., & Huss, J. (1974). *Sensorimotor evaluation and treatment procedures for allied health personnel.* Indianapolis: The Indiana University Foundation.

Farber, S. D., & Williams S. (1982). Neonatology. In S. D. Farber (Ed.), *Neurorehabilitation—A multisensory approach.* Philadelphia: W. B. Saunders Company.

Feldman, W. S., Manella, K. J., Apodaca, L., & Varni, J. W. (1982). Behavioral group parent training in spina bifida. *Journal of Clinical Child Psychology, 11*(2), 144–150.

Ferry, P. C. (1981). On growing new neurons: Are early intervention program effective? *Pediatrics, 67*(1), 34–41.

Fetters, L. (1981). Object permanence development in infants with motor handicaps. *Physical Therapy, 61*(3), 327–333.

Fewell, R. R. (1983). The team approach to infant education. In S. G. Garwood & R. R. Fewell (Eds.), *Educating handicapped infants: Issues in development and intervention.* Rockville, MD: Aspen Publishers, Inc.

Fewell, R. R., & Sandall, S. R. (1983). Assessment of high-risk infants. In E. M. Goetz & K. E. Allen (Eds.), *Early childhood education—Special environment, policy & legal considerations*. Rockville, MD: Aspen Publishers, Inc.

Filler, Jr., J. W. (1983). *Service models for handicapped infants*. Rockville, MD: Aspen Publishers, Inc.

Finkle, L. J., Hostetler, S. K., & Hanson, D. P. (1983). The assessment of profoundly handicapped children. *School Psychology Review, 12*(1), 75–81.

Finnie, N. R. (1975). *Handling the young cerebral palsied child at home* (2nd ed.). New York: E. P. Dutton.

Fiorentino, M. R. (1973). *Reflex testing methods for evaluating central nervous system development* (2nd ed.). Springfield, IL: Charles C Thomas Publishers.

Folio, M. R., & Fewell, R. R. (1983). *Peabody developmental motor scales*. Hingham, MA: Teaching Resources Corporation.

Ford, L. J. (1975). Teaching dressing skills to a severely retarded child. *American Journal of Occupational Therapy, 29*(2), 87–92.

Forness, S. R., & MacMillan, D. L. (1970). The origins of behavior modification with exceptional children. *Exceptional Children, 37*(2), 93–100.

Foster, R., & Tucker, D. J. (1974). *Camelot behavioral checklist*. Austin, TX: PRO-ED.

Foxx, R. M., & Azrin, N. H. (1973a). The elimination of autistic self-stimulatory behavior by overcorrection. *Journal of Applied Behavior Analysis, 6*(1), 1–14.

Foxx, R. M., & Azrin, N. H. (1973b). *Toilet training the retarded: A rapid program for day and nightime independent toileting*. Champaign, IL: Research Press.

Frankenburg, W. K., & Dodds, J. B. (1969). *Denver developmental screening test*. Denver: LADOCA Project and Publishing Foundation.

Fraser, B. A., Galka, G., & Hensinger, R. H. (1980). *Gross motor management of severely multiply impaired students, Volume 1, Evaluation guide*. Austin, TX: PRO-ED.

Fraser, B. A., & Hensinger, R. N. (1983). *Managing physical handicaps—A practical guide for parents, care providers, and educators*. Baltimore: Paul H. Brookes Publishing Co.

Fredericks, H. D., Baldwin, V. L., Grove, D. N., & Moore, W. G. (1975). *Toilet training the handicapped child*. Monmouth, OR: Instructional Development Corporation.

Fredericks, H. D., Riggs, C., Furey, T., Grove, D., Moore, W., McDonnell, J., Jordan, E., Hanson, W., Baldwin, V., & Wadlow, M. (1976). *The teaching research curriculum for moderately and severely handicapped*. Springfield, IL: Charles C Thomas.

Freeman, J., Gould, V., Markley, F., & Smith, M. (1975). *Project A.D.A.P.T.—A developmental curriculum for infants exhibiting developmental delay*. Santa Barbara: Tri-County Regional Center, Ventura County Association for the Retarded, Developmental Disabilities Projects Fund, State of California Health and Welfare Agency.

Frenkel, J. K. (1985). Toxoplasmosis. *Pediatric Clinics of North America, 32*(4), 917–932.

Fried, K. (1980). A score based on eight signs in the diagnosis of Down syndrome in the newborn. *Journal of Mental Deficiency Research, 24,* 181–185.

Frostig, M., & Horne D. (1964). *The Frostig Program for the Development of Visual Perception*. Chicago: Follett Publishing Co.

Fryers, T., & Mackay, R. I. (1979). Down syndrome: Prevalence at birth, mortality and survival. A 17 year study. *Early Human Development, 3*(1), 29–41.

Furrer, F., & Deonna, T. (1982). Persistent toe-walking in children. *Helvetica Paediatrica Acta, 73,* 301–316.

Furuno, S., O'Reilly, K. A., Hosaka, C. M., Inatsuka, T. T., Allman, T. L., & Zeisloft, B. (1985). *Hawaii early learning profile* (rev. ed.). Palo Alto, CA: VORT.

Gadow, K. D. (1986). *Children on medication, volume II: Epilepsy, emotional disturbance, and adolescent disorders*. San Diego: College-Hill Press.

Gallender, D. (1979). *Eating handicaps*. Springfield, IL: Charles C Thomas.

Gallender, D. (1980). The process of toileting. *Teaching eating and toileting skills to the multi-handicapped in the school setting*. Springfield, IL: Charles C Thomas.

Gardner, H. (1978). *Developmental psychology: An introduction*. Boston: Little, Brown and Company.

Garwood, S. G. (1983). *Educating young handicapped children: A developmental approach* (2nd ed.). Rockville, MD: Aspen Publishers, Inc.

Gearheart, B. R., & Weishahn, M. W. (1976). *The handicapped student in the regular classroom*. St. Louis: C. V. Mosby Company.

Geiger, W. L., & Justen, J. E. (1983). Definitions of severely handicapped and requirements for teacher certification: A survey of state departments of education. *The Journal of the Association for the Severely Handicapped, 8*(1), 25–29.

Gentry, D., & Adams, G. (1978). A curriculum-based, direct intervention approach to the education of handicapped infants. In N. G. Haring & D. D. Bricker (Eds.), *Teaching the severely handicapped, Vol. III*. Columbus, OH: Special Press.

Gesell, A., & Amatruda, C. S. (1947). *Developmental diagnosis* (2nd ed.). New York: Paul B. Hoeber.

Gesell, A., & Ilg, F. L. (1946). *Youth: The years from ten to sixteen*. New York: Harper & Row.

Gesell, A., Ilg, F. L., & Ames, L. B. (1977). *The child from five to ten*. New York: Harper & Row.

Giles, D. K., & Wolf, M. M. (1966). Toilet training institutionalized, severe retardates: An application of operant behavior modification techniques. *American Journal of Mental Deficiency, 70*, 766–780.

Gilfoyle, E. M., Grady, A. P., & Moore, J. C. (1981). *Children adapt*. Thorofare, NJ: Charles B. Slack.

Gilfoyle, E. M., & Hays, C. (1979). Occupational therapy roles and functions in the education of the school-based handicapped student. *The American Journal of Occupational Therapy, 33*(9), 565–576.

Gilfoyle, E. M., & Hays, C. (no date). *Training: Occupational therapy educational management in schools—A competency-based educational program, Volumes 1–4*. Rockville, MD: American Occupational Therapy Association.

Gisel, E. G., Lange, L. J., & Niman, C. W. (1984a). Chewing cycles in 4- and 5-year-old Down's syndrome children: A comparison of eating efficacy with normals. *The American Journal of Occupational Therapy, 38*(10), 666–670.

Gisel, E. G., Lange, L. J., & Niman, C. W. (1984b). Tongue movements in 4- and 5-year-old Down's syndrome children: A comparison with normal children. *The American Journal of Occupational Therapy, 38*(10), 660–665.

Glover, M., & Preminger, J. (1978). *Early learning accomplishment profile for developmentally young children*. Winston-Salem, NC: Kaplan School Supply Corporation.

Gluckman, S., & Barling, J. (1980). Effects of a remedial program on visual-motor perception in spina bifida children. *The Journal of Genetic Psychology, 136*, 195–202.

Goetz, E. M. (1982). Behavior principles and techniques. In K. E. Allen & E. M. Goetz (Eds.), *Early childhood education—Special problems, special solutions*. Rockville, MD: Aspen Publishers, Inc.

Goldberg, K. (1975). The high-risk infant. *Physical Therapy, 55*(10), 1093–1096.

Goldberger, J. M. (1975). *Tongue thrust correction*. Danville, IL: The Interstate Printers & Publishers, Inc.

Goldberry, E. (1987). Choosing clothes for your child. *The Exceptional Parent, 17*(3), 28–33.

Gomes-Pedro, J., deAlmeida, J. B., daCosta, C. S., & Barbosa, A. (1984). Influence of early mother-infant contact of dyadic behavior during the first months of life. *Developmental Medicine and Child Neurology, 26,* 657–664.

Gorski, P. A. (1984). Infants at risk. In M. J. Hanson (Ed.), *Atypical infant development.* Baltimore: University Park Press.

Gouvier, W. D., Richards, J. S., Blanton, P. D., Janert, K., Rosen, L. A., & Drabman, R. S. (1985). Behavior modification in physical therapy. *Archives of Physical Medical Rehabilitation, 66*(2), 113–116.

Green, M., & Solnit, A. J. (1964). Reactions to the threatened loss of a child: A vulnerable child syndrome. *Pediatrics, 7,* 58–60

Green, M. I. (1977). *A sigh of relief.* New York: Bantam Books.

Greenwald, C. A., & Leonard, L. B. (1979). Communicative and sensorimotor development of Down's syndrome children. *American Journal of Mental Deficiency, 84*(3), 296–303.

Gregg, C., Haffner, M., & Korner, A. (1976). The relative efficacy of vestibular proprioceptive stimulation and the upright position in enhancing visual pursuits in neonates. *Child Development, 47,* 309–314.

Griffin, P. P., Wheelhouse, W., Shiavi, R. & Bass, W. (1977). Habitual toewalker. *Journal of Bone Joint Surgery, 59*(A), 97–101.

Grimm, R. A. (1976). Hand function and tactile perception in a sample of children with myelomeningocele. *The American Journal of Occupational Therapy, 30*(4), 234–240.

Grossman, H. J. (Ed.). (1973). *Classification in mental retardation.* Washington, DC: American Association on Mental Deficiency.

Grossman, H. J. (Ed.). (1983). *Classification in mental retardation.* Washington, DC: American Association on Mental Deficiency.

Grossman, K., Thane, K., & Grossman, K. E. (1981). Maternal tactual contact of the newborn after various post partum conditions of mother-infant contact. *Developmental Psychology, 17,* 159–169.

Groves, I. D., & Carroccio, D. F. (1971). A self-feeding program for the severely and profoundly retarded. *Mental Retardation, 9*(3), 10–12.

Guerin, R. I. (1973). The management of drooling. *South Australian Clinics, 6,* 253–258.

Gunn, P., Berry, P., & Andrews, R. J. (1983). The temperament of Down's syndrome toddlers: A research note. *Journal of Child Psychology & Psychiatry & Allied Disciplines, 24*(4), 601–605.

Haberfellner, H., & Rossiwall, B. (1977). Treatment of oral sensorimotor disorders in cerebral-palsied children: Preliminary report. *Developmental Medicine and Child Neurology, 19,* 350–352.

Haeussermann, E. (1958). *Developmental potential for preschool children.* New York: Grune & Stratton.

Hales, D. J., Lazoff, B., Sosa, R., & Kennell, J. H. (1977). Defining the limits of the maternal sensitive period. *Developmental Medicine and Child Neurology, 19,* 454–461.

Hall, J. E., Salter, R. B., & Bhallask, S. K. (1967). Congenital short tendo calcaneus. *Journal of Bone Joint Surgery, 49*(B), 695–697.

Hall, R. V. (1975). *Managing behavior series: Basic principles, Part 2* (rev. ed). Austin, TX: PRO-ED.

Hall, R. V. (1974). *Managing behavior series: The measurement of behavior, Part 1* (rev. ed.). Austin, TX: PRO-ED.

Hall, R. V., & Hall, M. C. (1980). *How to use time out.* Austin, TX: PRO-ED.

Hallahan, D. P., & Kauffman, J. M. (1982). *Exceptional children: introduction to special education* (2nd ed.). Englewood Cliffs, NJ: Prentice-Hall.

Hanson, M. (1976). Tongue thrust: A point of view. *Journal of Speech and Hearing Disorders, 41*(2), 172–184.

Hanson, M. J., & Harris, S. R. (1986). *Teaching the young child with motor delays.* Austin, TX: PRO-ED.

Harbin, G. (1977). Education assessment. In L. Cross & K. Goin (Eds.), *Identifying handicapped children: A guide to casefinding, screening, diagnosis, assessment and evaluation.* New York: Walker and Company.

Haring, N. G. (1975). Educational services for the severely and profoundly handicapped. *Journal of Special Education, 9*(4), 425–433.

Harper, D. C. (1978). Personality characteristics of physically impaired adolescents. *Journal of Clinical Psychology, 34*(1), 97–103.

Harper, D. C., & Richman, L. C. (1978). Personality of physically impaired adolescents. *Journal of Psychology, 34*(3), 636–642.

Harris, M. M., & Dignam, P. F. (1980). A non-surgical method of reducing drooling in cerebral-palsied children. *Developmental Medicine and Child Neurology, 22*(3), 292–299.

Harris, S. R. (1980). Transdisciplinary therapy model of the infant with Down's syndrome. *Physical Therapy, 60*(4), 420–423.

Harris, S. R. (1981a). Effects of neurodevelopmental therapy on motor performance of infants with Down's syndrome. *Developmental Medicine and Child Neurology, 23,* 477–483.

Harris, S. R. (1981b). Physical therapy and infants with Down's syndrome: The effects of early intervention. *Rehabilitation Literature, 42*(11-12).

Harris, S. R., & Tada, W. L. (1985). Genetic disorders in children. In D. A. Umphred (Ed.), *Neurological rehabilitation, Vol. III.* St. Louis: C. V. Mosby Company.

Hart, V. (1977). The use of many disciplines with the severely and profoundly handicapped. In E. Sontage (Ed.), *Educational programming for the severely and profoundly handicapped.* Reston, VA: The Council for Exceptional Children.

Havighurst, R. J. (1972). *Developmental tasks and education* (3rd ed.). New York: McKay.

Hawcroft, J. (1976). Influence of screening for phenylketonuria on the incidence of mental retardation. In T. E. Oppe & F. P. Woodford (Eds.), *Early management of handicapping disorders.* New York: Associated Scientific Publishers–Elsevier.

Hayden, A. H., & Beck, G. R. (1982). Epidemiology of infants at risk. In C. T. Ramey & P. L. Trohanis (Eds.), *Finding and educating high risk and handicapped infants.* Baltimore: University Park Press.

Hayden, P. W., Davenport, S. L. H., & Campbell, M. M. (1979). Adolescents with myelodysplasia: Impact of physical disability on emotional maturation. *Pediatrics, 64*(1), 53–59.

Haynes, U. (1983). *Holistic health care for children with developmental disabilities.* Baltimore: University Park Press.

Henderson, A., & Coryell, J. (Eds.). (1972). *The body senses and perceptual deficit.* (Proceedings of the OT Symposium on Somatosensory Aspects of Perceptual Deficit.) Boston: Boston University.

Henderson, M., & Mapel, J. R. (1984). The colostomy and ileostomy. In J. A. Blackman (Ed.), *Medical aspects of developmental disabilities in children birth to three.* Rockville, MD: Aspen Publishers, Inc.

Henderson, S., & McDonald, M. (1973). *Step-by-step dressing.* Champaign, IL: Surburban Publications.

Henderson, S. E., Morris, J., & Frith, U. (1981). The motor deficit in Down's syndrome children: A problem of timing? *Journal of Child Psychology and Psychiatry and Allied Disciplines, 22,* 233–245.

Herskowitz, J., & Marks, A. N. (1977). The spina bifida patient as a person. *Developmental Medicine and Child Neurology, 19,* 413–417.

Hester, S. B. (1981). Effects of behavioral modification on the standing and walking deficiencies of a profoundly retarded child. *Physical Therapy, 61*(6), 907–911.

Heward, W. L., & Orlansky, M. D. (1980). *Exceptional children: An introductory survey to special education.* Columbus, OH: Charles E. Merrill Publishing Co.

Heward, W. L., & Orlansky, M. D. (1984). Early intervention. In *Exceptional children* (2nd ed.). Columbus, OH: Charles E. Merrill Publishing Co.

Hill, L. D. (1985). Contributions of behavior modification to cerebral palsy habilitation. *Physical Therapy, 65*(3), 341–345.

Holm, V. A., & McCartin, R. E. (1978). Interdisciplinary child development team: Team issues and training in interdisciplinariness. In K. E. Allen, V. A. Holm, & R. L. Schiefelbush (Eds.), *Early intervention: A team approach.* Baltimore: University Park Press.

Holser-Buehler, P. (1973). Correction of infantile feeding habits. *The American Journal of Occupational Therapy, 26*(6), 333–335.

Honig, A. S. (1984, May). Risk factors in infants and young children. *Young Children,* pp. 60–73.

Horner, R. D. (1971). Establishing use of crutches by a mentally retarded spina bifida child. *Journal of Applied Behavior Analysis, 4*(3), 183–189.

Horowitz, F. D. (1982). Methods of assessment of high-risk and handicapped infants. In C. T. Ramey & P. L. Trohanis (Eds.), *Finding and educating high-risk and handicapped infants.* Baltimore: University Park Press.

Horowitz, F. D., & Dunn, M. (1978). Infant intelligence testing. In F. D. Minifie & L. L. Lloyd (Eds.), *Communicative and cognitive abilities—Early behavioral assessment.* Baltimore: University Park Press.

Hoskins, T. A., & Squires, J. E. (1973). Developmental assessment: A test for gross motor and reflex development. *Physical Therapy, 53,* 117–126.

Hourcade, J. J., & Parette, Jr., H. P. (1984). Motoric change subsequent to therapeutic intervention in infants and young children who have cerebral palsy: Annotated listing of group studies. *Perceptual and Motor Skills, 58,* 519–524.

Howard, J. (1982). The role of the pediatrician with young exceptional children and their families. *Exceptional Children, 48*(4), 316–322.

Hreidarsson, S. J., Shapiro, B. K., & Capute, A. J. (1983). Age of walking and the cognitively handicapped. *Clinical Pediatrics, 22*(4), 248–250.

Hunt, G. M. (1981). Spinal bifida: Implications for 100 children at school. *Developmental Medicine and Child Neurology, 23,* 160–172.

Ilg, F. L., & Ames, L. B. (1955). *Child behavior.* New York: Harper & Row.

Illingworth, R. S. (1975). *The development of the infant and young child: Normal and abnormal* (6th ed.). New York: Churchill Livingstone.

Inge, K. L., & Snell, M. E. (1985). Teaching positioning and handling techniques to public school personnel through inservice training. *The Journal of the Association for the Severely Handicapped, 10*(2), 105–110.

Jaeger, L. (1987). *Home program instruction sheets for infants and young children.* Tucson, AZ: Therapy Skill Builders.

Jan, J. E., Ziegler, R. G., & Erba, G. (1983). *Does your child have epilepsy?* Baltimore: University Park Press.

Jedrysek, E., Klapper, Z., Pope, L., & Wortis, J. (1972). *Psychoeducational evaluation of the preschool child: A manual utilizing the Haeussermann approach.* New York: Grune & Stratton.

Jennett, R. J., Warford, H. L. S., Kreinick, C., & Waterkotte, G. W. (1981). Apgar index: A statistical tool. *American Journal of Obstetrics and Gynecology, 140*(2), 206–212.

Johnson, S. A. (1981). *First aid for kids.* New York: Quick Fox.

Johnson, V. M., & Werner, R. A. (1975). *A step-by-step learning guide for retarded infants and children.* Syracuse, NY: Syracuse University Press.

Johnson-Martin, N., Jens, K. G., & Attermeier, S. M. (1986). *Carolina curriculum for handicapped infants and infants at risk.* Baltimore: Paul H. Brookes Publishing Co.

Jones B. (1976). The perception of passive joint movements by cerebral palsied children. *Developmental Medicine and Child Neurology, 18,* 25–30.

Jones, P. R. (1982). The Meldreth dribble control project reassessed. *Child Care, Health and Development, 8*(2), 65–67.

Kaluger, G., & Kaluger, M. F. (1979). *Human development: The span of life* (2nd ed.). St. Louis: C. V. Mosby Company.

Kaminer, R. K., & Jedrysek, E. (1983). Age of walking and mental retardation. *American Journal of Public Health, 73*(9), 1095–1096.

Kansas Neurological Institute. (1985). *Feeding evaluation of oral function—adapted form.* Topeka: Author.

Kantner, R. M., Clark, D. L., Allen, L. C., & Chase, M. F. (1976). Effects of vestibular stimulation on nystagmus response and motor performance in the developmentally delayed infant. *Physical Therapy, 56*(4), 414–421.

Kantner, R. M., Kantner, B., & Clark, D. L. (1982). Vestibular stimulation effect on language development in mentally retarded children. *The American Journal of Occupational Therapy, 18*(4), 243–244.

Keele, D. K. (1983). *The developmentally disabled child: A manual for primary physicians.* Oradell, NJ: Medical Economic Books.

Kenny, W. (1963). Certain sensory deficits in cerebral palsy. *Clinicial Orthopedics, 21,* 193.

Kidd, J. W. (1983). The 1983 A.A.M.D. definition and classification of mental retardation: The apparent impact of the CEC-MR position. *Education and Training of the Mentally Retarded, 18*(4), 243–244.

Kinnealey, M. (1973). Aversive and nonaversive responses to sensory stimulation in mentally retarded children. *American Journal of Occupational Therapy, 27*(8), 464–471.

Kliewer, D., Bruce, W., & Trembath, J. (1977). *The Milani-Comparetti motor development screening test.* Omaha, NE: Meyer Children's Rehabilitation Institute.

Knoblock, H., & Pasamanick, B. (1974). *Gesell and Amatruda's developmental diagnosis: The evaluation and management of normal and abnormal neurophysiological development in infancy and early childhood* (3rd ed.). New York: Harper & Row.

Koch, R., & Friedman, E. G. (1981). Accuracy of newborn screening programs for phenylketonuria. *The Journal of Pediatrics, 98*(2), 267–269.

Koff, E., Boyle, P., & Pueschel, S. M. (1977). Perceptual-motor functioning in children with phenylketonuria. *American Journal of Diseases of Children, 131,* 1084–1087.

Kolderie, M. L. (1971). Behavor modification in the treatment of children with cerebral palsy. *Physical Therapy, 51*(10), 1083–1091.

Kolin, I. S., Scherzer, A. L., New, B., & Garfield, M. (1978). Studies of the school-age child with meningocele: Social and emotional adaptation. *Developmental Medicine and Child Neurology, 78,* 1013–1019.

Koontz, C. (1974). *Koontz child developmental program.* Los Angeles: Western Psychological Services.

Korabek, C. A., Reid, D. H., & Ivancic, M. T. (1981). Improving needed food intake of profoundly handicapped children through effective supervision of institutional staff. *Applied Research in Mental Retardation, 2,* 69–88.

Korner, A. F., & Thoman, E. B. (1972). The relative efficacy of contact and vestibular-proprioceptive stimulation in soothing neonates. *Child Development, 43*(2), 443–453.

Krumboltz, J. D., & Krumboltz, H. B. (1972). *Changing children's behavior.* Englewood Cliffs, NJ: Prentice-Hall.

Kuharski, T., Rues, J., Cook, D., & Guess, D. (1985). Effects of vestibular stimulation on sitting behavior among preschoolers with severe handicaps. *The Journal of the Association for the Severely Handicapped, 10*(3), 137–145.

Lamb, M. E., & Hwang, C. P. (1982). Maternal attachment and mother-neonate bonding: A critical review. *Advances in Developmental Psychology, 2,* 1–39.

Lancioni, G. (1980). Teaching independent toileting to profoundly retarded deaf-blind children. *Behavior Therapy, 11,* 234–244.

Lancioni, G. E., Smeets, P. M., Ceccarani, P. S., Capodaglio, L., & Campanari, G. (1984). Effects of gross motor activities on the severe self-injurious tantrums of multihandicapped individuals. *Applied Research in Mental Retardation, 5,* 471–482.

Langdon, H. J., & Langdon, L. L. (1983). *Initiating occupational therapy programs within the public school system: A guide for occupational therapists and public school administrators.* Thorofare, NJ: Charles B. Slack, Inc.

Langley, M. B. (1983). The implication of physical impairments for early intervention strategies. In S. G. Garwood (Ed.), *Educating young handicapped children: A developmental approach* (2nd ed.). Rockville, MD: Aspen Publishers, Inc.

Largo, R. H., Molinari, L., Weber, M., Pinto, L. C., & Duc, G. (1985). Early development of locomotion: Significance of prematurity, cerebral palsy, and sex. *Developmental Medicine and Child Neurology, 27,* 183–191.

Lasky, R. E., Tyson, J. E., Rosefeld, C. R., Priest, M., Krasinski, D., Heartwell, S., & Gant, N. F. (1983). Differences on Bayley's infant behavior record for a sample of high-risk infants and their controls. *Child Development, 54,* 1211–1216.

Lederman, E. F. (1984). *Occupational therapy in mental retardation.* Springfield, IL: Charles C Thomas.

Lee, J., Mahler, T. J., & Westling, D. L. (1985). Reducing occurrences of an asymmetrical tonic neck reflex. *American Journal of Mental Deficiency, 89*(6), 617–621.

Le Francois, G. R. (1983). *Of children.* Belmont, CA: Wadsworth.

Leibowitz, J. M., & Holcer, P. (1974). Building and maintaining self-feeding skills in a retarded child. *The American Journal of Occupational Therapy, 28*(9), 545–548.

Leifer, A. D., Leiderman, P. H., Barnett, C. R., & Williams, J. A. (1972). Effects of mother-infant separation on maternal attachment behavior. *Child Development, 43,* 1203–1218.

Lejeune J., Gautier, M., & Turpin, R. (1959). Les chromosomes humains en culture de tissues. *Comptes rendus hebdomadaires des seances de l'Academie des Sciences* (Paris), 248, 602.

Lemke, H. (1974). Self-abusive behavior in the mentally retarded. *The American Journal of Occupational Therapy, 28*(2), 94–98.

Lemke, H., & Mitchell, R. D. (1972). A self-feeding program—Controlling the behavior of a profoundly retarded child. *The American Journal of Occupational Therapy, 26*(5), 261–264.

Leo, J. (1982, August 2). The new scarlet letter. *Time,* 62–66.

Levine, M. H., & McColoum, J. A. (1983, July). Peer play and toys: Key factors in mainstreaming infants. *Young Children,* 22–26.

Levitt, S. (Ed.). (1984). *Pediatric developmental theory.* Boston: Blackwell Scientific Publications.

Lewis, B. J. (1978). Sensory deprivation in young children. *Child: Care, Health, & Development, 4,* 229–238.

Lewis, J. A. (1982). Oral motor assessment and treatment of feeding difficulties. In P. J. Accardo (Ed.), *Failure to thrive in infancy and early childhood*. Baltimore: University Park Press.

Lewko, J. H. (1976). Current practices in evaluating motor behavior of disabled children. *American Journal of Occupational Therapy, 30*(7), 413–419.

Ling-Fong Zee-Chen, E., & Hardman, M. L. (1983). Postrotary nystagmus response in children with Down's syndrome. *The American Journal of Occupational Therapy, 37*(4), 260–265.

Lovitt, T. (1970). Behavior modification: The current scene. *Exceptional Children, 37*(2), 85–91.

Ludlow, J. R., & Allen, L. M. (1979). The effect of early intervention and preschool stimulus on the development of the Down's syndrome child. *Journal of Mental Deficiency Research, 23*, 29–44.

Lussier, A. (1980). The physical handicaps and the body ego. *International Journal of Psychoanalysis, 61*, 179–185.

Lydic, J. S. (1982). Motor development in children with Down syndrome. *Physical and Occupational Therapy in Pediatrics, 2*(4), 53–74.

Lydic, J. S., & Steele, C. (1979). Assessment of the quality of sitting and gait patterns in children with Down's syndrome. *Physical Therapy, 59*(12), 1489–1494.

Lydic, J. S., & Windsor, M. M., Short, M. A., & Ellis, T. A. (1985). Effects of controlled rotary vestibular stimulation on the motor performance of infants with Down syndrome. *Physical and Occupational Therapy in Pediatrics, 5*(2-3), 93–118.

Lyons, B. G. (1984). Defining a child's zone of proximal development: Evaluation process for treatment planning. *American Journal of Occupational Therapy, 38*, 446–451.

MacKeith, R. (1973). The feelings and behavior of parents of handicapped children. *Developmental Medicine and Child Neurology, 15*(4), 524–527.

MacLean, W. E., & Baumeister, A. A. (1982). Effects of vestibular stimulation on motor development and stereotyped behavior of developmentally delayed children. *Journal of Abnormal Child Psychology, 10*, 229–245.

Magnusson, H. J., & Wernstedt, W. (1935). The infantile palmo-mentalis reflex. *Acta Paediatrica, 17*(Suppl. 1), 241.

Magrun, W. E., Ottenbacher, K., McCue, S., & Keefe, R. (1981). Effects of vestibular stimulation on spontaneous use of verbal language in developmentally delayed children. *American Journal of Occupational Therapy, 35*(2), 101–104.

Magrun, W. M., & Tigges, K. N. (1982). A transdisciplinary mobile intervention program for rural areas. *The American Journal of Occupational Therapy, 36*(2), 90–94.

Mahoney, K., Van Wagnen, R. K., & Meyerson, L. (1971). Toilet training of normal and retarded children. *Journal of Applied Behavioral Analysis, 4(3)*, 173–181.

Manella, K. J., & Varni, J. W. (1981). Behavior therapy in a gait-training program for a child with myelomeningocele. *Physical Therapy, 61*(9), 1284–1287.

Mann, W. C., & Sobsey, R. (1975). Feeding program for the institutionalized mentally retarded. *The American Journal of Occupational Therapy, 29*(8), 471–474.

Mans, L., Cicchetti, D., & Sroufe, L. A. (1978). Mirror reactions of Down's syndrome infants and toddlers: Cognitive underpinnings of self-recognition. *Child Development, 49*, 1247–1250.

Marinesco, G., & Radovici, A. (1920). Sur un reflexe cutane nouveau a reflexe palmo-mentonnier. *Revue Neurologique (Paris), 27*, 237.

Marks, N. C. (1974). *Cerebral palsied and learning disabled children: A guide to treatment, rehabilitation, and education*. Springfield, IL: Charles C Thomas.

Marotz, L. R., Rush, J. M., & Cross, M. Z. (1985). *Health, safety, and nutrition for the young child*. Albany, NY: Delmar Publishers, Inc.

Martin, J. E., & Epstein, L. H. (1976). Evaluating treatment effectiveness in cerebral palsy. *Physical Therapy, 56*(3), 285–294.

Martin, M. J. (1985). Children with mental retardation. In P. N. Clark & A. S. Allen (Eds.). *Occupational therapy for children.* St. Louis: C. V. Mosby Company.

Mason, R. M., & Proffit, W. R. (1974). The tongue thrust controversy: Background and recommendations. *Journal of Speech and Hearing Disorders, 39*(2), 115–132.

Matheny, M. M., & Ruby, D. D. (1963). A guide for feeding the cerebral palsied child. *Cerebral Palsy Review, 24*(2), 14–16.

Matthews, D. J. (1985). Developmental intervention and therapeutic exercise. In G. E. Molnar (Ed.), *Pediatric rehabilitation.* Baltimore:Williams & Wilkins.

Mayberry, W., & Gilligan, M. B. (1985). Ocular pursuit in mentally retarded, cerebral-palsied, and learning-disabled children. *American Journal of Occupational Therapy, 39*(9), 589–595.

Mazur, J. M. (1987, October). Early wheelchair training versus walking for high-level myelomeningocele patients. *Developmental Medicine and Child Neurology Abstracts,* (Suppl. 55), 8.

McAndrews, I. (1979). Adolescents and young people with spina bifida. *Developmental Medicine and Child Neurology, 21,* 619–629.

McBean, M. S. (1982). Problems of phenylketonuric children and their families. In T. E. Oppe & F. P. Woodford (Eds.), *Early management of handicapped disorders.* New York: Harper & Row.

McBride, A. B. (1973). *The growth and development of mothers, parents, and professionals.* New Haven, CT: Yale University Press.

McCann, J. R. (no date). Interdisciplinary approach to service. In M. A. H. Smith (Ed.), *Feeding the handicapped child.* Memphis, TN: Child Development Center.

McCollum, A. T. (1975). *The chronically ill child: A guide for parents and professionals.* New Haven, CT: Yale University Press.

McCormick, L., & Goldman, R. (1979). The transdisciplinary model: Implications for service delivery and personnel preparation for the severely and profoundly handicapped. *AAESPH Review, 4*(2), 152–161.

McCormick L., & Lee, C. (1979). Public Law 94-142: Mandated partnerships. *The American Journal of Occupational Therapy, 33*(9), 586–588.

McCormick, M. C., Charney, E. B., & Stemmler, M. M. (1986). Assessing the impact of a child with spina bifida on the family. *Developmental Medicine & Child Neurology, 28,* 53–61.

McCracken, A. (1975). Tactile function of educable mentally retarded children. *The American Journal of Occupational Therapy, 29*(7), 397–402.

McCracken, A. (1978). Drool control and tongue thrust for the mentally retarded. *The American Journal of Occupational Therapy, 32*(2), 79–85.

Melyn, M. A., & White, D. T. (1973). Mental and developmental milestones of non-institutionalized Down's syndrome children. *Pediatrics, 52*(4), 542–545.

Menolascino, F. J., & Egger, M. L. (1978). *Medical dimensions of mental retardation.* Lincoln: University of Nebraska Press.

Meryash, D. L., Harvey, L., Levy, H. L., Guthrie, R., Warner, R., Bloom, S., & Carr, J. R. (1981). Prospective study of early neonatal screening for phenylketonuria. *The New England Journal of Medicine, 304*(5), 294–295.

Michelsson, K., Ylinen, A., & Donner, M. (1981). Neurodevelopmental screening at five years of children who were at risk neonatally. *Developmental Medicine and Child Neurology, 23,* 427–433.

Miller, L. G. (1968). Toward a greater understanding of the parents of the mentally retarded child. *The Journal of Pediatrics, 73,* 699–705.

Miller, L. J. (1982). *Miller Assessment for Preschoolers*. Littleton, CO: The Foundation for Knowledge in Development.

Minde, K., Whitelaw, A., Brown, J., & Fitzhardinge, P. (1983). Effect of neonatal complications in premature infants on early parent-infant interactions. *Developmental Medicine and Child Neurology, 25,* 763–777.

Moen, J. L., Wilcox, R. D., & Burns, J. K. (1977). PKU as a factor in the development of self-esteem. *The Journal of Pediatrics, 90,* 1027–1029.

Molnar, G. E. (1974). Motor deficit of retarded infants and young children. *Archives of Physical Medicine and Rehabilitation, 55,* 393–398.

Molnar, G. E. (1978). Analysis of motor disorder in retarded infants and young children. *American Journal of Mental Deficiency, 83*(3), 213–222.

Molnar, G. E. (1979). Cerebral Palsy: Prognosis and how to judge it. *Pediatric Annals, 8,* 596–605.

Molnar, G. E. (Ed.). (1985). *Pediatric rehabilitation*. Baltimore: Williams & Wilkins.

Monreat, F. J. (1985). Consideration of genetic factors in cerebral palsy. *Developmental Medicine and Child Neurology, 27,* 325–330.

Montgomery, P. (1981). Assessment and treatment of the child with mental retardation. *Physical Therapy, 61*(9), 1265–1272.

Montgomery, P., & Gauger, J. (1978). Sensory dysfunction in children who toe walk. *Physical Therapy, 58*(10), 1195–1204.

Montgomery, P., & Richter, E. (1978a). Effect of sensory integrative therapy on the neuromotor development of retarded children. *Physical Therapy, 57,* 799–806.

Montgomery, P., & Richter, E. (1978b). *Sensorimotor integration program checklists*. Los Angeles: Western Psychological Services.

Morris, S. E. (1977). *Program guidelines for children with feeding problems*. Edison, NJ: Childcraft Education Corp.

Morris, S. E. (1978a). Section II—Assessment of children with oral-motor dysfunction. In J. M. Wilson (Ed.), *Oral-motor function and dysfunction children*. Chapel Hill: University of North Carolina, Division of Physical Therapy.

Morris, S. E. (1978b). Section III—Treatment of children with oral-motor dysfunction. In J. M. Wilson (Ed.). *Oral-motor function and dysfunction children*. Chapel Hill: University of North Carolina, Division of Physical Therapy.

Morris, S. E. (1982). *The normal acquisition of oral feeding skills: Implications for assessment and treatment*. New York: Therapeutic Media, Inc.

Morrison, D., Pothier, P., & Horr, K. (1978). *Sensory-motor dysfunction and therapy in infancy and early childhood*. Springfield, IL: Charles C Thomas.

Mueller, H. (1972). Facilitating feeding and prespeech. In P. H. Pearson & C. E. Williams (Eds.), *Physical therapy services in the developmental disabilities*. Springfield, IL: Charles C Thomas.

Mueller, H. (1975). Feeding. In N. Finne (Ed.), *Handling the young cerebral palsied child at home* (2nd ed.). New York: E. P. Dutton.

Mulliken, R. K., & Buckley, J. J. (1983). *Assessment of multihandicapped and developmentally disabled children*. Rockville, MD: Aspen Publishers, Inc.

Murphy, R. F., Nichter, C. A., & Liden, C. B. (1982). Developmental outcome of the high-risk infant: A review of methodological issues. *Seminars in Perinatology, 6*(4), 353–364.

Myers, G. J., Cerone, S. B., & Olson, A. L. (1981). *A guide for helping the child with spina bifida*. Springfield, IL: Charles C Thomas.

National Down Syndrome Society. (1984). *The Exceptional Parent, 14*(6), 47–48.

Neisworth, J. T., & Smith, R. M. (1973). *Modifying retarded behavior.* Boston: Houghton Mifflin Company.

Nelson, K. B., & Ellenberg, J. H. (1979). Neonatal signs as predictors of chronic neurologic disability. *Pediatrics, 64*(2), 225–232.

Nelson, K. B., & Ellenberg, J. H. (1981). Apgar scores as predictors of chronic neurologic disability. *Pediatrics, 68*(1), 36–44.

Nihira, K., Foster, R., Shellhaas, M., & Leland, H. (1974). *Adaptive behavior scales.* Washington, DC: American Association on Mental Retardation.

Norton, Y. (1972). Norton's basic motor evaluation. *The American Journal of Occupational Therapy, 26,* 176.

O'Brien, F., Bugle, C., & Azrin, N. H. (1972). Training and maintaining a retarded child's proper eating. *Journal of Applied Behavior Analysis, 5*(1), 67–72.

Oelwein, P. I., Fewell, R. R., & Pruess, J. B. (1985). The efficacy of intervention at outreach sites of the program for children with Down syndrome and other developmental delays. *Topics in Early Childhood Special Education, 5*(2), 78–82.

Offer, D., Ostrov, E., & Howard, K. I. (1981). *The adolescent: A psychological self-portrait.* New York: Basin Bodlin.

O'Flynn, M. E., Holtzman, N. A., Blaskovics, M., Azen, C., & Williamson, M. L. (1980). The diagnosis of phenylketonuria. *American Journal of Disabled Children, 134,* 769–774.

Ogg, H. L. (1975). Oral-pharyngeal development and evaluation. *Physical Therapy, 55*(3), 235–241.

Opitla-Lehman, J., Short, M. A., & Trombly, C. A. (1985). Kinesthetic recall of children with athetoid and spastic cerebral palsy and of non-handicapped children. *Developmental Medicine and Child Neurology, 27,* 223–230.

Oppenheim, J. F. (1984). *Kids and play.* New York: Ballantine Books.

O'Reilly, D. E., & Walentynowicz, J. E. (1981). Etiological factors in cerebral palsy: An historical review. *Developmental Medicine and Child Neurology, 23,* 633–642.

Orelove, F. P., & Sobsey, D. (1987). Toileting and dressing skills. In *Educating children with multiple disabilities—A transdisciplinary approach.* Baltimore: Paul H. Brookes Publishing Company.

Ottenbacher, K. (1981). An investigation of self-concept and body image in the mentally retarded. *Journal of Clinical Psychology, 37,* 415–418.

Ottenbacher, K. (1983a). Developmental implications of clinically applied vestibular stimulation: A review. *Physical Therapy, 63,* 338–342.

Ottenbacher, K. (1983b). Transdisciplinary service delivery in school environment: Some limitations. *Physical and Occupational Therapy in Pediatrics, 3*(4), 9–16.

Ottenbacher, K. J., & Short, M. A. (1985). Vestibular processing dysfunction in children. *Physical & Occupational Therapy in Pediatrics, 5*(2-3), 1–152.

Owens, J. R., Harris, F., Walker, S., McAllister, E., & West, L. (1983). The incidence of Down's syndrome over a 19-year period with special reference to maternal age. *Journal of Medical Genetics, 20,* 90–93.

Palmer, M. F. (1947). Studies in clinical techniques II—Normalization of chewing, sucking and swallowing reflexes in cerebral palsy. *Journal of Speech Disorders, 12,* 415–418.

Palmer, S., Thompson, Jr., R. J., & Linscheid, T. R. (1975). Applied behavior analysis in the treatment of childhood feeding problems. *Developmental Medicine and Child Neurology, 17,* 333–339.

Panyan, M. C. (1975). *Managing behavior series: New ways to teach new skills, Part 4* (rev. ed.). Austin, TX: PRO-ED.

Parham, D. (1985). Questions clinicians ask. *Sensory Integration News, 8*(2), 2–3.

Parker, A. W., & Bronks, R. (1980). Gait of children with Down syndrome. *Archives of Physical Medicine and Rehabilitation, 61,* 345–351.

Parmelee, A. H. (1963a). The hand-mouth reflex of Babkin in premature infants. *Pediatrics, 31,* 734–740.

Parmelee, A. H. (1963b). The palmomental reflex in premature infants. *Developmental Medicine and Child Neurology, 5,* 381–387.

Payne, P. J., & Durham, R. R. (1983). *Occupational and physical therapy home instruction manual.* Cincinnati: Children's Hospital Medical Center.

Payne, J. W., & Reder, R. D. (1983). *Occupational and physical therapy home instruction manual.* Cincinnati: Children's Hospital Medical Center.

Pearson, P. (1973). *Milani-Comparetti.* Omaha: Meyer Children's Rehabilitation Institute of University of Nebraska.

Pelletier, J. M., & Palmeri, A. (1985). High-risk infants. In P. N. Clark & A. S. Allen (Eds.), *Occupational therapy for children.* St. Louis: C. V. Mosby Company.

Pesch, R. S., Nagy, D. K., & Caden, B. W. (1978). A survey of the visual and developmental-perceptual abilities of the Down's syndrome child. *Journal of the American Optometric Association, 49*(9), 1031–1037.

Peterson, N. L. (1982). Early intervention with the handicapped. In E. L. Meyen (Ed.), *Exceptional children and youth—An introduction* (2nd ed.). Denver: Love Publishing Co.

Peterson, N. L. (1987). *Early intervention for handicapped and at-risk children: An introduction to early childhood-special education.* Denver: Love Publishing Co.

Petrillo, M., & Sanger, S. (1972). *Emotional care of hospitalized children: An environmental approach.* Philadelphia: J. B. Lippincott.

Physical Therapy Department. (1976). *Evaluation and treatment of developmentally disabled child.* Kansas City: University of Kansas Medical Center, University Affiliated Facility.

Pierce, R. B. (1978). *Tongue thrust—A look at oral myofunctional disorders.* Lincoln, NE: Cliffs Notes, Inc.

Pines, M. (1982, July). It's changing the lives of handicapped kids—Infant-stim. *Psychology Today,* 48–53.

Piper, M. C. (1983). Cerebral palsy II: New perspectives for physical and occupational therapists. *Physical and Occupational Therapy in Pediatrics, 3,* 15–24.

Popovich, D. (1977). *A prescriptive behavioral checklist for the severely and profoundly retarded.* Baltimore: University Park Press.

Powell, N. J. (1985). Children with cerebral palsy. In P. N. Clark & A. S. Allen (Eds.), *Occupational therapy for children.* St. Louis: C. V. Mosby Company.

Prechtl, H., & Beintema, D. (1984). *The neurological examination of the full-term newborn infant.* London: Spastics Society Medical Education and Information Unit with W. Heinemann Medical Books, Ltd.

Prensky, A. L., & Palkes, H. S. (1982). *Care of the neurologically handicapped child: A book for parents and professionals.* New York: Oxford University Press.

Preus, M. (1977). A diagnostic index for Down syndrome. *Clinical Genetics, 12,* 47–55.

Pringle, M. E., Kaninski, S. A., & Raymond, G. L. (1978). Survey of physical therapy provided to infants under three months of age. *Physical Therapy, 58*(9), 1055–1060.

Ramey, C. T., & Brownlee, J. R. (1981). Improving the identification of high-risk infants. *American Journal of Mental Deficiency, 85*(5), 504–511.

Ramey, C. T., Sparling, J. J., Bryant, D. M., & Wasik, B. H. (1982). Primary prevention of developmental retardation during infancy. *Prevention in Human Services, 1*(4), 61–83.

Ramsay, M., & Piper, M. C. (1980). A comparison of two developmental scales in evaluating infants with Down syndrome. *Early Human Development, 4*(1), 89–93.

Rapp, D. (1980). Drool control: Long-term follow-up. *Developmental Medicine and Child Neurology, 22*(4), 448–453.

Rapp, D., & Bowers, P. M. (1979). Meldreth dribble-control project. *Child: Care, Health and Development, 5*(2), 143–149.

Rapport, M. D., & Bailey, J. S. (1985). Behavioral physical therapy and spina bifida: A case study. *Journal of Pediatric Psychology, 10*(1), 87–96.

Ray, S. A., Bundy, A. C., & Nelson, D. L. (1983). Decreasing drooling through techniques to facilitate mouth closure. *The American Journal of Occupational Therapy, 37*(11), 749–753.

Redditi, J. S. (1983). Occupational and physical therapy treatment components for infant intervention programs. *Physical and Occupational Therapy in Pediatrics, 3*(3), 33–44.

Reis, D. J. (1961). The palmomental reflex. *Archive Neurology, 4,* 486.

Reynolds, G. S. (1975). *A primer of operant conditioning—Revised edition.* Glenview, IL: Scott, Foresman and Company.

Rice, H. K., McDaniel, M. W., & Denney, S. L. (1968). Operant conditioning techniques for use in the physical rehabilitation of the multiply handicapped retarded patient. *Physical Therapy, 48*(4), 342–346.

Richmond, G. (1983). Shaping bladder and bowel continence in developmentally retarded preschool children. *Journal of Autism and Developmental Disorders, 13*(2), 197–204.

Richter, E. (1986). Assessment: The client with mental retardation. *Sensory Integration—Special Interest Section Newsletter from the American Occupational Therapy Association, 9*(1), 4–6.

Riordan, M. M., Iwata, B. A., Finney, J. W., Wohl, M. K., & Stanley, A. E. (1984). Behavioral assessment and treatment of chronic food refusal in handicapped children. *Journal of Applied Behavior Analysis, 17*(3), 327–341.

Riordan, M. M., Iwata, B. A., Wohl, M. K., & Finney, J. W. (1980). Behavioral treatment of food refusal and selectivity in developmentally disabled children. *Applied Reserach in Mental Retardation, 1,* 95–112.

Roach, E. G., & Kephart, N. C. (1966). *The Purdue perceptual-motor survey.* Columbus, OH: Charles E. Merrill Publishing Co.

Robinson, N. M., & Robinson, H. B. (1976). *The mentally retarded child.* New York: McGraw-Hill Book Company.

Rogers, S. J., O'Eugenio, D. B., Brown, S. L., Donovan, C. M., & Lynch, E. W. (1977). *Developmental programming for infants and young children.* Ann Arbor: The University of Michigan Press.

Rosen, B. C., & D'Andrado, R. (1959). The psychological origins of achievement motivation. *Sociometry, 22,* 185–218.

Rostetter, D., & Hamilton, J. L. (1982). Risk factors beyond the child and family. In C. T. Ramey & P. L. Trohanis (Eds.), *Finding and educating high-risk and handicapped infants.* Baltimore: University Park Press.

Rutherford, F. W. (1971). *You and your baby.* New York: Signet Books.

Rutter, M. (1976). Early hospital admission and later disturbance of behavior. *Developmental Medicine and Child Neurology, 18,* 447–459.

Rutter, M. (1979). Maternal deprivation, 1972–1978: New findings, new concepts, new approaches. *Child Development, 50,* 283–305.

Salcedo, P. (1985). Parents' notes—An open letter to professionals. *Sensory Integration News, 13,* 3.

Sand, T., Mellgren, S. I., & Hestnes, A. (1983). Primitive reflexes in Down's syndrome. *Journal of Mental Deficiency Research, 27,* 39–44.

Sanford, A. R., & Zelman, J. G. (1981). *LAP: The learning accomplishment profile-A guide for individualizing educational programming, 36–72 months* (rev. ed.). Winston-Salem, NC: Kaplan Press.

Schafer, D. S., & Moersch, M. S. (Eds.), (1981). *Developmental programming for infants and young children* (rev. ed.). Ann Arbor: The University of Michigan Press.

Scheiner, A. P., & Abrams, I. F. (1980). *The practical management of the developmentally disabled child.* St. Louis: C. V. Mosby Co.

Scherzer, A. L., & Tscharnuter, I. (1982). *Early diagnosis and therapy in cerebral palsy: A primer on infant developmental problems.* New York: Marcel Dekker, Inc.

Schmidt, P. (1976). Feeding assessment and therapy for the neurologically impaired. *AAESPH Review, 1*(8), 19–27.

Schroeder, S. R., Mulick, J. A., & Rojahn, J. (1980). The definition, taxonomy, epidemiology, and ecology of self-injurious behavior. *Journal of Autism and Developmental Disorders, 10*(4), 417–432.

Schultz, F. R. (1984). Phenylketonuria and other metabolic diseases. In J. A. Blackman (Ed.), *Medical aspects of developmental disabilities in children birth to three.* Rockville, MD: Aspen Publishers, Inc.

Schwartz, J. L., Niman, C. W., & Gisel, E. G. (1984). Tongue movements in normal preschool children during eating. *The American Journal of Occupational Therapy, 38*(2), 87–93.

Scott, A. D. (1983). Evaluation and treatment of sensation. In C. A. Trombly (Ed.), *Occupational therapy for physical dysfunction* (2nd ed.). Baltimore: Williams & Wilkins.

Sears, C. J. (1981). The transdisciplinary approach: A process for compliance with Public Law 94-142. *The Journal of the Association for the Severely Handicapped, 8*(1), 22–29.

Segal, M. (1983). *Your child at play: Birth to one year.* New York: Newmarket Press.

Seidel, U. P., Chadwick, O. F. D., & Rutter, M. (1975). Psychological disorder in crippled children. A comparative study of children with and without brain damage. *Developmental Medicine and Child Neurology, 17,* 563–573.

Semans, S., Phillips, R., Romanoli, M., Miller, R., & Skillea, M. (1965). A cerebral palsied assessment chart. In *The child with central nervous system deficit.* Washington, DC: U. S. Government Printing Office.

Semmel, M., & Snell, M. (1980). Does toilet training belong in the public schools? A review of toilet training research. *Education Unlimited, 2*(3), 53–58.

Sensky, T. (1982). Family stigmata in congenital physical handicaps. *British Medical Journal, 285*(6347), 1033–1035.

Servnian, S. A., & Broman, S. H. (1975). Relationship of Apgar scores and Bayley mental and motor scores. *Child Development, 46,* 696–700.

Shapiro, B. K., Accardo, P. J., & Capute, A. J. (1979). Factors affecting walking in a profoundly retarded population. *Developmental Medicine and Child Neurology, 21,* 369–373.

Sheehan, R., & Gallagher, R. J. (1984). Assessment of infants. In M. J. Hanson (Ed.), *Atypical infant development.* Baltimore: University Park Press.

Shepherd, R. B. (1986). Spina bifida. In *Physiotherapy in pediatrics.* Rockville, MD: Aspen Publishers, Inc.

Shipe, D., Vandenberg, S., & Williams, R. D. B. (1968). Neonatal Apgar ratings as related to intelligence and behavior in preschool children. *Child Development, 3,* 51–74.

Sigal, J., & Gagnon, P. (1975). Effects of parent's and pediatrician's worry concerning severe gastroenteritis in early childhood on later disturbances in the child's behavior. *The Journal of Pediatrics, 87,* 809–814.

Sikes, R. K. (1982). Toxoplasmosis. *Journal of the American Veterinary Medical Association 108*(8), 857–859.

Silva, P. A., McGee, R., & Williams, S. (1982). The predictive significance of slow walking and slow talking: A report from the Dunedin Multidisciplinary Child Development Study. *British Journal of Disorders of Communication, 17*(3), 133–139.

Simeonsson, R. J. (1986). *Psychological and developmental assessment of special children.* Boston: Allyn & Bacon, Inc.

Sirvis, B. (1978a). Developing IEP's for physically handicapped students: A transdisciplinary viewpoint. *Teaching Exceptional Children, 10,* 78–82.

Sirvis, B. (1978b). The physically disabled. In E. L. Meyen (Ed.), *Exceptional children and youth: An introduction* (2nd ed.). Denver: Love Publishing Company.

Sittig, E. (1947). Chewing method applied for excessive salivation and drooling in cerebral palsy. *Journal of Speech Disorders, 12,* 191–194.

Smart, M. S., & Smart, R. C. (1967). *Children: Development and relationships.* New York: The Macmillan Co.

Smith, H. D., & Tiffany, E. G. (1983). Assessment and evaluation—An overview. In H. L. Hopkins & H. D. Smith (Eds.), *Willard and Spackman's occupational therapy* (6th ed.). Philadelphia: J. B. Lippincott.

Smith, P. S., & Smith, L. J. (1977). Chronological age and social age as factors in intensive daytime toilet training of institutionalized mentally retarded individuals. *Journal of Behavioral Therapy & Experimental Psychiatry, 8,* 269–273.

Smythies, J. R. (1953). The experience and description of the human body. *Brain, 76,* 132–145.

Snell, M. E. (1983). *Systematic instruction of the moderately and severely handicapped.* Columbus, OH: Charles E. Merrill Publishing Co.

Snyder-McLean, L., Sack, S. H., & Solomonson, B. (1985). *Parsons preschool curriculum* (experimental edition). Unpublished manuscript, University of Kansas, Bureau of Child Research, Lawrence, KS 66045.

Snyder-McLean, L. K., Solomonson, B., McLean, J. E., & Sack, S. (1984). Structuring joint action routines: A strategy for facilitating communication and language development in the classroom. *Seminars in Speech and Language, 5*(3), 213–228.

Soboloff, H. R. (1981). Early intervention—Fact or fiction? *Developmental Medicine and Child Neurology, 23*(2), 261–266.

Sobsey, R., & Orelove, F. P. (1984). Neurophysiological facilitation of eating skills in children with severe handicaps. *Journal of The Association for the Severely Handicapped, 9*(2), 98–110.

Solnit, A. J., & Stark, M. H. (1961). Mourning and the birth of a defective child. *Psychoanalytic Study of the Child, 16,* 523–537.

Somerton Fair, E., & Turner, K. (1979). *Pennsylvania training model: Assessment guide.* Slippery Rock, PA: Slippery Rock State College.

Sommerfeld, D., Fraser, B. A., Hensinger, R. N., & Beresford, C. V. (1981). Evaluation of physical therapy service for severely mentally impaired student with cerebral palsy. *Physical Therapy, 61,* 338–344.

Song, A. Y., & Gandhi, R. (1974). An analysis of behavior during the acquisition and maintenance phases of self-spoon feeding skills of profound retardates. *Mental Retardation, 12*(1), 25–28.

Spain, B. (1974). Verbal and performance ability in preschool children with spina bifida. *Developmental Medicine & Child Neurology, 16,* 773–780.

Sparling, J. W. (1980). The transdisciplinary approach with the developmentally delayed child. *Physical and Occupational Therapy in Pediatrics, 1*(2), 3–15.

Spaulding, B. R., & Morgan, S. B. (1986). Spina bifida children and their parents: A population prone to family dysfunction. *Journal of Pediatric Psychology, 11*(3), 359–374.

Spock, B. J. (1972). *Baby and child care* (rev. ed.). New York: Simon & Schuster.

Stagno, S. (1980). Congenital toxoplasmosis. *American Journal of Disabled Children, 134,* 635–637.

Sternat, J. (1987). Developing head and trunk control. In B. H. Connolly & P. C. Montgomery (Eds.), *Therapeutic exercise in developmental disabilities.* Chattanooga, TN: Chattanooga Corporation.

Sternat, J., Messina, R., Nietupski, J., Lyon, S., & Brown, L. (1977). Occupational and physical therapy services for severely handicapped students: Toward a naturalized public school service delivery model. In E. Sontag (Ed.), *Educational programming for the severely and profoundly handicapped.* Reston, VA: The Council for Exceptional Children.

Stillman, R. (1978). *Callier-Azuza scale.* Dallas: Callier Center for Communication Disorders.

Storey, K., Bates, P., McGhee, M., & Dycus, S. (1984). Reproducing the self-stimulatory behavior of a profoundly retarded female through sensory awareness training. *American Journal of Occupational Therapy, 38*(8), 510–516.

Stratton, M. (1981). Behavioral assessment scale of oral functions in feeding. *The American Journal of Occupational Therapy, 35*(11), 719–721.

Straub, W. J. (1951). The etiology of the perverted swallowing habit. *American Journal of Orthodonics, 37,* 603–610.

Strauss, M. S., & Brownell, C. A. (1985). A commentary on infant stimulation and intervention. In M. Frank (Ed.), *Infant intervention programs: Truths and untruths.* New York: The Haworth Press.

Sukiennicki, D. R. (1979). Mobility dysfunction and its management. In B. S. Banus, C. A. Kent, Y. Norton, D. R. Sukiennicki, & M. L. Becker (Eds.), *The developmental therapist.* Thorofare, NJ: Charles B. Slack, Inc.

Sweeney, M. J., & Lydic, J. S. (1985). Annotated bibliography—Toewalking in children without signs of spasticity. *Physical & Occupational Therapy in Pediatrics, 5*(1), 81–88.

Sweet, N., VandenBerg, K., & Flushman, B. (1982). Intervention with the very youngest. In J. D. Anderson (Ed.), *Curricula for high-risk and handicapped infants.* Chapel Hill, NC: TADS.

Switzky, H. N., Haywood, H. C., & Rotatori, A. F. (1982). Who are the severely and profoundly mentally retarded? *Education and Training of the Mentally Retarded, 17*(4), 268–272.

Tarratt, J. K. (1971). Pre-speech therapy techniques for the cerebral palsied child. *Journal of the Australian College of Speech Therapists, 10,* 49–53.

Taylor, D. C. (1982). Counseling the parents of handicapped children. *British Medical Journal, 284,* 1027–1028.

Teplin, S. W., Howard, J. A., & O'Connor, M. J. (1981). Self-concept of young children with cerebral palsy. *Developmental Medicine and Child Neurology, 23,* 730–738.

Thomas, C. L. (Ed.). (1985). *Taber's cyclopedia medical dictionary.* Philadelphia: F. A. Davis Company.

Tingey-Michaelis, C. (1983). *Handicapped infants and children.* Baltimore: Univeristy Park Press.

Toolte, A. (1987). President's message. *Interactions, C1*(6), 1.

Trause, M. A., & Kramer, L. I. (1983). The effects of premature birth on parents and the relationship. *Developmental Medicine and Child Neurology, 25,* 459–465.

Trombly, C. A. (Ed.). (1983). *Occupational therapy for physical dysfunction* (2nd ed.). Baltimore: Williams & Wilkins.

Uehling, D. T., Smith, J., Meyer, J., & Bruskewitz, R. (1985). Impact of an intermittent catheterization program on children with myelomeningocele. *Pediatrics, 76*(6), 892–895.

Urbanik, C. (1986). Sensory integrative treatment for people with developmental disabilities. *Developmental Disabilities—Special Interest Section Newsletter (American Occupational Therapy Association) 9*(1), 1–2.

Utley, B. (1982). Motor skills and adaptations. In L. Sternberg & G. L. Adams (Eds.), *Educating severely and profoundly handicapped students*. Rockville, MD: Aspen Publishers, Inc.

Utley, B. L., Holvoet, J. F., & Barnes, K. (1977). Handling, positioning and feeding the physically handicapped. In E. Sontag (Ed.), *Educational programming for the severely and profoundly handicapped*. Reston, VA: The Council for Exceptional Children.

Uzgiris, I., & Hunt, J. (1978). *Uzgiris-Hunt scales of infant psychological development*. Urbana: University of Illinois Press.

Van De Heyning, P. H., Marquet, J. F., & Creten, W. L. (1980). Drooling in children with cerebral palsy. *Acta Oto-Rhino-Laryngologica Belgica, 34*(6), 691–705.

Van Etten, G., Arkell, C., & Van Etten, C. (1980). Curriculum for the severely and profoundly handicapped. In *The severely and profoundly handicapped: programs, methods and materials*. St. Louis: C. V. Mosby Company.

Vincent, L. J., Dodd, N., & Henner, P. J. (1978). Planning and implementing a program of parent involvement. In N. G. Haring & D. D. Bricker (Eds.), *Teaching the severely handicapped, Vol. III*. Columbus, OH: Special Press.

Vulpe, S. G. (1977). *The Vulpe assessment battery*. Toronto, Ontario: National Institute on Mental Retardation.

Ward, D. E. (1984). *Positioning the handicapped child for function* (2nd ed.). St. Louis: Phoenix Press, Inc.

Webb, Y. (1980). Feeding and nutrition problems of physically and mentally handicapped children in Britain: A report. *Journal of Human Nutrition, 34*(4), 281–285.

Weber, N. J. (1978). Chaining strategies for teaching sequenced motor tasks to mentally retarded adults. *The American Journal of Occupational Therapy, 32*(6), 385–389.

Westervelt, V. D., & Luiselli, J. K. (1975). Establishing standing and walking behavior in a physically handicapped, retarded child. *Physical Therapy, 55*(7), 761–765.

Westmoreland, D., & Burlingame, D. (1977). A feeding spatula for cerebral-palsied children. *American Journal of Occupational Therapy, 31,* 260–261.

White, J. L., & Labarda, R. C. (1976). The effects of tactile and kinesthetic stimulation on neonatal development in the premature infant. *Developmental Psychobiology, 9*(6), 569–577.

Whitehead, W. E., Parker, L., Bosmajian, S., Garwood, M., Catalod, M. F., & Freeman, J. (1986). Treatment of fecal incontinence in children with spina bifida: Comparison of biofeedback and behavior modification. *Archives of Physical Medicine and Rehabilitation, 67*(4), 218–224.

Whitman, T. L., Scibak, J. W., & Reid, D. H. (1983a). Toilet training. In *Behavior modification with the severely and profoundly retarded*. New York: Academic Press, Inc.

Whitman, T. L., Scibak, J. W., & Reid, D. H. (1983b). Training self-help skills. In *Behavior modification with the severely and profoundly retarded*. New York: Academic Press, Inc.

Wiegerink, R., & Pelosi, J. W. (Eds.). (1979). *Developmental disabilities: The DD movement*. Baltimore: Paul H. Brookes Publishing Co.

Wiesser, S. T., & Domanowsky, K. (1959). Das Schreck verhalten des sauglins: Schreck und mora-reflex. *Archiv fur Psychiatrie und Nervenkr, 198,* 257.

Wilkie, T. F. (1967). The problem of drooling in cerebral palsy: A surgical approach. *The Canadian Journal of Surgery, 10,* 60–67.

Williamson, G. G. (Ed.), (1987). *Children with spina bifida: Early intervention and preschool programming.* Baltimore: Paul H. Brookes Publishing Company.

Wilson, C. B., & Remington, J. S. (1980). What can be done to prevent congenital toxoplasmosis? *American Journal of Obstetrics and Gynecology, 138*(4), 357–363.

Wilson, D. P., Carpenter, N. J., & Holcombe, J. H. (1985). Turner syndrome: Clinical investigations and review. *Oklahoma State Medical Association Journal, 78*(2), 37–42.

Wolraich, M. L. (1984a). Hydrocephalus. In J. R. Blackman (Ed.), *Medical aspects of developmental disabilities in children birth to three.* Rockville, MD: Aspen Publishers, Inc.

Wolraich, M. L. (1984b). Myelomeningocele. In J. A. Blackman (Ed.), *Medical aspects of developmental disabilities in children birth to three.* Rockville, MD: Aspen Publishers, Inc.

Wolraich, M. L. (1984c). Seizure disorders. In J. A. Blackman (Ed.), *Medical aspects of developmental disabilities in children birth to three.* Rockville, MD: Aspen Publishers, Inc.

Zinkus, C. (no date). Feeding skill training. In M. A. H. Smith (Ed.), *Feeding the handicapped child.* Memphis: University of Tennessee, Child Development Center, Department of Nutrition.

Index

AAMD, *see* American Association on Mental Deficiency
Abrasion, 242
ACTH, common side effects, 248
Activities of daily living (ADLs), 229
Acute distress syndrome, 15
Adaptive behavior ability
  deficits in, 305
  levels of, 305–307
  and mental retardation classification, 322
Adaptive Behavioral Scale, *see* American Association on Mental Deficiency Adaptive Behavior Scales
Adolescent, self-esteem of, effect of disability on, 12–14
Adrenocorticotropic hormone, *see* ACTH
Alpha-fetoprotein (AFP), 329
Amblyopia, 332
American Association on Mental Deficiency
  definition of mental retardation, 305
  medical classification of mental retardation, 308–309
American Association on Mental Deficiency Adaptive Behavior Scales, 322, 358
Anencephaly, 325
  description of, 328
Ankle, deformities of, 347
Ankle-foot orthosis, 342
Anoxia, *see* Hypoxia
Anticonvulsant, 246
Antigravity position, 45, 123–129
Apgar Scoring System, 77–78, 352
Apraxia, 333
Arm movement, training in, 113
Arnold-Chiari malformation, 327
Arousal state, 285
Assessment, 35, 278
  administration of selected tests, 38–39
  comprehensive, 43
  effects of development process and environment, 39–42

examiner
  role of, 38–39
  skills and characteristics, 39
  of general skill areas, 44–74
  method, selection of, 37
  phases of, 36–39
  pre-evaluation data collection, 36–37
  purposes of, 36
  results, sharing with other disciplines and parents, 39
  scoring, interpreting, and organizing data, 39
  in specific developmental disabilities, 74–94
  test environment, 37
  orientation of child and parents to, 37–38
  types of, 42–44
Asymmetric tonic neck reflex, 49, 55, 68, 152, 291
  effect on feeding skills, 160
  fading procedures for, 236
  obligate, 115–116
  persistent, 113
  effect on development, 97
At-risk infant
  acquiring information on, 273–277
  assessment strategies for, 273–275
  assessment tools for, 352–356
  criterion-referenced tests for, 275
  definition of, 263
  diagnostic test for, 274
  direct testing of, 273–275
  domain-referenced measures for, 275
  educational assessment of, 274
  intervention guidelines with, 280–285
  intervention techniques for, 279–280
  levels of risk, 263
  norm-referenced measurements for, 275
  observation of, 274, 275–276
  parental interview, 274, 276–277
  professional and parent roles with, 269–271
  risk factors for, 263–265
  screenings, 273–274